Fraser

Bridges

Pacific

Coast

Adventures

The Driver's Guide

Travel Guides by Fraser Bridges

British Columbia Adventures

Pacific Coast Adventures

Alaska-Yukon Adventures

Rocky Mountain Adventures (April 1992)

Pacific Coast Adventures

The Driver's Guide

Fraser Bridges

Western Traveller
p r e s s

Vancouver, British Columbia & Point Roberts, Washington

PACIFIC COAST ADVENTURES
THE DRIVER'S GUIDE

Fraser Bridges

Maps by Harry Bardal

First edition

Cover Photo by Thomas Kitchin / Image Finders
Sea stacks beside Highway 101 at Cape Sebastian, Oregon.
Highway 101 is the coast route which runs north from San Francisco, through
Northern California, Oregon and Washington, and in Canada along the
Sunshine Coast of British Columbia.

Cataloguing in Publication Data
  Bridges, Fraser, 1935-
    Pacific Coast Adventures
  Includes Index
  ISBN 0-9694136-3-7
    1. Automobile travel--Northwest Coast of North
  America--Guide-books. 2. Northwest Coast of North
  America--Description and travel--Guide-books.
  I. Title.
  F852.3.B74 1991   917.9504'43   C91-091116-9

Printed in Canada by Bowne of Vancouver Inc.

10 9 8 7 6 5 4 3 2 1

For Joyce
who introduced me to the Pacific Coast
and a continuing adventure

CONTENTS

CONTENTS

Welcome to your
Pacific Coast Adventure

People often ask me to identify my favorite part of the Pacific Coast. After several years of driving along this spectacular coastline, I can never answer the question properly. The coast is just too varied, with visual and recreational attractions changing so much with the seasons that it's a pleasure to drive the coastal routes at any time of the year. I usually wind up asking "What time of the year are we talking about"?

In the summers I like to explore Washington's Olympic Peninsula, or the placid islands of Puget Sound and the Strait of Georgia. The fall is a perfect time for walking the Oregon Dunes or visiting the seaside towns of Mendocino County. Winter brings a new cast to Washington State where the Olympics are covered with snow and outdoor activities turn to snowshoeing and cross-country skiing. But winter is also a great time to explore the coast wine country in northern California. Sonoma and Mendocino counties are fairly warm then but the summer crowds aren't there and the winemakers are in a more relaxed frame of mind for talking and introducing their wines. The Redwood Coast is wonderful at any time of the year but the spring is my favorite time for visiting this part of California.

The cities too have their seasons and it's possible to get a very different view of the great cities in this region (Seattle, Portland and Vancouver B.C.) from month to month. While the coastal cities are exciting to visit during the summer period, the winters bring on a rich cultural scene in each of these centers. And if you're hunting for a relaxed vacation with a cultural focus, including opera, ballet, symphony and art exploration, go in the off-season and join the local residents in their cultural pursuits and sports activity. For example, three ski mountains can be reached by 30-minute drives from downtown Vancouver B.C. (Cypress, Seymour and Grouse) and excellent mountain resorts are but an hour fromPortland and Seattle.

The Pacific Coast region is filled to the rim with outdoor adventure; beaches; forests; national parks; fine inns, hotels and restaurants; and a thriving cultural scene ranging from symphony orchestras to impressive museums which feature — among other themes — the history of the native peoples of this coastal region.

Enjoy your many Pacific Coast adventures!

Fraser Bridges

How to Use This Travel Guide

First, there's a short introduction to give you an overview of the entire Pacific Coast north of San Francisco. Then are chapters focusing on the coastal regions from the California North Coast to Washington and Southwestern British Columbia These regional chapters include some common elements:

The Highway Maps and Logs:

All but one chapter of the book (Puget Sound) include overview maps which are followed by strip maps and highway logs for the routes along the Pacific Coast, north of San Francisco. Use the highway log pages while you're traveling. They are meant to be read at the start of the day and especially while on the road. You'll discover the next picnic park, the gas stations ahead, state and provincial parks and campgrounds, and the scenic views along the way.

If you like getting out of the car and enjoying the natural environment, the logs will tell you where to stop to walk, hike, swim, fish, and to view wildlife. In addition to Highways 1 and 101, the main coastal highways, the log pages include scenic side-trips and alternate routes including a winery tour of parts of Sonoma and Mendocino counties in California.

Travel Planner Chapters:

The pages which cover the towns, cities and outdoor attractions contain the information you need to plan your coastal adventure trips. They include information on the cities and towns along the way, the things to do and see there and historical information on the fascinating places on the coast. We've included recommendations on a wide range of places to stay and eat, with a variety of prices for hotels, motels, inns, lodges and restaurants, ranging from deluxe to inexpensive. Private and public campgrounds and RV parks—in or close to the tourist destinations—are included in these pages We encourage you to enjoy your adventures by getting off the main routes and exploring the back roads and the recreational areas off the highways.

I have also tried to include as many distinctive local restaurants and watering holes as possible and I hope that you will enjoy the food and the local flavor of these unique places. I find that small, unpretentious restaurants and pubs along the coastal highways often offer superior and locally-flavored food (particularly the flavor of the sea) at extremely reasonable prices and often offer surprises which are remembered long after memories of high-priced gourmet restaurants have faded. Not that we neglect fine dining — and there is plenty of that along the routes, too!

A note about the British Columbia chapter: B. C. destinations are covered in much greater detail in the book "British Columbia Adventures". I have included a truncated chapter here for those venturing into B.C. from more southerly destinations. In addition, destinations in northern B.C. — including the province's North Coast and the Queen Charlotte Islands — are covered in detail in the book "Alaska-Yukon Adventures".

RECOMMENDATIONS & RATINGS

Places to Stay:

You'll find a broad selection of places to stay in the Travel Planner pages. Whether you're traveling deluxe or on a tight budget, there are recommended hotels, motels, inns, lodges and camping places listed for each of the cities and towns.

Accommodation:

Price ranges for hotel & motel rooms are based on double occupancy and are marked with dollar signs:

- Inexpensive: 40 - 60 dollars: Symbol: $
- Moderate: 61 - 100 dollars: Symbol: $$
- Deluxe: 100 dollars and up: Symbol: $$$

Deluxe accommodations are found in the large city hotels and in unique and specialized resort hotels, inns and lodges. We have included these but also have listed budget chains and resorts which feature housekeeping cabins.

There is a good supply of campgrounds and RV parks along the coast. Public campgrounds (national, state, provincial & local parks) have minimal facilities, sometimes with pit toilets and without hot water. Private campgrounds and RV parks are better equipped than public campsites, almost always with hookups, hot water, showers, flush toilets, water piped to sites and electrical supply. Prices for government campgrounds range from $4 to $8. Private facilities run from $10 to $20.

Places to Eat:

All restaurants, delis, cafes, and taverns are listed under the particular city or town in which you wish to eat.

We have not included fast food chains, as these are easy to spot along the roadsides and the prices are consistent.

Restaurants:

Three price ranges are listed:

- Inexpensive: 4 - 6 dollars per meal. Symbol: $
- Moderate: 7 - 11 dollars per entree-evening meals. Symbol: $$
- Expensive: Over 11 dollars per entree, at evening meals. Symbol: $$$

Many of the restaurants are to be found in hotels or attached to motels along the highways and these are identified in the hotel-motel listings. On the other hand, we have made an effort to include the smaller, more interesting local eating places which serve regional food including specialities found only in that location.

A selection of neighborhood bars or taverns which serve meals is included. We have found that pubs often serve simple, nourishing meals which are usually less expensive than in standard restaurants.

We encourage you to picnic along the way. Many scenic picnic parks are noted in the logs opposite the strip maps including road-side locations and state & provincial parks close to the coastal highways.

INTRODUCTION

PACIFIC COAST HIGHWAYS

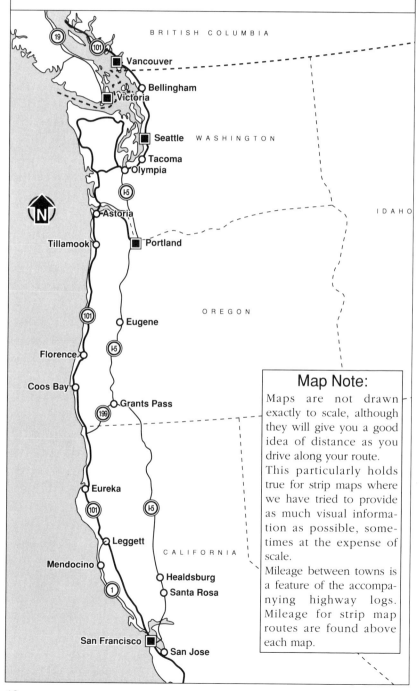

Map Note:

Maps are not drawn exactly to scale, although they will give you a good idea of distance as you drive along your route.

This particularly holds true for strip maps where we have tried to provide as much visual information as possible, sometimes at the expense of scale.

Mileage between towns is a feature of the accompanying highway logs. Mileage for strip map routes are found above each map.

A Pacific Coast DVENTURES

The word "Adventure" means many things to many people. The classic dictionary definition relates to risk-taking — endangering one's safety or even life to participate in battle or to seek out the unusual.

In recent years, Adventure has taken on another meaning — related to vacation travel. This is the kind of travel which brought about the writing of these "Adventures" books: finding the unusual and challenging in the out-of-doors; exploring new places & seeing new things; tracing local history as one visits for the first time; driving to unexpected pleasures on side roads and back roads — off the beaten track; finding physical challenge and aesthetic pleasure by walking, hiking, exploring, climbing, and paddling in natural surroundings including state, national and provincial parks and forests.

This is my definition of "Adventure" and I hope that it will become yours too.

The Pacific Coast, as far as this book is concerned begins at the Golden Gate Bridge and ends in Southwestern British Columbia. This part of the North American coastline stretches north from San Francisco, past the rocky headlands of northern California—through redwood country—to the shifting dunes and seastack sentinels of Oregon and the long sand spits along the southwest Washington coast. Our tour circles around the majestically rugged Olympic Peninsula; across the waters of Puget Sound — past wooded peninsulas and placid archipelagos—to the Strait of Georgia and Canada's Vancouver Island; and finally, the short but memorable Sunshine Coast of British Columbia as well as the B.C. Gulf Islands. We'll also make a detour beside the Columbia River to Portland Oregon.

Throughout these regions, the Pacific Coast provides some of the world's finest outdoor adventure experiences, in addition to scenic vacation centers which have captivated travelers for more than a hundred years. Nowhere else on the North American continent are there more fine inns and lodges for quiet getaways. The seaside towns along the Pacific are perfect for family vacations.

The major cities of the region are attractive pl;aces to visit: Seattle, Portland and Vancouver and Victoria B.C. The smaller centers along the way—I think of Bodega Bay, Eureka, Seaside, Long Beach and others— are charming, each in their own way.

This introduction sets out to briefly cover the regions from south to north, giving the highlights of each, which then can lead to many years of vacation experiences.

Introduction — Northern California Coast

The Marin Coast:

Our "North Coast" begins at the northern end of the Golden Gate Bridge and stretches for more than 200 miles to the Oregon border. Highway 1 branches off from Highway 101 in Sausalito and heads toward the Marin, Sonoma and Mendocino shoreline.

Marin County is a favorite play area for Bay area residents who take advantage of the fair weather at all times of the year for day trips to Mt.. Tamalpais and the seashore to the north. Interstate 101 is the way to get to your chosen vacation area quickly. Highway 1 is the scenic seaside route to explore at your leisure.

It is rare to experience dramatic changes in temperature along the Marin coast. Fog sometimes blankets the shore during morning hours, although less often in Marin County, as compared to farther north in Sonoma and Mendocino counties. Winters can be rainy along the coast, although many visitors prefer the uncrowded parks and beaches and the natural beauty of the Pacific shore at this time of year.

Taking Highway 1 west from its junction with Highway 101, the Muir Woods National Monument is a forest of pristine redwoods which are much visited. Some of the trees in the Cathedral and Bohemian groves are more than 1,000 years old and up to 250 feet tall. Named in tribute to famed naturalist John Muir, the park is on the original part of Highway 1 now separated by a landslide which occurred during the 1989 earthquake.

The seemingly permanent Highway 1 "detour" which leads to Stinson Beach and northward along the coast is actually a blessing. It winds over the mountains through Mt. Tamalpais State Park, a preserve of more than 6,000 acres with good camping and picnic facilities. A trail leads to the mountain top providing superb views of the surrounding countryside.

Descending from "Mt. Tam", Highway 1 leads to the village of **Stinson Beach**. The beach here is impressive with lots of white sand and swimming, fishing and windsurfing opportunities.

Three miles north of Stinson Beach is Audubon Canyon Ranch, a 1,000 acre bird sanctuary on the western slope of Mt. Tamalpais. Here, flocks of egrets and great blue herons nest on trees above the Bolinas Lagoon from March to the end of June.

Near **Olema** is Pt. Reyes National Seashore, another superlative nature preserve. This is an area of dunes and forest groves, hiking and horse trails and beached pounded with hard surf. The visitor center is adjacent to several trailheads for scenic routes throughout the park.

On the Pt. Reyes Peninsula is the fishing town of **Inverness** on Tomales Bay. Highway 1 snakes along the east side of Tomales Bay, with its oyster beds and salt marshes. The village of **Marshall** lies along the road offering rustic seafood restaurants and parks with boat launches and picnic spots. It pays to linger along the Marin Coast.

Introduction — Northern California Coast

Sonoma Coast:

While Sonoma County is best known for its wineries and Spanish history, the Sonoma Coast is a treasure which should be included on a Pacific Coast trip. The Russian River empties into the Pacific just west of Guerneville and this region is a favorite for tourists taking short holidays from the San Francisco Bay area.

The southern boundary of the county along the coast is at Bodega Bay. The northern county line is just beyond Sea Ranch, a resort complex with a hotel and vacation homes which are available for rental by visitors for a week or by the month.

Facets of this area are covered in both the Sonoma Coast and Wine Country chapters of this book. The Sonoma region between Highways 101 and 1 provide fascinating vacation opportunities, particularly in Russian River Country where huge redwoods mingle with relaxed riversiide reports and some of the notable Sonoma wineries.

Along the coast, Highway 1 takes you to **Bodega Bay**, a fishing village which has been in business since Spanish explorers came here in 1775. Deep sea fishing expeditions are for hire here. Restaurants along the waterfront serve fresh seafood year-round. Bodega Bay is connected to Highway 101 and **Santa Rosa** by Highway 12, another handy route for access to the coast.

Jenner to the north of Bodega Bay is a larger town. Several recently built inns offer excellent accommodation. A centerpiece of the area is Fort Ross Historic Park, the restored Russian fur trading fort, established in 1812. There is an excellent visitor center with interpretation programs and displays of historic artifacts including Russian arms and tools. Trails lead through the park which has a coastline much more rugged than the Marin coast to the south.

Jenner is the junction point for Highway 116 and the Russian River area — just inland. This watershed covers much of Sonoma and Mendocino counties. The river itself runs through rolling hills, covered with Redwood and Douglas fir forests. The resort villages of the area include **Guerneville, Forestville** and **Duncan Mills**. A three-minute drive north of Guerneville is Armstrong Redwood State Park, 752 acres with hiking trails, horses for hire, bike paths and several major redwood groves including Burbank Circle grove. There is camping within the park.

As in Mendocino County farther north, visitors flock to the Sonoma seashore to watch the California grey whales which migrate close to the shore on their southern trip from Alaska to Baja California during the winter months. Other special events include the Russian River Jazz Festival, held annually in September. There are comfortable and quaint places to stay as well as campgrounds along the winding roads which lead to the coast from the Sonoma interior. The northern Sonoma beaches have a distinctive character with small dunes and tufted grass above the high tide line.

Introduction — Northern California Coast

Mendocino Coast:

Mendocino County provides the gateway to the rugged shoreline of the real "North Coast" of California. The Mendocino coast stretches from the Gulala River north to Point No Pass and Humboldt County.

Point Arena is a tiny village at the southern end of the county. The Point Arena Lighthouse was built in 1870. Rebuilt after the 1906 earthquake, it is open for tours. Whale watching is a prime activity along the Mendocino coast, beginning in December. The rugged bluffs along the coast here provide good sighting spots.

Inland from Little River is Van Damme State Park, noted for its Pygmy Forest. The hard soil provides little nourishment for the cypress trees here. The village of **Mendocino** was settled around 1850 by lumbermen from Maine. The community is called the "New England of the West Coast" and its houses, shops and hotels are built in a New England style. Some of the best bed and breakfast inns in the region are in the Mendocino area.

This is the town which served as the backdrop for the television series "Murder She Wrote" and for numerous movies. The Mendocino Art Center has theater, dance and music programs throughout the year.

Ten miles north of Mendocino is **Fort Bragg**. When driving through, Fort Bragg seems to be one long strip development. But if you venture off the road, there are a number of attractions worth exploring. The Skunk Train, the successor to an old logging railway line, takes tourists through the redwood forests to the town of **Willits**, 40 miles inland.

The Mendocino Botanical Gardens, on the seaside bluffs, is a popular stop for rest and relaxation. **Noyo Harbor** at the south end of Fort Bragg is a working fishing village with several good seafood restaurants and the celebrated Fourth of July Salmon Barbecue.

Three miles north of Fort Bragg on Highway 1 is MacKerricher State Park which has pine forest and a campground.

Two highways connect Highway 1 and the coast with Highway 101 and the Mendocino interior. Highway 128 runs in a southeast direction from south of Mendocino, passing through the Anderson RIver Valley and Booneville, joining Hwy. 101 at Cloverdale. Farther north — Highway 20 connects Fort Bragg and Willits.

Humboldt & Del Norte Coast:

These two counties comprise the northwestern corner of California and together are known as the Redwood Empire. This is where Highway 1 moves inland, skirting the "Lost Coast" which is reached by side roads. Highway 101 is the route through the country's most famed redwood forests which begin at Garberville and run north to the Oregon border.

Introduction — Northern California Coast

Garberville is a good spot to begin an exploration of the Humboldt redwoods. Nearby is Humboldt Redwoods State Park and the Avenue of the Giants, an impressive drive parallel to Hwy. 101, through dense forest, the Kings Range Wilderness and Sinkoyne Wilderness State Park. There are several historic inns in the Garberville area.

Ferndale is the northern gateway to the **Lost Coast,** an extremely rugged coastline which is off the beaten track and accessed by back roads. For true outdoor adventure, the Lost Coast is supreme. At its southern edge is the Sinkyone State Recreation Area, a wilderness park on the ocean. The King Range of mountains provide a wide choice of hiking trails and forest campsites. The small village of Shelter Cove is the only community in the Lost Coast area. **Eureka** is the largest city on the north coast, with many Victorian homes, a historic 19th century town center and good hotels, bed and breakfasts and camping nearby.

Del Norte County to the north is the home of **Redwood National Park**, made up of three state parks: Prairie Creek, Del Norte Coast and Jedediah Smith redwood state parks. This complex of parks is 100 miles north of the Avenue of the Giants and is noted for its wildlife including Roosevelt elk and several of the world's largest trees — 340 feet tall and 20 feet in diameter.

The Klamath River descends from Oregon, attracting anglers who fish for king salmon and steelhead trout. The annual Klamath Salmon Festival lures thousands of anglers to the area.

Crescent City, named for its crescent-shaped beach, is the northern entrance to Redwood National Park. This is a fishing and lumber town. Fishing charters are available here. The Battery Point Lighthouse is the oldest working light on the Pacific Coast. Visitors can walk to this island lighthouse at low tide and there is a museum on the site.

Drive north from Crescent City along Highway 101 and you're in Oregon.

Coast Wine Country:

The chapter beginning on page 80 features a driving tour of Sonoma and Mendocino wine country. It's a tour which can be taken in stages, or as a long, leisurely vacation through striking scenery.

If you're an oenophile exploring the Pacific Coast route, you only need to venture an hour inland to sample some of California's best wines. Our tour begins in Sonoma, just north of San Francisco Bay and begins driving north through the Sonoma Valley — to Santa Rosa and then veering west toward the coast through the Russian River region.

Farther to the north, we cover the roads to wineries in Mendocino County and along Highway 101 which is the major route to the Northern California wine districts. We skipped the better known Napa Valley for two reasons: it's too far inland to consider part of the Pacific Coast region and there is a wealth of material available on the area

Introduction — Oregon Coast

South Coast:

21 miles north of Crescent City California, Highway 101 enters Oregon and the landscape quickly changes. To the east there are forested mountains as the Cascade range comes to join the sea. **Siskiyou National Forest**, a rugged and beautiful forest reserve, stretches from the California border north for almost 100 miles. It lies only a few minutes drive east of the highway.

On the west side of the highway lies the Pacific, bordered by some of the most striking natural seashore in the world, with state parks every few miles along the route. The 36 mile drive between **Brookings** and **Gold Beach** could consume a vacation on its own. **Boardman State Park** stretches for ten miles, offering high cliffs for ocean viewing. Harris Beach State Park just north of Brookings has a large campground overlooking an expansive beach.

Azalea State Park protects five varieties of wild azaleas. The Azalea Festival takes place on Memorial Day weekend. Daffodils are out in February and March while lilies bloom in July. This whole area is an attraction for sports anglers who are drawn to the fishing port of Brookings and to the Chetco River with its myrtlewood grove and redwood trees.

The **Rogue River** flows into the Pacific at **Gold River**. There are more sandy beaches here, as well as riverside parks and camping spots. Jet boats offer tours of the river with trips proceeding up-river for up to 52 miles. Sideroads take you along both sides of the Rogue. The small village of **Agness** is located in the National Forest and is the starting point for two outstanding walks: the 40-mile Rogue River Hiking Trail and the Illinois River Canyon Trail.

Moving northward along 101, **Port Orford** is the most westerly town in the lower 48 states. Cape Blanco—nearby—is the westernmost headland. There's a state park here alongside the Cape Blanco Lighthouse which has been in operation since 1870.

Bandon By The Sea prides itself on being the "Storm Watching Capital of the World". During the winter months the local "Storm Watchers" hold lectures and programs on the Oregon coast weather and Pacific Ocean storms in particular. Don't pass up a chance to see the ocean in all its fury. Summer vacationing is extremely polular too, in this and the other small towns of the Oregon Coast.

Coos Bay, North Bend and **Charleston** are neighboring communities on Coos Bay. Shore Acres State Park has floral gardens and a public campground is nearby. South of Charleston on Seven Devils Road, is the South Slough Estuarine Reserve, a 4,400-acre nature preserve which is the only estuary reserve of its type in the nation. Coos Bay is a large port and lumber town with a variety of m
breakfast inns.

Introduction — Oregon Coast

Central Coast:

This is one of the prime vacation areas on the Oregon Coast, with sand dunes in the center of it all. The **Oregon Dunes National Recreation Area** stretches for 47 miles south of Florence and north of Reedsport. The dunes roll to the seashore, some as tall as 500 feet. There are 14,000 acres of dunes and about half this area is open to off-road vehicles. You can bring your own dune buggy or rent them here.

Aside from dune walking and driving, there are vast ocean beaches, marshes, estuaries and coastal forests. The Oregon Dunes Lookout on Highway 101 is midway between Reedsport and Florence and is the best location for a g eneral orientation to the dunes region. You'll find more than adequate accommodations, particularly campsites, on or near the dunes. **Reedsport** on Winchester Bay is at the south end of the central coast. There is a large sport fishing charter fleet set beside a seafood cannery and some good seafood restaurants.

Florence is at the mouth of the Siuslaw River. There is a charming Old Town here with restored buildings and more restaurants. Florence hosts an annual Rhododendron Festival — in May through mid-June. Stellar sea lions are a popular feature north of Florence at Sea Lion Caves. Highway 101 north of Florence is a winding road along the rugged headlands. The road takes you to Cape Perpetua, an 800 foot-high coastal peak which is the highest point on the Oregon Coast. There is a park here, operated by the National Forest Serrvice with an information center, and a lookout trail to a view which can only be described in superlatives.

The town of **Hachats** (pronounced Yah-hots), north of Cape Perpetua, has more wide beaches, several family resorts and picnic sites.

This is a coastline with numerous seaside villages and towns, appearing every twenty miles or so. Typical of the seaside towns is **Waldport** which lies along Alsea Bay. Again, there is a good beach, boating facilities and campsites. The Alsea River accommodates salmon, steelhead and cutthroat trout anglers. Highway 34 runs along the river, leading to several private campgrounds and giving river access.

Newport is the largest Oregon coastal port, a sport and commercial fishing town with a full range of resort hotels, unique B & B homes and plenty to do if you're interested in more than beach activity and fishing. There's an annual Seafood and Wine Festival in February and the Sea Fair in May. Newport has become more of an established tourist center than most other Oregon Coast towns, with a Ripley's Believe It Or Not attraction and a wax museum. The Newport Performing Arts Center hosts classical and jazz concerts and drama.

The other major tourist town is **Lincoln City** with more than 50 motels and resorts spotted along the town's seven-mile coastline. **Depoe Bay,** just south of Lincoln City, is a center for fishing & California grey whale watching cruises.

Introduction — Oregon Coast

North Coast:

Oregon's early history is evident in the towns of the north coast, a region of expansive forests and the continuing beaches of the Pacific seashore. This is where early exploration occurred as the Spanish, Russians and British sailed on their 18th century voyages of discovery and fur trading. The Oregon North Coast stretches from Cascade Head — a 1,788 foot headland — to the mouth of the Columbia River and the city of Astoria.

Near Cascade Head is the small resort community of **Neskowin**, with its two golf courses, horse stable and several motels. **Pacific City**, a small and relaxed tourist town, is just south of the Three Capes Loop, a drive which will take you to: Cape Meares and an historic lighthouse as well as uniquely-shaped Sitka spruces; Cape Lookout — with a truly spectacular view; and Cape Kiwanda. This coast road leads through the town of Oceanside, the site of Three Rocks National Wildlife Refuge, a preserve for seabirds and sea lions. I'm using the word spectacular a lot here and I mean it! The Oregon Coast provides many a spectacle.

Over on Highway 101, the town of **Tillamook** is slightly inland but worth visiting for a tour of the famed Tillamook Cheese Factory, which produces Oregon's excellent cheddar cheese. There's a cheese shop at the factory as well as at the other cheese plant in town: the brie-making Blue Heron Cheese Factory. **Garibaldi** is a nearby deep sea port with charter fishing available and diving sites. **Nahalem**, on an estuary, is a fishing and crabbing village, with a local winery and a state park with campground.

As you drive north toward Astoria, you will pass by two more small tourist centers — but you may wish to stop.

Cannon Beach has become a major cultural center. There is a large art and crafts community here and summer brings music and art programs in addition to the Coaster Theater with its annual Dickens Festival. In May, the seven-mile long beach is the site of a sand castle competition. Haystack Rock — just offshore — is said to be Oregon's most photographed landmark. Ecola State Park is just north of Cannon Beach.

Seaside is a pleasant beach community to the north. The Broadway Street mall has a collection of shops, restaurants and arcades which ends at the beach and a turnaround viewpoint. The beach-side street runs for nearly two miles with old beach homes along the shoreline and the Seaside Aquarium is a popular family attraction. Just north of Seaside is **Gearhart**, little more than a famous resort hotel. The golf course here is historic and of championship caliber. Highway 26 takes you on a side trip up Saddle Mountain to picturesque mountain meadows.

Astoria is an historic city at the northern edge of the Oregon Coast. It was the first settled community in the state following the Lewis & Clark expeditions. It gets its name from the New Yorker who owned the fur trading fort: John Jacob Astor. A long bridge crosses the Columbia River from **Astoria** to the beaches of Southwest Washington.

Introduction — Oregon Coast

Astoria to Portland:

Highway 30 heads west beside the Columbia River to Portland. I've included this route in the Oregon chapter although the Lewis & Clark Trail isn't on the coast. However, many people will wish to visit Portland, the vibrant city at the confluence of the Willamette and Columbia rivers.

Astoria, at the mouth of the Columbia, is the site of the first permanent European settlement in the Oregon territory. It was here that the arrival of Lewis and Clark in 1805 set the scene for the permanent settlement of the Pacific Northwest. In the early days, Astoria rivaled San Francisco in size and in its culture.

Today the city named for the fur trader is a commercial fishing center and a major seaport. As the historic city of the Northwest, Astoria contains several major museums and historic homes to visit. The Columbia River Maritime Museum features one of the country's finest displays of ship models and early artifacts of the shipping trade in this area. The Heritage Museum is located in the former city hall. The partial reconstruction of old Fort Astoria — the first major outpost west of the Mississippi — is a block from the museum. There's a good walking tour with maps available at the Chamber of Commerce office.

Oregon's largest state campground is located at the tip of the state at **Fort Stevens**, now a park with 605 campsites. **Fort Clatsop National Memorial**, six miles south of Astoria, is the site of a replica of the fort where Lewis and Clark wintered in 1805-6. The park is open year-round. For history buffs, Astoria is a must!

On to **Portland** on Highway 30.

Set against an attractive waterfront on two rivers—the Willamette and the Columbia, Portland is a large clean city which is blessed with many parks and gardens. It really is the "City of Roses". A popular place for flower gazing is the Rose Test Garden in Washington Park. Portland's annual Rose Festival is held in June for 26 days. The city has good public transportation including a 15-mile light rail line and a free bus service through much of the downtown area. Portland's Chinatown offers shopping and restaurants and eachj of the city's districts have their own collection of distinctiove cafes, boutiques and antique stores.

Best of all, the city is a handy staging point for side trips through the Columbia River Gorge east of Portland to **Mt. Hood** and to **Mt. St. Helens**, across the Columbia in Washington state.

To the south, the Willamette Valley is serviced by Interstate 5 which runs the length of the valley. Here are wineries and other major Oregon centers including **Salem** and **Eugene**. **Oregon City** — just south of Portland — was the end of the Oregon Trail. Here too there are historic homes and museums related to Oregon settlement. More than 300,000 pioneers came to the west over the Oregon Trail and these hardy souls are commemorated in the National End-Of-The-Trail Interpretive Center.

Introduction — Washington Coast

Purists will point out that Washington has only one Pacific Coast and not the several coasts which are included in this book. However, the coastline of Washington state is a many splendored thing and for the sake of covering the entire Washington coastline, we must venture into Puget Sound as well as traveling to the *actual* Pacific Coast.

The real Pacific Coast includes the sections on Southwest Washington and the Olympic Peninsula. Then we move to the inland salt water of Puget Sound, including the Seattle/Tacoma area, the Kitsap Peninsula and the San Juan Islands.

Finally we drive along the eastern shore of the Gulf of Georgia, through the city of Bellingham to the resort town of Birch Bay and to Blaine, the border town just south of the greater Vancouver B.C. area.

Purists can stay close to the real coasts if they wish. However, there are many salt-water attractions on ths inland sea which is variously called Puget Sound, Georgia Strait and the Gulf of Georgia.

Southwest Washington:

This corner of the state is sometimes forgotten by travelers who want a seaside vacation in Washington. It's tucked below the Olympic Peninsula — north of the Columbia River and the Oregon border. It includes **Long Beach**, North America's longest sandy beach, a 28 mile stretch of sand spit, resort lodges, parks and fine scenery. **Ilwaco** at the mouth of the Columbia River is a deep-sea fishing port where charters are available to take salmon anglers out to the Pacific. **Ocean Park** and **Oysterville** are located in the middle and north end of the beach respectively — two more seaside resort communities. Early seafaring and exploration in the area are featured in several museums and state parks including the Lewis & Clark Interpretive Center at Ft. Canby State Park, the Fort Columbia Historical Museum and Gallery, and the Ilwaco Heritage Museum. Oysterville has a heritage district.

The Chehalis River empties into the Pacific near **South Bend.**

Venturing along the Columbia River to the coast should be considered when you're planning a drive in this area. Highway 4 is the major access road connecting Interstate 5 with the southwest Washington coast. This is an interesting drive in itself, with the road paralleling the north side of the Columbia River and passing through the small communities of **Cathalmet** and **Skamokawa**. There are historical highlights in both towns including the Skamokawa National Historic District and the Cathalmet Museum. The Gray's River bridge is the only covered bridge still in use in the state.

The last remaining ferry on the lower Columbia River takes visitors to beaches on Puget Island, and when you get near Long Beach, Bush Pioneer State Park offers a great spot for scenic picnics. Offshore in Willapa Bay is the Willapa National Wildlife Refuge, including an island preserve.

The route to Long Beach provides vistas of modern and traditional rural life including many old Victorian-era homes and antique barns.

IIntroduction — Washington Coast

Olympic Peninsula:

The Olympic Peninsula is a national treasure, the site of the impressive Olympic mountain range and **Olympic National Park**. The peninsula holds the largest and most impressive rain forest in the United States The national park and the Olympic National Forest provide superb outdoor adventure activity.

The national park surrounds the highest peak, Mt. Olympus and includes a host of slightly shorter peaks. There are more than 60 active glaciers in the range, many of them on Mt. Olympus. Within the park there are two accessible hot springs, including Sol Duc, a hot springs resort.

Olympic National Park and the wilderness areas of Olympic National Forest serve to preserve almost a million acres of mountains, glaciers, old-growth forest and wilderness coastline. The best way to explore the Olympic wilderness is by foot, and there are many campgrounds available in the wilderness area to make this easy. There are short trails suitable for short stays, or long hikes accessing the impressive alpine regions.

Highway 101 is the loop road which takes you around the peninsula, with the small but dramatic Olympic mountain range dominating the views in every direction.

At the southwestern corner of the peninsula is the Gray's Harbor area, including the ocean-side communities of **Ocean Shores** and **Ocean City**. Inland, where the Chehalis River empties into Gray's Harbor are the towns of **Aberdeen**, a deep water harbor and **Hoquiam**. **Westport**, at the southwest corner of Gray's Harbor is a fishing community and a tourist center with a public aquarium, several good seafood restaurants and fishing from the public docks. There are campgrounds here with ocean frontage.

Driving north along Hwy. 101, the rain forests appear near Lake Quinault. This is the gateway to the rain forests and three valleys — the Hoh, Queets and Quinault — in Olympic National Park.

The highway makes a turn to the west at the north end of the Peninsula — north of **Forks,** a lumber town — with **Clallum Bay** and **Neah Bay** providing salmon fishing opportunities and .more wilderness trails leading through deep forest to Cape Alava, at the very tip of the peninsula. This is an important archeological site.

The highway passes through the Sequim and the Dungeness valleys and on to **Port Angeles** on the Strait of Juan de Fuca where you can take the ferry to Canada's Vancouver Island.

The eastern shore of the peninsula becomes more civilized where there is more more sheltered water and several interesting towns are here, including **Port Townsend**, **Port Ludlow**, **Quilcena** and **Hoodsport**. Several wineries in this area can provide one or more good days of winery tours and tastings.

The Kitsap Peninsula lies across the Hood Canal: a long and slender fiord. More about the Kitsap in the Puget Sound pages.

Introduction — Washington Coast

Puget Sound:
This splendid body of water which laps against hundreds of miles of shoreline in the most populated corner of Washington was named for Peter Puget, an officer on Capt. George Vancouver's ship of exploration. Puget had a very short anchorage here, but the Sound has become the major center of activity for Washington commerce with not one but several port cities including Seattle and Tacoma.

The state capital city—Olympia — is nestled at the southern end of Puget Sound. Around the sound are large cities, scenic villages, naval bases, container ports and ferry terminals. Peninsulas, fiords and islands make the sound a fascinating place to live — and visit.

South Puget Sound:
The neoclassical dome of the Washington State Capitol Building is the landmark at the foot of Puget Sound. In the pleasant city of **Olympia,** the capitol building is open daily for tours and the open-air farmers market at the end of Percival Landing is worth visiting from April through December. Interstate 5 is the highway lifeline for the residents of the Sound and midway between Olympia and Tacoma, the Nisqually National Wildlife Refuge is an outstanding resting spot for migratory birds. Majestic Mt. Rainier looms over the whole region.

Tacoma is presently going through an updating. It's previously crumbling downtown area is being revitalized these days into a modern city-center. Point Defiance Park is a prime attraction for visitors. There are acres of Japanese, rose and rhododendron gardens and the Pt. Defiance Zoo has recently been joined by a new South Pacific Aquarium. The Camp 6 Logging Museum and Fort Nisqually — a restored Hudson's Bay Company fur-trading outpost — are here as well.

The route to the Kitsap Peninsula crosses the Tacoma Narrows Bridge, more stable now than when "Galloping Gertie" shook and fell apart in 1940, only three months after it was built. Across the bridge is **Gig Harbor**, a scenic small port town where an outstanding annual jazz festival takes place the second weekend in August.

The peninsula is bordered on the west by Hood Canal and on the east by Puget Sound. **Bremerton** was recently named the most livable city in the U.S.A. It's home to a large naval shipyard. **Poulsbo** — farther north on the peninsula — was settled by Norwegian immigrants and retains much of that country's culture. The Washington State ferries land at Kingston, a tiny old-fashioned seaport, and at Bremerton.

Port Orchard, located on Sinclair Inlet across from Bremerton, has a picturesque downtown with covered sidewalks and a good collection of antique, art and crafts shops. A passenger ferry runs between the two towns. The restored Port Gamble is a national historic site. **Port Hadlock** and **Port Ludlow** are small communities with golf, resorts and marinas, located between Port Townsend and the Hood Canal Bridge.

Introduction — Washington Coast

Central & North Puget Sound:

    Seattle is the vital city which serves as Washington's business hub. It's a center of commerce with a large working harbor and yet, Seattle always appeals to me as a great place for culture in a total sense. It is a fine place to eat with gourmet and popular seafood restaurants everywhere — in the city and the suburban areas including **Bellevue** which is on the east side of Lake Washington; a fine place to drink (there are several excellent micro-breweries here and the best coffee in the West). As a fine place to come for cultural stimulation, Seattle and environs host several notable festivals. My favorite is Bumbershoot, the annual Labor Day weekend cultural bash featuring hundreds of performers and artists of all genres from classical to blues in addition to art and craft displays. Seattle is a fine place to sightsee and browse: the downtown waterfront on Elliot Bay and the historic Pioneer Square district are adjacent attractions connected by a short street car line. Both are worthy of exploration. Also close-by is the famed Pike Place Market with farmers' stalls, fresh seafood, flower and local produce stands, and the market's own set of specialty restaurants.

    In short Seattle is just a fine place to visit — whatever your leisure pursuits.

    North of Seattle — off Interstate 5 — **Everett** boasts the largest one-storey building in the world: the huge aircraft assembly plant of the Boeing Company. The highway runs north toward the Canadian border, passing through the Skagit River Valley. **Mt. Vernon** is the tulip-growing center for the state and the valley is awash in color from early to mid April.

    Take a turn west at **Burlington** — north of Mt. Vernon — and you're on your way to Whidby Island, a long, slim piece of land with a fascinating mix of farming, resort life and small villages with historic main streets. The oldest of these towns is Coupeville, on the eastern side of the island with a Victorian main street and several rustic-but-modern resort hotels. Another such village is Langley, near the bottom of the island.

    Or keep driving west to the town of **Anacortes** and — by ferry — to the San Juan Islands: Orcas, Lopez, Shaw and San Juan. These quiet islands at the top of Puget Sound feature tranquil walks in dense parkland, relaxing water-side resorts, boating, and hiking on Orcas Island's Mt. Constitution. **Friday Harbor** — on San Juan Island — is a jazz festival venue.

    Bellingham is the largest population center in the extreme northwestern corner of the state. The Alaska Ferry terminal is in Bellingham, as is a huge shopping mall which you'll see from Interstate 5. **Blaine** is the small border and resort town at the end of I-5. Mt. Baker dominates this part of Washington. The North Cascades international loop drive provides a route over the Cascade Mountains with access to Mt. Baker and continues eastward to Lake Chelan National Recreation Area and the Okanogan National Forest. The loop enters Canada at the desert town of Osooyos and continues westward through southern B.C.

Introduction — British Columbia Coast

The Sea and the Mountains — these are the overwhelming elements in the coastal landscape of this huge province. British Columbia is as large as Washington, Idaho and California, all put together. B.C.'s weather is defined by its geography, particularly by the series of north-to-south mountain ranges which march across the province. The Coast and Cascade ranges protect the southern coast of B.C. from extreme weather and as a result the coastal communities are left in mild and temperate weather year-round.

As in the state of Washington, there are several "coasts" in southern B.C. There is the real coast — the west coast of **Vancouver Island** set against the Pacific Ocean. This is the wild coast with thundering Pacific surf, glistening sand beaches pilked high with driftwood and thick rain forests. Pacific Rim National Park is on the West Coast.

Then there is the east coast of this large island: sheltered by the mountain range which forms the spine of the island. Here, the calmer waters of the Strait of Georgia provide sandy beaches, clamming and Orca-watching. The city of **Victoria**, at the south end of the island is the most popular attraction for tourists in B.C. Across the strait on the B.C. mainland is **Vancouver**, Canada's third largest urban area, with 1.5 million people.

Near this cosmopolitan city (a short ferry ride north) is the **Sunshine Coast**: a collection of small fishing and resort towns slightly out of time.

The **Gulf Islands**—green, gentle and relaxed—lie between the mainland and Vancouver Island in Georgia Strait.

So this is our B.C. Coast—only a small part of the entire coastline of this province—and the routes are merely a continuation of the highways which bring tourists to this region from the United States. But within this confined area there is a wonderful variety of vacation experience waiting: from world-class skiing, mountain and forest hikes, relaxed beach activity, bucolic island getaways, all-seasons resorts, excellent restaurants, side road and back road adventure on forest roads, hot springs, wildlife viewing, and some of the best fishing in the world — for salmon, halibut, steelhead and cutthroat trout.

Snow does fall in this part of the world, but only sporadically and usually high on the mountains. It is common for vacationers and local residents to be able to ski in the morning and sun-bathe on a beach (or at the ski slopes) during spring months. The winters can be sometimes rainy, particularly in Vancouver, but spring rains and mists have a charm of their own in B.C., especially in Vancouver and Victoria when early spring blossoms are in view. The summers are generally sunny and warm with temperatures reaching into the eighties.

The B.C. chapter of this book covers the southwest corner of this vast and mountainous province. For those who wish to sample more than the southwest coast, our driver's guide "British Columbia Adventures" covers the entire province and should fill the bill for plotting further travel.

Introduction — British Columbia Coast

Sunshine Coast:

Highway 101 is a winding two-lane road which twists and turns beside the waters of the Strait of Georgia, a few kilometers north of Vancouver. You get to the Sunshine Coast by ferry — from the Horseshoe Bay terminal in West Vancouver. The entire length of the highway is 111 kilometers (69 miles). It stretches from the ferry terminal at **Gibsons** to a few kilometers north of **Powell River**, a pulp mill town.

Along the length of Hwy. 101, there are a number of small communities which offer a variety of accommodations from civilized resort hotels to rustic fishing camps. Because of its semi-isolation from the rest of the Lower Mainland area of B.C., the Sunshine Coast harks back to an earlier day. This is a relaxed part of the world where people don't hurry. The sea is an important source of revenue for the Sunshine Coasters — fishing is a prime occupation of local residents. Fishing also brings visitors to the area.

However, there are other things to do on the Sunshine Coast besides fishing. Mountain trails offer challenging hikes. Sailing and scuba diving are popular and the Sunshine Coast is a staging area for boat exploration to the north, into Princess Louisa Inlet — a long and beautiful fiord — and to Desolation Sound. **Sechelt** is the largest community on this coastline, situated on a large peninsula approximately half-way along the highway. A further ferry ride, north of Sechelt, takes cars and people to the northern section of the route and Powell River.

Vancouver Island:

The island is the emerging top of the Mackenzie range, an extension of Washington's Olympic Range. This range which is largely underwater also appears above the Pacific waters father north, as the Queen Charlotte Islands.

This backbone of mountains largely determines the way the weather behaves on the island and defines the sort of recreation which is available around the island's coastline. The mountains also provide two superior ski areas, near Nanaimo and Courtenay.

The east coast is placid and sheltered from nature's fury. The West Coast is wild, rugged and supremely beautiful, with strong Pacific waves pounding the seashore and thick rain forest flanking the mountain slopes which reach to the sea.

The southern tip and the southwest coast including the city of **Victoria** provides pleasant holidays with water sports, beach bathing and salmon fishing in Georgia Strait. The southern part of the island's west coast is less accessible but several roads take visitors to fine natural regions which are unique: **Port Renfrew** at the southwest tip of the island with its Botanical Beach; Barkley Sound and the seaside communities of **Tofino** and **Ucluelet** with the Long Beach section of Pacific Rim National Park lying between; and the extremely rugged and wild north coast at Cape Scott Provincial Park, near **Port Hardy**.

Introduction — British Columbia Coast

The city of **Victoria** is the grand dame of Vancouver Island, a staid dowager of a city which is reputed by no less than Conde Nast Traveler magazine as one of the best five cities to visit in the world. It's the capital city of B.C. and its parliament buildings are lit at night with hundreds of sparkling lights. The Inner Harbour provides a central focus for the city with hotels, restaurants and shopping nearby.

Victoria is a city of parks, gardens and golf courses, Victorian-era bed & breakfast homes and historic sites, including Fort Rodd Hill, a restored English fort which protected the British Columbia colony during the short and futile "Pig War" between the U.S. and British North America.

The city provides an excellent staging center for side trips to the southwest coast of the island — to **Sooke** on Juan de Fuca Strait and westward to **Port Renfrew**. North of Victoria is the Lake Cowichan resort district, as are the resort communities of **Parksville** and **Qualicum Beach** as well as the island's second largest city: **Nanaimo**.

"Up-Island" — north of Nanaimo — is Canada's finest salmon-fishing country in the **Comox/Campbell River** region. Father north at the northeastern tip is **Port Hardy** and nearby Orca (killer whale) watching which has become so popular that environmentalists are cautioning about the possibility of whale-watching cruises driving the whales out of their traditional home in Johnstone Strait.

For me, the gem of the island is **Pacific Rim National Park**, on the island's West Coast. This park is in three disconnected sections: Long Beach which is exactly that, lying between the villages of Ucluelet and Tofino. Both villages are places for taking charter cruises into the Pacific waters — for fishing and sight-seeing. The Broken Group islands lie within Barkley Sound, a pristine island environment protected as part of the national park. The third part of the park is the West Coast Trail, running along the coast between Port Renfrew and Bamfield. This was an early lifesaving trail, built to rescue foundering sailors. It's now a hiking magnet for tourists from around the world.

Vancouver and the Lower Mainland:

The Lower Mainland, also called Southwestern B.C., is the spreading urban area which includes the city of Vancouver, a number of suburban cities and towns and the wide Fraser River Valley which provides some of Canada's finest farmland.

Vancouver is the Lower Mainland's "downtown". Here is the large and impressive harbor which separates the city and the "North Shore" communities of **North** and **West Vancouver** which are nestled on the side of the Coast Mountains. The region extends northwest along Howe Sound to **Squamish** and **Whistler**, B.C.'s top ski resort. the drive to Squamish, less than an hour's drive from downtown Vancouver, offers fine views from the water's edge and several provincial parks which offer camping waterfall-viewing and picnicking opportunities

Introduction — British Columbia Coast

Vancouver, just over 100 years old, is now a grown-up city with impressive downtown architecture, a stupendous collection of restaurants serving food in every possible ethnic variation, parks and gardens, including Stanley Park, the city's top visitor attraction, and museums which are a must for history and native culture fanciers.

Vancouver sports several good beaches in the center of the city and most of them are placed around English Bay and are no more than ten minute's drive from the downtown core. Several beaches including those in Stanley Park are right in the downtown area. Wreck Beach is regarded by many as the finest clothing-optional beach on the continent. It's located below the bluffs of the University of British Columbia campus at Point Grey which separates English Bay from the **Fraser River** estuary.

The Fraser offers a variety of recreational pursuits including dining in river-side seafood restaurants, playing golf, boating and watching the busy work boats such as lumber-pulling tugs.

The Fraser River winds its way through the valley bearing its name after a tumultuous journey from northern British Columbia. Although much of the valley is devoted to farming, there are several fine provincial parks here including Chilliwack Lake and Cultus Lake parks.

80 minutes' drive from downtown Vancouver is **Harrison Hot Springs**, a cozy resort town set on the southern edge of Harrison Lake. The sulphur springs here have spawned a large resort hotel and a community which includes several private RV parks, motels and restaurants. Sasquatch Provincial Park is another place to camp and hike in the area. There is a public hot spring plunge pool in Harrison, a popular spot for Vancouver-area residents and tourists alike.

Farther to the northeast — a 2 1/2 hour drive from Vancouver — is **Manning Provincial Park**, a large wilderness area set high in the Cascade range, offering summer mountain hiking, canoeing on a small chain of lakes, riding, camping and a resort hotel. Winters bring cross-country and downhill skiing.

There are three mountain ski operations within a 30-minute drive of downtown Vancouver. Cypress Provincial Park in **West Vancouver** offers downhill and cross-country skiing. Grouse Mountain, accessed by a cable gondola ride in **North Vancouver**, is a downhill slope and summer view attraction. The next mountain to the east is Seymour which has ski runs at the top of the mountain in Mt. Seymour Provincial Park.

Golden Ears Provincial Park is a large and varied park north of the Fraser River near Maple Ridge. It offers mountain recreation and has a large campground. This park is accessed from Highway 7.

Vancouver has a full range of high-quality cultural organizations including the Vancouver Symphony, Ballet B.C. and several theater companies. The Queen Elizabeth Theatre hosts traveling musical productions. Several of the city's downtown hotels are among the best on the continent.

Travel Tips

Planning Your Trip: Auto Club Membership
Driving an automobile or recreational vehicle is the preferred way to experience the varied adventures the Pacific Coast regions have to offer, and this guidebook is designed to help you get the most out of your driving trip. An auto club membership is useful for planning your vacation and especially for coping with any problems you may have on the highways.

For help while traveling in Canada, should you not have an autoclub membership before you leave home, a convenient office of the American Automobile Association (B.C.A.A.) is located at 999 West Broadway in Vancouver. There are local B.C.A.A. offices in Victoria and Nanaimo on Vancouver Island.

Accommodation:
Depending on where you're planning to stay, we suggest you think about making advance reservations for the busy hotels and lodges in the tourist towns and cities. Resort community hotels and motels are often fully booked during the summer tourist season. The same holds true for the fishing and outdoor recreation lodges throughout the Paciufic Coast regions. That's why we've included recommendations for hotels, motels, campgrounds and RV parks in the travel planner pages of this book.

As a back-up to our recommendations, we suggest you obtain a copy of the state and provincial accommodation guides which are available at Chambers of Commerce and highway information centers along the U.S. coast and at travel infocentres in British Columbia.

Money:
The standard cautionary note is: avoid carrying large amounts of cash while on the road. Travelers' checks are widely available in the U.S. and British Columbia The two most widely used travelers' checks in Canada are American Express (available at banks and credit unions and at AAA offices in B.C.) and VISA. Banks and credit unions along the Pacific Coast routes affiliated with major credit card companies give cash advances on credit cards. Automatic bank teller machines (ATMs) are widely available in the urban centers servicing several networks including Cirrus, Interact and Plus.

The exchange rate for the Canadian dollar has been generally constant at about the 15% level during the past year although it has been rising in value recently. Americans get good value for their dollars in Canada except for gasoline prices. As well, smokers will be shocked at the cost of tobacco (the government's taxing smokers out of smoking).

To change U.S. dollars to Canadian money, we suggest you use a bank or credit union for the best exchange rates. Whereas U.S. dollars are accepted in most Canadian stores, hotels and restaurants, other currencies are not. Exchanging dollars in a retail store or hotel will generally bring a less favorable exchange rate than those charged in a financial institution.

Travel Tips

Budget Hostels:

Youth hostels are common in the Pacific Northwest. They cater to people of all ages who want to stay in low-cost accommodations and don't mind sharing a dormitory or want to have a communal kitchen and eating area for preparing some of their own meals. A directory of hostels is available from American Youth Hostels, 1332 Street NW, Suite 800, Washington D.C. 20005 (202-783-6161) and from the Canadian Hostelling Association, Pacific Region, 1515 Discovery St., Vancouver B.C. V6R 4K5 (604)-224-7111). Many hostels are mentioned further along in this book.

What To Wear:

Summer visitors to the Pacific Northwest states and southern B.C. require serviceable and comfortable light clothing While the summers are almost always sunny and warm, evenings can be cool and breezy so you may wish to bring along warmer outer wear (sweat shirts, windbreakers, etc.). The timid may want to bring rain gear as well. Visitors to the Pacific Northwest mountain areas — the Cascades, Olympics and Coast ranges — should be ready for cooler days and evenings than in the coastal regions. Nighttime temperatures in the mountains can get into the 40 degree range.

Winter travel in Northern California, Oregon and points north necessitates taking along warmer clothing, particularly if you're planning to camp or engage in long mountain hikes or storm-watching activity. Sweat suits and warm outer clothing, preferably down-filled, can be a comfort during the colder evenings.

Border Crossings:

For U.S. and Canadian tourists, visas are not necessary for the border crossings into Canada and the United States. If you are 18 or older, you may import goods into Canada duty free: 200 cigarettes or 50 cigars or three pounds of tobacco, 40 ounces of liquor or 24 bottles of beer, a small amount of perfume and other goods up to the value of $40. Seeds, plants and fruits are not allowed to cross the borders.

If you're passing through B.C., going into Washington state and are 21 or older, you may import free of duty the following: 200 cigarettes or 50 cigars or three pounds of tobacco and one U.S. quart of alcohol. All are entitled to take into the United States gifts to a value of $100. Plants, fruit and meat are not allowed past U.S. borders.

Firearms are not allowed to be taken across the Canadian border. Possession of "controlled substances" can result in fines, jail terms, and seizure of your vehicle—or all three. Tourists are strongly advised not to carry drugs or guns in vehicles. It's a bad way to abruptly end a vacation!

Camping:

This guidebook lists a wide variety of private and publiic campgrounds. We have included telephone numbers for all private campgrounds and RV Parks. Public campgrounds generally do not take reservations. California State Parks, however, use the MISTIX reservation system.

Travel Tips

Motoring Tips:
All of the highways along the Pacific Coast are paved and are in good condition. Side roads are another thing entirely, particularly in British Columbia where myriad forest roads offer recreational driving over routes which are used during the week by behemoth trucks which haul huge logs to sawmills and paper plants. These roads are not paved and most are dusty and require some care in driving. The same holds true for interior roads in the national and state forest reserves in Oregon and Washington. We suggest that you keep your headlights on while driving on forest roads, whether in Canada or the United States.

Major Ferry Crossings:
Ferries are a necessity for travel in Washington and British Columbia. There is an extensive ferry system operating across Puget Sound in Washington. Details on the Washington state ferry system for all Puget Sound destinations and the San Juan Islands, can be found in the Puget Sound chapter of this book, on page 193..

Briefly, these ferries operate: from Fauntleroy, south of Seattle to Vashon Island (Southworth) on the Kitsap Peninsula; from downtown Seattle to Bremerton on the Kitsap Paninsula and Winslow, on Bainbridge Island; between Edmonds, north of Seattle, and Kingston (also on the Kitsap); between Mukilteo, near Everett, and Clinton at the southern tip of Whidby Island; and ferries leaving Anacortes, south of Bellingham, docking at one or more of the various San Juan Islands and (sometimes) continuing on to Vancouver Island, B.C., landing at Sidney, near Victoria.

In British Columbia, large car ferries operate from the Vancouver area to Swartz Bay (near Victoria) and Nanaimo on Vancouver Island. Ferries cross Howe Sound from Horseshoe Bay to Langdale at the foot of the Sunshine Coast Mid-way alonmg the Sunshine Coast a ferry runs between Earl's COve and Saltery Bay. A ferry operates from Powell River at the top of the Sunshine Coast to Comox (mid-island). The car ferry Queen of the North plies the Inside Passage from Port Hardy at the northeast tip of Vancouver Island, sailing regularly to Prince Rupert on the B.C. North Coast. Please refer to the schedule of B.C. ferries located on page 212 of this book.

Traveling Seniors:
Pacific Northwest travel is increasingly appealing to seniors. Golf and fishing pursuits are ideal for older travelers and many seniors drive RVs which travel easily on most back roads and side roads.

Many hotels and local attractions provide discounted fares to seniors who need to show identification (driver's license, medicare card) to get these perks of age. **AAA** offers hotel and motel discounts to its older members as does the **AARP** (American Association of Retired Persons). Membership in the AARP brings hotel chain discounts and special tour prices in many centers. For information, write the AARP at 1909 K Street Northwest, Washington D.C. or phone them at (202) 872-4700.

California North Coast

For almost 400 miles the California North Coast stretches from San Francisco's Golden Gate until it meets the Oregon border. This coast is mostly unspoiled. Industry has left this part of the shoreline alone and wise governments have proclaimed long stretches of the coast to be national and state parks, reserves and recreation areas. This offers the possibility for many present-day voyages of discovery for modern landlubbers who drive the coastal routes in their cars and RVs.

North of the Golden Gate Bridge, the coast is reached by two routes. **U.S. Highway 101** is the inland road through Marin, Sonoma and Mendocino counties until it meets the ocean in Humboldt County. The scenic route is **Highway 1**, a two-lane state road which winds along the shore from the foot of Mt. Tamalpais near Stinson Beach until it meets Hwy. 101 at Leggett — in Redwood Country. It passes through scenic villages and towns including Bodega Bay, Jenner, Pt. Arena and Mendocino before turning inland just north of Westport.

Each person makes his or her own discovery of the North Coast and there are many kinds of discovery available. History abounds here, in the telling of the Russian fur trading adventure at Fort Ross Historic State Park and in several local museums along the way. Outdoor adventurers should explore the trails of Mt. Tamalpais and Pt. Reyes National Seashore or two delightful trails in nearby Tomales Bay State Park. Fanciers of art head for Mendocino with its New England heritage and profusion of artists and craftspeople. Flower and plant lovers visit Fort Bragg and its charming gardens.

The **Marin Coast** has a shoreline of remote beaches, shallow clamming bays, and rocky reefs — all of which is barely more than an hour's drive from San Francisco. The Golden Gate Recreation Area extends from the Golden Gate Bridge to Olema. The National Seashore at Pt. Reyes is a major ecological treasure and the Bear Valley trails offer more than 100 miles of trails for hikers and riders (horse and bicycle) from this park. The Audubon Canyon Ranch, 3 miles north of Stinson Beach, provides a refuge for thousands of migrating birds in the spring months, including great blue heron and egrets.

Past Tomales Bay, the **Sonoma Coast** is shorter and less busy than the Marin and Mendocino stretches of coastline. Fort Ross Historic State Park— north of Jenner — is its major attraction, south of the entrance to Russian River country at Jenner. A cluster of small beaches nestled between rocky headlands extend from Bodega Bay to the mouth of the river. Northern Sonoma beaches are found in Stillwater Cove County Park and Salt Point State Park, both between Ft. Ross and Stewarts Point.

The **Mendocino Coast** is forested for much of its length, with rocky heads dotting the shore. There are superb country inns in Westport, Little River and Elk and several New England colonial-style inns in Mendocino. Inland sideroads lead to wine country.

CALIFORNIA NORTH COAST HIGHWAYS

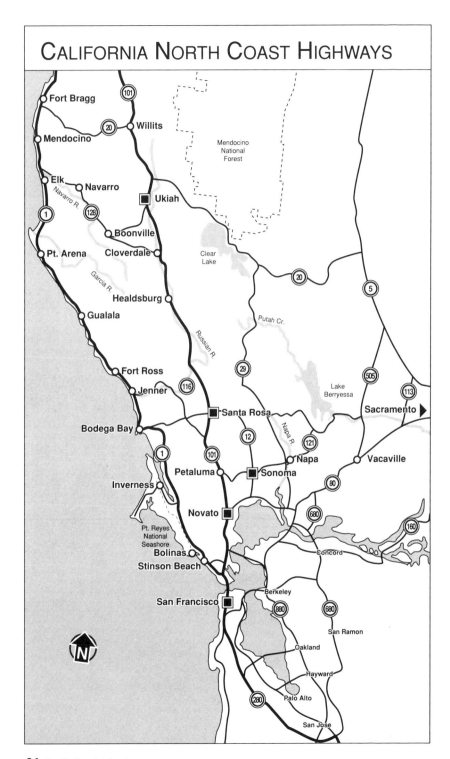

Fort Bragg · 101

20 · Willits

Mendocino

Mendocino National Forest

Elk · Navarro

Navarro R.

Ukiah

128

Boonville

1

Pt. Arena · Cloverdale

Clear Lake

Garcia R.

Healdsburg

20

5

Gualala

Putah Cr.

Russian R.

Fort Ross · 29

116

Jenner

Lake Berryessa

505

113

Santa Rosa

Sacramento ▶

Bodega Bay

12

Napa R.

121

1

101 · Petaluma · Sonoma · Napa

80 · Vacaville

Inverness

Novato

680

160

Pt. Reyes National Seashore

Concord

Bolinas
Stinson Beach

Berkeley

San Francisco · 880 · 680

San Ramon

Oakland

Hayward

280 · Palo Alto

San Jose

California North Coast — The Highway 1 Drive

Starting from the south at the Golden Gate Bridge, Highway 1 joins U.S. 101 in **Sausalito** (just north of the bridge) and heads west towards Muir Woods National Monument, an extremely popular preserve of redwoods and an excellent beach. Before the road curves down to Muir Woods there are detour signs for Highway 1. A nine-mile stretch of the road crumbled into the sea during the 1989 earthquake and this section has not been replaced to date. However, all is not lost; the detour is a thrilling drive through Mt. Tamalpais State Park, running past the park entrance. There is a campground here and trails lead through the park and to the Mt. Tam summit. The detour route descends to join the Pacific Ocean at **Stinson Beach** and you're back on Highway 1.

Stinson Beach is a small town lying exectly on the San Andreas Fault and is also a beach park which is part of the Golden Gate National Recreation Area. The popular day-use park is used for fishing and swimming between mid-May and late September. **Bolinas**, a tiny village across the lagoon from Stinson Beach, attracts visitors to Duxbury Reef, a good site for scuba diving, clamming and rock fishing.

The highway passes the entrance to Pt. Reyes National Seashore and the town of Inverness. The park is divided into two areas: beaches and farmlands are located north of **Inverness**, off the sideroad; and the Bear Valley trails are reached by stopping at the Park Headquarters off Highway 1, near **Olema**. At the end of the point is the Pt. Reyes Lighthouse, built in 1870.

Highway 1 continues northbound skirting Tomales Bay. **Marshall** and **Dillon Beach** are two villages on the way. Marshall is easy to miss unless you're looking for seafood restaurants. There are several rustic eateries beside the highway. Dillon Beach is a summer village at the mouth of the bay reached by taking a sideroad.

We're now entering Sonoma County and **Bodega Bay** provides shelter for pleasure and fishing boats. It's the only sheltered anchorage of substantial size between San Francisco and Mendocino County. This is a scenic town with good fishing, clamming, surfing and seafood restaurants. North of Bodega Bay, the Sonoma beaches extend to the mouth of the Russian River at **Jenner**. North of Jenner the landscape changes to a more rocky and rolling hillscape. Should you need to return soon to inland destinations, head east at Jenner through the Russian River area. **Fort Ross** is 13 miles north of Jenner. The state historic park commemorates early Russian history in the area and the park is also the point along the highway where beaches become accessible and Highway 1 heads north toward Mendocino County.

From **Little River** on the south to **Rockport** on the north, Highway 1 leads through popular vacation country. The two most populous towns are **Mendocino** and **Ft. Bragg**. North of Ft. Bragg is largely undeveloped. Tiny towns with weathered architecture provide occasional stopping points.

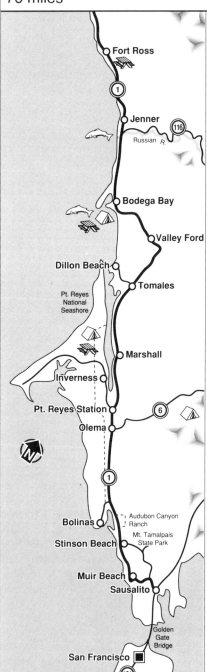

In our highway logs, we list the towns along the highway routes in addition to recreation sites and other prominent points of interest. Parts of this coastal route require careful driving over steep hills, around sharp curves and through fog at times.

Hwy. 1 joins U.S. 101 north of Sausalito and heads toward the sea, crossing — on a detour — through Mt. Tamalpais State Park. Before the detour, the old section of Hwy. 1 leads down the hill to

Muir Woods National Monument & Muir Beach This park commemorates the pioneering work of environmentalist John Muir through the groves of tall redwoods.

Mt. Tamalpais State Park The Hwy. 1 detour takes you through this impressive parkland. There are trails to walk, picnic tables, campsites & great panoramic views.

Stinson Beach Motel, restaurant, gas, book store. The village and the beach — where the road from Mt. Tam meets the sea. The day-use park provides sheltered swimming and fishing in Bolinas Bay.

Audubon Canyon Ranch 3 miles north of Stinson Beach, this park is a wildlife refuge. Bring your binoculars or use the ranch telescopes.

Turnoff to Bolinas This tiny town sits at the edge of Bolinas Bay, facing Stinson Beach.

Highway Log

Olema Gas, RV park, inns, restaurants. The village is just east of the National Seashore entrance.

Pt. Reyes Station Store, gas. This town owes its existence to a now-defunct narrow guage railroad. It now has a "wild west" flavor with saloon & nearby ranches.

Turnoff to Samuel P. Taylor State Park to 101 & Petaluma

Pt. Reyes National Seashore & Tomales Bay State Park Beaches and the point are accessed via Sir Francis Drake Blvd. through Inverness. Main park visitor center on Hwy. 1, one mile west of Olema, open 9 am to 5 pm, with Bear Valley trails nearby. Tomales Bay State Park is north of Inverness on sheltered bay-side of the peninsula. Boat launch, swimming.

Inverness Cozy village with 1900-era period buildings off the highway on Sir Francis Drake Blvd. Inns, lodge, stores, restaurants, oyster growers.

Marshall Village strung along Tomales Bay. Seafood cafes, oyster growers.

Tomales Village with hotel, gas, deli, restaurants, post office.

Turnoff to Dillon's Beach Turn west to reach this small seaside village. Clamming at low tide, fishing, RV park, tenting.

Valley Ford Tiny village with side roads to Petaluma & Santa Rosa. The village is slightly inland as Highway 1 leaves the sea for a few miles. Restaurant, B & B hotel.

Bodega Bay Village with marina, gas, inns, guest ranch, winery tasting room, restaurants, stores, art galleries & fishing charters.

Doran Beach County Park has camping, boat launch & beaches. This park is mainly on a sand spit lying across the bay, curving toward Bodega Head. Good walking on the spit, rock fishing, surfing.

Westside County Park has picnic tables & trails to beaches. Boat launch, moorage.

Sonoma Coast State Beach 14 miles of wild and uncrowded beach parks stretching from Bodega Bay to Jenner.

A large campground is found at the **Bodega Dunes** park. Another is at **Wrights Beach**, north of Duncan's Landing.

Junction with Hwy. 116 Road through Russian River area to Guerneville & Santa Rosa. There is lodging of all kinds in the Guerneville area in addition to wineries, campgrounds & parks.

Jenner Stores, gas, motels & inns, restaurants. Town at the mouth of the Russian River.

Fort Ross Historic State Park To west of highway. Visitor Center has interpretive displays. A short trail leads to the restored 19th century Russian fur-trading fort which overlooks the ocean. Picnic tables, bluff trail. Fort open 10 am to 4:30 pm daily.

Highway 101
133 miles

Fort Ross to Leggett
3 hours

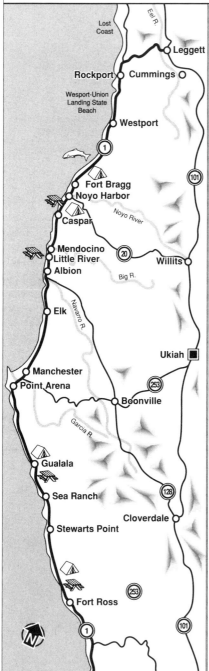

This part of the coast route is less settled than the route to the south. The landscape changes with wilder countryside, rolling hills and a seacoast of rocky headlands and forests reaching to the sea. The beach parks have a distinct charm of their own and side roads lead to interesting natural attractions.

Stillwater Cove County Park 3.5 miles north of Ft. Ross, this day-use park is located on the cove and creek-front. It's a favorite of scuba divers. There are picnic tables, a canyon trail and the old Ft. Ross schoolhouse.

Salt Pt. State Park midway between Jenner & Stewarts Point. There are secluded & open campsites, more scuba diving chances, beachcombing and miles of trails through pygmy pine groves & redwoods.

Kruse Rhododendron State Reserve Just south of Stewarts Pt., the reserve is at its most colorful in the April-June period with more than 300 acres of rhodos in bloom.

Stewarts Pt. A late 19th & early 20th century village with general store, hotel, gas & old school-house.

Sea Ranch This resort complex has modern vacation homes which may be rented for short or long periods, a fine resort hotel, restaurant and a golf course. There are miles of trails to walk and a fine seashore landscape.

38 Pacific Coast Adventures

Highway Log

Gualala An old lumber town and port. A county park lies beside the shore and a sand spit. There are campsites and steelhead fishing. The town (say Walalla) has an historic hotel, motels, gas, stores, cafes, RV park, bakery & deli.

Point Arena Gas, store, hotel, motel, B & B homes, RV park & campground, restaurants, deli. The old lighthouse, rebuilt after the 1906 earthquake, still shines and houses a museum with guest cottages on the site.

Turnoff to Mountain View Road This sideroad runs west from Pt. Arena for 27 miles, to Boonville and the Anderson Valley.

Manchester State Beach features a 7-mile beach with basic campground. A private campground is located beside the park.

Manchester a tiny village, 4.5 miles north of Pt. Arena. Inn, restaurant.

Elk Another small village with Victorian buildings. Restaurants, inns, store & Greenwood State Park (tidepools).

Turnoff to State Hwy. 128 & Boonville This is the main road connecting the coast with Boonville & Cloverdale on U.S. 101. It's 30 miles to Boonville, 52 miles to Ukiah & 58 miles to Cloverdale.

Albion A sheltered port and fishing village with gas, stores, restaurants, inns and B & B.

Little River Village, with inns.

Van Damme State Park On Little River with hiking through a pygmy forest & biking trails. Camping.

Sideroad to Comptche, Orr's Springs, Boonville This road runs south to join Hwy. 128 just north of Navarro.

Mendocino This village with New England architecture is an arts center with inns, motels, gas, and stores set above dramatic bluffs.

Mendocino Headlands State Park runs north from Little River past Mendocino town. It's perfect for sea-side walks & whale watching.

Russian Gulch State Park At Mendocino with waterfall trail.

Caspar Village with gas, camping, store & Jughandle State reserve is nearby.

Turnoff to Hwy. 20 — to Willits and Pygmy Forest Reserve.

Noyo Harbor At the south end of Ft. Bragg. Fishing charters.

Fort Bragg A sizeable town with motels on hwy., gas, stores, botanical gardens & Skunk Train railroad line to Willits.

MacKerricher State Park north of Ft. Bragg. Camping, dunes, trails, beaches, fishing lake.

Westport Tiny village with restaurant, gas (pumps!), store, motels. North is ghost town of Rockport and dirt road to the Lost Coast Trail & Sinkyone Wilderness State Park (summer only).

Westport-Union Landing State Beach just south of Rockport.

Leggett Humboldt County town is inland at junction of Hwys 1 & 101.

Marin County - Beaches & More

The beaches of the Marin Coast are a favorite holiday destination for San Francisco Bay/area residents. Only Dillon Beach at the northwest end of the county is more than one hour's drive from the Golden Gate Bridge and several beaches are within 30 minutes' drive via Highway 1.

From the sea, the Marin coast is forbidding. The shoreline is shoal ridden, the fog is frequent and winds tend to whine too much for safe passage through these waters. On the other hand, from the shore the coastline is made for recreational pursuits: the waves are made for watching and surfing, there's good rock fishing, rock hounding and clamming. Several sea-side parks invite swimming in warm, sheltered bays. And much of the shoreline has been preserved as park area, making it easy to find the holiday activity you wish to pursue.

Here's a short list of the Marin beaches with some of their special attractions:

- **Muir Beach**, part of the Golden Gate National Recreation Area, at the Muir Woods National Monument, is a small beach reached from Muir Woods. The Muir Beach Overlook, a small park, gives visitors a wonderful view of the Pacific Ocean.
- **Stinson Beach**, next to the village of the same name, is a larger day-use beach park with clean white sand. It offers swimming, surfing, fishing and picnics.
- **Point Reyes National Seashore**, with its headquarters near Olema, has several beaches on this geologically-interesting island separated from the mainland by the San Andreas Fault. **Drake's Bay** has beaches on almost the total length of the bay. **Limatour Beach** and estero provide additional spots for sunning on the sand. The estero is a marsh with abundant bird life. The **Point Reyes Beaches**, southwest of Inverness, have high surf and picnic facilities. **McClure's Beach** is also windy with tall waves and is unsuitable for swimming but is great for walking and wave-watching.
- **Tomales Bay State Park** near the National Seashore and Inverness, has warm and sheltered salt water swimming. There are beach areas along Tomales Bay in small coves.
- **Dillon Beach**, to the north via Highway 1, features clamming on an island at low tide and swimming for more hardy types.

Between these beaches are other attractions including several small towns and villages, each with its own character: Stinson Beach, Olema, Pt. Reyes Station, Inverness, Marshal, Tomales and Dillon Beach. Samuel P. Taylor State Park is on a sideroad just east of Olema — with a campground. The Audubon Canyon Ranch is a bird-habitat preserve. There are more inexpensive seafood restaurants than I can list here and most of the seafood comes straight to the cafes from Tomales Bay.

Stinson Beach & Bolinas

Stinson Beach is the first small town you reach when traveling along Highway 1 from the San Francisco area. It's at the foot of Mt. Tamalpais and is just north of Stinson Beach—the beach. This is a day-use park, part of the Golden Gate National Recreation Area. Anglers fish for ling cod, cabezone and blenny near the southern boundary of the park where it's rocky. Just at the entrance to the town is a swimming beach with warm water thanks to Bolinas Bay. The park is open from 9 am to 4:30 pm.

The town is small and has only a few places to stay and eat. The **Ocean Court Motel** (415-868-0212) has one-bedroom suites with kitchens and is close to the beach, restaurants and stores. **$$**. **Casa Del Mar** (415-868-2124) is a bed & breakfast home, a 1925 Mediterranean villa overlooking a garden with good views. **$$$**.

Eating in Stinson Beach is fairly basic but hunger can be cured at the **Parkside Cafe & Pizza Parlor**. It's open for breakfast, lunch and dinner. **$ to $$**. The **Sand Dollar** is a restaurant & cocktail lounge, open for lunch and dinner, serving seafood and other dishes. **$$**. The **Stinson Beach Grill** serves fresh California food including seafood, pasta, some Mexican dishes and steaks and has a good selection of California wines and regional micro-brewery beers. **$$ to $$$**.

Bolinas is off the highway via a short sideroad which leads around Bolinas Bay, two minutes' drive north of Stinson Beach. Bolinas people are a private bunch and tourism has not always been welcomed but there are accommodations here and the beach in front of the village offers good sunbathing, surfing and tidepools to explore during low tide periods. There's usually good fishing for striped bass at the mouth of the lagoon. Each end of the main street has access to the beach. The western approach to the beach is close to Duxbury Reef, which makes Bolinas a special place to visit.

There are cafes in town and a small historical and art museum. Hikers will find the Palomarin Trail offers an excellent walk from the trailhead at the end of Mesa Road. Hike along the shore for 3.5 miles and you reach Bass Lake, a scenic small lake with alders and cattails along much of the shore. A mile further is Pelican Lake where water falls down the rocky cliff to the ocean. Another 1.5 miles from Pelican Lake is a secluded ocean beach reached by a short side trail which leads down a bluff. From the foot of the bluff, head south a quarter of a mile and you come to the impressive Alamere Falls which form a pool on the beach before the water runs across the sand into the Pacific.

For accommodation in Bolinas, try one of several B & B homes, including **One Fifty-Five Pine** (415-868-0263), a beach cottage overlooking the reef. **$$**. **Thomas' White House Inn** 118 Kale Rd (415-868-0279) is a New-England style inn. There are two cafes on the main street of Bolinas: the **Bolinas Bakery & Cafe** and the **Blue Heron Inn Restaurant** which has a beer & wine bar.

Pt. Reyes National Seashore

First there was the fog and the Coast Miwok Indians, and the amazing travels of this strangely-shaped piece of land — shoved more than 300 miles north by the grinding of the huge Pacific and American plates whose opposition to each other formed the San Andreas Fault: the rift zone which characterizes this geological preserve. Sir Francis Drake visited the native encampment here in 1579, needing to beach his ship the Golden Hinde for repairs. Spaniards sailed the region from 1595 and in 1603 the explorer Don Sebastian Vizcaino named the headland "La Punta de Los Reyes". Spanish rule decimated the Miwok population of Point Reyes and the English never returned. The Mexican period was brief and uneventful. The Marin Coast became farmland.

Then came the lighthouse — in the late 1800s — to protect ships from the shoals and reefs of the Marin Coast. Its remote, rocky and fog-infested location drove its keepers mad during the early years of the light and summers are still foggy and windy. But the point had a haunting beauty of interest to naturalists and farmers alike, and to protect the unique geological and ecological zone, the National Seashore was created by Congress in 1962.

Sea lions bask along the shoreline. Deer are found in the Douglas fir and Bishop pine forests which stretch almost to the long beaches of the point. More than 350 species of seabirds nest in the park.

Inverness Ridge is a favorite place for summer hiking. Gray whales migrate to Baja California close to the lighthouse. Seals and migratory shore birds inhabit the estero (marsh) of Drake's Bay.

The best place to get an orientation to the park attractions is the Bear Valley Visitor Center (one of three in the park). It's just off Highway 1, at Olemo. Entering the park at this point, you cross the faultline. The visitor center contains interpretive exhibits on the National Seashore geology and wildlife. There are self-guided nature trails at the center in addition to a replica of a Coast Miwok Indian village. Be sure to pick up information on the park here, including guides to the trail systems.

The National Seashore is found in several parts. After a drive through the town of Inverness on Sir Francis Drake Highway, you may drive on to the end of this highway to the lighthouse and a small visitor center, then to Drake's Beach and the Kenneth C. Patrick Visitor Center which has been expanded and re-opened with new exhibits in the summer of 1991. The Pt. Reyes north and south beaches are on the ocean, just off the road.

A sideroad leads to the estero parking lot where the Estero Trail leads to the marsh for shore bird viewing. Another fork leads to two other parking areas for trails to Limantour Spit and beach. This same area can be reached by Limantour Road which intersects with Bear Valley Road near the main visitor center.

A network of trails, offering more than 100 miles of walking, fan out from the main Bear Valley Trail.

Pt. Reyes National Seashore

Things to See & Do:

Interpretation programs in the visitor centers change with the seasons. Winter programs focus on whale watching and viewing wintering shore birds. Earthquake trail walks are conducted year-round. Summer activity shifts to archaeology, longer trail walks, the marsh habitats and exploration of plant life in the park.

Pt. Reyes Light is on Francis Drake Highway, 20.5 miles from the main visitor center. There is an impressive view here and visitors may walk down the 300 steps to the lighthouse. Murres and sea lions live on the rocks below the light. The best place to see gray whales during winter months is from the lighthouse observation platform. The visitor center here is open Thursday through Monday, weather permitting.

Mt. Vision Overlook: At 8.7 miles on the Drake Highway a sideroad branches eastward to the Overlook which provides an outstanding view of Drake's Bay and the estero.

Pt. Reyes Ocean Beaches: This long beach is divided into two sections. The north beach is at 13 miles on the Drake Highway. The south beach is at 15.7 miles. Both are good places for beachcoming and picnics. They are not for swimming, however. The rip tides are fierce and waves are too high for water sports.

Drake's Beach: This beach is more protected and swimming is permitted. There is a cafe at the beach and the Kenneth C. Patrick Information Center is here too. The sideroad joins Francis Drake Highway between the north and south beaches.

Bear Valley Trails: The trailhead is at the Bear Valley Visitors Center. There are trail maps at the center and the longest one-way distance is 11.5 miles (Palomarin Trail). Shorter trails include: Arch Rock (4.1 miles); Sky Camp (2.7 miles); Wildcat Camp (6.3 miles); and Coast Camp (8.9 miles); these are all one-way distances.

Camping in the Park:

Camping with cars and RVs is not permitted within Pt. Reyes National Seashore. Walk-in tent camping is available in four locations: Sky Camp, 2.5 miles from the Bear Valley trailhead — a high campsite on Mt. Wittenberg; Coast Camp is on the ocean about 9 miles from the trailhead; Wildcat Camp is a group campground 6.3 miles from the Bear Valley trailhead; Glen Camp is a small wooded campground 5 miles from the trailhead. All campsites have drinking water and restrooms as well as a place to hitch your horse. Permits must be obtained at the visitor center.

There are car campsites available at Samuel P. Taylor State Park, on a sideroad near Olema as well as at several local private campgrounds & RV parks (see page 45 for Olema & Pt. Reyes Station details).

Tomales Bay State Park & Inverness

When I remember Tomales Bay, I always think of oysters — acres of oysters. The native oysters were enjoyed by the Miwok Indians for thousands of years. Today, West Marin oysters are cultivated and grown by oyster farmers — and served on the shell or in a dozen other ways in the seafood restaurants which are clustered around the bay. Some of these are in the town of Inverness which lies on the Pt. Reyes peninsula — but on the sheltered side. Tomales Bay State Park is also on the quiet side of the peninsula, with swimming beaches and picnic sites. It is reached by taking Sir Francis Drake Highway past Inverness. There are several sandy-bottom coves — Indian, Hearts Desire (the main beach), Pebble, and Shell — with good swimming and sunbathing. There is a stand of Bishop pine in the park, a species not found off the peninsula. Rock cockles are abundant along the shore, below the sandstone bluffs.

Inverness was founded as a summer resort by James Shafter, a lawyer and ranch owner who was a partner in the narrow gauge railway operation. He landed in debt and paid it off by subdividing his land, creating a summer resort community in 1889. A museum in the library building displays artifacts of this early Inverness development.

This is a cozy town, with period architecture. There are oysters for sale in town at Johnson's Drake Bay Oysters and local seafood restaurants offer the catch of the day. Several B & B homes and inns offer comfortable lodging.

For accommodations, we suggest two inns: **Manka's Inverness Lodge** (415-669-1034), built as a hunting lodge with a restaurant serving dinners and Sunday brunch, rooms in the main building and cabins with fireplaces. **$$ to $$$**. The **Blackthorne Inn** (415-663-8621), is a building which grew like topsy with a windowed tower above the main building. Breakfast served. **$$$**. **Ten Inverness Way** (415-669-1648) is a B & B home with four rooms in a redwood shingle cottage with library,bar and whirlpool. **$$**. The **Inverness Motel** (415-669-1081) has budget accommodation with restaurants nearby. **$ to $$**. For very cozy accommodations (one room only) you may wish to stay at **Rosemary Cottage** (415-663-9338) a French country cottage furnished with antiques with a full kitchen and wood stove **$$** or at **Arbor Cottage** (415-663-8020) a private cottage with full breakfast **$$;** or try **The Ark** (415-663-8276) another private cottage with breakfast **$$**.

The restaurant at Manka's Inverness Lodge in the hills above Inverness serves dinners and Sunday brunch **$$ to $$$**. **Barnaby's By The Bay** specializes in seafood with a Tomales Bay view, including oysters served on the restaurant's decks during summer months. Open from 8 am for breakfast and serving lunch and dinner daily. **$$ to $$$**. **Vladimir's Czechoslovakian Restaurant** in downtown Inverness features schnitzel and other central European entrees. Bar. **$$ to $$$**. The **Gray Whale Bakery & Pizzeria** serves soups, sandwiches, pizza and salads. **$ to $$**.

Olema & Point Reyes Station

These two small towns service the needs of local residents and the hundreds of thousands of visitors who come each year to Pt. Reyes National Seashore. They began their existence as market towns for the farmers and ranchers of West Marin; now these towns are now geared for tourist traffic and each has its own atmosphere.

With a population of 55, tiny **Olema** is a mere shadow of its former feisty self when the weekly steamer brought people and freight from San Francisco, and the bi-weekly stage ran to San Raphael. In the 1860s and 70s, Olema had six bars, two hotels, and a lusty and sometimes dangerous population. There are still hotels and a bar or two, but the cowboys from local ranches are well-behaved these days.

There are several good places to stay in and near Olema. The best of these is **Pt. Reyes Seashore Lodge**, 10021 Costal Highway (415-663-9000), a big country lodge built in a turn-of-the-century style with large rooms and suites, some with whirlpools & fireplaces. Free breakfast served. The lodge is next to a National Seashore trail at Olema Creek **$$$**. **Roundstone Farm** 9940 Sir Francis Drake Blvd. (415-663-1020) is a bed & breakfast home set in a working horse ranch. There are four comfortable rooms and full breakfast is served. **$$**. The **Olema Inn** (415-663-9559) is an old hotel, built in 1876. **$$**. RV and tent camping is available at the **Olema Ranch Campground** (415-663-8110) with wooded and open sites, full hookups, laundry, store, propane, firewood and RV pads.

In such a small village, restaurants are few. However, the **Olema Farm House** on Hwy. 1 is a restaurant and bar which serves seafood, local lamb and pasta dishes with breakfast from 8 am. It's closed on Tuesdays. **$$**

There's a little more to choose from in Pt. Reyes Station, which compared to Olema is a johnny-come-lately town — founded in 1875. Pt. Reyes Station was a stopping point on the narrow gauge railway which wound its way along through West Marin to Sausalito. At that time, the station was alone in the middle of a large pasture. The railway is gone but the village remains, with a decided "old-west" atmosphere. There are operating ranches close by. The "Feed Barn" store is a main street landmark and the Old Western Saloon maintains the ambience.

There are several very good B & B operations here. **Fernando's Hideaway** (415-663-1966) has three rooms in a house and cottage with fireplaces & hot tub. **$$**. The **Holly Tree Inn** (415-663-1554) has five rooms with full breakfast in a Swedish atmosphere in 19 wooded acres with antique furnishings and gardens. There's a private cottage in the woods. **$$ to $$$**. **Thirty-Nine Cypress** (415-663-1709) has 3 rooms, one with shared bath. **$$**. To reserve at six inns in the area call 415-485-2649.

The **Palace Market** has fresh food, a deli and cooked food to go. The **Station House Cafe** is a superior cafe and bar, open at 7 am for breakfast. **Chez Madelaine**—on Highway 1—specializes in French country cooking along with hamburgers and other such comfort food. All are **$ to $$**.

Marshall, Tomales, Dillon Beach & Valley Ford

The village of **Marshall** is hard to find. As a collection of buildings — oyster farmers, homes, restaurants and stores scattered along Highway 1 — it sort of sneaks up on you. You know you're in Marshall when you see **Tony's Seafood Restaurant**. I believe that Tony's is the best casual seafood place in the country and it's mainly because of the atmosphere of the place. When you get out of your car and try to find the door, you have to run through a gauntlet of several oyster shuckers on the sidewalk, preparing your lunch or dinner. Inside, the ambience is decidedly rustic but the view of Tomales Bay is great and the food is terrific: oysters on the half shell, or in a dozen other ways — barbecued and pan fried. Add scallops and various fish dishes along with the best French fries you've eaten in a long time and your hunger will be well-satisfied. There are other seafood places in Marshall and beyond. You may wish to try **Nick's Cove**, along the road west of Tony's. It has an antique bar and claims to be the "Home of the Horny Oyster" (whatever that means).

The village of **Tomales** is small but there are reasons for staying, at least overnight. The **Tomales Country Inn** (707-878-9992) is an old 1899 Victorian farmhouse, a B & B home with an English garden and gabled guest rooms. **$$.** An old historic hotel built in 1866 as the Continental and then re-built as the United States Hotel in the 1890s has AGAIN been rebuilt as the **U.S. Hotel** and opened to the public in 1990. This is a bed & breakfast operation with eight upstairs rooms and continental breakfast.**$$.** Ron and Gary Davis own the hotel and also own the **Village Coffee House** across the street. It's open for breakfast, lunch and dinner. **$ to $$.** The **William Tell House** is a bar and restaurant in Tomales which has been here for a long time. There's a long bar and the dining room features prime rib, roast duck, seafood pasta and other filling items. **$$ to $$$.** There's a deli in Tomales, named **Country Delights**, serving breakfast and stocking meats, cheeses and such for take-out. It's open for breakfast at 7 am and closes at 6 pm.

Valley Ford is a hamlet slightly inland between Tomales and Dillon Beach, just inside Sonoma County. For historic hotel fans, the **Valley Ford Hotel** (1-800-696-6679 or 707-876-3600) is worth attention. This ancient (1864) inn is now a B & B operation in this rural village of 126 people. Remodeled in 1990, the hotel has six upstairs bedrooms and one room downstairs — all with private baths. **$$.** North of Valley Ford and 3 miles south of Bodega Bay, the **School House Inn** (707-876-3257) is indeed an old rural school which now has rooms with private bath and breakfast. The schoolhouse was featured in Alfred Hitchcock's "The Birds" which was filmed in Bodega Bay & area. **$$.** Returning to the seashore via Highway 1, Dillon Beach offers excellent fishing and crabbing as well as clam digging and looking for abalone. This is a favorite spot for rock fishing. **Lawson's Resort** (707-878-2204) has housekeeping cottages for rent by the weekend or week. There's a campground and general store. Restaurants are nearby.

Sonoma Coast — The Drive

The western part of Sonoma County is a diverse landscape of rivers, dense forest, farm-studded valleys and rugged coastline.

The first settlement of the area was on the coast when Russian trade explorers came here looking for furs. Fort Ross was established in 1812 as a Russian trading post.

By the late 1800s, railroads ran through the countryside, connecting the redwood forests with San Francisco. The rail lines brought settlers and tourists, as well as a large redwood lumber industry.

The rail lines have disappeared from the coast but U.S. Highway 101 and State Highway 1 provide north/south corridors for the region with state roads connecting the two.

The Russian River flows through the heart of western Sonoma County and the valley is the heart of the region's agricultural activity. This is apple country and, in recent years, wineries have been established in the Russian River Valley — 57 at last count — some of the most notable devoted to sparkling wines. This is also fishing country, on the coast and in the Russian River Valley. The valley is covered in detail — including accommodations and food — in the Coast Wine Tour chapter which begins on page 80.

Visitors come to the coast during the summer months to enjoy the rugged beaches north of **Bodega Bay** and from January through March to watch the great grey whales on their southern migration from Alaska to Baja California waters. Whale watching excursions are a popular feature of the harbor at Bodega Bay.

Jenner, an underrated town at the mouth of the Russian River, is a fine spot for experiencing the vagaries of nature. Killer whales and white sharks can be seen just off the rocky headlands. The river mouth harbors seals which grow to huge sizes (some weigh in at 300 pounds), terns and pelicans. They all gather for the prime seafood dining. By late April and early May, the seals give birth and the pups are seen frolicking at the river's mouth. There are several inns and good seafood restaurants in Jenner, one perched on a hill overlooking the sea where it's joined by the Russian River.

To the north, on Highway 101, **Fort Ross** has been restored as a national historic park. The fifteen miles of Highway 1 between Jenner and Fort Ross may be the most slow-driving stretch along the northern California coast. The route contains winding hill-climbs, steep drops from cliffs as high as 900 feet and few amenities along the way. Drivers of RVs and cars pulling trailers are advised to take it easy along this stretch.

The State Park at **Salt Point** is one of the newest parks in the California State system — 6000 acres of beaches, rocky coast and forest. There are car sites and walk-in tent campsites in ocean-side and forest campgrounds. Driving through sparsely-settled countryside, the north end of the county features rolling hills in the **Stewart's Point / Sea Ranch** area. This is a place for cozy getaway lodges and strolls along the untamed coastline.

Bodega Bay

The town was made famous (or notorious if you wish) by Alfred Hitchcock when he shot his film "The Birds" in Bodega Bay. I can assure you that now, many years later, the birds are friendly and only looking for fish in the picturesque Bodega Bay harbor.

There are two chief attractions for visitors to Bodega Bay: the fishing docks and the sea-side golf course. The golf course was designed by Robert Trent Jones in the Scottish style, with rolling hills and heavy roughs. The fishing docks are perfect for relaxed strolling and looking at the busy fishermen bringing in their catches each day.

The fishing industry has a side benefit: some of the best seafood restaurants along the coast, perched in scenic locations on the slopes which lead to the harbor. The Fisherman's Festival & Blessing of the Fleet is held during the third week of April. There is a winery in the town, although the grapes are purchased from vineyards farther inland. The tasting room on Highway 1 features a saltwater aquarium which will keep the kids amused while wine tasting proceeds.

Bodega Bay is a good place to shop for food and other supplies when traveling north to the state beaches and campgrounds in the area. The Crab Pot Fish Market, on Highway 1, is a handy place to buy fresh and smoked seafood. McGaughey Bros. General Store at the Spud Point Marina is a real old-fashioned general store with groceries, fishing supplies and hardware. There are several art and crafts stores in the town, including the Branscombe Gallery, on the northeast side of the bay at 1588 Eastshore Road.

Places to stay include the **Bodega Coast Inn** on Highway 1 (707-875-2217), a cluster of 44 rooms and suites with a view of the bay and marsh. All units have private baths, some have fireplaces. **$$ to $$$**. **The Inn At The Tides**, also on Hwy. 1 (707-875-2751) has twelve lodges set on a slope above the bay. Across the road is a fishing dock and the Inn's restaurant and bar. The 86 rooms have fireplaces and room service is available. There's an indoor-outdoor pool and sauna. **$$ to $$$**.

Bodega Vista Inn at 17699 Hwy. 1 (707-876-3300) is a bed & breakfast home in a geodesic dome with four units, full breakfast and a rural setting. **$$**.

For seafood, go straight to **Lucas Wharf Restaurant and Bar**. It's on the waterfront, opened in 1984 and built over the water. The white boards serve as a daily catch sheet but a full menu is also available. A full-service deli is next door to the main restaurant, as is a take-out seafood stand with fish & chips, shrimp, clams and calamari. It's located in the south harbor area. **$ to $$$**. The **Sandpiper Dockside Cafe** is at the north end of town, down the hill from Hwy. 1. with outdoor dining during warm months. **$ to $$**.

A more homey local restaurant is **Nunu's TNT**, at 1400 Hwy. 1. The Nuno family now have four restaurants in Sonoma County. This one is typical, serving Mexican dishes including seafood specialties. **$$ to $$$**.

Sonoma Coast State Beach

The beaches north of Bodega Bay are among the most scenic in the state. Collectively they are Sonoma State Beach, a sort of disconnected state park which is accessible from more than a dozen points along Highway 1.

The beaches extend for more than 13 miles: a prime location for anglers as well as picknickers, beachcombers, hikers and campers.

There are 30 campsites at **Wright's Beach** and a much larger campground with 100 sites at **Bodega Dunes**. This is a more developed campground with showers, restrooms, a sani-station and campsite center. Its 1/2 mile south of Salmon Creek. Reservations should be made in advance during the busy summer season at any of the California MISTIX ticket outlets which are found in stores around the state. Summer stays are limited to seven days, 30 days at other times.

The park headquarters and information center is located at the Salmon Creek site. The beach at Salmon Creek curves around a lagoon with eel grass sheltering many birds in the shallows. You'll see European beach grass on the dunes in the area, the result of a dunes stabilizing effort started in 1951.

There are no lifeguards along these beaches and swimming is not recommended. The waves are high and rip tides in many places make for strong undertows. Goat Rock, at the northern end of the park, is a particularly dangerous place.

The **Sonoma Coast Trail** runs along the blufftops and connects many of the beaches. It begins at the north end on the bluffs overlooking Blind Beach and there is a further access point 1/2 mile north at Goat Rock. A causeway connects the rock and the mainland. There is a small parking lot at the end of Goat Rock Road and signs point to the trail which heads south along the bluffs. You climb over a stile and cross a pasture. The trail climbs up Peaked Hill and then comes down and over a ravine bridge to sheep grazing fields. The trail continues south into Furlong Gulch and from here the trail and the beach leads to Wright's Beach campground and the south trailhead.

Supplies (food and otherwise) can be purchased in Bodega Bay and the smaller community of **Duncans Mills**, just off the highway south of Jenner. There's a private campground in Duncans Mills, on Moscow Road. The **Casini Ranch Family Campground** (707-865-2255) with full hookups, showers and laundry.

For those who require indoor accommodation in the beach area, **Bodega Bay** and **Jenner** provide a number of good inns and motels. Bridgehaven Restaurant and Lodging, south of Jenner on Highway 1, provides rustic two-bedroom bungalow accommodation at a good price. **$ to $$**. The restaurant across the highway serves burgers, soup, salads and seafood dishes. Other places to eat are two minutes away — in Jenner.

Just north of the beaches lies the mouth of the Russian River, the gateway to **Guerneville** and the other towns of the Russian River region.

Russian River Country

The Russian River resort region offers a wide variety of accommodations, restaurants, parks and wineries. Details on this region are found in the Wine Tour chapter (page 80) but coastal travelers should think about taking a side-trip along the Russian River or plan to make the Russian River Valley a stop-over spot as you explore the coast route. This is an area of great natural beauty as the river winds through orchards and vineyards and through forests of giant redwoods. This part of Sonoma County is covered in much greater detail in the Coast Wine Country chapter of this book with the lower Russian River section beginning on page 103.

Below are three tiny villages which are close to the coast, offering quaint views of Russian River rusticity.

Duncans Mills:

In 1886, Sam and Alex Duncan founded this tiny community after being flooded out of their sawmill site at Salt Point. The mill and post office were barged to the present site in 1886. Today, there's a general store, campground, several restaurants and the old post office. This spot on Moscow Rd. is handy for Sonoma Beach campers to pick up provisions or to go for a lunch or dinner. As mentioned on the previous page, the Casini Ranch Family Campground has full facilities for RVs and trailers.

The **Blue Heron Inn** is a small cafe in Duncans Mills — a turn of the century restored tavern. The redwood-finished dining room features fish, chicken and vegetarian dishes. The **Gold Coast Oyster & Espresso Bar** roasts its own coffee. In summer days, grilled and barbecued oysters are served in the garden courtyard. The **Duncans Mills General Store** also serves breakfast and carries a full stock of supplies for campers and anglers, along with a good selection of regional wines. Duncans Mills is the epitome of rural America.

Cazadero:

On Cazadero Hwy., north off Hwy. 116, there's a general store with picnic supplies and Sonoma wines as well as fishing supplies, gasoline and hardware. **Cazanoma Lodge**, at 1,000 Kidd Rd (707-635-5255) has overnight accommodations including continental breakfast **($$)** and its restaurant has dinner rates from $12 to $16.

Monte Rio:

South off Hwy. 116 on the Bohemian Hwy., this village has an historic three-story inn, built in 1906 which served as "Holiday Inn" in the 1940s film of the same name. Now called the **Village Inn**, the hotel has basic rooms as well as 1-bedroom suites in two buildings and a large lobby with fireplace. **$ to $$**. There is a restaurant here with an outdoor deck. The menu is includes seafood specialties.

The other Inn in Monte Rio, the **Highland Dell Inn**, also dates from 1906 (a good year). This hotel is slightly more luxurious. Breakfast is served and if you want to splurge, ask for the Bohemian Suite which covers the entire third floor. **$$ to $$$**.

Jenner

This fishing village is located in one of the most impressive natural environments in California. This is where the Russian River meets the sea and a wealth of wildlife inhabits the mouth and the banks of the river — as it winds through the forested region which is known as Russian River Country. As the gateway to this resort area and to the northern beaches, Jenner is a handy place to stop for a meal or for gas and picnic supplies before heading elsewhere.

An enduring attraction of the town are the seals which mate and bring up their young on several rocky offshore islands. The seals come to the mouth of the river when fish are returning, late in the fall.

The river mouth has a fascinating annual life cycle. The river is some 90 miles long with its source in Mendocino County. During winter storm periods, the river is a rushing torrent. But during the spring and summer, the river is quiet and the waves of the Pacific overcome the flow of the river. The mouth is closed each year with a low sandy berm — a natural bridge which visitors use to walk from Goat Rock to the north shore of the river. The rains of fall — sometimes with the help of a bulldozer — clear the rivermouth again, fish move upstream, the seals come to eat the fish and the cycle continues. During the prime seal season, state park rangers are handy to conduct seal-watching excursions.

Murphy's Jenner Inn (707-865-2377) located on the Coast Highway (#1), is an extremely popular bed and breakfast operation. Cottages next to the lodge have been made into 10 rooms and suites. All have private baths and most have decks and ocean views. Several have hot tubs. **$$ to $$$**. Their restaurant is a noted seafood place and has a full bar. **River's End Lodging** (707-865-2484 or 879-3252) is another restaurant/cabins combination, this one less sophisticated than Murphy's with rooms and cabins but no breakfast (coffee is provided). Brunch is served on the weekends. **$$ to $$$**. The **Lazy River Motel** on Highway 1 (707-865-2409) is an unpretentious, rustic place with rooms and cabins at the river's edge. Several of the rooms have decks overlooking the river. Morning coffee available. **$ to $$**.

Jenner is definitely a place to eat — with several scenic restaurants serving good food. **Murphy's Jenner Inn Restaurant** is mentioned above. The cuisine is continental and fresh seafood is a daily feature. **$$ to $$$**. The **River's End Restaurant** is perfectly situated, overlooking the mouth of the Russian River. The cuisine is an interesting mixture of Indonesian cuisine and American game dishes including venison, duck, and, of course seafood with a daily catch list. The view from the restaurant is impressive, especially at the end of the day as the sun sinks into the Pacific. **$$ to $$$**. For informal, outdoor eating, the **Seagull Giftshop and Espresso Bar** is located on Highway 1 close to the river mouth. There's a small deli here and outdoor picnic tables with hot dogs, clam chowder, sandwiches and desserts available.

Fort Ross Historic State Park

Ten miles north of Jenner, a promontory surveys the ocean and much of the Sonoma Coast. This site was chosen by Russian fur-trading explorers for the first permanent Russian settlement south of Alaska — in 1812. The explorers brought with them 40 sea otter hunters.

The Russians established a stockade fort on this point of land and established farms around the fort. Social life here was rich and varied. World travelers stopped at the Russian fort which contained a superb stock of French wines, a fine library and imported European furnishings. But by 1841, the sea otter stocks had been almost extinguished and the Russians were forced to sell the fort. Sonoma had been under Mexican control but General Vallejo — the governor of Sonoma — demurred and the property was sold to Captain John Sutter (of Sutter's Mill fame).

Fort Ross Historic State Park is open for tours every day except for major holidays from 10:00 am until 4:30 pm. The visitor center at the park entrance contains exhibits of Russian history which include artifacts from the early Russian community. Inside the fort, a short walk from the visitor center, the buildings of 1812 have been restored. Conducted tours are available.

Today's visitors unknowingly enjoy the fruits of the early Russian settlement. The famed Gravenstein apples of Sonoma County are derived from seed stock which the Russians originally planted in their Ft. Ross orchards. Needless to say — a lot of apple pie is served in Sonoma restaurants and it's highly recommended.

Three miles north of Ft. Ross and 13 miles north of Jenner, the **Fort Ross Lodge** (707-847-3333) has modern, deluxe accommodation with ocean views, fireplaces, hot tub, sauna and access to the coast. There's a store gas station and deli across the road. **$$$**. The **Timber Cove Inn** (707-847-3231), three miles north of Ft. Ross, has 49 rooms on a 26-acre headland with a fine view of the sea and the cove. The Inn is beautifully laid out with a massive entrance room with stone fireplace and a Japanese pond. There is a dining room with a varied wine list and full bar. **$$$**.

Travelers who may wish to spend several days or a week in the area might reserve a vacation home or cabin by calling **Sea Coast Hideaways** (707-847-3278). The people who run Timber Cove Boat Landing & Campground (see below) also operate a reservation service for vacation homes in the area, a good deal for anglers and others who wish to linger in northwest Sonoma.

Camping is available in the Ft. Ross area. **Timber Cove Boat Landing** has campsites, suitable for overnight camping, with showers, boat launch, a hot tub and fishing supplies.

Twenty miles north of Jenner and ten miles north of Ft. Ross is **Salt Point State Park**. This is one of the northern beach parks covered on the next page. The park has campgrounds — the nearest public campsites to Fort Ross.

Northern Beaches

The landscape is increasingly wild on the drive north from Fort Ross along Highway 1. The northern beaches are for the most part small, secluded coves — separated by long stretches of cliffs, bluffs and rocky headlands which reach into the sea.

Stillwater Cove Regional Park is a small sea-side day-use and camping park set in a redwood grove with a forest trail to the beach. An historic schoolhouse is located in the park's canyon — via another trail.

Salt Point State Park, just north of Stillwater Park offers, 6,000 acres of forest, grassland, a rocky shoreline and several beaches tucked into the rock landscape. There is a large campground (Woodside) suitable for trailers & RVs. It's on the east side of the highway. Moonrock Campground is located to the west — at ocean-side. At night, with the moon shining, this can be an awesome, eerie scene. The park also contains 20 walk-in sites on the inland side of the highway with hikes of up to 1/2 mile. The park is known for its tide pools, diving and fishing opportunities, for this is one of the first underwater parks created by the State of California. Trails cross the park — for hiking and riding. Although there is not a store next to the park, supplies are available in Fort Ross, Stewarts Point and Ocean Cove. For park information, phone (707) 847-3222.

The **Kruse Rhododendron Reserve**, off Kruse Road — 10 miles north of Ft. Ross—features 317 acres of wild rhodos which bloom from April to June. Telephone707- 865-2391 for blooming information.

Gulala Point State Park is at the northern edge of the county, at the mouth of the Gulala RIver. There are hiking and bike paths as well as steelhead and rock fishing. There's a campground here and the point is a good spot for whale watching. Park Information: 707-785-2377.

Between these parks is **Sea Ranch**, a long expanse of private land, dotted with large vacation homes which are often available for private rental. Public access trails lead to the shore with $2.00 charged for trail use.

There are several places to stay along this stretch of road, ranging from rustic to super-deluxe. **Timber Hill Ranch** (707-847-3258) is a new country inn and tennis center perched high above the ocean, with gourmet food, private cottages, pool and spa. **$$$**. **Stillwater Cove Ranch** (707-847-3227), six miles north of Ft. Ross, is more rustic and designed for groups and couples. Some units have kitchens and the Dairy Barn is a genuine bunkhouse. **Salt Point Lodge** (707-847-3234) is at the south entrance to the state park with 16 comfortable and inexpensive rooms. **$ to $$**. The restaurant features seafood and mesquite-grilled dishes at a good price. The **Sea Ranch Lodge** offers deluxe accommodation and a fine dining room with a golf course, hiking trails and several unspoiled, unpopulated beaches. **$$$**. For those who prefer to rent a vacation home for their stay at Sea Ranch, there are several companies which arrange reservations: Ram's Head Vacation Rentals (707-785-2427); Sea Ranch Escapes (707-785-2426); & Sea Ranch Vacation Rentals (707-785-2579).

Mendocino South Coast

Mendocino County is an uncrowded and mostly-uncultivated land of redwood forest, wild and rocky ocean shore and rivers which wind their way to the sea. In this natural setting have sprung up some of the finest small inns in the country. Few modern towns impede the appreciation of the natural beauty of the Mendocino coast but the towns which are there are picturesque and entirely in keeping with the rest of the landscape.

South Mendocino Coast:

The Mendocino Coast can best be separated into two sections: south of Mendocino town, and north of Mendocino to the Humboldt County line. Activity in the south section is dominated by the rivers which flow to the sea: Gualala, Garcia, Navarro, Albion and Big. Each of these rivers has recreation facilities at its mouth and for several miles inland. Some of the finest lodging in the Northwest can be found in this region.

The small town of **Gualala** (pronounced Walalla - a Spanish version of the Pomo Indian word Walali — "meeting of the waters") is just north of the southern county line on the north shore of the Gualala River. It was a redwood lumber town until the 1960s. The Art Center here is well-known for its annual Art in the Redwoods and Summer Fair — held in mid-August. There are trails to the riverside beaches which are popular with steelhead anglers. The **Gualala Hotel** (707-884-3441) is an old landmark on Highway 1 with 18 rooms on the second floor (13 with shared bath), antique beds and other furniture and a good Italian restaurant with bar and wine shop on the main floor. **$$**. **Seacliff** (707-884-1213) is a more deluxe place to stay, on the bluff with private whirlpools, decks with a view, fireplaces and fine dining. **$$$**. The **Gualala Country Inn** (707-884-4343) has ocean views, fireplaces and whirlpools. Bed and Breakfast inns include: **North Coast Country Inn** (707-884-4537) a rustic redwood home on a hillside with hot tub and ocean views. **$$**; **Whale Watch Inn** (707-884-3667) an 18-room inn on the ocean shore with deluxe accommodations, continental breakfast. **$$$**; **Saint Orres** (707-884-3303) is a Russian-style inn with 19 rooms, ocean views, cottages with fireplaces, whirlpools and a garden **$$ to $$$**. **Gualala River Park** is an RV park & campground, with hookups, showers, propane & laundry. Take County Rd. 501, south of Gualala, east for 1 mile.

Driving north on Hwy. 1, the **Point Arena** lighthouse marks the most westerly point in the lower 48 states. The town of Point Arena is a quiet community, often shrouded in fog. It was a lumbering and fishing town which is focussing these days on welcoming tourists. The light is an attraction, as is Manchester State Beach, a long swath of curving sand to the north with 650 acres of dunes and meadows and trails. There's a large private KOA campground and RV park — south of the park (707-882-2375).

Lodging in Pt. Arena includes the **Coast Guard House** (707-882-2442), an historic life-saving station converted into a B & B home with six rooms **$$**, and rental homes on the site of the Point Arena Lighthouse (707-882-2777) with 3 bedrooms & ocean views **$$ to $$$**.

Mendocino South Coast

Just north of the Garcia River, Mountain View Road cuts cross-country to intersect with Hwy. 128 near Boonville — a handy side route to the Anderson Valley. By taking Hwy. 53 at Boonville, you can drive to Ukiah and join U.S. 101.

Between Pt. Arena and the town of Mendocino, there are several scenic villages placed at the mouths of the rivers of the region. There are two parks along the way. Manchester State Beach lies between the sleepy village of Manchester and Elk, an old mill town with several significant Victorian buildings. This is prime inn country and much of the next few pages will be a listing of the fine inns of the Mendocino coast — mostly bed & breakfast operations. In Elk: **Harbor House** (707-877-3203) is one of these heritage buildings, built in 1916 as a guest lodge for the Goodyear Redwood Lumber Co. There are ten units and four cottages with dinner and breakfast served. **$$ to $$$**. **Greenwood Lodge** (707-877-3422) provides a quiet stay beside the ocean with breakfast served in the 1920s-era private cottages. **$$ to $$$**. The **Sandpiper House Inn** (707-877-3587) was also built in 1916 on a superb ocean-front site. Breakfast, afternoon tea and evening cheer are served. **$$ to $$$**. **Greenwood Pier Inn** (707-877-9997) has great service and excellent food. The Inn has 11 rooms in cottages with ocean views. **$$ to $$$**.

Albion, the village at the mouth of the Albion River, was founded in 1853 around another lumber mill. There are two outstanding inns here: the **Albion River Inn** (707-937-1919) has a magnificent location on a bluff overlooking the sea, with lodge rooms and cottages. **$$$**. Their dining room is renowned and so popular that reservations should be made. **Fensalden Inn** (707-937-4042) is on Navarro Ridge Rd., another B & B inn with ocean views and fireplaces. **$$ to $$$**.

The village of **Little River** is a favorite vacation town, with several fine parks in the area and unique inns to stay in. Another mid-19th century lumber town, Little River's cove is a good spot for diving and abalone gathering. Van Damme State Park is a wonderful natural area, with its 1,825 acres set on both sides of the river — around Fern Canyon. The canyon trail is a popular walk, a five-mile round trip which crosses the river eight times leading to several walk-in natural campsites. This trail also leads to a pygmy forest and a short loop trail through the stunted cypress trees.

The traditional place to stay is the **Little River Inn** (707-937-5942), almost 150 years old, with a fine dining room and cozy accommodation in the lodge, annex and cottages. **$$ to $$$**. Another antique inn is the equally-famous **Heritage House** (707-937-5885), on Hwy. 1 with 70 units with dinner and breakfast included in the daily rate. **$$ to $$$**. Two restaurants serve excellent fresh cuisine: **Ledford House** features modern "California" dishes. **$$ to $$$**. The **Little River Restaurant** is a small, respected restaurant with a French flair. It's open Friday—Monday in the summer and Friday—Sunday during the winter. **$$ to $$$**.

Mendocino

Mendocino gets much mention as the "New England Village of the Pacific Coast". The town was founded by loggers and lumber barons from Maine who built their homes, stores and inns in the New England style.

Set on a beautiful headland facing the ocean, the town began as a lumber port at the mouth of the Big River with most of the houses constructed between 1840 and 1860. Mendocino had a rowdy past, as did most logging towns, but by 1910 the lumber boom ended and the town settled down to a dowdy and faded period which stretched from the 20s until the mid 1960s. It then become an attractive center for arts and crafts, bolstered during the 1960s when the flower children of the San Francisco Bay Area found Mendocino to their liking and brought an artistic renaissance to the area.

A good place to start your visit to Mendocino is the **Ford House Visitor Center**, a 1854 home which now is the town information center. Mendocino Headlands State Park winds along the ocean shore, with several trails leading to small beaches carved into the rocky walls of the headlands.

The **Mendocino Art Center and Gallery**, 45200 Little Lake St., offers exhibits of photography, painting and crafts and is open year-round. Summer performances feature drama, dance and musicals. **The Kelley House Historical Museum & Library**, 45007 Albion St., provides historical views of the region in another old home built in 1861 for settler William Kelley. The museum's gardens feature plantings from a century ago. The building and gardens are open daily, during afternoon hours.

There are just so many fine places to stay in and close to Mendocino that we can't cover them all here. For a full listing, write the Fort Bragg/Mendocino Chamber of Commerce at 332 N. Main St., Fort Bragg CA 95437. However, we'll try now to give you a sampling of the best:

The **Mendocino Hotel** (707-937-0511) is the largest of the "period" inns, near the ocean with 51 rooms (some with shared bath, fireplaces, balconies and ocean views). The hotel's Garden Cafe and Bar is popular for lunch and dinner. **$$ to $$$**. The **Mendocino Village Inn** (707-937-0246) on Main Street has 12 rooms in an 1882 building with a full breakfast and reasonable rates. **$ to $$**. **Headlands Inn** (707-937-4431) is also in the village with 5 rooms (three with private bath) and full breakfast. **$ to $$**. A small, cozy B & B operation is the **Whitegate Inn** (707-937-4892) overlooking Headlands State Park with double parlors, deck and garden. **$ to $$**. The very impressive **Stanford Inn By The Sea** (Big River Lodge) (707-937-5615) is just south of Mendocino at the mouth of the Big River. It's a large redwood lodge with fireplaces, ocean views and decks. Accommodations come at a high price and this inn is worth the extra tab. This is one of the most deluxe and scenic resorts on the coast. **$$$**.

Campers stay in **Van Damme State Park** south of town at Little River, at **Caspar Beach RV Park**, north of town at 45201 Pt. Cabrillo Dr. (707-964-3306) or **MacKerricher State Park,** 3 miles north of Ft. Bragg.

Fort Bragg

On the drive between Mendocino and Fort Bragg, the **Jug Handle State Reserve** is a must for people with a geological interest. The reserve protects a giant staircase with five terraces leading from the sea — at 100-foot intervals — each 100,000 years older than the one below. There are Bishop and Monterey pine, Sitka spruce and western hemlock on the terraces. The round trip on the "staircase" takes three to four hours.

You'd never know it from traveling along the strip development along Highway 1 in Fort Bragg, but this town has scenery with a distinct charm. Its charm is found at the edges of Fort Bragg where the seafaring and logging history of the area comes alive, as do the flowers and shrubs of an impressive botanical garden. **Noyo Harbor** is directly south of town, at the mouth of the Noyo River. A picturesque fishing village, Noyo Harbor is a place for chartering fishing boats and a great place to eat while you're looking at the busy fishing fleet in the harbor. **The Wharf** (780 Harbor Dr.) has a great view with its seafood, chowder and beef sandwiches. **$$**. **The Noyo River Inn** on South Harbor Dr. serves pasta and prime rib along with the local seafood. **$$**. The **Cliff House Restaurant** overlooks Noyo Harbor from a bluff at the south side of the Noyo bridge. **$$ to $$$**. In Fort Bragg, **The Restaurant**, across from the train station, is recommended. The chefs who own the restaurant serve fresh, seasonal food. **$$ to $$$**.

The most popular attraction in Fort Bragg is the **Skunk Train**. In 1885, lumber magnate C.R. Johnston built a railway line from the settlement to Willits — 40 miles east. Steam engines pulled the logging trains in 1904 and in 1925, passenger service was extended to Willits, using gas-powered "Skunk" railcars. The name came from the powerful gas odor given off by the engines. The California Western Railroad operates today's Skunk Train, using historic diesel and steam logging locomotives and open observation cars on the trip to and from Willits. It's a full-day round trip and half trips can be taken from either station. A light meal is served at Northspur. The train runs through the dense forest — much of it redwood.

Three miles south of Fort Bragg, the **Mendocino Coast Botanical Gardens** feature year-round displays of rhododendrons, azaleas, hydrangeas, heather, daisies and ferns in a wooded setting. This is one of the finest gardens in Western America. The paths wind through the floral and wooded displays and picnicking is available on the expansive meadows overlooking the ocean and in the fern canyons.

The **Grey Whale Inn** in Fort Bragg (1-800-382-7244) is a large B & B operation housed in what was the Redwood Coast Hospital. The rooms are large and private. **$$**. **Pudding Creek Inn** (707-964-9527) has two Victorian homes joined by a garden courtyard. There are ten rooms here decorated in period style. **$$**. **Harbor Lite Lodge** (707-964-0221) is a motel with 70 units and views of Noyo Harbor. **$$**. Pine Beach Inn (707-964-5603) has 51 rooms & suites and an informal restaurant. **$$**. There's a large campground in **MacKerricher State Park**, 3 miles north of Fort Bragg.

California's Lost Coast

Samoa
Eureka
101
299
Redwood Cr.
Trinity R.
Loleta
Ferndale
Grizzly Bluff Rd.
Fortuna
Mad River
Rio Dell
Van Duzen R.
Cape Mendocino
Scotia
Bear River
Pepperwood
Holmes
36
Weott
Humboldt Redwoods State Park
Petrolia
Punta Gorda
Honeydew
Mattole R.
Phillipsville
Ettersburg
Redway
Garberville
Briceland
Whitethorn
Benbow
Eel River
Shelter Cove
Sinkyone Wilderness State Park
Smithe Redwoods
Leggett
Cummings
N
1
Eel River
101

The Lost Coast

Some of California's most impressive, rugged and unspoiled landscape is on what is called the "Lost Coast". The area extends from the northwest edge of Mendocino County to just south of Ferndale in Humboldt County. Much of the area is included in the King Range Conservation Area including Sinkyone Wilderness State Park which makes up the southern end of the region.

This area is so remote that there is only one organized community: **Shelter Bay**. The rest of the conservation area is virtually uninhabited with the King Mountains sealing it off from the east. Hiking, fishing, sea-watching and camping are the reasons people come to visit the Lost Coast. Those who take the trouble to venture into this area are impressed with rugged beauty and the truly spectacular vistas along the coastline. A 16-mile trail, in several sections, takes hikers along the coast.

There are three ways to get into the Lost Coast.

From the south, Usal Road branches off Highway 1, three miles north of the hamlet and ghost town of Rockport. This road is unsigned and unpaved. For the first six miles, Usal Road winds and rises to more than 1,000 feet and then descends to the Usal Beach Campsite.

From the east and Highway 101, take either the Garberville or Redway exits, drive through Redway and turn west on Briceland Road. After 12 miles of driving, turn on the left fork to the hamlet of Whitethorn. One mile past Whitethorn the pavement ends but you can continue on the dirt road for another 3.5 miles to the Four Corners, a junction. Left is Usal Rd. Right is a road climbing into the mountains. Drive straight ahead and you come — in another 3.5 miles — to the Sinkyone Wilderness State Park Visitor Center. This last part of the road may be impassable during winter months. The state park headquarters has trail maps and camp site information. There are camping areas at Needle Rock: near the visitor center where trails lead to the beach and at the Jones Beach site. There are drive-in campsites four miles south of Needle Rock — at Bear Harbor. This is where the road ends and the Lost Coast Trail begins. For advance information, write to the California Dept. of Parks & Recreation, Eel River District, P.O. Box 100, Weott CA 95571 or phone 707-946-2311.

The third access route is from the north but this route is recommended only for intrepid drivers with 4-wheel drive or off-road vehicles, and then only during the dry summer and fall months. Mattole Road runs south from the Victorian town of Ferndale and past Cape Mendocino. It's impossible to get to the King Range Conservation Area except by the mostly impassible Wilder Ridge Rd. While it provides a unique mountain drive, I suggest that anyone wishing to take it should get up-to-date advice from the Ferndale Chamber of Commerce office (707-786-4477), the BLM offices or from the state police.

The community of Shelter Cove is at the western end of the Briceland/Shelter Cove Road. More on Shelter Cove on page 61.

Lost Coast Trails

Although it is possible to walk almost the entire 100 miles of the Lost Coast, most hikers concentrate on the southern portion in Sinkyone Wilderness State Park and the King Range Conservation Area. The trail in the state park extends for 16 miles, from Bear Harbor, leading along the shoreline to the Usal campground near the southern boundary of the park.

The most popular method of handling the trail is to set up camp at Bear Harbor and/or Needle Rock campsites and spend several days walking two or three sections of the trail and the other trails which lead into the King Range Conservation Area.

Needle Rock to Whale Gulch (4.5 miles round trip):

This section of the Lost Coast Trail provides an easy introduction to the state park trail. The trailhead is behind the barn, near the park road. The trail leads north from behind the barn, through a gully and after 1/4 mile to Streamside Camp, a wilderness campsite. Passing Low Gap Trail, our trail moves through the forest, travels beside Low Gap Creek to Usal Rd. and Low Gap Camp. The trail continues along the bluffs to Jones Beach and another campsite. A left fork leads to the beach. The right fork descends through a canyon. Here are two ponds and Whale Gulch, a small lagoon that is the end of this section of the Lost Coast Trail. Another trail which climbs up Chemise Mountain leads from Whale Gulch and into the King Range Conservation Area.

Bear Harbor to Wheeler Campsite (9 miles round trip):

This part of the trail leads through canyons with redwood groves and through prairie grasslands. Start at the end of Bear Harbor, 2 1/2 miles from the visitor center. Cross Orchard Creek to a grove of giant eucalyptus at Railroad Creek Camp. The path crosses the creek and leads along the old Bear Hartbor Railroad railbed. The path continues near the old corral and up the Railroad Creek canyon. You cross the creek and climb to an old logging road — a short distance to Wheeler Campsite.

Usal Campsite to Anderson Gulch (5 miles round trip):

This is the southern portion of the Lost Coast Trail (you can also access this part of the trail by walking south from Wheeler Camp). To walk this trail from the south, take Usal Road from Hwy. 1 and park at Usal Beach Camp. The trail ascends through redwoods and onto a ridge and climbs again to near the top of Timber Point (1,300 feet). The trail descends through fern-laden Dark Gulch and then moves up to grassy land. The trail swings east to Anderson Gulch and a small campsite set beside a stream in the meadow.

Mattole River to Punta Gorda Lighthouse (6 miles round trip):

From the northern access route (Mattole Rd.), drive to Petrolia and turn west on to Lighthouse Rd. and drive five miles to the Mouth of the Mattole Recreation Site. From the rivermouth, the walk heads south along the dunes, past waterfalls cascading to the beach and to Punta Gorda, a sea lion rookery, the old lighthouse and another 20 miles of unspoiled beach.

Lost Coast — Shelter Bay

The village of **Shelter Bay** is the only organized community on the 100-mile stretch of pristine wilderness called the "Lost Coast". Founded around 1855 as a small seaport to service the farms and interior Humboldt communities, Shelter Bay became a fishing village in 1928 when the San Francisco Fish Company bought the pier and surrounding land and started landing salmon for shipping to San Francisco. The Machi family bought the company's 40 acres and set up their own fish house. Today, the Machis operate several of the Shelter Cove enterprises.

Anglers come to the cove for many reasons: deep sea fishing for salmon, ling, rock cod, red & black snapper, abalone, crab and other shellfish, as well as surf-fishing for ocean perch and rock fish. There's a sheltered boat ramp in the cove. People with trailers and RVs head for the **Shelter Cove Campground** (707-986-7474) where there are 100 serviced sites.

There are several motels, including the **Shelter Cove Motor Inn** (707-986-7521) on Wave Drive, with ocean-front units with a view. **$$**. The **Shelter Cove Beachcomber Inn** (707-986-7733) has units with brass beds, fireplaces, stoves and kitchens on Shelter Cove Rd. **$$**. **Mario's Marina** (707-986-7432) has a nine-unit motel in addition to trailer units with kitchens beside the marina which services sport fishermen with gas, supplies and bait. **$$**.

Seafood is the prime diet for those eating in the restaurants of Shelter Cove. **Pelican's Landing Restaurant** has its own fish boats which guarantee very fresh fish every day. **$$ to $$$**. The **Beachcomber Inn** has its own restaurant (**$$**) as well as the town general store on Shelter Cove Rd. You can buy fresh (off-the-boat) fish and shellfish from the **Shelter Cove Seafood Company** on Machi Rd. The **Shelter Cove Campground** has a deli and market, a good place for picnic supplies.

Shelter Cove Rd. provides access to several side roads and hiking trails in the King Range Conservation Area. For current information on the trail network, contact the Bureau of Land Management offices in Arcata or Ukiah. The **Chemise Mountain Trail** is reached via Shelter Cove Rd . and Chemise Rd. Park at the Wailaki Recreation Site. The upper trail (3 miles round trip) crosses over Bear Creek and ascends for 1/4 mile along a ridgetop to the top of Chemise Mtn (2,596 feet). This is a 3-mile round trip. If you continue west along the trail you come to a meadow after 2 miles. The trail switchbacks down the slope, through a dense old-growth Douglas fir forest. The trail ends 1/4 mile from the beach, stopped by landslides. The walk back to your car is a stiff climb. The **King Crest Trail** is accessed by taking Shelter Cove Rd. to Horse Mtn. Rd. Take this road. for seven miles and turn on Saddle Mtn. Rd. for another seven miles to the trailhead. The narrow path leads along a ridge, through a madrone (arbutus) forest and up through several switchbacks. At a junction, the right fork leads to Maple Camp and water. The left fork leads to the summit and magnificent views. This is a five-mile round trip.

REDWOOD COAST HIGHWAYS

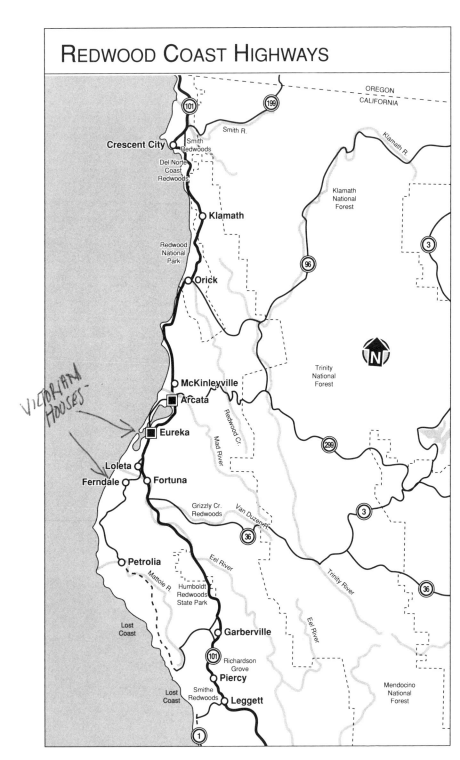

OREGON
CALIFORNIA

101
199

Smith R.

Crescent City
Smith Redwoods

Del Norte Coast Redwoods

Klamath R.

Klamath National Forest

Klamath

Redwood National Park

3

96

Orick

N

Trinity National Forest

VICTORIAN HOUSES

McKinleyville

Arcata

Redwood Cr.

Mad River

Eureka

299

Loleta

Ferndale

Fortuna

Grizzly Cr. Redwoods

Van Duzen R.

3

36

Petrolia

Mattole R.

Eel River

Humboldt Redwoods State Park

Trinity River

Lost Coast

Eel River

36

Garberville

101

Richardson Grove

Piercy

Mendocino National Forest

Lost Coast

Smithe Redwoods

Leggett

1

THE REDWOOD COAST

Although redwoods are seen far to the south, the largest stands of the Giant Sequoia (*Sequoiadendron giganteum*) and Coast Redwood (*Sequoia sempervirens*) are found north of Leggett in Humboldt and Del Norte counties and on into Oregon's Curry County. This inspiring stretch of redwoods continues for more than 200 miles from the Mendocino County line to southern Oregon, linked by Highway 101 which joins the national and state parks throughout the region. Coast Redwoods, the largest of all the sequoias, have grown in the region for more than 20 million years.

Our itinerary through Redwood Coast Country is a south-to-north trek, the first major redwood stand preserved in **Richardson's Grove State Park**. The neighboring communities of **Benbow**, **Garberville** and **Redway** are all tourist centers in south Humboldt county. The south entrance to the amazing Avenue of the Giants is just north of Garberville. This alternate road leads drivers through Humboldt Redwoods State Park, a large forest containing some of the largest redwoods in existence. The Avenue Of The Giants passes by the small villages of **Myers Flat, Weott** and **Redcrest**, re-joining Highway 101 just west of the lumber towns of **Scotia** and **Rio Dell**. Past the town of **Fortuna** is the sideroad to the Lost Coast and to the picturesque Victorian village of **Ferndale**.

The city of **Eureka** is the largest community in the northern redwoods area and is the hub of commerce for the region. With its fascinating old town — which is well preserved — Eureka is situated on Humboldt Bay, a large protected harbor. To the north, this body of water becomes Arcata Bay, and the town of **Arcata** is situated on the northern shore. Arcata's marshes and Dune Preserve are outstanding places for outdoor recreation.

The City of **Trinidad** (with 410 residents but still incorporated as a city) was once a logging port and whaling station and is now home of a small fleet of fish boats, as well as a thriving artists' community. Patrick's Point State Park has a large campground and scores of picnic sites along forested and meadow-side headlands.

A few miles south of **Orick**, a town renowned for its sport fishing, the southern entrance to Redwood National Park points the way to the finest stands of redwoods in the United States. The national park is composed of three separate state parks with joining segments — stretching across the Humboldt line and through the length of Del Norte County. Highway 101 weaves in and out of Redwoods National Park, past Lady Bird Johnson Grove and through Prairie Creek, Del Norte and Jedediah Smith state parks. **Crescent City** is the last large town before arriving at the Oregon border.

To the west of the highway are several outstanding ocean parks with campgrounds, pristine beaches and special ecological zones. Two major rivers in this northern redwood country — Klamath and Smith — are noted for steelhead and salmon. Above all, there are the redwoods. This is a mystical place where time stands still, and the giant old trees seem to make inconsequential our relatively recent human history.

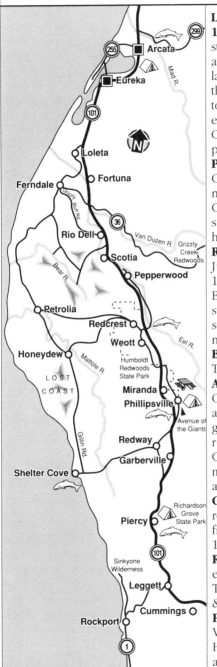

Leggett, Junction-Hwy 1 & Hwy. 101: Gas, motels, RV parks, stores. The small town of Leggett attracts hordes of anglers in the late fall, during salmon season at the mouth of the Eel River. The town is inland after Hwy. 1 turns east to join U.S. 101. The Chandelier Drive-Thru Tree is a popular attraction.

Piercy 11 miles north of Leggett. Gas, store, cafes, camping. The northernmost town in Mendocino County, Piercy is also a prime salmon fishing spot with steelhead & trout as well.

Richardson's Grove State Park Just inside the Humboldt line, 1,000 acres of redwoods along the Eel River with campground, swimming, visitor center, food and scenic walks. A private RV park is next door.

Benbow Gas, store, hotel, golf. The **Benbow State Recreation Area** 5 miles north of Richardson Grove Park has 786 acres of forest and a reservoir lake. Campground, hiking, trail riding, boat rentals, swimming, fishing. Outdoor Shakespeare festival in mid-summer. The Benbow Inn is an historic hotel.

Garberville Gas, motels, restaurants, campgrounds, stores, fishing. Visitor center is off Hwy. 101 at south end of town.

Redway Adjacent town, Hwy. 101 exit to Lost Coast. Tourist facilities. Take Briceland Rd to Whitethorn & Shelter Cove.

Phillipsville Gas, store, cafe. Village at south entrance to Humboldt Redwoods State Park and the Avenue of the Giants.

Highway Log

Avenue of the Giants — South Entrance: Just north of Phillipsville, take this 31-mile road for the drive through Humboldt Redwoods State Park. The north exit/entrance is at Pepperwood. There are several exits to Hwy. 101 along the length of the Avenue.

Humboldt Redwoods State Park The park has 51,000 acres with 70 memorial redwood groves, visitor center, picnic sites, walking trails, 3 large campgrounds, interpretive exhibits. Food & lodging in towns along the route.

Miranda The first of the small towns along the Avenue of the Giants - inn, food & gas.

Weott Gas, motels, stores, cafe. Exit to and from Hwy. 101 freeway. Eel River trails.

Rockefeller Forest, five miles west of Hwy. 101, via Mattole Rd. This 13,000 acre redwood forest joins Founder's Grove and Bull Creek Flat in Humboldt Redwoods State Park. Walking trail beside Bull Creek. Mattole Rd. is the back-road route to Ferndale & sections of the Lost Coast. The Mattole River is a prime steelhead stream.

Redcrest Village on the Avenue of the Giants with gas, store, motel.

Pepperwood At the north end of the Avenue of the Giants, with gas, store, cafe, Newton B. Drury Grove.

Scotia Lumber mill town on Hwy. 101. Demonstration forest 4 1/2 miles south off the highway. Gas, stores, cafes, hotel.

Sideroad to Bear River Ridge & Capetown Take the backroad south of Rio Dell to Bear River Ridge Rd. which cuts west toward Cape Mendocino. This is another alternate and scenic backroad route to Ferndale and portions of the Lost Coast.

Rio Dell Town across the Eel River from Scotia. Gas, stores, cafes, motel. RV park, B & B inns.

Junction—Grizzly Bluff Rd. Just north of Rio Dell, west off Hwy. 101. To Ferndale & Fortuna.

Junction—Hwy. 36: Take exit just south of Fortuna. Hwy. 36 leads southeast to villages of Carlotta & Bridgeville. **Grizzley Creek Redwoods State Park** is between the two villages — 393 acres of redwoods, swimming, campground, trails, fishing in the Van Duzen River. **Van Duzen County Park** is 12 miles east of Hwy. 101 with old growth redwoods, campgrounds, picnic sites, good swimming.

Fortuna Small city with gas, stores, cafes, motels, RV park, golf, museum, rodeo in late July. Rohner Park in the city has picnic sites & playground.

Junction—Road to Ferndale & Lost Coast: The well-preserved Victorian village of Ferndale makes for an interesting side-trip. The village has restaurants, shops, cafes, hotel, motels, B & B homes and an RV park at the fairgrounds. Mattole Rd. is the northern route to the Lost Coast.

Loleta Small dairy community, 12 miles south of Eureka. Gas, store, camping, cheese factory.

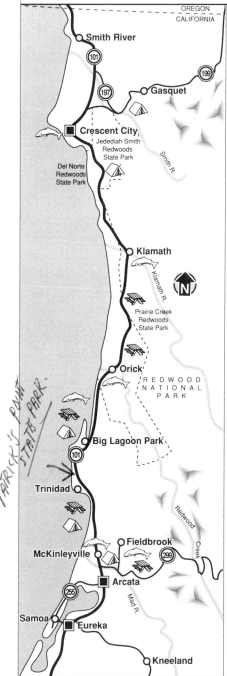

Eureka City on Humboldt Bay, the largest population center in redwood country. Gas, stores, restaurants, hotels, motels. Large shopping mall at south end of town on Hwy. 101. Eureka has an outstanding historic downtown area via 4th or 5th streets. This area is worth exploring with a walking tour map from the Chamber of Commerce—2112 Broadway. Sequoia Park, on the south end of town, has a zoo and picnic sites.Other picnic tables on campus of the College of the Redwoods, also at south end. Take Samoa Bridge to the Woodley Island Marina, with fishing fleet & marina cafe. Clarke Museum & Fort Humboldt have historical displays. The National Wildlife Refuge is at the south end of Humboldt Bay.

Junction-Route 255—To Samoa Bridge, Samoa Peninsula (famous Samoa Cookhouse restaurant) & scenic route to the city of Arcata.

Junction— Kneeland Rd. North of Eureka, to the east, sideroad to villages of Kneeland & Bridgeville.

Junction-Fickle Hill Road—Exit off freeway between Eureka & Arcata. This back road leads southeast through the Mad River valley—to Kneeland and across the Mad River bridge to Maple Creek Rd. (Korbel & Blue Lake).

Arcata Redwood lumber town just north of Eureka. Gas, cafes, stores, motels, camping.

Lamphere-Christensen Dune Preserve Take Arcata exit & drive west of town. Arcata Marsh & Wildlife Preserve, off Samoa Rd.

Highway Log

Junction-Hwy. 299, Road to Blue Lake. Hunting and fishing center in the Trinity Alps. Mad River Hatchery on Hatchery Rd. open daily with picnic tables. Old railway station restored as a museum of the Mad River Railway & local history. **Fieldbrook** is a rural village at the end of a side-road running north from Hwy. 299. The respected Fieldbrook Valley Winery has a new tasting room.

McKinleyville Gas, motels, restaurants, shopping, RV park, 18-hole golf course. A town set between the Little and Mad rivers. The Hammond Trail (hiking, biking) follows the Mad River. Little River State Park, just north of town, has good fishing. Turn off on North Bank Road for the Azalea State Reserve.

Clam Beach (at McKinleyville) Clam Beach County Park has fishing, swimming, tent camping & overnight parking for RVs.

Trinidad Gas, cafes, stores, motels, B & B inns. Sea-side community with scenic attractions including Trinidad Head, lighthouse, trail from Mill Creek to Elk Head at Trinidad State Beach, fishing pier, boat charters.

Patrick's Point State Park 25 miles north of Eureka. 632 acres on wooded plateau overlooking ocean and beach. Campground, fishing, tidepools, sea lion over-look, trails, outdoor museum.

Humboldt Lagoon State Park North of Patrick's Pt., a wildlife refuge, hosting more than 200 species of birds using the Pacific Flyway. Dry Lagoon and Stone Lagoon are suitable for fishing. Stone Lagoon has overnight camp-sites.

Big Lagoon County Park A campground for tents and RVs.

Redwood National Park The southern entrance to the park is just south of Orick and a visitor center is located west of the highway at Freshwater Lagoon (campsites). The center has information on park camping & reservations. Bus tours to the Tall Trees area leave from here daily (June-Labor Day).

Redwood Creek Trail This 8.5 mile trail leads to the world's tallest known tree.

Orick 41 miles north of Eureka with gas, motels, cafes, stores, fishing.

Lady Bird Johnson Grove Turnoff just north of Tall Trees Trail — one-mile loop trail.

Prairie Creek Redwoods State Park 10 miles north of Orick, with 55 miles of forest trails, information center, picnicking.

Klamath 18 miles north of Orick. Gas, motels, cafes, stores. Fishing (steelhead), jet boat tours, museum.

Del Norte Redwoods State Park 7 miles south of Crescent City, this is the northern part of Redwood National Park with trails & campground.

Crescent City Gas, motels, restaurants, stores, fishing pier. museum, Battery Pt. Lighthouse.

Jedediah Smith Redwoods State Park 9 miles east of Crescent City. Camping & hiking trails.

REDWOOD PARKS

The tall trees begin as soon as you cross the south fork of the Eel River. Just north of Leggett, before you see the Humboldt County line, the **Standish-Hickey State Recreation Area** marks the southern entrance to Redwood Country and from this point north, Highway 101 becomes the main street leading to the redwoods parks of Humboldt and Del Norte counties. After this overview, the parks are covered in detail on further pages of this chapter.

Between Leggett and Piercy, **Smithe Redwoods State Reserve** protects a grove of old-growth redwoods. Just across the Humboldt line, **Richardson Grove State Park** offers both the Eel River for recreation and an outstanding 2,000 acre redwood forest. Along the highway are shops selling burl products and the first of several drive-through trees, although it's not the most impressive.

Humboldt Redwoods State Park is an accessible and huge (51,000 acres) forest which is accessed by turning off Hwy. 101 and taking the **Avenue of the Giants** (Route 254) which winds through the park, passing several small communities. This park alone could prompt a vacation of several days — swimming and fishing in the Eel River, camping, hiking the park trails and relaxing in several historic and comfortable inns along the way, beginning with the renowned Benbow Inn, just south of Garberville. The huge tree at Myers Flat is the one to drive through. There's a visitor center on the Avenue. Garberville is the main tourist center for this area.

Redwoods National Park is a tribute to the foresighted preservation-minded environmentalists who lobbied for many years, and the state and federal governments which worked together to preserve the best of the northern Coast Redwood groves. This unusual park includes three self-contained state parks as well as the connecting pieces which are under federal control. The main visitor information center is at the southern entrance to the National Park, just south of the town of Orick and about 40 miles north of Eureka. From the south, **Lady Bird Johnston Grove** offers an east two-mile loop walk to some very tall trees. About 10 miles north of Orick is **Prairie Creek Redwoods State Park**, first seen as a wide meadow. Here there's a visitor center and museum which gives information on the park's hiking trails, camping and fishing possibilities. The 1-mile Revelation Trail is a self-guided trail which is planned for the handicapped. The Fern Canyon Trail is a wonderful 5-mile walk through lush ferns and tall redwoods. There are 28 miles of walking trails in **Del Norte Redwoods State Park**, just south of Crescent City. The most northern information centre for the national park is in Crescent City, at 1111-2nd Street. Continuing the drive north on Highway 101, the last of the state parks within the national park is **Jedediah Smith Redwoods State Park**, 9560 acres reached by taking U.S. Highway 199 for 9 miles from the junction with Hwy. 101. The ranger station, just off Hwy. 199, gives out trail maps and conducts interpretive programs.

GARBERVILLE

This southern Humboldt town, along with Benbow Lake just south and Redway to the northwest, is the main tourist center for the region. It's a handy staging point for excursions to California's Lost Coast including vacationing at Shelter Bay.

Conveniently situated at the southern end of the Avenue of the Giants, Garberville has a lot to offer: an arts festival in the late spring, Shakespeare in the great outdoors at mid-summer, and a rustic ambience to the town itself.

The **Benbow State Recreation Area** is centered on a six-mile lake created by a dam. This is the site of the June Arts & Crafts Fair, and a well-known jazz festival. While there are several motels in the region, the **Benbow Inn** (707-923-2124) should be considered for at least one night's stay. It's a Tudor-style inn, two miles south of Garberville, overlooking the south fork of the Eel River. **$$ to $$$**. There's a nine hole golf course, a cozy quasi-Victorian atmosphere and a dining room with a considerable reputation. In Garberville, accommodations are more ordinary although there are several respectable motels, and cafes with a natural touch. **The Humboldt House Inn,** a Best Western motel, has 56 units and a swimming pool at the north end of Redwood Drive, the main street. **$$**. Up the street are several older but comfortable motels including **Motel Garberville**, at 948 Redwood Drive (707-943-2422) which has a restaurant on-site and special deals for steelhead anglers. **$$**. The **Rancho Motel**, a few doors away, has a heated pool and modest rates. **$ to $$**.

A few miles south of Garberville, in Piercey, the **Hartsook Inn** (707-247-3305) has 62 cabins set in the forest next to Richardson Grove State Park. Some cabins have kitchens. **$**. There is a respected dining room here.

Campers will find campgrounds in the neighboring redwood parks. For those who require full hookups, **Dean Creek Resort** in Redway (707-923-2555) has serviced sites on the river with hookups, cable TV, a whirlpool and sauna. The **Benbow Valley Resort** (707-923-2777) is 2 miles south of Garberville: a deluxe RV park with its own 9-hole golf course, paved RV sites, full hookups, a cafe, whirlpool, sauna, laundry and all the other trappings. There are a few more private campgrounds & RV parks along the Avenue of the Giants (see later pages).

Eating in the Garberville area can be very rewarding, especially at the aforementioned **Benbow Inn**. The **Hartsook Inn** at Piercey has a good restaurant which is unlicensed but diners are encouraged to bring their own wine with them. In Garberville itself, the **Waterwheel Restaurant** is the one next to the Motel Garberville, open for breakfast, lunch and dinner with daily specials. **$$ to $$$**. **Calico's Cafe**, also on Redwood Drive is a small cafe with fresh baked goods, soup, sandwiches, etc. **$ to $$**. **Sicilito's** at 445 Conger Street behind the Humboldt House Inn serves both Italian and Mexican food, in addition to seafood and steaks. It's open for dinner only during winter months. **$$ to $$$**.

AVENUE OF THE GIANTS

Since Europe's medieval age, the redwoods of Humboldt Redwoods State Park have been the silent sentinels of northwest California. The Avenue of the Giants, a route which parallels U.S. Hwy. 101, weaves in and out of the forest groves leading visitors to gaze in awe at these giant sequoias — many of which have been standing here since before the birth of Christ. The freeway speeds you past these impressive groves, but to get the true feeling of majesty in this forest, you must take the Avenue of the Giants.

I have come here again and again, as have millions of other visitors to the Humboldt redwoods. Yet even with all the tourist activity, the forest is so vast that the human element is lost in its space and grandeur

The Avenue of the Giants has its southern entrance off Hwy. 101 just south of Phillipsville at Sylvandale and runs for 31 miles to the north exit/entrance south of Scotia.

Along the way, there are several small villages which offer tourist services: burl shops, cafes, stores and a few rustic inns and resorts. North of Miranda, at Myers Flat, the Shrine Drive-Thru Tree is a popular spot — the result of a fire which burned through the bottom of the 2,000 year old tree, leaving a hole large enough to drive through. At Miranda, the **Miranda Gardens Resort** (707-943-3011) has 16 cottages nestled in the forest along with a heated pool and whirlpools. **$$ to $$$**. The **Whispering Pines Lodge** (707-943-3182) is in the Avenue with rooms and suites with kitchens and a heated pool. **$$**.

Weott is the closest town to the park visitor center and Founder's Grove. The **Sequoia Motel** in Weott (707-946-2276) has standard units close to a store and walking trails by the Eel River. Opposite Founder's Grove a turnoff leads into Rockefeller Forest, another must-see grove (more a large forest than a grove).

Redcrest to the north has several places to stay including the **Redcrest Motor Inn** (707-722-4208) which has cabins, a motel, store, cafe and a campground. **$$**.

The Avenue of the Giants exits to U.S. Highway 101 just south of the mill town of **Scotia. Rio Dell** is the neighboring town across the highway and most of the tourist facilities are in Rio Dell. However, if you have an interest in old hotels, Scotia is the place to go. The **Scotia Inn** (707-764-5683) is an historic building in this town owned by the Pacific Lumber Company. The inn which opened in 1888 serves dinners Wednesdays through Sundays. The company operates a visitor tour through their huge redwood lumber mill which includes a visit to their museum.

The **Humboldt Gables Motel** (707-764-5609) is across the highway in Rio Dell with standard motel units. **$$**. **Nally's RV Park**, also in Rio Dell (take the Davis exit) is on the Eel River with full hookups.

The **Wildwood Cafe** on Rio Dell's main street (Wildwood Ave.) is open for breakfast, lunch and dinner — an unpretentious restaurant. **$ to $$**.

HUMBOLDT REDWOODS STATE PARK

Possessing an impressive series of 70 memorial groves, this park is the best-known of California's redwood parks. With campgrounds, picnic sites, trails and interpretive sites, the park attracts hundreds of thousands of visitors each year. Some whistle through on the freeway, missing most or all of the natural grandeur of the park. Others shoot through on the Avenue of the Giants, not staying to walk in the redwoods or to take the sideroads through the forest. The more I visit the park, the longer I stay and I hope that you will stay long enough to catch the spirit of the forest.

About half-way along the Avenue of the Giants is the park Visitor Center, near the village of Weott. This is a natural starting place for a full exploration of the park. There are interpretive exhibits — outside and inside — and a full range of information including trail maps, guided walks, junior programs and campground information is available from the rangers here.

At the south end of the park is the **Chimney Tree**. A campfire accident in 1914 started a fire in a great redwood. The fire continued to burn inside the tree until the entire interior of the trunk was burned. The tree's top was torn off by a windstorm, exposing the "chimney". The tree still lives and continues to send out new shoots. Many of the memorial groves throughout the park are in memory of the organizations which raised money to aid the "Save the Redwoods League" which from 1918 purchased forest land from lumber companies and other local owners to create the park. **Founder's Grove** commemorates the leaders of the movement. This grove, north of Weott, has its own parking lot with a short trail from the foot of the **"Founder's Tree"**. There are self-guiding brochures available at this point for the trail which passes the **Dyerville Giant** and other notable specimens.

The **Rockefeller Forest** has been called the nation's finest forest. It's 13,000 acres extending for five miles west of the Avenue of the Giants. Take the road across from Founder's Grove. There is a parking lot at Bull Creek with a pleasant walk beside the creek.

Farther north along the Avenue of the Giants is Redcrest, a small village where you will find the **Eternal Tree** (about 70 feet around) and the **Immortal Tree**.

There are three campgrounds within the park and all are suitable for family camping. The visitor center is near the Burlington Campground. There are environmental campsites in addition to the large family campgrounds. These are walk-in tenting sites where the camper leaves no trace of his or her stay. Many say that camping in the dark interior of the forest is the only way to truly appreciate the wonder of the ancient redwoods.

The campgrounds are full for the whole summer period and those intending to camp in the park must reserve their site at least eight weeks in advance by phoning 1-800-444-PARK, the MISTIX ticket service.

FORTUNA & FERNDALE

Two small towns in central Humboldt typify the history and current activity of the area.

Fortuna is a market town — the real Humboldt — servicing the needs of the agricultural areas in the southern part of the county. It's a business-as-usual town. Ferndale serves another purpose. It's a tourist center, the result of well-preserved heritage architecture and a canny tourist promotion program.

The town of **Fortuna** was established around 1875 by farmers who came to the area from northern Humboldt. Originally called Slide, the town's name was later changed to Springville due to the fresh water springs in the area, and then to Fortuna. The town is 250 miles north of San Francisco and there are motels, cafes and stores for stocking up on your way through.

A half-hour's drive east of town on State Hwy. 36 is **Grizzly Creek Redwoods State Park**, a 234-acre recreation area with memorial groves, short nature trails, swimming and fishing in the Van Duzen River. There is a campground here and reservations are required during summer months. This road which leads to the Trinity Alps mountain range offers views of several rustic rural hamlets along the way including Carlotta, Bridgeville and Dinsmore. The **Fortuna Motor Lodge** is the newest motel in town, at 175 12th Street (707-725-6993). The rooms are of the ordinary type but larger than others in the area with King and Queen beds. **$$**. The **6 Rivers Motel** is a less modern place at the south end of town on Business 101 (707-725-1181) **$ to $$**. A handy place to eat, especially if you're speeding along Hwy. 101, is the **Hungry Hutch Restaurant** at Main and 12th streets — open 24 hours. Take the 12th Street exit from the highway.

Ferndale calls itself "The Victorian Village". Aside from the restored downtown of Eureka, Ferndale boasts the best preserved Victorian architecture in California, a tidy Main Street looking as if the village had locked in time, and some interesting places to stay, eat and shop for antiques, gewgaws and art from local artists and crafts people. It's only 20 miles south of Eureka so Ferndale makes a good alternative place to stay when visiting this area. The local museum displays early village artifacts.

Ferndale is a perfect place for B & B lodging and there are several good homes to consider. The **Victorian Village Inn**, 400 Ocean Ave. (707-786-9400) has twelve rooms in an 1890 building which also contains a fine restaurant. **$$**. The **Gingerbread Mansion**, 400 Berding St. (707-786-4000) has nine rooms in a restored 1899 mansion with garden, fireplaces and antique furniture. **$$ to $$$**. The **Shaw House Inn** is on a large property with an 1854 gothic house with garden, fireplaces, and three shared-bath bedrooms out of the seven rooms available. An expanded continental breakfast is served at all three B & Bs.

For eating, there is **Henry Ford's** in the **Victorian Village Inn** on Ocean Ave. **($$ to $$$)** and a genuine soda fountain at the **Fern Cafe** on Main Street.

EUREKA & AREA

Of all the early logging and lumber towns of northwestern California, Eureka is the most interesting to visit. Its logging industry is not altogether defunct and the heritage of the area is remembered in several good museums. Part of the downtown core of Eureka is the **"Old Town"**, several blocks of restored and re-created buildings from the late 1800s which are positioned near the waterfront. The city fathers moved during the 1960s to preserve the decaying area and it's an outstanding tribute to their foresight.

First and Second (Two Street to history-minded locals) are the central streets in the preserved quarter. Here are several good restaurants including the **Carter House Inn** — a recreation of an historic San Francisco mansion — and the **Romano Gabriel Sculpture Garden** at 2nd and D streets. The **Humboldt Cultural Center** is a restored warehouse building on 1st Street and the scene of a regular series of concerts and art exhibitions. The **Carson Mansion** is worth a gaze for it is one of the state's best examples of Gingerbread Victoriana. This state historical landmark at the head of 2nd street is now a private men's club and the inside is not accessible to outsiders. Outside of the downtown area, **Sequoia Park** at Glatt and W streets, includes a modest zoo with sea otters, elk prairie dogs and other wildlife as well as picnic sites, trails through the trees and flower gardens.

Eureka is an excellent focus for history buffs, with several unique and worthwhile museums to visit. The **Clark Memorial Museum** is located in a columned building (a former bank) at Third and E streets in Old Town. The museum contains the general history of the region, including an extensive collection of artifacts of the Yurok, Hupa and Karuk tribes, such as woven baskets and dance regalia. These tribes inhabited the forests, shores and mud flats of Humboldt Bay long before the gold searchers and loggers arrived in these parts.

Another replica building, this one the recreation of the first home built in Eureka—the McFarlan House—is the **Humboldt Bay Maritime Museum**. The first version of the house was built in 1852. This museum includes lighthouse displays and other memorabilia of the sea. The museum operates its own cruise boat, a former ferry, the Muskadet. Across the bay is the famed **Samoa Cookhouse**, an old-fashioned logging cookhouse and museum. The **Fort Humboldt Museum and State Historical Park** is on Fort Avenue, at the south end of town. The original fort was the most northerly military post on the Pacific Coast during the mid 1880s and was commanded by general Ulysses S. Grant for a while. There are steam-era engines and other artifacts, old logging equipment and a wood-burning steam engine which offers rides during summer months.

For a small city of 25,000 people, Eureka is well supplied with shopping and entertainment facilities, including the large Bayshore Mall on Hwy. 101 at the south end of town. The Eureka Chamber of Commerce, at 2112 Broadway (707-442-3738) has a walking tour map of Old Town, as well as a variety of other information on Eureka attractions.

EUREKA

The scenic drive in the area is the road which crosses Humboldt Bay via the Samoa Bridge. The bay is hemmed in by two long peninsulas with a channel to the ocean between the two spits of land. The road crosses to the Samoa Peninsula and then turns north towards Arcata.

For a rustic and entertaining eating adventure, visit the **Samoa Cookhouse**, just across the bridge. This relic of the 1890s logging era serves bountiful meals at large tables covered with oil cloth. Waiters arrive at your table with large loaves of bread, hearty soups and platters of meat and vegetables. **$$**. As mentioned earlier, there is also a logging museum here. To get there, turn left after crossing the bridge from Eureka and look for the cookhouse signs.

In Eureka, the **305 Coffee Shop** on Hwy. 101 (corner of 5th & G) is a good place for breakfast with fresh biscuits & gravy, good hashbrowns and other filling food. Seafood is available in several restaurants of varied stages of sophistication. For fine dining, try two places in Old Town: the **Carter House Inn** serving seafood in addition to an elegant breakfast. **$$ to $$$** and the **Hotel Carter** (across the street) with an excellent dining room which wins raves from gourmets and gourmands. **$$$**. The **Sea Grill** on E Street in Old Town serves seafood & steaks. **$ to $$$**. For more rustic but scenic dining, try the **Cafe Marina** on Woodley Island overlooking the marina (**$$**) or **Lazio's** at 327 Second Street in Old Town. This is a fairly new location for this long-established seafood restaurant. **$$ to $$$**. **The Landing Seafood Restaurant**, at the foot of C Street, has a good view of the bay and a raft of oyster and clam appetizers along with whatever is caught on the day you're there plus hamburgers and standard breakfasts. **$ to $$**.

The city operates an **18-hole golf course** at 4750 Fairway Drive.

Eureka is a good B & B town with several historic mansions converted to Bed & Breakfast operations. These include the **Carter House** and **Hotel Carter** in Old Town (707-444-8062) two Victorian re-creations which have cozy rooms and full breakfast. **$$ to $$$**. **An Elegant Victorian Mansion** (707-444-3144) is probably the best preserved house in Eureka and is operated with panache by its innkeepers, Doug and Lily Vieyra. This was the Queen Anne home of William Clark, a former mayor and county commissioner. Non-smokers only. The house has a sauna and croquet field. **$$**. The **Daly Inn** (707-445-3638) is located at 1125 H Street in Old Town, a Colonial Revival home built in 1905. Full breakfast is supplied. **$$**. A small B & B home at 2154 Spring Street is the **Shannon House**, with two rooms (private & shared bath) at reasonable rates, a full breakfast and afternoon tea. **$$**. There are standard motels in Eureka, including the **Best Western Thunderbird Lodge** (707-443-2234) at 5th & Broadway. This is a large modern motel with heated pool, whirlpool and coffee shop. **$$**. The **Carson House Inn** (707-443-1601) is next door to the Carson Mansion with 60 rooms and suites, some with whirlpool, heated pool and sauna. **$$**.

ARCATA

In 1850, Union Town was founded on the north shore of Humboldt Bay to service the lumber industry in addition to the gold miners and prospectors heading for the Trinity Alps gold fields. Arcata, as it's now called, is still a lumber town with redwood continuing to fuel an important local industry.

The town has an interesting downtown plaza with some important buildings facing a statue of President McKinley. The most notable is the old **Jacoby's Storehouse**, built of stone and brick with decorative ironwork and shutters. The building has been lovingly restored and decorated by several local artists and crafts people.

There are several worthwhile natural attractions in the area. On the east side of town, **Redwood Park** and the **Arcata Community Forest** provide a living museum of some 600 acres of second-growth redwood including ten miles of walking trails. This is still a working forest, harvested by the city but available for recreational use. The historic logging trail takes visitors on a walk from the west side of the parking lot. **Mad River Beach** offers sunning and gazing at the crashing surf. The **Lamphere-Christensen Dune Preserve** contains some of the most impressive dune plant life on the California coast. Tours are available from the Friends of the Dunes society. Another fine place to view wildlife is the **Arcata Marsh & Wildlife Sanctuary** at the south end of I Street. This is a sewage treatment plant which shows how a municipality can take care of its waste — and birds as well — through marsh restoration. It's an important stopping place for egrets, loons, great blue herons and marsh wrens. Wood chip trails lead to several blinds.

Arcata is home to **Humboldt State University** which includes an excellent historical museum full of natural history displays. The museum is located at 13th and G streets.

The **North Coast Inn** is a full-service hotel at 4975 Valley West Blvd (707-822-4861). The hotel has a dining room, coffee shop, cocktail lounge, indoor pool , sauna, whirlpool and laundry. **$$**. The **Plough & The Stars** (707-822-8236) is a bed & breakfast inn with 5 rooms (3 with shared baths) and full breakfast. This is an 1852 farmhouse with gardens, antique furnishings and fireplaces. It's closed from late December until the end of January. **$$**. The **Lady Anne** (707-822-2797) is another B & B home, in a turreted 1888 building at 902-14th Street. **$$**.

Interesting places to eat include **Crosswinds**, open for breakfast and lunch, with Victorian decor and an art gallery at 860-10th St. **$$**. The **Plaza Grill** is in the restored Jacoby's Warehouse building on the Plaza with evening jazz. **$$ to $$$**. Beer fans head straight to the **Humboldt Brewery**, a brew pub with four of its own original ales and food including burgers and pasta dishes **$ to $$**. Chamber of Commerce Information centers are found on G Street in downtown Arcata and in the Valley West Shopping Center (off Hwy. 101 at the Giuntoli Lane exit).

NORTH HUMBOLDT BEACHES

From Arcata north to Orick, a distance of 34 miles, the ocean is apparent and the coast is studded with a number of beaches and lagoons. The north Humboldt coast is an underrated part of the Pacific shoreline and worth spending some time to explore. Most of the coast in this area is accessible from the highway with several state and county parks which provide access to the beaches, campgrounds, hiking and bicycle paths and picnic facilities. Several small towns provide tourist accommodations.

McKinleyville, just north of Arcata, is a fast-growing residential community. Although a rural village has been here since the 1860s, it is only within the past twenty years that the population has boomed to 10,000. The town is still tied to Arcata and Eureka for jobs. Local agriculture includes tree, bulb and dairy farms. Goat cheeses with an international reputation are made at the Cypress Grove Chevre cheese factory. There's golfing at the 18-hole Beau Pre course on Norton Road.

The **Azalea State Reserve** is close to the highway, east on North Bank Rd at McKinleyville. This park is wooded and on the edge of the forest grows an extensive range of wild azalea. Two loop trails lead through the reserve to several scenic overlooks. There are two picnic areas beside the parking lot.

Although McKinleyville is a residential town, the **Bella Vista Motel** (707-839-1073) offers 16 standard and housekeeping units overlooking the ocean on Central Ave. **$ to $$**. For dining, **Merryman's Dinner House** on Moonstone Beach offers the best prospect, with a menu which includes fresh seafood and steaks. **$$ to $$$**. The **Silver Lining Restaurant & Lounge** is a better than average airport eatery, at the Humboldt County Airport. **$$ to $$$**.

Clam Beach north of McKinleyville is a popular place for locals and for passing visitors. This is a county park with camping, hiking and riding trails, fishing and beachcombing. The beach affords long views of the Humboldt coastline. The Hammond Trail starts at the Mad River, following an old railway roadbed to arrive at Clam Beach.

Within two miles of Clam Beach is **Little River Beach** and you're close to the town of **Trinidad**, a small sea-side community with much to offer the traveler. Discovered by Portugese explorers in 1595 and re-explored by the Spanish in 1775, this is a salmon fishing town with a long fishing pier, lighthouse and several beaches within a short drive. **Trinidad State Beach** is right in town with a trail which starts at Mill Creek and ends at Elk head at the state beach. The **Marine Laboratory** of Humboldt State University is in Trinidad and is open for self-guided tours.

The **Redwood Inn** (707-677-3349) is on St. Patrick's Pt. Drive, in a redwood grove with moderate to deluxe accommodations. **$$ to $$$**. Also on St. Patrick's Pt. Drive, the **Bishop Pine Lodge** is a collection of cottages, including new units with their own hot tubs. Many of the cabins have their own kitchens and a cafe is close at hand. **$$**.

TRINIDAD & ORICK

The **Trinidad Bed and Breakfast** (707-677-0840) is a Cape Cod-style home on Edwards Street. The house has four rooms with views of the bay and expanded continental breakfast. **$$**. The **Lost Whale Bed & Breakfast** has much the same ambience with four suites with an ocean view on St. Patrick's Pt. Drive. **$$ to $$$**.

Private campgrounds and RV parks in Trindad include **Deer Lodge RV Park & Motel** (707-677-3554) on St. Patrick's Pt. Drive. **Sylvan Harbor** (707-677-9988) has cabins in addition to an RV park with full hookups, on St. Patrick's Pt. Drive. The **Trinidad Bay Trailer Court** (707-677-3647) is one block west of the freeway off-ramp. Although there are several modest cafes in Trinidad serving basic meals, the **Larrupin' Cafe** on St. Patrick's Pt. Drive has gained a strong reputation for its innovative cuisine including seafood. It's open Wednesday through Sunday during summer months. For pier dining, the **Seascape Restaurant** is located on the fishing pier, open for three meals a day with seafood and steaks taking up most of the menu.

Five miles north of Trinidad, **Patrick's Point State Park** includes a large campground with 123 family sites. There are also 20 walk-in and bike-in sites in the park. Unlike other state parks in the region, the forest is made up of trees other than redwoods. Here Sitka spruce, fir, pine and hemlock dominate the landscape. Rim Trail runs from the parking area at Agate Beach along the coast, through woods and meadows to Palmer's Point where several short trails lead to the shore. For information on camping at St. Patrick's Point Park, call 707-677-3570.

As Highway 101 leads north from St. Patrick's Point, the road runs through **Humboldt Lagoons State Park** and beside fifteen miles of sand beaches, rocky headlands, old-growth forest and freshwater lagoons and marshes. Like Patrick's Point Park, the Lagoons are extremely popular during summer months as beach fans and campers congregate along the shoreline. There are only 20 campsites in this park and RV owners tend to park their vehicles along the road, next to the beach. **Big Lagoon County Park**, 7 miles north of Trinidad, has 11 campsites. The lagoons and marshes here attract thousands of birds on their migrations — more than 200 species have been identified.

Past the south information center for Redwood National Park (see next page), the town of **Orick** is situated in a beautiful valley — a magnet for anglers who come here from far and wide to fish in the rivers of the area and in tyhe ocean and lagoons just to the south. Redwood Creek flows through the center of the valley and the town is close to several major salmon streams including the Smith, Klamath and Eel rivers. Orick has several standard motels, all with some kitchen units. These include the **Park Woods Motel** (707-488-5175) on Hwy. 101 **($$)**, the **Prairie Creek Motel** (707-488-3841) which has a cafe **($$)**, and **Rolf's Prairie Creek Motel & Park Cafe** (707-488-3841) where German food specialties are served along with game (elk, buffalo, boar) and barbecue dishes.

REDWOODS NATIONAL PARK

1968 and 1978 were monumental years for the Californians who had campaigned — for many years — for the preservation of the state's redwood forests. On October 2, 1968, President Lyndon Johnson created Redwoods National Park, 50,000 acres of supreme forest land in Humboldt and Del Norte counties. Then the battles began in earnest and for ten years the Save the Redwoods League and lumbering interests struggled to gain the upper hand for further preservation (or lumbering). In 1978, President Carter signed the Redwood National Park Expansion Act which increased the size of the park to 106,000 acres. Redwood National Park is an unusual combination of federal and state interests for the national park includes three self-contained state parks: **Prairie Creek Redwoods, Del Norte Redwoods and Jedediah Smith Redwoods.**

This whole area had been occupied for millennia by several Indian tribes. The Karok were inland people, living on the upper reaches of the rivers which flow through the park. The Yurok lived along the shoreline and the Hoopa lived where the Klamath and Trinity Rivers meet. There were Indian Wars in the area until around 1870 with massacres and bad feeling all-round.

Today, this huge forest is preserved for future generations and the national and state parks provide prime recreation possibilities for present visitors. Highway 101 links the various components of the national park, from south of Orick in Humboldt County to just south of the Oregon border.

The southern visitor information center for Redwood National Park is to the west of the highway at **Freshwater Lagoon.**, south of the town of Orick. It's open daily except on major holidays. This is a good spot to reserve campsites in California State Parks in the region and to get hiking trail maps for the national park. The northern park office is located in downtown Crescent City, just a block from Hwy. 101. Along the way there are information and interpretation centers in each of the state parks.

Much of the federal land was logged before the 1978 proclamation, leaving 39,000 acres of logged landscape within the park, including more than 200 miles of old logging roads. The park will regenerate in these areas but it will take 100 years or more for the new forest to grow into a natural state.

While there are campgrounds in the three state parks, there is no developed camping on federal lands. There are no lodgings within the park at all and visitors to the park who wish to stay in motels and lodges stay in the Eureka/Arcata area, in the limited Orick accommodations, or stay in or near Crescent City at the northern end of the park. There are hiking trails throughout the forests, including the southern national park areas. The south information center on Hwy. 101 is your best location for trail information in the area and bus tours leave the center for the **Tall Trees Trails** which are southeast of Orick as is the **Redwood Creek Trail**.

PRAIRIE CREEK REDWOODS STATE PARK

55 miles of trails cut through the most southerly of the state parks within the national park: Prairie Creek Redwoods. The small visitor center and museum is located 10 miles north of Orick, close to the campground and trailhead for the **Revelation Trail**. This self-guiding trail has been constructed especially for handicapped people, with guide ropes for the blind and braille interpretation signs. Walking this trail is a great way for everyone to have an introduction to the park.

Just south of the visitor center is a narrow, winding road which leads to the head of the **Fern Canyon Trail**. This trail is on the west side of the highway, leading for less than a mile past a flat prairie via the **James Irvine Trail** and past the former site of a small mining camp. Hiking the James Irvine Trail from the visitor center takes about three hours. This trail leads to ocean bluffs and several good whale-watching sites.

For those who wish to take a complete vacation hiking the length of the national park, the **Coastal Trail** begins off Hwy. 101, west of **Lady Bird Johnson Grove** and follows the Pacific Coast, ending at Enders Beach, just south of Crescent City. There are campsites along the way and the trail ranges in difficulty from Class 1 (easy) to Class 5 (extremely rugged). Portions of the trail can be taken from trailheads along the highway. The national park has a trail map available, giving locations of more than 55 trails including sections of the Coastal Trail.

Campgrounds are available in the park with 100 sites. There are back-country sites along the Redwood Creek Trail, in federal lands south of the state park.

A long stretch of beach can be reached by park trails which have their trailheads along Highway 101, including the James Irvine Trail. Other trails to beaches include the **Boat Creek Trail** and **Butler Creek Trail** which branch out from a highway trailhead north of the visitor center.

The **Ossagon Trail** to the north leads to a tidal flat and connects with the Coastal Trail.

A network of trails to the east of the visitor center includes the **Rhododendron Trail** (3 hours — 6.3 miles), and the **Foothill Trail**, a shorter walk which is the return part of the Rhododendron Trail (2 hours — 2.6 miles).

One of the most convenient shorter trails is the **Cathedral Trees Trail** which begins at the visitor center and winds for 1.5 miles beside streams and through meadows. Elk are often seen along this trail which takes about 35 minutes to walk and which connects with the Rhododendron and Foothills trails.

A more difficult but rewarding loop trail at the north end of the Prairie Creek park is the **Ten Taypo Trail**, a 3 hour (6.4 miles) hike for the full loop. The trail follows a fern path beside a creek through old-growth forest to a high ridge. A shorter 4-mile loop is possible by connecting with the **Hope Creek Trail**. The Ten Taypo Trail has a difficulty rating of 4.

Klamath & Del Norte Redwoods State Park

Ten miles north of the edge of Prairie Creek Redwoods State Park, Highway 101 crosses into Del Norte County and moves down into the Klamath River Valley.

Del Norte exhibits a change in the air (fog) and in the landscape (dense forest) as you travel north. By this time it is certain that we have left the semi-arid California scene and have come into the Pacific Northwest.

Most of Del Norte Redwoods State Park is thick, virgin forest and this is the least developed part of Redwoods National Park. However, this park has its own attractions and should not be skipped as you tour the area.

As Highway 101 approaches the town of Klamath, it moves slightly inland and crosses the river over a bridge which is flanked by four grizzly bear statues. This is historic country, with the trail (literally) blazed by Jedediah Smith as he and his group of mountain men worked their way along the Klamath River from the Central Valley near Sacramento to Oregon.

Klamath is a steelhead fishing center, a growing town which has based its economy on hosting visitors: with jet boat trips up the Klamath River, operating camping and RV parks and operating attractions including the **Tour-Thru Tree** (south of town) and a Paul Bunyan theme park called **Trees of Mystery** (north of town). This attraction includes a large gift shop and the **End-of-the-Trail Indian Museum**, holding one of the nation's largest collections of Indian artifacts including masks, jewelry and woven baskets. Don't be misled by the garish nature of the entrance to Trees of Mystery. It's a very interesting place with an educational trail through the woods. A restaurant is located across the highway.

Klamath makes a good place to stay when visiting Redwoods National Park. It's in just about the center of the park. The **Requa Inn** (707-482-8205) is one mile off Hwy. 101 west of town with 16 rooms in an historic building overlooking the Klamath River. The nightly charge includes a full breakfast. **$$**. Four miles north of Klamath is the **Motel Trees** (707-482-3152), across the road from the Trees of Mystery. This motel has 23 units with tennis courts, a lounge and restaurant. **$$**.

Klamath attracts thousands of outdoors lovers each year and the town is well-supplied with places to camp. The **Camp Marigold Motel & RV Park** (707-482-3585), on Hwy. 101, has housekeeping cabins, six rooms inside the lodge (**$$**) and RV hookups, showers and laundry. **Steelhead Lodge** (707-482-8145) on Terwer Riffle Road, has eight motel units with kitchens (**$ to $$**) as well as tent sites and RV spaces with hookups. **Chinook RV Resort** (707-482-3511) on the highway, has 72 sites with full hookups and tent sites on the river with showers, laundry, store and liquor store. The state park campground is seven miles south of Crescent City.

In Del Norte Redwoods State Park, two trails are accessible from the road. **Damnation Creek Trail**, for hardy hikers, climbs from the sea through a forest. It's 2.5 miles long but takes about three hours for the round trip. The **Alder Basin Trail** is easier: a 45-minute round trip.

JEDEDIAH SMITH REDWOODS STATE PARK

East of Crescent City, the third of the state parks within Redwood National Park is reached by turning east on U.S. Highway 199 and driving for nine miles. You may also take a sideroad drive to the park by taking Elk Valley Road, south of Crescent City and continuing on unpaved Howland Hill Road. The advantage of the latter drive is that you get to experience more of the park scenery, especially as the road follows Mill Creek. The road traces part of the route of an old stagecoach road. **Stout Memorial Grove** is along Howland Rd. This was the first of the park's memorial groves and contains the park's largest redwood — 340 feet high and 22 feet across. This is also the trailhead for the **Stout Grove Trail** — an easy walk which takes about 30 minutes. The forest is dense and dark but it is also accessible to wheelchairs. In summer, the trail can be accessed from the Jedediah Smith campground.

The **Hiouchi Ranger Station**, the park's visitor center, is at the Hwy. 199 entrance. There are trail maps available here, as well as interpretive programs and exhibits. It's not open during winter months.

The **Hiouchi Trail** starts at the ranger station and moves northwest to link the visitor center with several loop trails. The **Simpson Reed-Peterson Trail** provides a loop path through old growth redwood forest, over several small creeks which have ferns lining the banks. There are several large redwood burls along the way.

The **Leiffer Loop & Ellsworth Loop** trails have their trailhead on the left side of Walker Road, just off Hwy. 199. These moss-covered loop paths take you through big-leaf maple groves and old growth redwood. The Ellsworth Loop starts about 2 miles down the Lieffer trail. It takes about an hour to do both loops. There are several benches beside the trails.

A much more difficult trail (Class 6) is the **Little Bald Hills Trail** which has its trailhead 1/2 mile east of Stout Grove, off Howland Road. This trail makes a nine-mile round trip, taking about four hours. This old former road crosses prairies — past what was once a ranch — and ends at the park boundary. There is a spring at the site of the former ranch.

For anglers, the **Mill Creek Trail** offers several side-trails to good fishing. The trailhead is at the campground. Cross the bridge and take the left fork of the **Jensen Loop Trail** to reach the Mill Creek Trail. You can also park along Howland Road at the west side of the Mill Creek bridge. The side trails to the creek are not marked but are easy to spot. Old growth redwoods line the stream.

Another trail accessed from Howland Hill Road takes you to a waterfall. The trailhead for the **Boy Scout Trail** is beside the road and is signed. This is a 4-hour round trip (7.4 miles) leading through old growth forest. There is a fork after three miles and the right fork leads to the Boy Scout Tree. The left fork continues to Fern Falls. Local historians believe that small gold mines were operated by Chinese immigrants in this area in the late 1880s and 90s.

CRESCENT CITY

18 miles south of the Oregon border and just north of Del Norte Redwoods State Park is Crescent City. The gold search in southern Oregon and the Trinity mountains brought miners and settlers from San Francisco in the 1850s and a small community of stores and warehouses was established on the crescent-shaped bay.

The small, isolated pioneer community has survived several disasters. In 1865, the side-wheel steamer Brother Jonathan foundered on St. George's Reef and sank with 232 people aboard. 203 bodies from the wreck lie in the Brother Jonathan Cemetery. On Good Friday of 1964, the day of the great Alaska earthquake, a tsunami crashed over the town and destroyed the downtown business section with four great waves which arrived at a speed of 500 miles an hour.

Two museums operated by the Del Norte Historical Society display exhibits of the town's changing fortunes. The **Main Museum** is located at 577 H street in an old jailhouse. Here are exhibits of North American Indian artifacts, logging memorabilia and displays on pioneer life in the county. The museum is open Monday through Saturday from 10am to 4 pm (summers). Winter hours vary, call 707-464-3922 for information. The second museum is the **Battery Point Lighthouse Museum**, located at the foot of Front Street. The museum has a guided tour of the lighthouse, shipwreck displays and books. Its open hours are Wednesdays through Sundays from 10 am to 4 pm (summer months).

Crescent city is the seat of Del Norte County and the headquarters and visitor center for **Redwood National Park** is located at 1111-2nd Street, downtown. **Crescent City Harbor** at the south end of town offers restaurants, charter fishing trips, boat launching and tackle shops. The harbor is flanked by beaches reached by taking Pebble Beach Drive (south beaches) and Scenic Drive north of downtown. The **Rumiano Cheese Factory**, at 9th and E streets, is the largest producer of Dry Monterey Jack Cheese in the country. You can tour the plant and sample several types of cheese. The 18-hole (par 71) **Del Norte Golf Course** is at 130 Club Drive.

The best places to stay in the area are outside of Crescent City (see Smith River page) but there are more-than-acceptable lodgings in town including the **Crescent Travelodge** (707-464-6106 or 1-800-255-3050) with easy access at 725-Hwy. 101. The **Crescent City Motel** (707-464-5436) has a scenic location on the beach at 1455 Redwood Hwy. South (Hwy. 101). The rooms have patios and decks. **$$**. The **Best Western Northwoods Inn** (707-464-9771) is located just south of town at 655-Hwy. 101. Also at the south end of town is **Curly Redwood Lodge** (707-464-2137), a motel built from just one "curly redwood" tree. Rates here are low and the boat harbor is adjacent. **$**.

Campers who require hookups close to town stay at the large **Redwoods KOA**, at 4241-Hwy. 101 North (707-464-5744). This RV park also has secluded tent sites, nature trails, a playground and farm animals.

SIX RIVERS NATIONAL FOREST / HIOUCHI & GASQUET

For anglers, Highway 199 which heads east through the Six Rivers National Forest is a route to be seriously considered. The road follows the path of the Smith River as it wends its way toward the Pacific. This route is the direct way to reach Grants Pass, Oregon and Interstate 5. Along the way there are outstanding fishing opportunities and much fine scenery.

There are two hamlets in this valley which offer interesting lodging and lots of information on local fishing in addition to licensed guides, of which there are at least a score.

Hiouchi is just outside the boundary of Jedediah Smith Redwood State Park and is a quiet and scenic place to stay while visiting the park. The park has its own campground — with 108 campsites. RV owners can hook up to services at the **Hiouchi Hamlet RV resort** (707-458-3321). This modern RV park is five minutes' drive from both the Smith River and the state park. The resort has 120 RV spaces with daily and monthly rates, hookups, showers, laundry. A store is next door and the nearest golf course is four miles away.

The **Hiouchi Motel** (707-458-3041) has standard rooms and a cafe. **$**.

The Six Rivers National Forest covers a large section of the Siskiyou mountain range — from a few miles inland from the ocean to the Rogue River National Forest to the east. The town of **Gasquet** is located in the National Forest and is a good startng place for trips into the forest which has numerous wilderness campsites and river access points. There is a ranger station in Gasquet where trail maps and campsite information are available.

Gasquet was a thriving resort town in the 19th century. 18 miles from the coast, Gasquet has sunnier, warmer days than the coastal communities and people from central California head here to relax in the fine weather and fish. In late July, the Gasquet Raft Races take place over a two-mile course on the Smith River. The **Patrick Creek Lodge & Historical Inn** is situated in the national forest, a 30-minute drive from Crescent City on Hwy. 199. The lodge contains comfortable rooms and the dining room is open for three meals a day — to day visitors as well as for lodgers. There is a cocktail lounge and the staff are great at helping to plan driving and hiking excursions into the forest. The **Wagon Wheel Motel** (707-457-3314) is a short walk from the river with housekeeping units at low prices. **$**. There's a cafe here as well. The village has a deli, grocery store with propane and fishing supplies and a burger stand.

There are remnants of old mining operations in the area. Del Norte County has a history of futile mining attempts, among them searches for gold and copper. Ten mining companies were operating by 1860 but they were all soon defunct. In 1874, possibilities of silver in the area attracted a flurry of speculation but by 1880, only one mine remained in the county.

There are three national forest campgrounds east of Gasquet: Panther Flat, Grassy Flat and Patrick Creek, all within two miles of each other.

DEL NORTE COAST & SMITH RIVER

The eighteen miles of highway between Crescent City and the Oregon line provides scenic highlights and more good fishing opportunities. However, before leaving Crescent City, you may wish to explore lakes Earl and Talawa which are just north of town via Northcrest Drive. These landlocked lagoons are a prime stopping place for more than 250 species of birds using the Pacific Flyway. The park includes 2500 acres of ponds, dunes and marshes. There is environmental camping in the park and limited duck hunting. Kellogg Beach is just north of the marsh area with impressive dunes.

The tiny village of **Smith River** is 13 miles south of the Oregon border, where the Smith meets the Pacific. The flat riverlands brought farmers to the valley in the mid-1800s. It's still an important dairy center. It's also the Easter Lily "capital of the world" with acres of blooms covering the farms in July. Smith River residents celebrate the lily with an "Easter in July Festival", each second weekend in July.

The Arcata Lumber company has its tree nursery in the village.

The Smith is famous for its steelhead and salmon and is the last completely undammed river in California. It's called the "Crown Jewel" of the state's scenic rivers. The Rowdy Creek Fish Hatchery is the only hatchery in the states operated by a non-profit society. It's next to the post office on Fred Haight Drive and is open to the public for tours, Monday through Saturday.

Smith River is an excellent place to stay while traveling in the area. The popularity of fishing here is responsible for several outstanding resorts. The **Ship Ashore Resort** (707-487-3141) is a Best Western motel with 50 units, hot tubs, a penthouse and several units with kitchens. The motel includes a restaurant and lounge. **$$ to $$$**. The resort holds two salmon derbies each year with proceeds going to the Rowdy Creek Fish Hatchery. The resort also operates an RV park. The **Pelican Beach Motel** (707-487-7661) on Hwy. 101, has ocean views from its units and a restaurant and cocktail lounge are right on the beach. **$ to $$**. The **Sea Scape Motel** (707-487-7333) is also beach-side and on Hwy. 101 with kitchen units and a private beach. **$ to $$**.

The **Salmon Harbor Resort** is an RV park with river-front sites, boat launch & dock, and other facilities.

North Bank Road, heading northeast from Smith River, could be a scenic backroad drive to Grants Pass Oregon. However, bridge construction makes it impossible to do the whole trip on this road and there is a detour via Hwy. 199. This is a favorite winter fishing area for salmon and steelhead. **Ruby Van Deventer County Park** features picnicking, fishing, river-kayaking and float trips during summer months.

Pelican Beach, just south of the Oregon line, is your final place to soak up the northern California sun before leaving the state. The beach offers good walks and beachcombing.

Coast Wine Country Tours

Scenic farmland, rustic architecture, fresh food, Victorian bed and breakfast inns, small town life, art and music festivals and relaxed vacations: these are all benefits of a tour through northern California wine country. The nearness of the Pacific Coast makes it all the better!

When I began exploring the Pacific coastline a half-dozen years ago, I found that I was increasingly drawn off my coastal travels to the nearby wineries and vineyards of Sonoma and Mendocino counties. Since then, I have used every opportunity while in the area to devote a day or two to wine explorations.

The character of the winery towns in these two counties makes a visit rewarding. There is a relaxed ambience to wine country which is special and visiting several wineries a day — with picnics and long lunches in modern California cafes in-between — makes a wine tour most enjoyable. The evenings can be devoted to exploring local and state parks, more fine meals in the inns and restaurants of the region and strolling through vineyards (particularly in the fall). Ahh! More than a year without a wine tour is too long.

On the next page is a map which shows the various routes through the two counties which provide our wine tours. The four tours shown on the map can be done in a day but we suggest you plan for more time — even if you have to come back several months or a year later to do the rest. Wine touring, like wine itself, is to be savored in a relaxed fashion.

I have not included the much praised and much sampled Napa Valley wineries. Perhaps Napa is for another book but in any event I chose the counties which border the Pacific Coast and have restricted this chapter to Sonoma and Mendocino. Together, they contain more than 1/3rd of all of the wineries in the state.

Sonoma County contains two major grape-growing districts. The southern part of the county is the Sonoma Valley, a wide swath of land north of the town of Sonoma. This valley, however, does not hold the majority of the wineries in the county. That distinction is reserved for the Russian River region, on both sides of U.S. Highway 101 and close to the Russian River, which lazily winds its way from north of Geyserville, through Healdsburg (the centre of this wine-making region) and then turns west to the Pacific passing through the town of Guerneville, ending its journey at Jenner.

Mendocino County has a different landscape: this is redwood country. Highway 101 continues north as a corridor to many wineries. The scenic Anderson River Valley provides an alternate, scenic route to the coast along State Highway 128.

I believe that wine touring in these regions provides an excellent way to enjoy nature at its best — fishing in trout streams, camping in redwood parks, walking on river-side trails — while learning about and sampling some of the products of nature.

ROADS TO COAST WINE COUNTRY

Willits

Mendocino

MENDOCINO NATIONAL FOREST

101

Elk

Navarro

Navarro R.

128

Ukiah

Russian R.

Boonville

Pt. Arena

Cloverdale

Clear Lake

Geyserville

Garcia R.

Healdsburg

20

Putah Cr.

Gualala

116

29

Fort Ross

Geurneville

Jenner

River Rd.

Lake Berryessa

Santa Rosa

Bodega Bay

Kenwood

Napa R.

121

1

101

12

Napa

Petaluma

Sonoma

Inverness

Novato

6

Pt. Reyes National Seashore

N

Bolinas

Stinson Beach

San Francisco

Berkeley

Coast Wine Country

The above title may seem like another oxymoron — there are no wineries right on the coast — however many of California's finest vineyards and wineries are situated within an hour's drive of the Pacific Coast in Sonoma and Mendocino Counties. For wine fanciers, it makes sense to combine a drive along the coastline with a tour of these accessible wineries.

To help make sense of one or more possible winery tours, we have separated a jaunt through coast wine country into three distinct drives.

The first drive covered in the next few pages is the **Sonoma Valley**, a bucolic trip from south-to-north through the popular vineyard region north of the town of **Sonoma** and ending north of Kenwood, as Highway 12 veers westward to the city of **Santa Rosa**.

The second drive is concerned with **Russian River Country,** the generic title for that area serviced by both U.S. Highway 101 (from **Petaluma** to **Healdsburg** and **Cloverdale)**, and then west along Highways 12 and 116 from Santa Rosa, following the course of the Russian River as it winds its way to the Pacific Coast at Jenner. This is the region for some of California's best sparkling wines.

To the north, the by-ways of **Mendocino County** provide routes to Mendocino wine country with drives through the scenic **Anderson Valley** — through the town of **Boonville** along State Highway 128 — and then through redwood forests to the Mendocino Coast just south of the town of **Mendocino**. Here too, Highway 101 leads us to many of the northern wineries and vineyards, many centered around **Ukiah**.

Touring California wine country is not a new or even recent recreational pursuit. Since the mid 1700s, when the first wineries were established in Sonoma County and far to the south near San Diego, people have spent vacation time visiting wine country. Winery visits and tastings now provide a major industry in northern California as wineries compete for prime space along the major highway routes and provide increasingly-fancy shops and tasting rooms, as well as tours of the wine-making operations. It sounds like snobbish activity, but it isn't. You don't need to know a lot about wines to thoroughly enjoy a wine tour and after your drive and visits to a score of wineries, you'll be knowledgeable about the gastronomic glories and benefits of wine consumption.

The wine tour can take place at any time of the year, and there are certain benefits to off-season travel. Summer is the heavy tourist season. Spring and Fall provide smaller crowds and more leisurely talks with the wine makers and sellers. Autumn is a wonderful time for traveling through the vineyards. I have done a Sonoma wine tour in the moderate chill of winter and enjoyed it thoroughly, having the wineries mostly to myself.

Having spent some time on tasting sprees, I can only caution that while you may choose to explore a score of wineries in a day's drive, your appreciation (and driving ability) soon becomes deadened and could be deadly. Four or five tastings a day seem to offer optimum enjoyment.

SONOMA VALLEY

Less well-known and traveled than its more sophisticated sister, the Napa Valley next door to the east, the Sonoma Valley is a sprawling and less-organized area which has diversified agricultural activity. So, between vineyards, there are vegetable farms, dairy farms and hamlets, all of which make touring this valley most enjoyable. It's a scant hour north of San Francisco.

In planning a wine-tasting trip through the valley, I think of an itinerary with three stages: sampling the Spanish colonial atmosphere of the town of Sonoma where the largest long-established wineries have their operations; moving half-way up the valley to Glen Ellen, with time to explore the beautiful and historic Jack London State Park; and finally moving to the north end of the valley — to Kenwood— the location of the newer and smaller family-operated wineries.

The valley is easy to get to — from several directions. From San Francisco, the best route is via the Golden Gate Bridge, driving north on U.S. Highway 101. From Hwy. 101, there are two roads leading directly to the valley. **Highway 37** intersects Hwy. 101 at Novato (eight miles north of the town of San Raphael) and a turn to the north on Highway 121 leads to Highway 12 at Schellville. Turn north and four miles later you're in Sonoma. The less-traveled route is **Highway 116**, exiting Hwy. 101 at Petaluma, crossing placid farming land until arriving at Highway 121. Drive east for a mile and turn north on Highway 12. This leads to the south end of Sonoma and the town Plaza. Preferring sideroads, I usually take Highway 37 from Petaluma. From other directions, **Highway 12/121** runs east from Napa. From the north, **Highway 12** joins U.S. 101 at the south end of Santa Rosa. Take your pick.

The valley is only 17 miles long but a stay of several days can be filled with rewarding activity in and out of the wineries and tasting rooms. The town of Sonoma is a marvelous historic center, the site of the Mexican colonial government for northern California under General Mariano Vallejo.

The adobe buildings around the Sonoma Plaza, the historic hotels in the downtown area and the parks of the valley provide fascinating tours. The last of the mineral spas , the **"Agua Caliente Mineral Springs"** (707-996-6822) and **"Morton's Warm Springs"** (707-833-5511) are still in operation in Kenwood during summer months. Horseback riding is available in both Jack London State Park and Sugarloaf Ridge State Park (phone 707-996-8566). The **Sonoma Valley Visitors Bureau**, on the Plaza, is a good place to begin your visit to the valley. Special events and festivals are staged in the valley, year-round. These include an Ox Roast in early June in the town Plaza. The "Salute to the Arts" features wine, food and art in the Plaza in mid to late June, the valley's Wine Festival is held in mid-July; and the renowned Sonoma County Wine Auction in August. There are chamber music and jazz concerts held during the summer at several of the wineries and the Vintage Festival winds up September.

SONOMA

The town of Sonoma is filled with history and exploring the Spanish period provides an exciting alternative to winetasting. I find myself spacing wine-tasting sessions with tours of historic buildings and there are plenty to see. The early Spanish history of Sonoma was centered around the town Plaza, created by General M.G. Vallejo in 1835. Much of the original Plaza remains, including **"Casa Grande"**, the original adobe home of the Mexican governor. Other significant buildings on the Plaza include **Mission San Francisco Solano de Sonoma**, the last of California's 21 Spanish missions, built in 1823; the **Sonoma Barracks**, constructed in 1836; and the **Bear Flag Monument**, marking the site where then original Bear Flag was raised in 1846, proclaiming the "California Republic".

A self-guided tour of 59 historic buildings around the Sonoma Plaza has been developed by the Sonoma League for Historic Preservation. The map is available at the **Sonoma Valley Visitors Bureau**, located in the Plaza park or at **Vasquez House**, the former home of General Joseph Hooker and now a library and shop devoted to historic preservation.

For historical overnight stays, the **El Dorado Hotel** (707-996-3030) offers accommodation on the Plaza. Built by M.G. Vallejo's brother, it's a deluxe inn with a fine dining room. **$$$**. Across the street, the **Sonoma Hotel** (707-996-2996) offers lower rates for rooms in an old Victorian building. The rooms have private and shared baths, interesting old furnishings and an informal dining room and bar. **$$**. The valley's paramount luxury resort is the **Sonoma Mission Inn and Spa** (707-938-9000), a sprawling pink palace devoted to relaxing in whirlpool tubs, taking spa programs, swimming in the Olympic-size pool, or dining in the Grill Room restaurant — one of the valley's finest. **$$$**. Close to the entrance to Jack London State Park in Glen Ellen is the **Jack London Lodge** (707-938-8510). This is a high-quality motel with 22 rooms, a country ambience, restaurant and (of course) the Jack London Saloon.

There are B & B homes in each of the valley's communities. In Sonoma, the **Thistle Dew Inn** (707-938-2909) features two restored homes filled with antiques near the Plaza with fireplaces, whirlpool and full breakfast. **$$**. The **Hidden Oak** (707-996-9863) is at 214 E. Napa St., a block from the Plaza with three cozy rooms, private baths and full breakfast **$$**.

In Glen Ellen, the **Glenelly Inn** (707-996-6720) has eight rooms in a quiet setting with outdoor whirlpool and full country breakfast. **$$ to $$$**. For even quieter stays, try the **Stone Tree Ranch** on Sonoma Mtn. Rd. (707-996-8173) with only one cabin; the **Beltane Ranch** (707-996-6501) with four rooms; or the **Gaige House Inn** (707-935-0237) on Arnold Drive. All are in the **$$ to $$$** range. For a one-call B & B reservation, phone 1-800-284-6675 or 707-996-INNS. Campers and RV owners have little choice. **Sugarloaf Ridge State Park** (1-800-444-7275) is on Adobe Canyon Rd near Kenwood. **Spring Lake Regional Park** on Summerfield Dr., has campsites with no reservations. There are no resort-type RV parks in the valley.

SONOMA VALLEY WINERIES

The oldest-established wineries are within walking distance from the downtown Plaza in Sonoma.

Sebastiani Vineyards, at 389 Fourth Ave. East, is one of northern California's largest producers of inexpensive wine. The winery has been here since Samuele Sebastiani immigrated from Italy around 1890 and bought the vineyards which had been planted by General Vallejo in 1835. Son August Sebastiani fully developed the winery which now produces more than a million cases each year. The winery has an excellent tour and a large tasting room. Samuele handed the winery down to his son Sam, who lost a family battle and was fired by his mother. Don Sebastiani is now in charge and Sam operates another winery in the Carneros area, south of Sonoma.

At the end of Old Winery Road, a short drive from the Plaza, is **Buena Vista**, the oldest existing winery in the state. It was founded by the intrepid Hungarian Agoston Haraszthy who brought in the first European cuttings to be planted in California. The vineyards survived blights and the winery survived fires and the 1906 earthquake. It now produces some of the state's finest wines and tours are led through the winery's limestone caves with tastings held in one of the original stone buildings. As is the case with several other wineries in the valley, there is a picnic ground on-site. Buena Vista now has its main winery in the Carneros area while the original caves are still used as aging cellars.

A smaller winery, **Hacienda**, is situated on an historic property at 1000 Vineyard Lane, 1 1/2 miles northeast of the Plaza. This is a beautiful location for a winery, set in a grove of oaks with a garden and tasting room. The tasting room is open from 10 am to 5 pm and there is a picnic area here as well. Tours are by appointment only (phone 707-938-3220). Don't be put off by the necessity to arrange tours in advance. Many of the wineries have limited staff and tours made by appointment are often more complete and enjoyable than those more readily available.

Gloria Ferrer Champagne Caves is located south of the town of Sonoma in the hills of the famed Carneros region. The winery is located at 23555-Highway 121. The tasting room is open from 10:30 am to 5:30 pm and tours are given from 11 am to 4 pm. Operated by a Spanish family who first imported Freixenet wine to the U.S., the Sonoma winery was completed in 1986. The winery itself could have been transported from Spain. The tour takes visitors through underground aging rooms and tastings are conducted in the Sala de Catadores (Hall of The Tasters), with tapas served in addition to the sparkling Ferrer wines.

The **Gundlach-Bundschu Winery** is in the hills east of town, off Denmark Street. This is another of the historic Sonoma wineries, founded in the 1850s. Prohibition in the 1930s forced the winery to close but in 1970, Jim Bundschu began rebuilding the operation, opening to the public again in 1976. The old stone facade remains with a modern winery behind.

SONOMA VALLEY WINERIES

As you drive north along Highway 12, you come upon the village of Glen Ellen, five miles northwest of Sonoma. Here are some of the finest wine-making operations in the Valley including old, established wineries and new family operations.

Arrowood Vineyards & Winery is entered by a lane to the east — directly off Highway 12 as you approach Glen Ellen. This is a small winery which does not have a tasting room but has guided tours by appointment (phone 707-938-5170). Owned by Richard and Alis Arrowood, the operation produces limited quantities of very high-quality Chardonnay, Cabernet Sauvignon and Merlot. In 1975, Bruce Cohn established his **Olive Hill Vineyard** in a beautiful and very old olive grove (over 100 years old). This small winery produces estate wines including Cabernet Sauvignon and Chardonnay. There is a picnic area beside the winery and the fine old olive grove makes picnics here quite memorable.

The Parducci family of Mendocino wine fame were responsible for taking vineyards — acquired in 1941 — and turning them into one of the most successful medium-sized wineries in the state — **Valley of the Moon**. Harry Parcucci, the son of Enrico, has been the manager since 1971. Valley of the Moon is situated beside Sonoma Creek on Madrone Rd. down the road from **B.R. Cohn**, four miles west of the highway. The winery produces sparkling wines as well as a variety of estate-bottled varietals including Chardonnay and White Zinfandel. There is a tasting room, picnic area, and tours are given during harvest-time.

Turn onto Arnold Drive and then take London Ranch Road to two of the area's best-known wineries. **M.G. Vallejo Winery** upholds the legend of General Mariano Vallejo who founded the town of Sonoma, was the Spanish Governor of the region and then cooperatively surrendered to American forces and became a leader of the new state of California. He was also one of the state's first commercial vintners. This winery produces moderately-priced wines which have won international favor. The manager is Val Harasthy, a descendent of Agoston Harazthy who founded Buena Vista. There is a tasting room at the winery, open from 10 am until 4:30 pm, and a picnic area.

Continue west on London Ranch Road and you pass **Glen Ellen Winery**, one of the best known of the Sonoma wineries. There are two types of wine bottled by the Benzinger family in their winery: The Glen Ellen label covers a wide variety of moderately-priced Cabernet Sauvignon, Sauvignon Blanc and Chardonnay. Under the Benzinger label are a series of "super premium" wines. The winery property has a fascinating history. This was a 122 acre farm given to Julius Wegener by M.G. Vallejo in the 1860s. Wegener built two residences which were restored and now house the Benzinger families. The grapevines suffered neglect over the years and most vines have been replanted. There is a picnic area and a tasting room. A self-guided tour takes you through the winery.

Sonoma Valley Wineries

Any traveler who stops at the two wineries on London Ranch Road should spend some time exploring the nearby **Jack London State Park**. This park is a major attraction — for good reason. The writer finished his days living and writing on a ranch in these hills west of Glen Ellen from 1904 to 1916. He built "Wolf House" which burned to the ground before the Londons could occupy it. The ruins remain in the park. His widow built the large stone house which now serves as a Jack London museum. Above the house on the hill is the old working ranch which London built around several old brick buildings which had previously been the Kohler & Froeling Winery.

There is a curiosity at the junction of Highway 12 and Warm Springs Road. Dick and Tom, the Smothers Brothers, have a shop and sell wines under their own labels. The shop offers tastings and a selection of Smothers Brothers memorabilia.

On a more serious note, the **Kenwood Winery** is accessed from Hwy. 12 (turn east at the winery sign). This is an excellent producer, beginning its operations in 1970, having modernized an old 1906 winery founded by the Pagani Brothers. This winery, under Martin Lee, has become a thoroughly modern facility, with a range of wines including estate wines from their notable Jack London Vineyard including excellent Zinfandels. There is a large tasting room and shop which sells a fine series of posters taken from their artist-series labels. The winery produces Chardonnay, Chenin Blanc, Riesling, Sauvignon Blanc, Cabernet Sauvignon, Pinot Noir and Zinfandel. The Kenwood Restaurant (no relation to the winery) is just across the highway.

The next property to the north is **Chateau St. Jean.** The name is French, the building is designed in the French villa style but the winery is now owned by Suntory, the Japanese whiskey and restaurant mega-company. The operation was founded by a group of Californians, one of them giving his wife's name to the winery. There's a wine tasting room and store, along with a self-guided tour. Picnic grounds are also on the property.

The **St. Francis Winery** and Vineyards are across the Highway from St. Jean. This is a 100-acre estate with superb award-winning Merlots and Chardonnays. There is a tasting room and picnic area. **Landmark Vineyards** is on the highway in line with Kenwood and Chateau St. Jean. Landmark produces Chardonnays — exclusively. Landmark's first operation is in the Russian River area. This new operation marks their entry into the valley with their superb Damaris Reserve Chardonnay.

If you're not into picnicking in Kenwood, you could try the abovementioned **Kenwood Restaurant ($$ to $$$)** or drive along Adobe Canyon Rd. to **Oreste's Golden Bear Lodge**. With a mainly-Italian menu, this cozy place serves excellent food indoors and outdoors under the trees, overlooking a creek (**$$ to $$$.**

SONOMA VALLEY WINERIES

At the north end of the valley, the vineyards run up the slopes of the mountains on two sides. Highway 12 leads on to the city of Santa Rosa, the county seat and trading center. Sugarloaf Ridge State Park anchors the northeast section of the valley with its hiking and riding trails and picnic areas. There is a campground here.

Several wineries hug the southwest edge of the highway. **Grand Cru Vineyards** is one of several Sonoma wineries which was re-built using old cellars built during the 1800s. The Lemoine Winery was established here in 1886. In 1970, the new owners put in a series of stainless steel fermentation tanks next to the old concrete fermentors. A self-guided tour takes you through the ultra-modern process. The winery is well known for its excellent varietal wines. There is a tasting room and a picnic area on the lawn, shaded by oaks with a fine view of the vineyard.

Wines produced here include Zinfandel, Cabernet Sauvignon, Sauvignon Blanc, Gewurztraminer, Chenin Blanc. A special Gewurztraminer is a late harvest wine which is botrytised. Botrytic cinera or noble mold affects grapes which are left for winter harvesting. The result is a large concentration of sugar and pungent flavor which makes for a fine dessert wine.

The **Adler Fels** winery is located at the extreme north end of the valley, on Los Alamos Road. A steep road winds up the mountain to the winery gate and then even higher to the winery, where there is a spectacular view of the valley. Wines produced here include Chardonnay, Gewurztraminer, late-harvest Riesling and Cabernet Sauvignon. There is no tasting room at Adler Fels and tours are arranged through appointment (phone 707-539-3123). The view is worth the drive, let alone the good wines made here.

Across the valley, on Bennett Valley Road, is the **Matanzas Creek Winery**. For the past 13 years, Sandra and Bill MacIver and their winemakers have been producing excellent Burgundy-style Chardonnays, Merlots and Sauvignon Blancs. This is another scenic location, just across the ridge which separates the Sonoma Valley from the Russian River watershed. The building is a high-tech wonder, producing Chardonnay, Merlot and Sauvignon Blanc. There are guided tours, a tasting room and a picnic ground.

Getting to and from the this winery provides a scenic backroad loop drive. After driving on **Bennett Valley Road** to the winery, I suggest that you return via **Sonoma Mountain Road** which intersects with Bennett Valley Road again just before reaching Highway 12.

Another interesting backroad adventure leads across the western ridge from Glen Ellen to the Napa Valley. **Trinity Road** departs from Highway 12 south of Grand Cru Vineyards. Should you not want to go all the way across the hills, return to Highway 12 on **Cavedale Road** thus completing another scenic loop.

RUSSIAN RIVER WINE COUNTRY

The majority of the Sonoma wineries are not in the Sonoma Valley but in the Russian River watershed which stretches from Santa Rosa in the south for more than 40 miles to Cloverdale and the Mendocino county line.

Highway 101 is the main street of Russian River Country, passing through the middle of the grape-growing countryside. However, as convenient as Highway 101 is to travel from town to town, you must explore the sideroads and backroads of the region to fully appreciate the range of wines which are produced in the area. As is the case in other California wine regions, it is this backroad wandering which makes a wine tour so memorable.

This wine tour attempts to separate what could otherwise be a confusing search for wineries into several drives off Highway 101, departing from the highway at Santa Rosa, Healdsburg and Geyserville. Viticultural areas in this region include Chalk Hill, Alexander Valley and Dry Creek.

We move into lower Russian River country by taking two roads which lead to the town of Guerneville and then — if you wish — to the Pacific Coast at Jenner. **River Road** is a winding and scenic drive from Santa Rosa, passing through forests beside the river with several rustic wineries on sideroads. **Highway 116** which departs from U.S. Hwy. 101 north of Petaluma is another — more direct — route to Guerneville from the south.

The newest of the Sonoma wine-making areas is the **Anderson Valley**. This formerly-remote valley is now the scene of an explosion in vineyards and winery construction. For travelers to the Pacific Coast, **Highway 128**, the rural road which snakes northwest from Cloverdale on Hwy. 101, provides an ideal route to explore the wineries of the Anderson Valley, arriving at Highway 1 just south of Mendocino. The small towns of the area — Boonville, Philo and Navarro — are still sleepy villages, still unused to tourist traffic although there are several restaurants, country inns and an outstanding cottage brewery worth visiting. It's possible to take a loop drive through Boonville and then back to Highway 101 at Healdsburg.

Our listings for cities and towns begin at the south with **Petaluma**, a convenient place to stay when approaching Russian River Country. It's also near enough to the Sonoma Valley, Marin County and San Francisco to be a center for several days of activity. **Santa Rosa**, the county seat, is the city at the southern end of this wine region and a convenient take-off point for River Road & Highway 116 wineries and to the coast. But Healdsburg, 17 miles north of Santa Rosa, is the real center of viticulture in the Russian River region with wineries in every direction.

The Sonoma County Wineries Association is building a tourist-oriented wine information and education center complete with a small working winery. It is expected to be built by the end of 1991 in Rohnert Park, south of Santa Rosa. It will be particularly handy for travelers to purchase the wines made by many small family wineries which do not have tasting rooms and which produce many of the county's most memorable vintages.

PETALUMA

An hour's drive from San Francisco and 20 minutes from Sonoma, Petaluma is well-situated for exploring the more southern wine regions of Sonoma County.

This is a country town. Dairy farms ring the city and there are still the chicken farms which made the city famous a century ago when the incubator was invented here. The town celebrates Butter & Egg Day each April.

Petaluma grew up along the riverfront in the 1850s. The river — actually a tidal slough — was used for transporting lumber in the 1800s and is now used by pleasure boats. There is a new 200-berth public marina and boat launch at Lakewood Hwy. and Baywood Drive, a block from Hwy. 101. The city has a visitor center at the marina, open daily from June through September. The Chamber of Commerce visitor center is at Washington & Howard streets (phone 707-762-2785). Maps are available for a walking tour of the city's Victorian homes and the historic downtown core. There are 122 restaurants in Petaluma, with cuisine for every taste. A country farms trail leads to dairy operations, a llama farm and to vegetable and flower growers. The trail map is available at the visitor center.

The **Eagle Ridge Winery** is located on Goodwine Road in Pengrove, north of town, on the historic Denman Ranch. Vines were first planted in 1920 and this is the only winery in the United States growing the German Ehrenfelser grape. Other wines available at the tasting room and store here are Sauvignon Blanc, Zinfandel (including a late-harvest Zin.) and Charmat Champagne. The **Braren Pauli Winery** is west of town on Spring Hill Road (take Western Ave.) Wines produced here include Chardonnay, Cabernet Sauvignon, Gewertztraminer and Merlot. Tastings and tours are arranged by appointment (phone 707-778-0721).

History fans will require a visit to **Petaluma Adobe State Historic Park**, the site of the largest adobe building in California. The "Old Adobe" was built in the 1830s by General Vallejo. The park is at the corner of Casa Grande and Adobe roads. The oldest structure in town is the Great Petaluma Mill, a landmark by the river which has been converted into shops and restaurant space. The **7th Street Inn** is a 1892 B & B home at 525 7th St. west of Highway 101 via G. Street (707-769-0480). **$$**.

The **Best Western Petaluma Inn** (707-763-0994 or 1-800-528-1234) is at 200 S McDowell Blvd, to the east of Hwy. 101, with 75 rooms, a pool, restaurant and cocktail lounge. **$ to $$**. The **Casa Grande Motel** (707-762-8881) is a modest place with several kitchen units at 307 Petaluma Blvd **$**.

Campers who wish to visit the Sonoma Valley wineries may want to pitch their tents or park their RVs in Petaluma because of the shortage of camping space in the valley. The **KOA campground and RV park** is located at 20 Rainsville Road (707-763-1492 or 1-800-992-CAMP). There are 312 sites here with full hookups and tenting sites, a heated pool, whirlpool, playground and petting farm.

Santa Rosa

While it is the geographical and trading center of the county, Santa Rosa is best known for Luther Burbank who settled here around 1900 and conducted his renowned botanical experiments in the area. Downtown gardens bear his name and display the results of his research. The **Luther Burbank House and Gardens** provide a quiet retreat. The home is open to the public with information on the famous botanist and the gardens are both beautiful and educational.

The **Old Railroad Square** area is the historic section of town, now restored with a pleasant mixture of hotels, stores and restaurants. The Sonoma County Museum displays artifacts of Sonoma history.

Just north of Santa Rosa, at 5007 Fulton Road (just off the highway in Fulton), is **Chateau De Baun**. This family-owned winery produces estate-grown Chardonnay, Pinot Noir and the new Symphony varietal wine. The tasting room and shop are open daily from 10 am to 5 pm. There's a large picnic ground at the winery, offering great hill-top views of the surrounding valley. The tasting room and shop are in a chateau-style building.

There are two routes to reach the Pacific Coast from Santa Rosa — and to sample wines on the way. River Road links a series of forest parks and small villages along the Russian River, joining Hwy. 116 at Guerneville. The Bodega Highway, (# 12) connects with Hwy. 116 (for the wineries) and then continues west to the coast at Bodega Bay.

Fans of the Peanuts comic strip will want to visit the **Redwood Empire Ice Arena**. The rink is owned by Charles Schultz and adjacent to the arena is a large Snoopy and Peanuts store.

The **Gables Bed & Breakfast Inn** (707-585-7777) is a striking heritage building at 4257 Petaluma Road, dating from 1857. There are fifteen gables on the house which contains seven bedrooms & suites (a 2-storey cottage) with private baths and antique furnishings including claw-footed bath tubs. The home is set on 3 1/2 acres of country landscape and full breakfast and afternoon tea are provided. **$$ to $$$**. The **Los Robles Lodge** (1-800-552-1001, CA or 1-800-552-6330, outside CA) is at 925 Edwards Ave., a resort and convention hotel with dining room, lounge and whirlpools. **$$**.

The **Vintner's Inn** (1-800-421-2584-CA or 1-800-351-1133) is a remarkable town-house lodge amidst the vineyards north of Sonoma at 4350 Barnes Rd. **$$ to $$$**. The inn includes the **John Ash & Co.** restaurant (707-527-7687). The **Red Lion Inn** (707-584-5466) is in nearby Rohnert Park. This resort hotel, surrounded by the Mountain Shadows Golf Course, has 245 rooms, heated pool, whirlpool, restaurant and lounge. The **Best Western Garden Inn** (707-546-4031) is moderately-priced with 78 rooms in five small buildings, coffee shop and two pools. **$**. Campers stay at the **Petaluma KOA** (see page 95) or in **Austin Creek State Rec. Area**, north of Guerneville or **Spring Lake County Park** which is east of Santa Rosa via Newanga Avenue (call 707-539-8092). For downtown food, try **La Gare** with French cuisine at 208 Wilson St. in the Railroad Square district. **$$**.

HEALDSBURG

Healdsburg, a rural town, is the center of the Russian River winery district. It's a mecca for people who love their wines, especially those from the smaller, more intimate family-owned operations. The Dry Creek Valley is to the north and west, the Alexander Valley to the north and east. The Chalk Hill area and Knight's Valley are to the south and east.

The center of Healdsburg is reminiscent of the Plaza in Sonoma. The Healdsburg Plaza is smaller but has the same ambience with historic buildings, inns, restaurants and stores ringing the square.

Three wineries have operations right in the downtown area. The **William Wheeler Winery** has a store-front wine room on Plaza St. Tasting hours are from 11 am to 4 pm. **Clos du Bois** has a tasting room in its winery at 5 Fitch Street (at Haydon). Tastings are held from 10 am to 5 pm with winery tours by appointment (phone 707-433-5576). **White Oak Vineyards** is around the corner from Clos du Bois at 208 Haydon St., with a tasting room which is open from 10 am to 4 pm daily. Tours are given by appointment, phone 707-433-8429. Three separate drives to other wineries in the immediate Healdsburg area are covered in detail on the next three pages.

For a small, rather rural community, Healdsburg has a number of very good places to stay. The **Dry Creek Inn** (707-433-0300 or 1-800-222-KRUG) is located at 198 Dry Creek Road, just off Hwy. 101. The hotel, part of the West Western chain, serves a continental breakfast and boasts a heated pool and whirlpool. **$$**.

The town has several fine bed and breakfast operations including the historic **Healdsburg Inn On The Plaza** (707-433-6991), located right on the town square. This building was originally a Wells Fargo express office built in 1900. It has a roof garden, fireplaces, antique furnishings and full breakfast is served. **$$ to $$$**. **Madrona Manor** (707-433-4231) is a wonderful B & B operation: a four-storey 1881 Victorian home with orchards, garden and swimming pool. **$$ to $$$.** The inn has a renowned restaurant — the best in the area — with always-fresh food including fish, poultry and special pizzas from the brick oven. Full breakfast is served to stay-overs. There's another great overnight experience at **Belle De Jour** (707-433-7892), a B & B operation with four rooms in white cottages which include fireplaces, antique furniture, whirlpools and gardens in a treed setting. Full breakfast is served and picnic baskets are prepared on request. **$$ to $$$**. A 1900 Queen Anne house is the **Grape Leaf Inn** (707-433-8140) at 539 Johnston St. This is an elegant home with gardens, whirlpools and (again) antique furnishings. Full breakfast is provided, and picnic baskets on request. **$$**. The **Camelia Inn** (707-433-8182) is an 1869 Italianate house at 211 North St., with double parlors and swimming pool with terrace. A doctor's house, this was Healdsburg's first hospital. Many of the camelias on the grounds are attributed to Luther Burbank, a friend of the doctor's family. **$$ to $$$**.

The next three pages are devoted to three drives through the countryside around Healdsburg which will lead you to some of the more prominent wineries in this wine region. All of the wineries have tasting rooms which are open daily and most have picnic grounds and winery tours (either self-guided or by appointment). The gently rolling landscape provides relaxing sideroad drives through vineyards and mixed-farm country.

The first drive explores the Chalk Valley area to the east of the Russian River by taking Chalk Hill Road, south of Healdsburg. Start by taking Old Redwood Highway (off Hwy. 101), turn east on Pleasant Ave. and then turn north on Chalk Hill Rd. The **Chalk Hill Winery** is a modern building set on rugged terrain. 278 acres of the 1,100-acre Frederick Furth estate are planted with vines. The "Chalk" in the winery's name is volcanic ash which intensifies the flavor of grapes such as Chardonnay and Sauvignon Blanc. Cabernet Sauvignon wine also benefits from this soil. Tastings and tours are available by appointment only — call 707-433-4774. There is a picnic ground as well.

The **Field Stone** Winery is on Highway 128 to the north, at the junction with Chalk Hill Road. This unique underground facility was constructed by excavating a shallow trough, building the winery and covering the roof with the excavated earth which then was planted with grass. Field stones unearthed during construction were used for the entrance wall. The winery is well-known for its fine Cabernets and a wonderful Petite Sirah. It also produces Chardonnay, Sauvignon Blanc and Gewurztraminer, including late harvest bottlings. The tasting room is open daily from 10 am to 5 pm. There is a scenic picnic area and concerts are held on summer weekends. Two minutes north on Highway 128, the **Alexander Valley Winery** mixes several architectural styles in its buildings: adobe, Old West and modern California-style. The vineyard and winery are located on the original homestead of Cyrus Alexander who settled here in the 1840s. Tours are by appointment (call 707-433-7209) but the tasting room is open daily from 10 am to 5 pm. Wines produced range from Zinfandel (including their popular "sin-zin") and Merlot, Pinot Noir and Cabernet Sauvignon, to Chardonnay, Johannisberg Riesling and Gewurztraminer. There are picnic tables available on request.

Johnson's Alexander Valley Wines is across the highway and slightly north. The tasting room contains a 1920-era theater pipe organ which is played during concerts in the room. Outdoor concerts are held in the summer. The estate wines are bottled in limited quantities and can be tasted from 10 am to 5 pm daily. Farther north on the highway is the **Sausal Winery** which started out as a bulk-wine business and then developed into a fine estate winery. The renowned Zinfandel is still the mainstay with Chardonnay and Cabernet Sauvignon added more recently. Tastings from 10 am to 4 pm. There is a picnic area here too.

Russian River Wineries — Healdsburg

The Dry Creek Valley lies west of the Russian River and most of the wineries are set along West Dry Creek Road. The first on our drive is located on Lambert Bridge Rd. To get to the **Dry Creek Vineyard**, take the Dry Creek Rd. exit from U.S. 101. Drive west 2.5 miles and turn west on Lambert Bridge Rd. Dry Creek's tasting room is open from 10 am to 4:30 pm daily. The original masonry-block building was built in 1973; the new wing was added in 1978 and the tasting room in 1988. Wines include Chardonnay, Chenin Blanc, Sauvignon Blanc, late harvest wine most years, and a range of red wines. There's a picnic area at the winery and tours are booked by phone (707-433-1000).

The **Robert Stemmler Winery,** across Lambert Bridge Road, specializes in Pinot Noir. The tasting and sales room is open daily from 10:30 to 4:30 pm daily with picnicking by reservation, call 707-433-6334.

Now, drive west and turn south on Westside (West Dry Creek) Road. The **Lambert Bridge Winery** is on the west side of the road with its tasting and sales room open from 10 am to 4:30 pm daily. Wines produced include Chardonnay, Fume Blanc, Merlot and Cabernet Sauvignon. There is a picnic area. **Alderbrook Winery** is on Magnolia Dr., just off Westside Rd. The tasting room is open 10 am to 5 pm daily, with a picnic area and tours by appointment (call 707-433-9154). Alderbrook has an annual production of 22,000 cases including Chardonnay, Sauvignon Blanc, Semillon and Muscat Canelli. **Mill Creek Vineyards,** at 1401 Westside Rd., is open daily from 10 am to 4:30 pm except for Dec.- Feb. when it's Tuesday to Thursday. Wines include a Cabernet Blush, Merlot, Chardonnay and Gewurztraminer. **Hop Kiln** features a restored 1905 hop-drying barn on 240 acres of land with vineyards producing eight estate wines. The tasting room is open from 10 am to 5 pm daily and a picnic area is situated on these historic and scenic grounds. Other small wineries on Westside Rd. include **Belvedere**, **Bellerose** and **Rochioli**.

Two well-known wineries are located on Old Redwood Highway, just west of Highway 101 and south of the Russian River bridge. Rodney Strong has developed two of the seminal Sonoma wineries, and has trained many of the successful winemakers in the region. The **Rodney Strong** tasting room is high above the winery and guided tours are available daily. Wines include the famous Alexander's Crown Cabernet Sauvignon and Pinot Noir, Sauvignon Blanc, Chardonnay, Riesling and Zinfandel. The winery's picnic ground, the scene of summer concerts, is a popular spot. The larger **Piper Sonoma Cellars** is adjacent and is a state-of-the-art facility. Here too, tours are available daily and it's a pleasure to walk through the vineyards and floral gardens and then to relax in the terrace picnic grounds. Light lunch is available by reservation (call 707-433-8843). Visiting these two wineries can take half a day. **Foppiano Vineyards**, north of Rodney Strong, is the longest-held family winery in Sonoma County. The tasting room is open daily from 10 am to 4:30 pm. For tours, call 707-433-7272.

RUSSIAN RIVER WINERIES — HEALDSBURG

There are six wineries located near Highway 101, all north of Healdsburg and all within a few minutes' drive of each other by using Hwy. 101 as your access route. We'll visit them by driving south-to-north from downtown Healdsburg and by the time you've finished at the Nuervo barn, you're almost in Geyserville.

The **Simi Winery** is accessed by taking the Dry Creek Rd. exit from Hwy. 101 to West Healdsburg Ave. and driving one mile north. Simi is an old winery started in 1890. The original stone winery is used as aging cellars. The tasting room is open from 10 am to 4:30 pm with tours at 11, 1 and 3. Driving north, take the Lytton Springs exit to the west and you come upon the **Lytton Springs Winery** (at Chiquita Rd.). This operation concentrates on one wine: Zinfandel. Founded in 1975, the vineyard is now known as Valley Vista. A tasting room and picnic area were built in 1987 and this is an ideal place to deeply explore the making of the quintessential California red wine. The tasting room and shop are open daily from 10 am to 4 pm. The **Mazzocco Vineyards** are also located on Lytton Springs Road with tastings and retail sales from 10 am to 4 pm. This is a family operation which produces Chardonnays, Zinfandels and Cabernet Sauvignons. For information, call 707-433-9035.

While the Lytton Springs operation is housed in a factory-type building, **Chateau Souverin** is something else. Designed after the old hop barns, this large building commands the surrounding area. The winery has been designed for tours with walkways running through the winery, passing the steel fermentation tanks and then over the Slovenian oak tanks and French and American oak barrels. There is a tasting room on the upper level. The winery was founded in 1971 by the Pillsbury Co. which sold the operation in 1976. Tastings are held from 10 am to 4 pm daily. There is an excellent open-air restaurant which serves lunch and dinner as well as Sunday Brunch. For reservations, call 707-433-3141. The restaurant has wonderful views of the vineyards and surrounding countryside.

Geyserville Avenue is located east of Highway 101, just across from Chateau Souverin (take the Independence Lane exit from Hwy. 101). The **Trentadue Winery** at 19170 Geyserville Ave. is a small family operation which produces Chardonnay, Chenin Blanc, white Zinfandel, Cabernet Sauvignon, Carignane, and Merlot. The winery also produces sherry and late harvest wines when the year is right. There is a large tasting room on the second floor with a good view down to the cellars and the store includes a large stock of wine-related merchandise. The **Nervo Winery**, now part of the Geyser Peak operation, is housed in an old stone barn, a short drive north of Trentadue. The winery was sold by former owner Frank Nervo in 1974 but the **Nervo** name has been retained as a separate label and Frank Nervo manages the vineyard. The barn serves as a tasting room and aging cellar. The sales and tasting room is open daily from 10 am to 5 pm. A specialty is late-harvest Winterchill wine.

GEYSERVILLE & CLOVERDALE

At the north end of Sonoma County, Geyserville is home to several historic family winemaking operations. Cloverdale is the junction point for traveling west to the Pacific Coast and via Highway 128 through the Anderson Valley wine region to Albion and Mendocino.

Geyserville is a small town with limited accommodations. However, lack of numbers is more than offset by quality and ambience in the few places available. These include two related bed and breakfast homes. The **Hope Merrill House** (707-857-3356) is a Victorian inn, a frequent subject of several slick homes magazines, with private whirlpools, swimming pool, its own vineyard and garden. **$$ to $$$**. Bob and Rosalie Hope are the innkeepers. The **Hope-Bosworth House** (707-857-3356) is the sister B & B operation, a 1904 Queen Anne house with gardens and swimming pool. **$$**. Both homes serve a full breakfast.

The **Isis Oasis Lodge** (707-857-3524) is a resort-type inn with gardens, spa program, pool, sauna, several acres for walking and breakfast served. There's a cottage available as well. **$$ to $$$**. The **Campbell Ranch Inn** (707-857-3476) is at 1475 Canyon Rd., set in 35 acres in the country with great views, gardens, swimming pool, tennis court, whirlpool, spa and bicycles. There are five rooms here with full breakfast served on the terrace when weather permits — which is most of the time. For reservations at eleven inns in the Russian River area, the **Wine Country Inns of Sonoma County** offers a one-call service. Call 505-433-INNS or write P.O. Box 51, Geyserville CA 95441. The **Hoffman Farm House Restaurant** in Geyserville serves continental cuisine in a former stagecoach stop. The restaurant is open for lunch and dinner with a good list of California wines. **$$ to $$$**.

In Cloverdale, the **Vintage Towers Inn** is a distinctive bed and breakfast home listed on the U.S. registry of historic places. There are three towers on this 1913 mansion with a choice of seven rooms including tower rooms. Each room is furnished with antiques and the 40-foot veranda is perfect for sitting in the evening. A full breakfast is served. **$$**. The **Cloverdale KOA** (707-894-3337) is a well-equipped campground and RV park at 4350 Barnes Road. The park has full hookups and 58 tent sites, showers, store, summer swimming pool and miniature golf. The **Sonoma Lake Recreation Area** has more than 220 campsites west of Cloverdale.

Hamburger Ranch is a long-time landmark at the junction of U.S. 101 and Hwy. 128. This used to be called the Top-Of-The-Hill Texaco and the Hamburger Ranch emerged in 1986. In good weather, the burgers are served on a patio which contains an eclectic collection of ranch memorabilia. If you're a burger, hot dog & fries fan, this is a perfect place to contemplate a drive through the Anderson Valley. From Cloverdale, wine-travelers have a choice of heading north along U.S. 101 to Ukiah and the heart of Mendocino wine country or driving northwest along Hwy. 128 to Boonville and onward to the Anderson Valley wineries.

Russian River Wineries — Geyserville

To begin this tour from Geyserville, drive north of town and exit at Canyon Road. Turn on Chianti Road for a one-mile drive. The **Geyser Peak Winery** was founded in 1880 by Augustus Quitzow and is now owned by the Trione family of Santa Rosa and Penfolds Wines of Australia. The grapes come from the Trione Family Vineyards in the Alexander Valley and the nearby Russian River area. There is a tasting room open daily from 10 am to 5 pm and a picnic ground next to the winery. The winery shop sells a number of small bottlings and rare varieties as well as a selection of Chardonnay, Cabernet Sauvignon and Merlot which are widely available.

The **J. Pedroncelli Winery** is located at 1220 Canyon Road (west of Hwy. 101), on a ridge which divides the Dry Creek and Russian River valleys. The Pedroncelli family has owned the property since 1927, began selling grapes to local wineries and developed their first wines in 1934. The tasting room is open from 10 am to 5 pm. The winery produces generic wines called Sonoma Red, Rose and White, as well as a range of varietal red and white wines. Tours are not available.

Driving west on Canyon Rd. into the Dry Creek Valley, then turning north on West Dry Creek Road, you come to a small family operation, **Preston Vineyards & Winery**, specializing in producing Sauvignon Blanc and Zinfandel. The tasting room and store are open from 11 am to 3 pm on weekdays and 11 am to 4 pm on weekends. Tours are available by appointment, call 707-433-3372.

Retrace the route south and drive east on Yoakum Bridge Road , then turn north on Dry Creek Road to reach the **Ferrari-Carano** Vineyards and Winery. The winery has vineyards in the Alexander V alley as well as on this property, and produces a range of varietal wines. The tasting room is open from 10 am to 5 pm daily and tours are available by appointment, call 707-433-6700.

Lake Sonoma is a large reservoir created by the Warm Springs Dam and near the dam is the small **Lake Sonoma Winery.** Lake Sonoma should be visited because the wines made here are available nowhere else in California although they are sold in other states. This operation produces about 6,000 cases each year, including Chardonnay, Sauvignon Blanc, Cabernet Sauvignon and their blended wine "Hillside White".

Fritz Cellars is an outstanding piece of architectural sculpture, located on Dutcher Creek Road which runs between Dry Creek Rd. and U.S. 101. This is the local winery with picnic tables beside a pond and on sunny days wines are tasted at umbrella-tables in the entrance courtyard. The tasting room is open daily from 12 noon until 4:30 pm. Wines produced in this scenic winery include Petit Sirah, Gamay Beaujolais, Pinot Noir Rose, Sauvignon Blanc and Chardonnay.

Here's another note for Smothers Brothers fans: the **Pat Paulson Vineyards** tasting room is located in Asti Village, to the east of Hwy. 101 north of Geyserville.

Russian River Country via River Rd. & Hwy. 116

Although the Healdsburg and Geyserville wine area is part of the Russian River wine region, travelers don't see much of the Russian River itself until driving west of Healdsburg and Santa Rosa on the routes which lead from U.S. Highway 101 to the Pacific Coast. To me, this is the real Russian River Country — where the river winds slowly through the redwood forests — with state parks providing handy and restful stopping places and camping spots and the small villages and towns of the Russian River Valley offering quaint and historic inns and lodges.

From Santa Rosa, the Bodega Highway (Hwy. 12) leads west from the city. To reach the Russian River turn northwest on Highway 116 at the town of **Sebastopol**. The highway passes through **Forestville** and then crosses the river between **Guerneville** and **Rio Nido**. Both towns are good places to stay while exploring the wineries of this area.

The most useful route to the Russian River vineyards and wineries is River Road which leads west from U.S. Highway 101, south of Healdsburg. Here, the wineries appear shortly after starting down the road and they continue to be spaced along River Road and on sideroads as far as Guerneville. River Road joins Highway 116 at Guerneville and they continue together to meet the Pacific Ocean at **Jenner**. It is 14 miles from Highway 101 to Korbel Vineyards and another four miles to Guerneville. This is 18 miles of some of the most scenic country in the state, with a number of wineries along the way in addition to lovely forest road and places to stop for picnics. Any of the sideroads in the area provide fascinating sightseeing in this hilly countriside.

Because there are the two routes to Guerneville, our Russian River wine tour is divided into two parts. River Road could serve for both. Most of the wineries accessed via Highway 116 from Santa Rosa are in the Forestville area. There is a lot to do in this region besides wine tasting. The Russian River is used as a canoeing and kayaking course. Each year thousands of anglers fish for steelhead and salmon. **Armstrong Redwoods State Reserve** north of Guerneville is a superb forest preserve with hiking and riding trails, and camping. Some of the most interesting historic inns in California are located in the trees beside the Russian River. There's a golf course beside the river at the Highway 116 bridge, plus a private campground and RV park in Guerneville.

Two small villages should receive special mention. Both **Monte Rio** and **Rio Nido** are scenically-located resort towns with excellent inns and rustic but satisfying restaurants. Closer to the coast is the tiny Victorian-revival village of **Duncans Mills** with another eccentric inn.

The best place to obtain detailed information on things to see and do along the river is in Guerneville, at the **Russian River Region Tourist Information** office. The office is located on Armstrong Woods Rd., downtown. To reach them by telephone, call 707-869-9212 or 1-800-253-8800.

RUSSIAN RIVER COUNTRY

The two villages on the banks of the Russian River have distinct charms which make them popular getaway resorts. Like their larger cousin Guerneville, Rio Nido and Monte Rio are close enough to the San Francisco Bay area to attract a large number of day trippers and especially weekend holidayers who come here to enjoy the riverside forest settings and the relaxed lifestyle of the quaint inns and lodges of the area.

Rio Nido is situated on the north bank of the river — accessed by River Road. It is just east of Guerneville, close to river activities and near Armstrong Redwoods State Reserve. The resort hotel here is the **Rio Nido Lodge** (707-869-0821), an intimate and moderately-priced resort in the redwoods. The lodge has a swimming pool, restaurant and cocktail lounge.

Due south of Monte Rio, the Bohemian Highway — a sideroad — winds its scenic way to meet Highway 12 (the Bodega Highway). On the way it intersects several other backroads and at a major intersection is the tiny village of Occidental. If you're partial to out-of-the-way overnight experiences, the **Heart's Desire Inn** (707-874-1311) offers B & B accommodation in a renovated 1867 Victorian home with private baths, antique furnishings and a country breakfast. The backroads in this area provide fascinating drives through this wooded countryside in addition to alternative ways of reaching the coast.

Monte Rio is a larger community — but still a village — on the south bank of the Russian River. To get there drive along Highway 116 southwest of Guerneville to the Bohemian Highway, take the Bohemian Highway across the Russian River bridge, and you're there. Monte Rio is definitely a resort town. It has a good selection of historic, rustic and modern accommodations in addition to good restaurants. It makes an interesting alternative to Guerneville for an overnight stay, or for several days if you're serious about winery visits, fishing or recreation in Armstrong Woods park. The Northwood Golf Course is located just off Highway 116 with a scenic layout beside the river.

The **Highland Dell Inn** (707-767-1759 or 1-800-767-2454)) is an historic, fully restored 1906 building. The inn boasts fine stained glass windows, fireplaces, spacious living room areas and its ten rooms are individually decorated with antique bricabrack and furnishings. There is a swimming pool and continental breakfast is served to overnight guests. **$$**. **Huckleberry Springs** (707-865-2683) is a country inn on 56 acres, one mile from the river. All the cottages and cabins comne with private baths and, as well, there's a swimming pool and whirlpool. This is a full-service operation with a restaurant and complimentary breakfast is served to overnighters. Huckleberry Springs also has a modified American Plan with breakfast, dinner and lunch included in the fare.

Angelo's Resort (707-865-2215) has housekeeping cabins with a beach on River Blvd. **$**. The resort includes a restaurant serving seafood and Italian cuisine in a rustic setting overlooking the river.

GUERNEVILLE

The geographical center of the Russian River valley west of Highway 101 is Guerneville, a small town which offers an inexpensive alternative to the more deluxe resort towns in Napa and Sonoma counties. Accommodations here are more on the rustic side and restaurants are basic but quite adequate. What Guerneville has is the Russian River atmosphere: thick forests, river recreation, golf and several of Sonoma's more interesting wineries including the famed Korbel Champagne Cellars. The area was adopted years ago by the gay community of the San Francisco Bay area as a weekend and vacation center.

The prime outdoor attraction is **Armstrong Woods State Reserve**, a 752 acre stand of old growth redwoods. There are trails to several groves and recreational pursuits include biking, riding, walking and picnicking. There's a park amphitheater with interpretive programs during summer months. Guided trail rides are available. Two miles north of Guerneville on Armstrong Woods Road is **Austin Creek State Recreation Area**, which has developed and primitive (walk-in) campsites in 4,236 acres of forest and scrub lands. There's also a horse camp. For information on these state facilities, phone (707) 869-2015 or 865-2391.

Guerneville has several motels and a good selection of B & B homes for overnight stays. The **Creekside Inn & Resort** (707-869-3623) gives you a choice of rooms in the B & B house or a housekeeping cottage. The resort has a swimming pool, fireplaces and exceptionally low rates. **$**. **The Estate** is a B & B with ten rooms in a 1922 mission revival building in the redwoods with antique furnishings, fireplaces, pool, whirlpool and gardens. **$$**. If you want to have quantities of Champagne on hand for breakfast, you couldn't be nearer to the source than by staying at **Ridenhour Ranch House Inn** (707-887-1033). Next to the Korbel Winery on River Road, this 1906 Victorian farmhouse B & B has a garden, antique furnishings and library. **$ to $$**. **Santa Nella House** (707-869-9488) is a smaller B & B with four rooms and full breakfast in an 1870 Italianate farmhouse with redwoods all around. Picnic baskets are available. **$ to $$**.

For those who prefer the anonymity of a motel and the amenities of a resort, the **Brookside Lodge** (707-869-2874) should fill the bill. There are standard motel rooms and several separate cottages with kitchens available. One has a private whirlpool. There is a swimming pool in addition to a sauna and whirlpool. Morning coffee. **$$ to $$$**.

For campers, **Johnson's Beach Resort** (707-869-2022) is at 16241 First Street, with 50 RV and tent sites with electrical hookups, showers, laundry and picnic area. There are also housekeeping and standard motel units at the resort **($)**. A much larger and more fully equipped RV park is located in Duncans Mills which is west of Guerneville — near the coast — on Moscow Road. The **Casini Ranch Family Campground** (707-865-2255 or 1-800-451-8400) has 225 RV spaces and is open year-round with full hookups, showers, laundry, store, propane and boat rentals.

RUSSIAN RIVER WINERIES — VIA RIVER ROAD

From its junction with Highway 101 south of Healdsburg, River Road provides the most scenic and interesting drive between the freeway and the Sonoma Coast. The road runs through the business district of Guerneville and follows the river — leading along its north side — to the Pacific Coast.

This winery tour begins near the Highway 101 junction. On the south side of River Road is the **Z Moore Winery**. This operation is housed in an old redwood hop kiln which overlooks the vineyards and apple orchards. The winery produces Chardonnays, Gewurztraminer, a Zinfandel-Petite Sirah blend and Pinot Noir. There is a picnic area and the tasting room and store are open daily from 10 am to 5 pm. Close-by is the **Martinelli Winery**, at 3350 River Road. This winery is also housed in an old hop barn. The vineyard has been here since the turn of the century when the grandparents of Lee Martinelli (the present owner) planted grape vines. The winery produces estate wines which are available to taste from 10 am to 5 pm, daily. The **Sonoma-Cutrer** winery requires an advance booking for a tour and tasting. It is located on Slusser Road, less than a mile from River Road. Built in 1981 by founder Brice Jones, this winery is devoted to one varietal and produces three distinctive Chardonnays. The winery's architectural design is truly amazing. The many small and sometimes unique features add to the quality of the wine. Phone (707) 528-1181.

Approaching Forestville, the **Mark West Vineyards** are located at 7,000 Trenton-Healdsburg Road, with the winery perched on the crest of a rolling hill. The building has a rustic style with redwood siding and a shake roof. There is a not only a picnic area on the premises but a deli in which to buy your picnic fixings. The tasting room, open daily from 10 am to 5 pm, features current offerings and several older vintages. The winery bottles estate Chardonnays, Gewurztraminers, Johannisberg Rieslings and Pinot Noirs.

After driving farther west on River Road, we cross the Russian River, approaching Guerneville. The **Korbel Champagne Cellars** (F. Korbel & Bros.) is a prime tourist attraction in the area, not only because of the internationally-known sparkling wine but for the winery itself. The winery was founded in 1882 by Francis, Joseph and Anton Korbel, brothers from Bohemia. First involved in a redwood logging operation, the Korbels planted grapes on the cleared hillsides above the Russian River. The winery was bought by the Heck family in 1954. The Heck's Alsatian background has fostered the production of sparkling wine since that time. The sparkling wines feature four grades of dryness (Sec, Extra Dry, Brut & Natural). There are two specialty wines: Blanc de Blanc, from Chardonnay grapes, and Blanc de Noir, from Pinot Noir. Korbel winery tours start from the restored railway depot (bought from the Northwestern Pacific in 1935) and lead to the tasting room which is situated in a restored former brandy barrel warehouse. The winery's rose garden brings flower lovers from afar and provides yet another reason to drive to Guerneville via River Road.

WINERIES — VIA HWY. 116 OR RIVER ROAD

From a start in San Francisco, State Highway 116 is the most direct route to Guerneville and the south Sonoma Coast. It departs from U.S. 101 south of Santa Rosa, leads through the agricultural town of Sebastopol (apples), and then passes through Forestville, giving access to several wineries which are clustered around this small town. It then moves northwest to cross the Russian River at Monte Rio and leads directly to Guerneville. The highway turns west at Guerneville and ends at the coast, in Jenner. The **De Loach Winery** can be accessed from River Road or via Hwy. 116. From Forestville, drive eastward on Guerneville Rd. and turn north on Olivet Rd. All the wines are varietal: Zinfandel (red & white), Pinot Noir, Gewurztraminer (regular and late-harvest), Chardonnay, Fume Blanc, Cabernet Sauvignon. This is a true family operation: father Cecil De Loach is the winemaker, sons John and Michael operate the vineyard and sales operations.

The **Martini & Prati Winery** is located at 2191 Laguna Rd., north of Guerneville Rd. and south of River Road. While the winery has little aesthetic appeal — from the outside — the cellars hold a huge assortment of aged redwood tanks, oak casks and other barrels. Dating back to the 1800s, the winery was taken over by the Martini family in 1902. The Pratis came later. Most of the wine made here is sold in bulk but the winery does sell wines under its own label in bottles and jugs and the Fountain Grove label is reserved for the winery's most prized varietals. The tasting room is open daily from 11 am to 4 pm (except January) but tours are available only by appointment (phone 707-823-2404).

At the northeast corner of Guerneville Road and Vine Hill Roads in Sebastopol is the **Dehlinger Winery**. The entrance is on Vine Hill. This is a small operation, specializing in estate wines including Chardonnay, Pinot Noir and Cabernet Sauvignon. Older wines and reserved lots are available only at the winery store which is open from 10 am to 5 pm daily. Tours are available by appointment (phone 707-823-2378). **Iron Horse Vineyards** have come on the scene more recently than most of the family operations in the Russian River area. This winery was founded in 1978 and produces three sparkling wines from vineyards which were planted much earlier: Blanc De Blanc, Brut and Blanc de Noir. Other (still) wines include Chardonnay, Fume Blanc, Pinot Noir and Cabernet Sauvignon. The Iron Horse name comes from a previous owner — a train hobbyist — who had a narrow gauge railroad running around the property. Tours and tastings are available by appointment only (phone 707-887-1507).

Finally, **Topolos at Russian River Vineyard** is located at 5700 Gravenstein Hwy. N, on the southern edge of Forestville. This historic winery has a deliberately-offbeat look with tall Russian-style wooden towers beside a concrete cellar. The winery lab is atop one of the towers. The tasting room and a restaurant with indoor and outdoor seating are open daily from 11 am. This pleasant restaurant is open for dinner as well.

MENDOCINO WINE COUNTRY — ALEXANDER VALLEY

For those wine lovers who enjoy backroad and sideroad travel, Mendocino County offers several fine experiences. This is not a finely-tailored landscape. The valleys are smaller than in Sonoma and Napa wine country, there are fewer towns and the countryside has a wild touch which provides fascinating travels through a large and scattered territory. In the years following the end of prohibition, the Parducci family were just about the only prominent Mendocino winemakers and all of the few wineries were within a few miles of U.S. Highway 101. Now, the county has more than 25 wineries scattered across the sprawling landscape.

While the geographical center of Mendocino wine country is the town of Ukiah (see page 114 and the Hwy. 101 wineries), the **Anderson Valley** is attracting growing interest from winemakers and travelers. This scenic valley wanders from Cloverdale at the north end of Sonoma County to the Pacific Coast at Albion, just south of the town of Mendocino. What was only a few years ago a remote and private string of small settlements along Highway 128 is now a preferred alternative route to the coast for many tourists — for good reason.

The first two Anderson Valley wineries opened in 1971 and a score had developed by the late 1980s, with more being opened each year. The wineries range from the large Roederer sparkling wine operation — established in 1987 as a subsidiary of the French Champagne company Louis Roederer — to the tiny Lazy Creek Vineyards which produces about 500 cases per year.

There are three communities in the valley. **Boonville** is the largest, with a range of visitor facilities. West of Boonville, **Philo** and **Navarro** serve as book-ends for the wine district with the wineries flanking the highway between the two villages. Traveling through the valley is the western equivalent of touring through Kentucky hill country. North of Philo, on Greenwood Ridge Road, **Hendy Woods State Park** has campsites and picnic areas under the redwoods. The park is located on the Navarro River with swimming and fishing available. There's a sani-station for trailers and a nature trail by the river.

Indian Creek County Park is a smaller day-use picnic park near Philo on Hwy. 128 with a trail through the redwood forest. **Dimmick State Park**, 10 miles west of Navarro, has overnight camping beside the Navarro River. With the recent interest in traveling through the Alexander Valley, the towns are gradually developing motels, bed and breakfast operations and other tourist services. There are good restaurants in Boonville and the excellent cottage brewery offers a pleasant stop to tour the plant and quaff their several fine beers. For those who want to visit the Alexander Valley wineries but wish to continue north to Ukiah on U.S. Highway 101, it is possible to get back to Hwy. 101 by taking Highway 253 which wanders northwest from its junction with Highway 128, just south of Boonville. As a route to the coast or as a sidetrip, the Alexander Valley is hard to beat.

BOONEVILLE, PHILO & NAVARRO

25 miles northwest of the Cloverdale turnoff, **Boonville** is the center of an agricultural area based on orchards and sheep farming. Recently, the establishment of a growing wine industry here has broadened the economy and brought many more travelers to the Anderson Valley. Not always friendly to visitors, Boonville residents invented a language of their own in the late 1800s — called Boontling — to keep their conversations private. The language has become a part of the valley folklore. There's a handy guide to Boontling titled "A Slib of Lorey" (A Little Bit of Folklore) which is available at local stores. The telephone is "telef" or "Buckey Walter"; men are "kimmies"; women are "dames"; a meal is a "gorm".

Apart from Boontling, Boonville is home to 700 people and has developed several good bed and breakfast homes. The **Toll House Inn** (707-895-3650) is the best of the lot — a 1912 Victorian farmhouse on 360 acres with fireplaces in the rooms, a garden with a hot tub, antique furnishings, and full breakfast served. **$$**. Dinner is available in the excellent restaurant. Another fine place to stay is the **Anderson Creek Inn** (707-893-3091), a modern ranch house with four rooms, fireplaces, swimming pool, library, bicycles for exploring the countryside and full breakfast. Picnic baskets are available on request. **$ to $$**. **Bear Wallow Resort** (707-895-3335) is four miles west of town on Mountain View Road with one and two-bedroom cabins set in the redwoods. Prices are moderate, including the cost of meals served in the Dinner House restaurant **$ to $$**. The restaurant is closed during winter months.

The dining room in the **New Boonville Hotel** is the best place in the downtown for lunch or dinner. This rustic and ramshackle place has quite a remarkable restaurant with California cuisine the specialty, using locally grown fresh vegetables and herbs, in addition to local lamb.

West of Boonville, **Philo** marks the beginning of the winery area and here the **Anderson Valley Inn** (707-855-3325) provides B & B accommodation in its seven rooms. The inn is located on Highway 128. **$$**. The **Blackberry Inn Bed & Breakfast** (707-895-2961) has four rooms in a modern home with swimming pool. **$$**. The Anderson Valley has become home to a growing group of artists and crafts people. The **Philo Pottery Inn** (707-895-3069) offers the intriguing combination of a bed & breakfast operation with a pottery gallery and store which displays local crafts. **$ to $$**.

West of Philo, **Greenwood Road** offers a sideroad drive — south of the Navarro River — as an alternate route to the coast, meeting Highway 1 at Elk. This is the road to take to reach **Hendy Woods State Park** and the public campground. The village of **Navarro** is closer to the coast, past winery row, a place to get gas or to buy picnic supplies. From Navarro it's a short drive to the coast and the junction with Highway 1 which is just south of Albion. Another alternate sideroad route is **Flynn Creek Road** which leads north from Hwy. 128 to Comptche and Mendocino.

ALEXANDER VALLEY WINERIES

All of the Anderson Valley wineries are located on either side of Highway 128, west of Philo and east of Navarro. The first wineries (Edmeades and Husch) opened in 1971. Now there are more than a score with new operations opening each year. Wine production has grown to equal the size of the traditional apple orchard farming in the valley. Most of the wineries are family owned and operated.

Deron Edmeades, the founder of **Edmeades Vineyards**, is a pioneer of the valley wine industry in more ways than one. From vines which his father had planted on the property in the 1960s, grapes were first sold to Parducci. Then, winemaking commenced in 1972 and the winery developed a number of special proprietary Anderson Valley wines including Rain Wine (1975) and later Opal (Pinot Noir) and Whale Wine. Aside from the proprietary wines, several varietals are produced including Chardonnay, Gewurztraminer and Zinfandel, as well as a Cabernet-Fume blend. The tasting room is in a rustic building next to the winemaker's house which used to be a garage. The winery is open from 10 am to 6 pm in the summer and 11 am to 5 pm October through May. It's on the south side of the highway and guided tours are available by appointment. For tasting and tour reservations, call 707-895-3232.

Navarro Vineyards (north of the highway) was an early valley operation, opening in 1975. The distinctive wine tasting room is next to the highway with the winery buildings down the lane. Tours are available by appointment and this winery should be visited (call 707-895-3686). The winery buildings are clad in weathered wood, designed to match an existing barn. The two cellars are devoted to reds (small amounts of Pinot Noir and Cabernet Sauvignon), and whites (Gewurztraminer, Chardonnay, Riesling and Edelzwicker Vin Gris (a specialty). The tasting room is open daily from 10 am to 5 pm and there is a picnic site.

Greenwood Road runs southwest from Philo to the Pacific Coast. **Green wood Ridge Vineyards** has a dramatic site off this road, 7.8 miles from the highway. The lane into the winery is equally dramatic and at the winery, the view is spectacular. The winery also has its tasting room in Philo but guided tours of the operation are available by appointment (call 707-877-3262). Among the wines produced are Riesling, Merlot and Cabernet Sauvignon.

Husch Vineyards is now operated by the Oswald family and this winery makes a pleasant stop, particularly at lunch time with picnic tables located under the trees and a grape arbor. The winery may be toured by appointment (call 707-895-3216) but the tasting room and store are open daily from 10 am to 6 pm (summer) and 10 am to 5 pm (winter). What must be among the smallest wineries in Mendocino County is **Pullman Vineyards**. John Pullman grows grapes mostly for sale to large wineries but also produces small lots of his Boonville White and Boonville Red each year. He's been doing this since 1983. For an appointment, call 707-895-3565.

ALEXANDER VALLEY WINERIES & A BREW-PUB

On the north side of Highway 128, west of Philo, is the tiny **Lazy Creek Winery**, the operation of Hans and Teresa Kobler who produce about 500 cases of wine each year. To have a look at a true cottage winery, call 707-895-3623. Tours are given by appointment only.

The **Christine Woods Winery**, on Highway 128 approaching Navarro, was named after a former township which was the headquarters for tan-bark and railroad tie businesses which existed in the 1800s. Winery founder Vernon Rose discovered many artifacts of this era while clearing his land and you may see them at the tasting room. For tours, call 707-895-2115. Wines produced include Zinfandel and Cabernet Sauvignon.

The largest winery in the valley is the **Roederer** sparkling wine operation near Philo. This subsidiary of the French Champagne firm Louis Roederer was established in 1987. 350 acres of Pino Noir and Chardonnay vines supply the 44,000 square foot winery. There is a tasting room at the winery which is four miles west of Philo.

Pepperwood Springs is a distinctive redwood building built in the California barn style. This winery, in a natural setting with a copse of oaks outlining the rows of vines, is on Holmes Road, east of Highway 128, 5.5 miles northwest of Philo. For information on tours and tastings, call 707-895-2250.

The story of **Handey Cellars** is a tale of perseverance over several years by Milla Handley who started operations in a basement before building her winery here in 1987. The tasting room is next to Hwy. 128, on the north side of the highway. Look for the tower as you drive along the road. The winery produces Chardonnay (barrel-fermented) as well as Sauvignon Blanc and in recent years a selection of sparkling wines including Brut Rose. This is the northernmost winery in the Anderson Valley and the first to be sighted when driving from the coast toward Philo and Boonville.

Now to the brewery and other local attractions!

Boonville — aside from the nearby wineries — is a treasure trove of local color and memorabilia. The **Anderson Valley Historical Museum**, the 1891 Conn Creek School House and other buildings display pioneer artifacts and native relics from the area. **The Anderson Valley Brewing Company** is a recent arrival in the community but it takes its place as part of the local color. Prominently located on Highway 128, the brewery operates its own pub in which lunch and dinner are served. Light and dark ales which are not widely available outside of the valley are produced here. Beer lovers shouldn't miss this opportunity to taste some of the best beer available in the western states.

Next door to the brewery is the Farrer General Store, built around the turn of the century and still in operation with a bakery, wine boutique and ice cream shop. The Rookie-To Gallery is one of several places to look for Anderson Valley handcrafted items.

MENDOCINO WINERIES — VIA HIGHWAY 101

The heart of Mendocino wine country is **Ukiah**, a rural town situated on U.S. Highway 101 in the fertile Yokayo Valley. The Parducci family has long been the prominent wine family in this area since planting their first vines following Prohibition. They have been joined by several large wineries including Hidden Cellars and the Weibel sparkling wine company, plus more then thirty smaller, mostly family-owned vineyard and winery operations.

The first winery in the region was founded in 1879 by Louis Finne near the present-day town of Hopland, south of Ukiah. The large Fetzer winery is close to the site of the original Finne winery. By 1990, more than 3,000 acres of grapes were being harvested. Prohibition stopped the winemaking operations and only a few farmers held on to their vines. Several wineries resumed operations when prohibition was repealed in 1933. Adolph Parducci was among the first to open new wineries in the area and family vineyards are still prominent.

Aside from the Anderson Valley, there are five wine regions surrounding Ukiah. The **Sanel and McDowell valleys** are found where Highway 101 enters Mendocino County from the south and then along Highway 175 leading toward Lake County. The **Ukiah Valley** is found farther north, along U.S. 101. This is where the larger wineries are located and where Mendocino winemaking began. The **Redwood and Potter valleys** are at the north end of Mendocino Wine Country, lying along Highway 101 and State Highway 20.

For full information on these and other wineries in the region, contact the Mendocino County Vintners Association, P.O. Box 1409, Ukiah CA 95482, or call (707) 463-1704.

Ukiah provides a good base for wine explorations throughout Mendocino county including those on the scenic side roads of the region.

Lake Mendocino is a man-made reservoir which fills a large valley north of Ukiah. The lake has three recreation areas which are accessed via highways 20 and 101. The parks have swimming beaches, picnic sites, boat launches and fishing opportunities. The Russian River—above the lake—also has fish, primarily trout. The municipal park in Ukiah is a pleasant spot for picnics.

Our tour of the inland wineries begins at the southern border of the county at **Hopland** and moves north through Ukiah to the northern edge of the grape-growing region. We then drive north to the town of **Willits,** where is is possible to rejoin the coastal route by taking Highway 20 west, joining Highway 1 at Noyo — at the southern edge of Fort Bragg — after a drive of slightly more than 40 miles. This is a particularly scenic route, passing through the redwoods of Jackson State Forest for more than half of the trip. This drive is located to the south of the route of the famous Skunk Train railway which runs daily between Fort Bragg and Willits. The Mendocino County Museum is located in Willits.

Beginning near Hopland at the southern edge of Mendocino Wine Country, the **Milano Winery** is found in one of several old kilns which are survivors of the earlier days of wine production in the area. James Milone founded the winery in 1977 and built the operation in a building which his grandfather had constructed. The tasting room and store is located in the upper level. You'll find one of the Milones here, pouring wines including Chardonnay, Cabernet Sauvignon and their prime wine — Zinfandel. The winery is located on Highway 101, 2 miles south of Hopland west of the junction with Mountain House Road. The tasting room is open Tuesdays through Sundays from 10 am to 5 pm. Guided tours are available by appointment, call 707-744-1396.

One of the largest and most prominent of the Mendocino wineries is **Fetzer**, with its tasting room and store located in what used to be Hopland High School on the west side of Highway 101. The winery itself is farther north, beyond Ukiah in Redwood Valley. The tasting facility in Hopland includes gift shops exhibiting Mendocino crafts and a range of wine items. There is a picnic area as well. The wines to be tasted include Chardonnay, Sauvignon Blanc, Cabernet Sauvignon, Petit Sirah, Zinfadel and Pinot Noir. Fetzer also markets blends called Premium Red & Premium White as well as another label "Bel Arbre". The tasting room on Highway 101 is open daily from 10 am to 5 pm. For guided tours of the winery and directions, call 707-485-7634.

McDowell Valley Vineyards offers an interesting sideroad drive along Highway 175 into a small valley where the solar winery is located. Yes, the winery is solar-powered and the low sleek building is an attraction in itself. The tasting room in the upper level of the winery is a combination of art deco design and redwood and oak accents. This room has been designed for parties, complete with grand piano. Two wooden decks with picnic tables provide another location for wine tasting. Wines produced here include Sauvignon Blanc, Chardonnay, Cabernet Sauvignon and Syrah. The second label is "Soleil". The winery is open daily from Tuesday through Sunday from late June until October 1. Tours are arranged by appointment, call 707-744-1053.

Three miles north of Hopland on Highway 101 is **Jepson Vineyards**, where guided tours and tastings are held daily from 10 am to 4 pm. The original farmhouse — more than a century old — serves as a restaurant and conference center. The architecture is eccentric as is the winery operation which produces brandy as well as Chardonnay, Sauvignon Blanc and a sparkling Chardonnay. Brandy is distilled from French Colombard. **Tijsseling Winery & Tyland Vineyards** are located on McNab Ranch Road. Turn off Hwy. 101, 6 miles south of Ukiah and drive west 2.5 miles. Both of these related wineries have tasting rooms which are open Wednesday through Sunday from 10 am to 5 pm, as well as picnic sites. Tijsseling produces two *methode champénoise* sparkling wines.

UKIAH

Ukiah is the county seat and the largest community in Mendocino County. The city has a population of 14,000 and services a region of 32,000 people.

Lumber was the reason for Ukiah's founding in the mid 1800s when the building of San Francisco demanded all the wood available from the area. Lumbering is still a major industry and Ukiah is home to the large Georgia Pacific lumber and Masonite mill. Redwood furniture and artifacts (clocks, tables, stump items) are also part of the economy.

While it is a modern city, Ukiah reflects its history over the past 150 years. Some of the descendants of the Pomo Indians still live here.

Anglers flock to the area in great numbers, particularly to Lake Mendocino and the Upper Russian River. The city has five parks. County and state parks close to Ukiah include Low Gap Regional County Park, Mill Creek County Park, the Cow Mountain Recreation Area and Montgomery Woods State Reserve. Lake Mendocino has three recreation areas which offer swimming, boating and fishing, with 300 campsites in the park areas.

There are two major celebrations which provide a "down-home" flavor: the **Hometown Festival** is held in late May and early June with a rodeo, regatta, races and a food fair. It's possible to tour Victorian homes of the area during this period. The **Redwood Empire Fair** is held annually in August. The **Grace Hudson Museum** is located in Sun House, the home of John Hudson and his wife Grace Carpenter Hudson. Grace Hudson was a noted painter who specialized in paintings of Pomo Indian life. The museum, at 431 South Main Street, is open Tuesdays through Sundays.

There are several motels in Ukiah including the **Discovery Inn** (707-462-8873), a large lodge at 1340 State Street, across from the Crossroads shopping center one mile from downtown. The motel has rooms and suites, a heated pool, sauna, whirlpool, tennis court and laundry. **$ to $$**. The **Manor Inn Motel** (707-462-7584 or 1-800-922-3388) is at 950 N. State Street (Hwy. 101) with standard rooms, family suites, a large swimming pool, restaurant and lounge. **$**. The **Ukiah Travelodge** (707-462-6657 or 1-800-255-3050) is at 1070 State Street with 31 units, swimming pool, restaurant and lounge. **$**.

For a special treat complete with hot spring pool, plan to stay at **Vichy Springs Resort Bed & Breakfast,** located at 1605 Vichy Springs Road. The cottages date from 1854, the lodge from 1865. There are miles of walking and mountain bike trails on the 700-acre property as well as picnic sites and easy access to Lake Mendocino. **$$ to $$$**.

For eating in Ukiah, the **Coach House Restaurant** serves the kind of food that "Mother used to cook", at 131 East Mill Street. **$$**. **Basilios**, at 1090 South State St., serves Italian cuisine in large quantities in a relaxed, gregarious ambience. **$$ to $$$**. Moore's Flour Mill and Bakery (1550 South State St.) is a good place to pick up muffins and other baking, to have a cup of coffee and also to tour the century-old mill.

MENDOCINO WINERIES — UKIAH

In 1983, **Hidden Cellars** owner Dennis Patton moved his winery from a remote site to the historic Hildreth Ranch. This new, modern winery is in the midst of orchards and vineyards just south of Ukiah, less than two miles from Highway 101 via Talmage Rd. and Ruddick-Cunningham Rd. The winery's tasting room is open daily from 12 noon until 4 pm. Hidden Cellars has become well known for its late harvest botrytised white wines. Wines produced here include Chardonnay, Riesling (also as a late harvest wine) and Zinfindel. The Chevrignon D'Or is a late harvest blend of Semillon and Sauvignon Blanc. For tours by appointment, call 707-462-0301. **Scharffenberger Cellars** have not one but three locations: two separate wineries and a tasting room on Highway 128 in Philo in the center of the Anderson Valley. Visitors who phone in advance (707-462-8996) are shown through the two Ukiah facilities (one is in an industrial park and the other in a warehouse) and are shown the way to the tasting room in Philo. It might be better, however, to visit Philo while touring other Anderson Valley wine operations (see page 109). The company produces still and sparkling wines including Eagle Point Chardonnay and Sauvignon Blanc from grapes grown in the Eagle Point Ranch vineyards. Scharffenberger Brut is a blend of Pinot Noir and Chardonnay. The Blanc de Blanc is all Chardonnay and the Brut Rose is totally Pinot Noir. Their Blanc de Noir is a still rosé.

The best-known winery in the Ukiah region, and a pillar of the northern California wine industry, is **Parducci Wine Cellars**. On the north side of Ukiah, the winery is an extension of the operation founded in 1916 by Adolph Parducci who settled in Cloverdale and began the Parducci dynasty. Three generations of the Parducci family have been involved in the growth and development of the family business, a growth which has been remarkable. In the early 60s, 100 acres of vineyards had been planted. Five years later, more than 200 acres had been cultivated. By 1987, the acreage had grown to more than 500, including four separate vineyards. The mainstay is still the Sun Valley Ranch, first planted by Adolph Parducci during the prohibition days when he survived by making sacramental wine for the Catholic Church.

To visit the winery, drive north from Ukiah on Highway 101 and take exit E to North State Street. Drive north for .5 mile to Parducci Road and turn west to reach the winery. This is one of the few wineries in the state which ages its wines in large redwood and oak tanks. They are featured on the guided tour which is given hourly. The tasting room is open daily from 10 am to 6 pm (9 to 5 in the winter). There is a large tasting room and store as well as an art gallery in a Spanish-style building. In the back is a summer picnic area with tables on an adobe patio.

Parsons Creek Winery is a small winery in an industrial warehouse at the south end of town. For a tour and tasting, call 707-462-8900. Two Chardonnays and a Riesling are produced.

REDWOOD VALLEY & WILLITS

Lake Mendocino is located five miles north of Ukiah, on Highway 20 east of Highway 101. Created in 1958 by the construction of the Coyote Dam, the lake is the widening of the Russian River which provides flood control and water supply, in addition to many recreational opportunities. There are two boat launching ramps, three swimming and picnic parks and more than 300 campsites around the lake. The Shakota Trail is 3.5 miles in length, the Kayeo Trail is 7 miles. There are two horse camps on the lake and the horse trail leads beside the lake on its north and east sides. The recreation area is administered by the Army Corps of Engineers.

The beautiful **Redwood Valley** runs parallel to Highway 101. This is a high valley which favors grape-growing and wineries have produced wines here since before Prohibition. There are five major wineries in the valley.

23 miles north of Ukiah, the small, rustic town of Willits is famed chiefly as the eastern terminus of the Skunk Train, an old logging railway which takes tourists on a 40-mile trip between Willits and Fort Bragg on the Pacific Coast. Now, Willits is famous for something else: as the site of the transplanted old archway which used to announce Reno Nevada as the "Biggest Little City in the World" and now hails Willits as the "Gateway to the Redwoods".

The **Mendocino County Museum** on East Commercial Street is open Wednesdays through Sundays with an excellent collection of Pomo Indian artifacts and displays on early pioneer life in the county. This is a rural town and the Frontier Days Rodeo, held each July 4th, provides residents and visitors with a midsummer country celebration. It's the oldest established rodeo in the state.

Unlike Ukiah, Willits has several places to stay which have a distinctive ambience. **Brooktrails Lodge** (707-459-5311) is nestled in the redwoods on Sherwood Road, 3.5 miles north of town. There are 20 motel units and 10 cottages with one and two-bedroom accommodations. There's a cafe, a swimming pool, tennis courts and a nine-hole golf course. **$ to $$.** The **Old West Inn** (707-459-4201) on Hwy. 101 is all done up in Wild West decor, pretending to be a re-created western town. It's near the Skunk Train depot. **$$.** The **Holiday Lodge Motel** (707-459-5361) is at 1540 South Main Street with standard motel units at reasonable prices. **$ to $$.**

Campers and RV owners can stay at two private campgrounds in Willits. The large **KOA Kampground** is on Highway 20, 1.5 miles from the Highway 101 junction. There are full hookups, tenting sites, a summer pool and store. For information and reservations, write to P.O. Box 946, Willits CA 95490 or phone 707-459-6179.

Hidden Valley Campground is on Highway 101 north of the town center with hookups, showers and laundry. For reservations write 29801 N. Hwy. 101, Willits CA 95490 or phone 707-459-2521 or 1-800-458-8368 (CA only).

MENDOCINO WINERIES — REDWOOD VALLEY

The wineries of the Redwood Valley range from tiny family operations to large operations such as the Weibel sparkling wine facility.

Lolonis Vineyards is located on Road B east of Highway 101. It's one of the finest vineyards in the state. The Lolonis family came here in 1915 from Greece and planted the vineyards in 1920. Several north coast wineries get their grapes from these vineyards and the Lolonis' make their own Greek-style wine. For information and directions, call 707-485-8027.

Take Road A and then turn on Road B to reach **Olsen Vineyards**, on a site with fine vistas overlooking Lake Mendocino and the Redwood Valley. Donald and Nancy Olsen (he was a a retired engineer) founded the winery in 1971. After selling their grapes to other wineries, their first vintage was produced from their 1982 harvest. The winery produces less than 10,000 cases per year, including Chardonnay, Sauvignon Blanc, Riesling and a Napa Gamay Blanc. They produce several reds including Zinfandel, Petite Sirah and Cabernet Sauvignon. The winery's Glacier Blanc is a blend of Riesling, Chenin Blanc and French Colombard. Their low-priced red is Viking Zin. The tasting room is open daily from 10 am to 5 pm and there is a picnic site at the winery. A second tasting room is on the east side of Highway 128, 10 miles south of Boonville in the Anderson Valley. There is a picnic site here as well.

Weibel Vineyards is a well known and long-time producer of sparkling wines, starting in Mission San Jose in Alameda County and moving north to establish a winery north of Ukiah in 1973. The tasting room here is in the shape of an upside-down champagne glass. While the Ukiah winery produces white and red wines, the sparkling wines are still produced in the southern winery but they are available for tasting here as well. You'll find the Weibel tasting room on Highway 101, 6 miles north of Ukiah, just north of the Highway 20 junction. It's open daily from 9 am to 6 pm.

The Redwood Valley is home to the northern portion of the **Braren Pauley Winery** operation. The southern winery is near Petaluma (see page 95). It's quite a drive to get to this winery but it provides a fascinating back road tour. Take Highway 20—east from Hwy. 101—and turn north on East Side Potter Valley Rd to the village of Potter Valley. Take Main Street to the end and then drive .2 miles to the winery which is at 12507 Hawn Creek Rd. Tastings and tours are arranged by appointment, call 707-778-0721.

Dolan Vineyards is another "appointment-only" winery, located 1.6 miles north of Redwood Valley via West Rd. & Inez Way. Located on a steep slope of the Redwood Valley, this tiny winery makes Chardonnay and Cabernet Sauvignon in small lots. Informal tours are arranged by phoning 707-485-7250.

Blanc Vineyards and **Frey Vineyards** are found on West Road (Tomki Road) which runs almost due north up the Redwood Valley from the village. Phone 707- 485-7352 (Blanc) and 707-485-7525 (Frey) for information.

Oregon Coast Highways

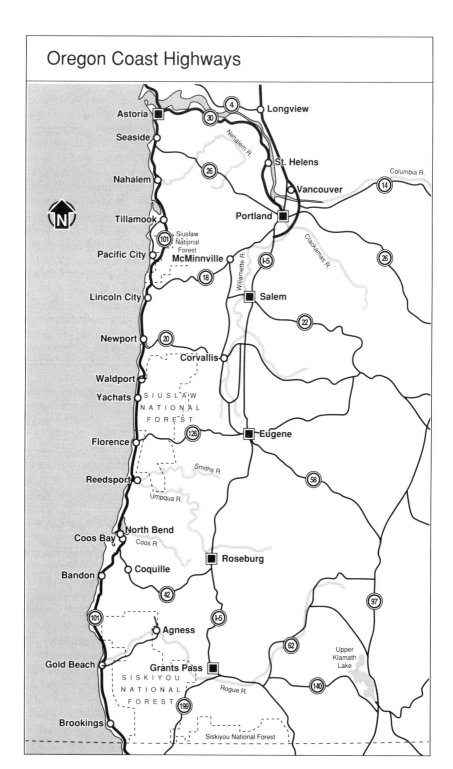

Oregon Coast — The Drive

Although our route maps and logs continue along the Columbia River to Portland, the real Pacific Coast drive starts at the California border and ends at the historic city of Astoria. For 350 miles, Highway 101 passes by some of the most magnificent scenery in the Pacific Northwest, including the most protected and accessible shoreline of any state in the lower 48.

The Oregon Coast drive takes you to national parks and forests; long, wide beaches with tall, shifting dunes; picturesque fishing villages; tranquil sea-side vacation towns; superb resort lodges and inns; and the majesty of nature throughout the well-defined seasons of the year.

Basically, the attraction of the Oregon Coast can be separated into two vacation seasons. Summers are for leisurely beach-walking, relaxation at scenic and distinctive sea-side resorts, and hiking in the two national forests which touch Highway 101: Siskiyou and Siuslaw. Oregon Coast winters are elemental in their savagery with strong winds, thundering surf and awesome storms blowing in from the northwest. Anyone who has not experienced the Oregon Coast during winter months has missed much of the attraction of this wild and wonderful part of the country.

The Highway 101 drive is as varied as the overall topography of this atypical Pacific Northwest state. Just north of the California border, the town of **Brookings** sits near the southern end of Siskiyou National Forest. State parks and beaches stretch from the border, past **Gold Beach, Port Orford** and **Bandon**. Coos Bay — at the mouth of the Coos River — harbors the neighboring towns of **Coos Bay**, **Charleston** and **North Bend**. The bay marks the southern edge of the **Oregon Dunes National Recreation Area**. For 48 miles, the huge dunes dominate the coastline providing unexcelled beachcombing, opportunities for hiking and dune buggy travel, and observing the unique plant life of this sandy shore.

Just north of **Florence**, the highway enters the **Siuslaw National Forest**, another prime recreation area. It leads past the fishing village of **Yachats** and the town of **Waldport** to **Newport**, one of Oregon's long-standing summer vacation centers. The northern portion of Siuslaw National Forest is adjacent to both **Lincoln City** and **Pacific City**.

While Highway 101 now takes a turn inland to pass through **Tillamook**, the **Three-Capes Loop** takes you to more rugged Oregon seashore characterized by rocky headlands with haystack and seastack rocks in the ocean surf. The loop road provides access to the small vacation villages of **Netarts** and **Oceanside**.

The most northerly part of the coast continues the steady succession of wayside parks and state beaches, as Highway 101 passes **Rockaway Beach**, **Cannon Beach** and **Seaside** before ending in Astoria at the bridge over the Columbia River. All of these small towns have their own distinctive charms and are favorite vacation spots for Oregonians and people from farther-away who return each year to savor the natural delights of the sea and the nearby forests of western Oregon.

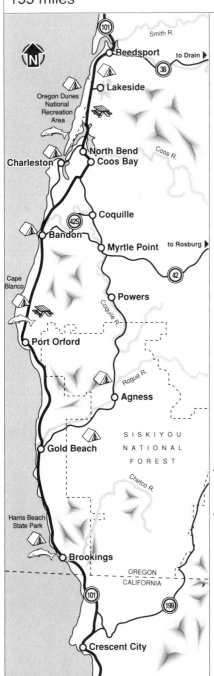

Oregon Border. Just 2.4 miles north of the border is the world's largest cypress tree.

Brookings-Harbor 4.5 miles from the California border, Brookings has stores, gas, restaurants, RV & camping parks and fishing. **Azalea State Park** on Hwy. 101 has 5 varieties of azaleas & picnicking. **Loeb Park**, 8 miles northeast of town has camping & picnic tables. Visitors Center on Hwy. 101.

Harris Beach State Park 2 miles north of Brookings. Overnight campsites, picnic sites, trails, swimming.

Boardman State Park south access point 8 miles north of Brookings. Nine miles of ocean beaches, picnic sites.

Pistol River Park 19 miles from Brookings. Dunes, trails, picnicking, 11 miles of parkland.

Cape Sebastian State Park 23.5 miles from Brookings. Forest park area with 700 ft. headland.

Gold Beach town at mouth of Rogue River. Gas, stores, motels, RV parks, fishing, ocean views.

Junction-South Bank Rd. Leads along the river to Illinois River & Agness. Resorts, RV parks.

Junction-North Bank River Rd. follows river to Agness.

Siskiyou National Forest Geisel Monument

Otter Point Wayside 4 miles north of Gold Beach (day-use)

Nesika Beach State Park Exit to village of Nesika.

Rest Area 10 mi. from Gold Beach. **Humbug Mtn. State Park** 6 mi. south of Port Orford. Camping.

Highway Log

Humbug Mtn. Trailhead leads to summit (1,750 feet).
Port Orford Gas, motels, camping, stores, cafes. Roads along Elk & Sixes rivers lead to parks & mountain trails. **Garrison Lake State Park** has a boat ramp.
Paradise Point - Beach access.
Cape Blanco State Park 9 miles north of Port Orford, with access to historic lighthouse, scenic views, picnic area & campground.
Floras Lake Loop road.
Langlois 13.5 miles from Port Orford. Gas, store.
Bradley Lake Boat launch.
Beach Loop South exit to beaches, motels, golf course & **Bandon State Park** (day-use).
Bandon-by-the-Sea Resort town, gas, stores, motels, camping, RV parks, historic Old Town restoration, cheese factory.
Junction-Hwy. 42S to Coquille & Roseburg. Coquille River offers 20 miles of good tidewater fishing.
Bullards Beach State Park 1 mi. north of Bandon. Picnic area, campground, hike & bike camp.
Seven Devils Rd. to Charleston, Cape Arago, & **Seven Devils State Park** (coastal day-use park with beach). Scenic route to Coos Bay.
Junction - Hwy. 42 - exit for Coquille loop road - to I-5 at Roseburg.
Junction-Coos River Rd. - to Gold & Silver Falls. Access to village of Allegany & waterfalls.
Coos Bay Lumber shipping port with gas, motels, restaurants, RV parks, camping, museum. Visitor Center on Hwy. 101.
Take the Cape Arago Highway (via.

Newmark Ave.) for **Cape Arago State Park** with beaches, surf fishing, picnicking, hiker/biker camp, sea lion & whale watching. Also Sunset Bay Park with swimming, picnicking, overnight camping.
Take Newmark Avenue for the scenic fishing village of **Charleston** (boat basin, B & B homes, South Slough Estuarine Sanctuary, fishing charters, Coast Guard Station).
North Bend 3.5 miles north of Coos Bay. Gas, motels, cafes, stores.
Oregon Dunes National Recreation Area South access just north of McCullough Bridge across Coos Bay channel. Dunes stretch for 48 miles, from here to the town of Florence.
Horsefall Dune & Beach Access with campground & dune buggy staging center. This is the south entrance to the National Rec. Area.
Saunders Lake 7.3 miles from McCullough Bridge. Boat ramp.
Spinreel Campground Forest Service campground, dune buggy area.
Lakeside Small community with tourist facilities. Tenmile Lake & Eel Lake provide boating, swimming, fishing & 115 campsites with partial hookups.
Eel Creek Campground Forest Service campsite.
Tugman State Park 19 miles north of Coos Bay. Picnicking, hiker/biker camp.
Access Rd. to Umpqua Lighthouse & Park, dunes access, & village of Winchester Bay.

Reedsport At mouth of Umpqua & Smith rivers in the heart of the Oregon Dunes. Gas, motels, B & B homes, restaurants, stores, Oregon Dunes National Recreation Area headquarters & visitor center. Highway 38 leads east to Drain and on to connect with I-5.

Bolon Island Wayside Park 11-acre day-use park at north end of Umpqua bridge with trail to island overlook.

Junction-Smith River Rd. A possible scenic sideroad route to Eugene.

Gardiner Just north of Reedsport. Fishing, clamming.

Tahkenitch Lake & Forest Camp Siuslaw Forest campground, boat ramp, fishing.

Dunes Overlook 11 miles from Reedsport. Picnic tables, trails to beach.

Carter Lake Forest Camp Dune access, campground, boat ramp.

Siltcoos Trail Head Beach access.

Siltcoos Lake Forest Service campground, beach access, fishing.

Jessie M Honeyman State Park 522 acres, 2.5 miles south of Florence. Coastal lake & dune area with rhododendrons, fishing, swimming, day-use & camping facilities. Hiker/biker camp.

South Jetty Road Beach & dune access.

Florence 21 miles north of Reedsport. Town on Siuslaw River. Gas, motels, B & B homes, cafes, stores. 17 fishing lakes in area. Old Town on waterfront & museum. Take Rhododendron Dr. for scenic 9-mile loop drive. Rhodos bloom in May & June.

Highway Log

Junction, Hwy. 126-to Mapleton & Eugene

Ocean Beaches Access to Harbor Park, 2 miles north of Florence.

Junction - Munsel Lake Rd. Dunes in **Munsel Rd. Park**.

Heceta Junction to beach area and loop drive to Florence.

Darlingtonia State Wayside Park 5 miles north of Florence, home of "Cobra Lily" plant. Picnic area, viewing platform.

Siuslaw National Forest-Alder Dune Campground Camping, fishing, swimming.

Heceta Head & Devils Elbow State Park 545 acre park with ocean views, beach, picnicking. Heceta Head & lighthouse named for Spanish explorer. Picnic tables, gardens.

Carl G Washburne Memorial Park 14 miles north of Florence. 2 miles of beach, picnic areas, trails, RV & tent sites.

Ponsler Wayside Park 16 miles north of Florence. Beach access, picnicking, fishing.

Rock Creek Campground 1 mile from Ponsler Park. Forest campsites, trail to ocean.

Stonefield Beach Wayside 19-acre day-use park, 6.5 miles south of Yachats. Beach access.

Neptune Park 302 acres, picnic area, surf fishing.

Cummings Trailhead-Cook's Chasm Just north of park.

Cape Perpetua Visitor Center, trail to Giant Spruce, auto tour, drive or walk to top of cape.

Yachats Ocean Wayside 79 acres south of Yachats. Picnic tables.

Yachats Tiny fishing village at mouth of Yachats River. Gas, motels, B & B homes, cafes, stores.

Yachats State Park just south of river off Hwy. 101. Surf fishing, picnic tables.

Smelt Sands Park Coastal access.

Tillicum Campground Beach access, picnic tables.

Beachside Park 4 miles south of Waldport. Camping, picnicking.

Waldport On Alsea Bay. Gas, stores, motels, B & B, cafes. Good fishing, crabs & clams, golf.

Junction-Hwy. 34 To Corvallis.

Ocean Parks: between Waldport & Newport, there are several day-use parks. Campsites at **South Beach State Park**.

Newport Seaside resort town, 50 miles north of Florence. Gas, hotels, motels, B & B homes, stores. **Yaquinna Lighthouse** is north of town. **Yaquinna Bay State Park** & lighthouse is in town with beach & picnicking.

Depoe Bay Village with gas, store, cafes & a tiny harbor. **Depoe Bay Park** has picnic tables & good views.

Boiler Bay Wayside Just north of village with picnic tables, marine gardens, views.

Fogerty Creek Park Beach access & picnicking.

Gleneden Beach Day-use park, beach access & Salishan Resort.

Drift Creek National Forest access.

East Devil's Lake Rd. Loop drive to **East Devil's Lake State Park** & **Sand Point County Park.**

Lincoln City See page 142.

Lincoln City 7.5 miles of resort town and beaches.

East Devil's Lake Rd. This is the south access to the loop drive around this lake. **Devils Lake State Park** has picnicking, fishing & a boat ramp. Campsites are on Hwy. 101. **"D" River Wayside Park** has a picnic site on the world's shortest river.

Road's End Beach Park Wayside picnic park, 1 mile north of downtown. Beach access.

East Devil's Lake Rd. North access. **Three Capes Loop:** This 38-mile loop drive ending at Tillamook is a must for ocean watchers. Drive to the loop on one of three roads north of Lincoln City. The loop takes you to **Pacific City,** a small vacation town & **Bob Straub Park**, 484 acres of sand spit; **Cape Kiwanda** Park, with great views of the cape; **Sand Lake Dunes & Park**, off the loop road; the **Cape Lookout Trail** (2.5 miles to the cape) and **Cape Lookout Park** (camping, picnicking); the sea-side towns of **Netarts** and **Oceanside**; **Cape Meares State Park** (lighthouse, picknicking, sea lion and cape viewing); **Cape Meares** (take Bay Ocean Dr., just west of Tillamook).

Cascade Head Rd. To mouth of Salmon River. East on scenic old Hwy. & return to Hwy. 101 a few miles north.

Cascade Summit Take access road 2 miles to viewpoint.

Cascade Head Rd. North access. **Neskowin Beach Wayside Park Neskowin** Small town 10 miles north of Lincoln City with sandy beach, stream fishing, golf course.

Highway Log

Little Nestucca River Fishing for salmon, steelhead & cutthroat trout.
Sand Lake Dunes Access Rd.
Cloverdale Small dairy town with gas, stores, cafe.
Hebo Village with gas, store.
Junction-Hwy. 22 To Hwy. 18 & McMinnville.
Beaver Village near forest campgrounds & Nestucca River fishing.
Trask River Fishing for trout, salmon & steelhead.
Tillamook Gas, stores, cafes, motels, RV park. Town famous for its cheese factories. Visitor center on Hwy. 101.
Wilson River Fishing.
Kilchis River Trout & steelhead.
Bay City Gas, store, cafe. Small town on Tillamook Bay.
Miami River Trout fishing.
Garibaldi Fishing village with tours at fish & shrimp plants.
Barview/County Park Jetty fishing—flounder, perch, rock cod.
Rockaway Beach Park Picnics.
Rockaway Beach Gas, stores, cafes, motels, RV park. Vacation town with wide beaches, lake fishing, view from Neahkanie Mtn.
Lake Lytle Just north of Rockaway Beach. Fishing, boating, swimming.
Manhatten Beach Park Beach access, picnicking.
Wheeler Village with public dock on Nehalem Bay.
Junction-Hwy. 53 To Mohler & Portland via Hwy. 26.
Nehalem Riverside town with gas, stores, motel, B & B, cafes.
Nehalem Bay Park 828 acres, 3 miles off Hwy. 101. Six miles of beach, boat ramp, horse trail, camp-ground, picnic area.
Manzanita Gas, store, motels, cafes. Small resort town with seven miles of sandy beach.
Heah-Kah-Nie Beach West of the highway at Manzanita.
Viewpoints on Hwy. There are several high pull-off viewpoints offering good views of the beaches and ocean.
Oswald West Park 4 miles north of Manzanita, with walk-in camping, drive or hike to summit of Mt. Neahkanie. Agate caves, fishing.
Short Sand Beach State Park has hike-in campsites.
Cove Beach, Falcon Cove Off the highway via access roads.
Arch Cape Beach access with surf & stream fishing.
Hug Point Park 42 acre picnic park, 4 miles from Cannon Beach.
Arcadia Beach Park Beach access, picnicking.
Tolvana Park & beach South access to beach loop road.
Cannon Beach Gas, motels, B & B homes, stores, restaurants. Seaside resort town & arts center with 9 miles of beach. Summer music and art programs.
Ecola Park Six miles of beach with sea lion & bird rookeries.
Seaside Resort town with gas, motels, B & B homes, cafes, stores.
Gearhart On loop road north of Seaside. Golf course & condo-style resort hotel.
Fort Clatsop National Memorial Replica of Lewis & Clark fort.
Fort Stevens State Park On Warrenton—Hammond Rd. Camping, fishing, picnicking, swimming.
Astoria (see page 148).

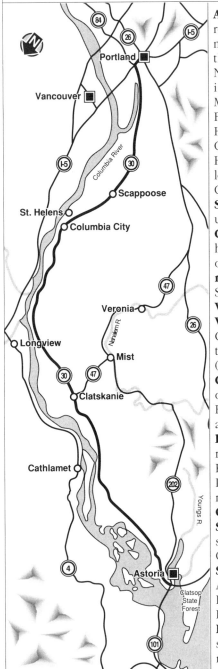

Astoria Gas, hotels, motels, restaurants, B & B homes, stores, museums. This historic city was the first community founded in Northwest Oregon. Things to see include the Astor Column, Maritime Museum, the Victorian Flavel House museum and the Heritage Center in the restored old City Hall.

Hwy. 30 begins in Astoria and leads along the north bank of the Columbia River.

Svensen Small river-side community off the highway.

Clatsop State Forest The highway touches the northern tip of this large state forest. There is a **roadside picnic park** east of the Svensen turnoff.

Westport & Rd. to Cathalmet WA. Turn north to cross the Columbia River for a shorter route to southwest Washington beaches (Long Beach, Ocean City).

Clatskanie Small town at junction of Hwy. 101 & Hwy. 47. Take Hwy. 47 south to village of Mist & alternate route to Portland.

Bridge to Longview (WA) Turn north for bridge to Longview, Kelso and the short route to Interstate 5, Seattle and points north.

Columbia City Gas, cafe, store.

St. Helens Gas, motels, cafes, stores. Town on the bank of the Columbia River.

Scapoose Village with gas, store. Alternate sideroad route to Pittsburg, Clatskanie & return to Hwy. 101.

Portland Gas, hotels, motels, stores, restaurants, parks, museums (see pages 149 to 151).

Northwest Oregon Drives

While not as awe-inspiring as Washington's Olympic Peninsula, the northwest corner of Oregon has its own scenic charms, including several national and state forest preserves and a network of sideroads and backroads which wind through the hills and forests of this corner of the state. Between Astoria and Portland, Highway 30 touches the northern corner of Clatsop State Forest. The forest preserve runs in a north/south direction and is crossed by several sideroads.

Highway 202 begins in Astoria and leads through the **Klaskanne River Valley** which offers prime fishing opportunities just southeast of the hamlet of Olney. Hwy. 202 then runs through part of **Clatsop State Forest**, reaching the village of Jewell and turning northwest for 17 miles to the village of **Mist**. From here, it's 12 miles north on **Highway 47** to Clatskahie and **Highway 30** for the drive back to Astoria. Or turn east on Highway 30 and drive through St. Helens to Portland.

Highway 47 provides an interesting side-road drive to Portland from Clatskahie, by-passing Columbia City and St. Helens. It takes you south to Mist and then on to the village of Pittsburg before joining Highway 26 which leads south to Portland.

The **Tillamook State Forest** is a large preserve which doesn't quite touch the Pacific Coast. It's north of the town of Tillamook and due east of the seaside towns of Rockaway Beach and Garibaldi. **Highway 6** runs through this forest. Its western junction with coastal Highway 101 is in Tillamook and the road leads in a general northeast direction through the Tillamook Forest. It connects with State Highway 8 at Glenwood. You can then take Highway 8 to Portland. If you're adventurous and wish to get back to the coast, turn left (north) on the backroad to the village of **Timber** and then continue until reaching Highway 26. Turn left on **Hwy. 26** and drive northwest through the northern part of Tillamook Forest and through a small arm of Clatsop State Forest to reach the coast between Seaside and Cannon Beach.

A loop tour takes you through part of **Oregon Wine Country**, connecting the Pacific Coast with the Willamette Valley. Start in Newport by taking **Highway 20** which runs east to Corvallis. Now, you're in wine country and if you drive south and north along **Hwy. 99W**, you'll be able to sample the wines of the Willamette Valley. The wineries are found along sideroads in the valley and include **Alpine Vineyards** and **Broadley Vineyards**, near the village of Alpine (south of Corvallis). **Springhill Cellars** is off Hwy. 20 (east of Hwy. 99W), northeast of Corvallis near Albany. To the north: Airlie Road runs west from Hwy. 99W leading to the village of Airlie. The **Airlie Winery** and **Serendipity Cellars** are both on Dunn Forest Road. Near the town of McMinnville, **Amity Vineyards** has its tasting room on **Hwy. 18**, nine miles southwest of town. From McMinneville, Hwy. 18 returns to the coast at Lincoln City. Turn east and you're on your way to Portland.

SISKIYOU NATIONAL FOREST

Established as a national forest in 1907, Siskiyou is a huge tract which takes up most of the southwestern corner of Oregon. As you drive along Highway 101, you'll see signs that the forest parallels the Pacific Coast from the California border to the Sixes River—just north of Port Orford—a distance of more than 65 miles. At most points along the highway, the forest is only a few miles to the east.

The name Siskiyou comes from the Cree/Chinook language and means *Bobtail Horse*. The mountains were named after a Hudson's Bay Company horse which died while on a trapping expedition.

The forest covers more than a million acres and 232,495 of these acres have the wilderness designation. The Rogue River is protected within one of the wilderness areas. More than 10,000 people float down the Rogue each summer and fall.

Two ranger stations are located on the coast: in Brookings at 555 Fifth St. (Chetco District), and in Gold Beach (Gold Beach District) at 1255 S. Ellenburg Ave. Both of the ranger stations have detailed information on hiking trails, forest campgrounds and access to other recreation sites with a short drive off Highway 101.

There are more than thirty hiking trails within the two ranger districts. Several readily-accessible trails are reached by driving from Gold Beach on Jerry's Flat Rd. (County Rd. 595) which turns into Forest Service Road # 33. The road runs 30 miles to the village of Agness which is close to several trailheads. Agness is the dividing point between the **Upper and Lower Rogue River trails**. These trails run for a total length of 54 miles.

The upper trail (42 miles) follows the "Wild & Scenic" Rogue River through protected land. The walk is filled with vistas: the Rogue River Canyon with much whitewater, vertical walls, high cliffs, and then old-growth Douglas fir and cedar forests. Animals—including black bear, deer, raccoon and river otter—may be seen beside and in the river.

The Lower Rogue Trail heads down-river from Agness. The trailhead is just west of the post office. This trail through the coastal rain forest has a gentle grade and mountain bikes are popular on this 12 mile stretch to Forest Road #340, near Silver Creek.

Jerry's Flat Road, from Gold Beach, is also the access road to the **Shrader Old Growth Trail** which has its trailhead at the **Lobster Creek Forest Campground**. The **Quosatana Campground** is about four miles past Lobster Creek. There is a 1-mile loop with numbered interpretation posts showing the species and the ways in which they are related. Species include Douglas fir, the Port Orford cedar, myrtlewood and tanoak. There are wild rhododendrons which bloom in the spring. The two campgrounds have developed sites, flush toilets and picnic areas. Other campsites along the river are primitive and tents may be pitched at other suitable locations along the Rogue River. For more information, call the Gold Beach Ranger Station at (503) 247-6651.

OREGON COAST TRAIL

The Oregon Coast trail is now a partial reality: a long-time dream which will eventually be completed to cover the 350 miles of the Oregon Coast from the California border to the Columbia River.

The trail is well-developed in Curry County and starts (at the south) on Cape Ferrelo. The trail touches Highway 101 every few miles, making it easy to hike in short stages if that is what you prefer, or should you not have time to complete the distance to just north of Humbug State Park, near Port Orford (about 40 miles). Several sections offer parking for your car and short, scenic walks:

Cape Ferrelo to Whalehead Park:

At the south end, the trail starts at the Cape parking lot, crosses grassy fields and then moves into wooded areas. This 1.5 mile trail ends at the House Rock viewpoint which also has a parking lot.

From House Rock, the next 3-mile trail section touches Hwy. 101 before descending to the beach for the final 1.5 miles to Whalehead Park. At Whalehead, there is a 1-mile loop trail.

Natural Bridge to Miner Creek:

There's another parking lot at Natural Bridge. For 1/2 mile, the trail heads north through woods to a fork where you turn left to find a scenic viewpoint. Continuing on the main trail (right fork) the trail has another fork with the left path leading to Thunder Rock Cove, a small scenic cove. The right fork leads to Hwy. 101. Should you want to continue from Thunder Rock, after this 1/2-mile walk, the Oregon Coast Trail continues to Miner Creek—a 3/4 mile hike. Take the left fork of the trail which passes by and overlooks Secret Beach, a stretch of beautiful secluded shoreline. The next part of the trail leads to Miner Creek and you can walk down to Secret Cove from here. An old road leads from Miner Creek to Hwy. 101.

Cape Sebastian Trail:

A portion of the trail which provides panoramic scenery is at Cape Sebastian, south of Gold Beach. The trail runs up (or down) the cape and the easier way to walk it is to drive to the top of the road and walk down the 1-mile trail. The Myer's Creek parking lot is at the lower end of the trail. To continue from the same park, begin walking from the north parking lot and the trail comes out at Hwy. 101, about 1/3 mile away.

Rogue River to Otter Point:

In Gold Beach, walk along the beach from the north shore of the river to the first creek, south of Otter Point. The trail crosses the bluff area and ends at the parking lot on Otter Point. You can continue on to the Geisel Monument.

Detailed descriptions of these and other sections of the Curry County section of the trail are found in a leaflet compiled by trail volunteer Walt Schroeder. It is available at the Gold Beach Ranger Station of Siskiyou National Forest. The short, easy sections of this trail provide alternatives to the longer and more rugged trails within Siskiyou National Forest.

BROOKINGS & GOLD BEACH

Brookings is actually two communities: Brookings, an old lumber town founded in 1908—on the north side of the Chetco River's mouth—and Harbor, on the south side. Thus, the area is often called Brookings-Harbor. The river offers excellent fishing opportunities for salmon, trout and steelhead and flows into the Pacific Ocean at Harbor where there are charter boats for hire. Other attractions include the nearby **Siskiyou National Forest** (there's a ranger station in Brookings), **Azalea State Park** with 36 acres of wild azaleas, and **Loeb Park**, 8 miles northeast of town, with access to the beach and camping near more wild azaleas.

The **Brookings Inn** (503-469-2173) is a Best Western motel with 68 standard units and suites and a restaurant on Hwy. 101. **Nendels Inn On the Beach** (503-469-7779) is indeed on the beach with rooms, suites (with whirlpools) & kitchens. It's in the port area of Brookings. The **Ward House B & B** (503-469-5557) is at 516 Redwood St., with Scandanavian decor, a hot tub and sauna. Campers have a choice in Brookings. There is public camping at **Harris Beach State Park**, north of town. In Brookings, the **Chetco RV Park** (503-469-3863) is on the highway with 120 sites and full hookups, laundry & showers. **Driftwood RV Park** (503-469-3213) has 100 full hookups at 16011 Lower Harbor Rd., with beach access, showers and laundry. The **Flying Gull Restaurant** serves seafood dishes along with more standard fare. It's a family place and is open for breakfast at 6 am.

Gold Beach, 30 miles north of Brookings is a busier, tourist-oriented town where the jet boats take visitors up the Rogue River for an unforgettable trip. But that's not all there is to do here. First of all, the fishing is renowned. Then there are the roads into the Siskiyou National Forest, including the road to the village of **Agness** which lies within the national forest 32 miles up-river.

There's a **Best Western Inn** here too (503-247-6691), and this one is on the beach with good views, an indoor pool & hot tub with restaurants nearby. **$$**. The **River Bridge Inn** (503-247-4533 or 1-800-759-4533) is a modern 50-room motel overlooking the river. The inn has suites with whirlpools, an indoor spa and free coffee. **$$ to $$$**. **Endicott Gardens** (503-247-6513) is a B & B home with four private rooms on Jerry's Flat Rd. The whole property is a scenic garden. **$$**. Camp on the river at **Indian Creek RV Park** (503-247-7704), **Kimball Creek Bend Resort** (503-247-7580) or **4 Seasons RV Resort** (503-247-4503). All have full hookups.

Staying in **Agness** gives you the special flavor of Pacific Northwest forest country. The Rogue River adds another special touch. Agness is easy to drive to—take Jerry's Flat Rd. **Cougar Lane Lodge** is located on the river across from the village. It's a newly-built replacement for a long-time lodge with a lounge, a dining room and a deck overlooking the river. **$$**. The **Lucas Pioneer Ranch** (503-247-7443) is a country inn on the Rogue with rustic cabins and rooms. **$ to $$ Singing Springs Ranch** (503-247-6162 has seven cottages, some with kitchens. **$ to $$**.

PORT ORFORD & BANDON

Port Orford has the distinction of being the most westerly incorporated city within the lower 48 states. The fall salmon runs in the Elk and Sixes rivers draw thousands of anglers each year. Access roads up both rivers open up the wilderness of the Siskiyou National Forest. There are forest campgrounds along the Elk River. Battle Rock City Park commemorates the early efforts to colonize this wild country. Humbug Mountain, with its trail, is just south of Port Orford.

Cape Blanco State Park is 9 miles north of town, offering camping in addition to hiking trails and beachcombing. Cape Blanco is six miles west of Hwy. 101. It was discovered by Spanish explorer Martin De Aguilar in January 1603. Drive to the lighthouse on the Cape and you'll be farther west than anyone else in the contiguous United States. The **Shoreline Motel** (503-332-2903) is located at Battle Rock Beach with standard rooms. **$$**. For camping, the **Arizona Beach Resort** (503-332-6491)is open year-round, on the beach with full hookups, showers, etc.

Bandon By The Sea is a calm, charming town with quite a turbulent history. It was the site of a gold rush at nearby Whiskey Run. Bandon has endured two disastrous fires. In 1936 fire wiped out all but 16 buildings which now comprise the restored "Old Town" core of the community. Bandon was re-developed into a beautiful little town which is a popular vacation spot. There are 26 miles of the Coquille River to explore. Bandon State Park and Bullard State Park are the beach "bookends" for the town. There is public camping at Bullard, just north of town. The beach south of town is reached via Seabird Drive. The town has a golf course (9 holes), a museum and cheese factory. 'Old Town' features boutiques and cafes.

There are ample accommodations in Bandon, including several good B & B homes. The **Cliff Harbor Guest House** (503-347-3956) has two units on the ocean—one with kitchen—on Beach Loop Rd. **$$**. Also on the beach is the **Seabird Inn** (503-347-2056) with two rooms and private baths. **$$**. **Lighthouse B & B** (503-347-9316) is on Jetty Road with four rooms, one with a whirlpool. **$$**. The **Inn at Face Rock** (503-347-9441) is on the beach, near the golf course. This large resort motel has ocean-view suites with kitchens and fireplaces, as well as standard rooms. **$$ to $$$**. The **Sunset Motel** is also on the beach with oceanfront rooms, restaurant, lounge and whirlpool, standard rooms and rooms with kitchen units.**$$**. There's a hostel in Bandon—at 375 Second Street (503-347-9632)—open to all ages with a few family rooms. There are two private campgrounds: **Driftwood Shores** (503-347-4122) is open year-round with full hookups at 935 East 2nd St.; the **Blue Jay Campground** is a summer operation on Beach Loop Rd. with trailer hookups, tent sites and showers.

There are several good places to eat in Bandon, including **Andrea's Old Town Cafe** on Baltimore in the restored area. It's popular and we suggest reservations (347-3022) **$$**. The **Boatworks** serves seafood, steaks & prime rib on the south jetty with a good view (347-2111) **$$ to $$$**.

COOS BAY, CHARLESTON & NORTH BEND

The three towns in the Coos Bay area offer a wide variety of recreation and places to stay and eat. **Coos Bay** is Oregon's lumber port with ships sailing into the bay from around the Pacific. **Charleston** is a scenic old community at the mouth of the bay, close to another trio—of state parks—on the headlands overlooking the ocean. **North Bend** is just north of Coos Bay and the two towns run into each other.

The three towns are just south of the **Oregon Dunes National Recreation Area**. The dunes flow for 48 miles offering wonderful vacation opportunities including dune buggy riding, hiking and beachcombing.

The three state parks on the Cape Arago Highway, southwest of Charleston offer camping—at **Sunset Bay Park**, beautiful botanical gardens at **Shore Acres Park**, and the ruggedness of rocky headlands at **Cape Arago Park**. I suggest that you save most of a full day to visit the three parks. Sunset Bay and the north cove at Cape Arago have tidepools. Fossil shells can be found on the coaledo sandstone walls of Sunset Bay Park. There's golfing at an 18-hole and two 9-hole courses in thearea. TThe three lighthouses in the region have historic significance. **Umpqua Lighthouse** is north of North Bend. Built in 1857, this was the first lighthouse on the Oregon Coast. The **Cape Arago Lighthouse** was built in 1866 and was rebuilt in 1934. The **Coquille Lighthouse**—at Bullard's Beach—began operations in 1866 and abandoned in 1963.

There are also three museums to visit. The **Coos Art Museum**, at 235 Anderson Street in downtown Coos Bay is open Tuesday through Sunday. The **Coos County Historical Museum**, founded in 1891, is at Simpson Park in North Bend. The museum collects artifacts of the region's pioneer past and is open Tuesday through Saturday. The **Marshfield Printing Museum**, at Front St. & Hwy. 101 in Coos Bay is open Tuesday through Saturday.

The **Oregon Coast Music Festival** is held each year in late July. And for motor fans, the Coos Bay International Speedway holds a variety of hot-rod events, drag racing and ATV racing throughout the summer.

Bird watchers come to the area to see migratory waterfowl and shorebirds at several locations including Cape Arago and Shore Acres state parks, Horsfall Beach, Kentuck and Pony sloughs and the South Slough Sanctuary. The area is also a center for myrtlewood products.

Whale watching has become a popular visitor attraction from December through May as the great grey whales migrate past the Cape Arago headlands. Charter trips leave from Charleston's harbor. Whales may also be spotted from the Umpqua Lighthouse and Shore Acres Park.

Fishing is good here, as it is along the whole southern and central Oregon coast. Offshore charter boats are available and fish caught in the area include salmon, striped bass, steelhead, sturgeon, trout, bluegill and shad. Shellfish is plentiful, including crab. Restaurants in the three towns serve local fish and shellfish with daily fresh sheets in several seafood cafes.

COOS BAY, CHARLESTON & NORTH BEND

There are several large chain motels in the area and the best of these is the **Red Lion** Coos Bay Inn on Virginia Ave, five blocks west of Hwy. 101. The motel has 144 units, a dining room and lounge, a heated outdoor pool and a laundry. **$ to $$**. Another good motel is the **Coos Bay Inn** (503-267-7171 or 1-800-635-0852) on Hwy. 101 with views of the bay and free continental breakfast, sauna, fitness rooms and laundry room. **$$ to $$$**. The **Edgewater Inn** (503-267-0423 or 1-800-233-0423) is a new and inexpensive motel at 175 E. Johnson in Coos Bay with indoor pool and whirlpool, kitchen suites & good views of the waterfront. **$ to $$**.

The **Pony Village Motor Lodge** (503-756-3191) is on Virginia Ave (Hwy. 101) in North Bend next to a large shopping mall. This motel has 119 units with large rooms and a restaurant attached. **$**. The **Plainview Motel** (503-888-5166) is in Charleston, on Cape Arago Highway two miles from the boat basin. Some units in this small motel have kitchens. **$**. There are a number of bed and breakfast places in the area which offer a homey alternative to the more standard downtown motor hotels. These include the **Blackberry Inn Bed & Breakfast** (503-267-6951) at 843 Central Ave. in Coos Bay. This home was built in 1903 and renovated in 1989. There are four rooms and continental breakfast is served. **$**. **The Captain's Quarters B & B** (503-888-6895) is a Victorian house built in 1892. It has a bay view, two rooms and shared bath. It's located at 265 South Empire Blvd in Coos Bay. **$**.

The **Sherman House B & B** (503-756-3496) is at 2380 Sherman in North Bend. This is another 1903 house and the three rooms here are furnished with antiques. **$**. Another Victorian house from the turn of the century is **This Olde House B & B** (503-267-5224) at 202 Alder Ave. (corner of North 2nd St. in Coos Bay). There are antique furnishings here too. **$**. The **Coos Bay Manor** (503-269-1224) is a colonial-style house with five rooms, each decorated in a different style and located at 955 S. 5th Street in Coos Bay. **$ to $$**. **Baywood On The Water** (503-756-6348) is a charming B & B in North Bend which has two rooms and a large hot tub overlooking the bay. **$**. **The Highlands B & B** (503-756-0300) is at 608 Ridge Rd. in North Bend with two large rooms, private baths and a family room. **$**.

For RV owners and campers, there is a good choice in the area. Private parks include the **Lucky Logger Park** (503-267-6003) in Coos Bay with 78 spaces and full hookups close to downtown, the large **Charleston Travel Park** (503-888-9512) on Kingfisher Dr., with 104 RV sites, full hookups and all the rest, and **Seaport RV Park** (503-888-3122) on Boat Basin Dr. in Charleston, with 26 spaces, full hookups, propane and laundry.

You can camp in **Coos County Park** at Bastendorff Beach (503-888-5353), with 25 tent and 30 trailer sites. As mentioned earlier, there is a campground at **Sunset Bay State Park**. The **Bluebill Forest Service Campground** is four miles north of North Bend in the Horsfall Beach area. The 19 tent & trailer sites are set amongst the dunes.

REEDSPORT

Set half-way along the **Oregon National Dunes Recreation Area**, Reedsport is a handy place to stay and shop while exploring the vast stretch of protected dunes along the Pacific shore. To the south, there is **Tugman State Park**. Right at Reedsport, the dunes provide a curving spit of sand which serves as a breakwater for the bay. To the north of Reedsport, the dunes stretch on, including **Honeyman State Park**. The headquarters and visitor center for the Dunes Recreation Area is in Reedsport The main corner in Reedsport is the junction of Highway 101 and State Hwy. 38. This is a scenic road which leads east along the Umpqua River, to the small village of Drain and then joins Interstate-5 just south of Eugene.

There is an active harbor here as tugs push barges up the river. Fishing charter boats are available to take you river fishing for striped bass and other fish. Loon Lake is nearby but the dunes are the chief attraction of this little town which is joined by the town of Gardiner (to the north) and Winchester Bay (to the west on a loop road).

The **Winchester Bay Motel** (503-271-4871) is located on the harbor. It has 52 units including suites; and restaurants, shops, beaches and the dock are nearby. **$ to $$**. The **Fir Grove Motel** (503-271-4848) is at 2178 Winchester Ave. with standard rooms and family units with kitchen. There is a pool. **$**.

Reedsport has a good supply of campgrounds and RV parks, largely because of the popularity of the place for fishing. Private campgrounds include the **Fisherman's RV Park** (503-271-3536) with 70 full hookups and a short walk to Winchester Bay. The **Surfwood Campground** (503-271-4020) is on Highway 101 with tent and trailer sites and the **Umpqua Beach Resort & RV Park** (503-271-3443) has cottages as well as pull-through RV spaces, full hookups and a store—all on the bay. There are several public campgrounds along the stretch of dunes in the Oregon Dunes National Recreation Area. There's overnight camping at **Umpqua Lighthouse Park**, just south of Winchester Bay on the loop road. Farther south, at **Lakeside**—a small community next to Tenmile Lake & Eel Lake—there is a large campground with 115 sites with electricity, showers, laundry & trailer dumping station. Just north of Lakeside is the Forest Service's **Eel Lake Campground** which offers access to the dunes and a hiking trail. **William M. Tugman** State Park, 10 miles south of Reedsport has a hiker/biker campground. Eight miles north of Reedsport, The **Tahkenitch Forest Camp** has campsites in addition to a boat ramp and picnic tables. The fishing is particularly good here, year-round. The **Carter Forest Camp** is 12.8 miles north of town and has camping facilities, dune access, a hiking trail, boat ramp and more good fishing. There are more public camping spots before you get to Florence at the northern end of the dunes area.

For dining in Reedsport, I suggest the **Windjammer**, a large place for families with a salad bar (**$$ to $$$**), and **Jim's Waterfront Restaurant & Lounge** (**$$ to $$$**..

SIUSLAW NATIONAL FOREST

The national forests in Oregon are among the foremost treasures of the state. Siuslaw is not only a resource for the forest industry but is a prime recreation area which includes the northern half of the **Oregon Dunes National Recreation Area** as well as some 640,000 acres of Douglas fir forest. On the coast, **Cape Perpetua** and the **Cascade Head Scenic Area** are the scenic highlights with the **Dunes Overlook** providing a viewing platform and a trail through the high half-mile wide dunes to the beach. Inland, there are myriad streams which offer superb fishing opportunities. Along the forest roads are trailheads and campgrounds.

The forest name comes from the Yakona Indians, meaning *far-away waters*. This forest area is full of history: several bands of Indians inhabited the coast range forests. The tribes included the Alsea, the Lower Umpqua, Siuslaw, Coos and the Yakona. The first European explorers included Bartolomew Ferrelo who is said to be the first white man to reach the Siuslaw when he sailed the Oregon Coast in 1543. Capt. Bruno Heceta followed in 1775 and the cape bears his name. Fur trader Jedediah Smith, for whom the nearby Smith River was named, traveled through the area in 1828 reaching the mouth of the Umpqua River. In 1850, gold was discovered up the Rogue River and miners traveled through the area to reach the high sites in the coast mountains. The Umpqua served as a transportation route and the first villages were founded at that time. The first lumber operations came in the mid 1800s when the town now called Gardiner was established at the mouth of the Smith River. The forest was extensively logged during the First World War period. There had been many fires in the forest previous to this, including the Nestucca Fire in 1853 and the huge Coos Fire in 1868.

Highway 34, running east from Waldport, runs beside the Alsea River through the village of Tidewater to Alsea and then to Corvallis. There are three developed campgrounds in this area. The largest of these is **Blackberry**, with 32 tent and trailer sites. For hikers who like to be challenged, **Mary's Peak** (4,007 ft.) offers two hiking trails, including a new 2.5 mile trail up the east ridge. The North Ridge Trail provides a 3.5 mile hike.

The Meadow Edge Trail, near the summit of Mary's Peak is an easier walk—for 1.6 miles. The summit offers superb panoramic views. To get there, take Hwy. 34 north of Alsea and turn to the west (left) on the signed road. There is a campground with six sites—for tenters and suitable for small trailers but not for RVs.

The village of **Mapleton**—on Hwy. 116 east of Florence—has a forest ranger station. Here you can obtain the forest map ($2.00) and lists of trails and campsites. The Mapleton ranger district features three developed campgrounds. The **Alder Dune Campground** has 39 sites, flush toilets and a hiking trail to a beach. There are picnic areas on the Smith River and on Sutton Lake. A new hiking trail, the Pawn Trail, is now open with the trailhead located 16 miles along the North Fork Siuslaw Rd.

OREGON DUNES NATIONAL RECREATION AREA

The north half of the Dunes Recreation Area extends from Reedsport to Florence and is managed by the staff of Siuslaw National Forest. Information on trails and campgrounds is available from the forest offices at Cape Perpetua and Mapleton and the Dunes headquarters father south in Reedsport.

There are campgrounds located conveniently along Hwy. 101 in the Dunes Area, with trails leading out of each campground.

Tahkenitch Landing Campground is about seven miles north of Reedsport (15 miles south of Florence) with graveled parking pads but no piped drinking water. The **Tahkenitch Dunes Trail** leads 3/4 mile from the trailhead at the campground's south loop, across open sand along a stabilized dune. The total distance from the campground to the beach on this trail is 1.5 miles. There's a picnic area at the trailhead.

Driftwood Campground is 12 miles north of Reedsport on Siltcoos Dune & Beach Access Rd. The campground has 70 sites with a flush toilet and drinking water. The trailhead for Chief Tsiltcoos Trail is at the north campground loop. The **Lagoon Campground** is closer to Hwy. 101 on the same road, with 40 tenting sites and a flush toilet and water. The River of No Return Trail circles the campground and follows a fresh water marsh. **Waxmyrtle Campground** is in the same area with 56 campsites suitable for tents and trailers. The **Waxmyrtle Trail** runs west along the riverbank (start at the bridge) and ends at a viewpoint overlooking the estuary. There is good fishing here.

Tyee Campground is a mile north of the above sites, east of Hwy. 101 on Westlake Rd. There are 14 paved sites here with pit toilets only. There's a .5-mile trail to Siltcoos Lake.

Carter Lake Campground is just south of the Siltcoos cluster of campsites—11 miles north of Reedsport. There are 22 campsites with a flush toilet and drinking water. The Carter Dunes Trail leads over the open sand past shorepine forests, offering viewing of birds, reptiles and amphibians on the dry and wet hummocks.

There are other hiking trails in the Dunes area which do not connect directly to the beach. One of the most popular is the **Bluebill Trail** which circles the 40-acre Bluebill Lake. To get to the trailhead, drive 2.5 miles east of Hwy. 101 on Horsfall Beach Road at the southernmost end of the Dunes Area (just north of Coos Bay). There's a horse camp in this area as well as tent and trailer sites at **Horsfall Beach Campground**.

The **Umpqua Trail** is reached from the **Eel Lake Campgrounds** near Lakeside, 8 miles south of Reedsport. This trail leads through an evergreen forest and breaks out into open sand. The magnificent, high dunes are at least 1/2 mile wide at this point. There's backcountry camping along the **Threemile Lake Trail,** accessed from the Tahkenitch Dunes Trail. **Siltcoos Lake Trail** offers an extended hike or a loop walk from Hwy. 101, east of the Siltcoos Dunes Access Rd.

FLORENCE

Located mid-way on the Oregon Coast, Florence is on a bend in the Siuslaw River as it enters the Pacific. To the south is the Oregon Dunes National Recreation Area. To the north, the Oregon Islands National Wildlife Reserve. To get to the Dunes, take South Jetty Road which joins Hwy. 101 just south of the Siuslaw River Bridge. You'll find six parking areas with access to the Dunes and beaches.

The Siuslaw and North Fork rivers are fishing favorites, particularly for steelhead. 17 lakes in the immediate area are stocked with bass, trout, catfish, perch and bluegill. 12 miles north of town are the **Sea Lion Caves**, a commercial attraction where a herd of Stellar sea lions live, in and around the largest sea cave in the United States. Florence has a picturesque **"Old Town"** located on the waterfront with seafood restaurants and boutiques in restored Victorian buildings. Other recreational pursuits include golfing (there's a championship 18-hole course as well as several 9-hole courses), bay clamming and crabbing. The **Rhododendron Loop**—starting in downtown Florence—provides a tour of wild rhododendron groves in a 9-mile drive. The loop ends at Hwy. 101, four miles north of town.

There's a wide range of accommodation in and near Florence including several larger motels. These include the **Pier Point Inn** (503-997-7191), a Best Western motel which overlooks the river. It has a restaurant, lounge, sauna, whirlpools and a handy location in Old Town. **$$**. The **Driftwood Shores Inn** (503-997-8263 or 1-800-824-8774) is set on the ocean overlooking Heceta Beach, with 136 rooms, indoor pool, whirlpool, restaurant and lounge. **$$ to $$$**. On Hwy. 101, the **Americana** (503-997-7115) has standard rooms and units with kitchens, an indoor pool and whirlpool, with a trail to the dunes. **$$**. The **River House Motel** (503-997-3933) is as close to the river as you could get, one block from Old Town with a large whirlpool and balcony views of the river. **$$**.

The **Johnson House** is a Bed & Breakfast home (503-997-8000) at 216 Maple St. Hosts are Ron and Jane Frasee. **$ to $$**.

Campers and RV drivers have the choice of three private campgrounds. **Woahink Lake Resort** (503-997-6454) has pull-through spaces with full hookups, showers, laundry and access to the Dunes. **Rhododendron Trailer Park** (503-997-2206) has full trailer and RV hookups at 87735 Hwy. 101. **Heceta Beach RV Park** is a quiet campground close to the ocean on Heceta Beach Road, with full hookups, pull-through sites and showers. To the north of town, within eight miles are several **Forest Service campgrounds**: Sutton Lake, Sutton Creek and Alder Dune. All have water access, fishing, picnicking and basic campsites.

Seafood dining is available at **Mo's** restaurant, built on a pier on the Florence bayfront. Here you'll get clam chowder, fish and shellfish dishes and a good view of the river. **$$**. All-day breakfast is served at **Morgan's Country Kitchen** on Hwy. 101, 1/2 mile south of the bridge. **$ to $$**. The **Blue Hen** on Hwy. 101 is a charming cafe with outstanding breakfasts. **$ to $$**.

YACHATS

Pronounced "Yah-Hots", this small fishing village is a very scenic little town located at the mouth of the Yachats River. Yachats calls itself "The Gem of the Oregon Coast" and they may be right. The population is around 550. The pace here is slow and the beaches are, for the most part, uncrowded. There are rocky promontories which feature high surf, particularly during winter months.

Just south of the village is one of the striking scenic highlights of the whole Oregon Coast, Cape Perpetua. This is the highest point on the coast and Hwy. 101 winds its way up the cape through a series of switchbacks. There's a short trail to a stone lookout with remarkable views. The U.S. Forest Service operates an information center and campground at the cape.

All summer, silver sea-run smelt appear at Yachats where local fishermen capture them with special nets. The annual run is celebrated with a community smelt-fry. The Little Log Church By The Sea is now a museum and was built with donated logs, shingles and labor in 1932.

For its small size, Yachats has a wide range of accommodation, from forest campgrounds and rustic cabin-type lodges to romantic inns and B & B homes. The **Adobe Resort** (503-547-3141 or 1-800-52-Adobe) is on the ocean's edge with rooms and suites (some with fireplaces), a dining room, sauna and whirlpool. **$ to $$**. The **Yachats Inn** (503-547-3456), on Hwy. 101, also has good ocean views. Some of the rooms have kitchens and fireplaces and there is an indoor pool. **$$**. The **Dublin House Motel** (503-547-3200) on Hwy. 101, has rooms with kitchen units and an indoor pool. **$$**.

If you're interested in a more private, remote place, **Oregon House** (503-547-3329) is located on a scenic property 9 miles south of town off Hwy. 101. Set in a forest close to the beach, this inn has eight units, most with kitchens, fireplaces and reasonable rates. **$ to $$**. The **Shamrock Lodgettes** (503-547-3312) is closer to the village at the south end, with individual log cabins as well as rooms—on the beach—with a whirlpool, hot tub and sauna. **$ to $$**.

There's a striking pyramid-shaped B & B home called **The Ziggurat** (503-547-3925), six miles south of town on Hwy. 101. It's on the beach with glassed-in decks, a sauna and full breakfast served. **$ to $$**. **Burd's Nest Inn** (503-547-3683) is a B & B home with two rooms in the village at 664 Yachats River Rd. There are private baths and a full breakfast is served. **$$**. **Serenity B & B** (503-547-3813), at 5985 Yachats River Rd. is nestled in a quiet valley on a 10-acre property and a European ambience. Some of the rooms have a whirlpool. **$$**.

For campers, there are several Forest Service campgrounds including one at **Cape Perpetua** (mentioned above). The **Rock Creek Campground**—in Siuslaw National Forest—is located 10 miles south of Yachats, with a creekside trail to the Ocean. The **Tillicum Campground** is five miles north of town on Hwy. 101, with a picnic area and beach access.

WALDPORT AND SEAL ROCK

Waldport is located on Alsea Bay, eight miles north of Yachats. Another picturesque town on the coast, Waldport is a sports fishing center, well-known for its steelhead, salmon and trout. For beach diggers, there are crabs, razor and bay clams. The pace is gentle here. It's a small, friendly town lacking the busier resort atmosphere of the larger places such as Newport (15 miles to the north) and Lincoln City.

The central Oregon beaches continue through the Waldport area. Just south of town is **Patterson Memorial Park,** a ten-acre park named for a former Oregon governor. The park has good trails, a sandy beach and picnic areas. Beach access just north of town is available at **Driftwood Beach**, a day-use state park located on a sandy bluff with a trail to the beach and picnic areas. **Seal Rock Park** is 5.5 miles north of Waldport, set on a rugged coastline with good fishing and ample picnic facilities. Seal Rock is a small community north of the park. **Sea Gulch** is a commercial attraction in Seal Rock. It's owned by Ray Kowalski, a humorous chainsaw artist who carves large figures and displays them in this rustic place. He has built the shop into something of a theme park and a trail leads to more than 300 of these chainsaw creations.

The small riverside community of Tidewater is east of Waldport on Highway 34 which continues to Corvallis and Interstate-5. The **Crestview Hill Golf Course** is one mile south of Waldport—a 9-hole layout.

Most places to stay in the area are in Waldport. The **Alsea Manor Motel** (503-563-3249) is next to the bay and is close to the beaches. Restaurants are nearby and the motel has free coffee. **$ to $$.** The **Bayshore Inn** (503-563-3202 or 1-800-782-0683)) is a large motel, also on the bay, with 91 units, restaurant and lounge. **$$. Cape Cod Cottages** (503-563-2106) have one and two-bedroom oceanfront cottages with kitchens and decks at 4150 SW Pacific Coast Hwy (Hwy. 101). **$$.** For the ultimate in privacy, **Heather Cottage** (503-563-3620) is a one bedroom cottage by the sea at Hwy. 101 and Adahi Ave, just south of Waldport. **$$. Cliff House Bed & Breakfast** (503-563-2506) is located on eight miles of beach south of Waldport, just west of the Forest Service unit. Full breakfast is served. **$$.**

The restaurants in Waldport and area are relaxed, informal places whose prime mission is serving seafood. The **Galley Ho Restaurant & Lounge** is at the foot of the Alsea Bridge. **$$.** The **Kozy Kove Floating Restaurant** is 9.5 miles east of Waldport in Tidewater and getting there makes a pleasant sidetrip. **$$. Leroy's Blue Whale** restaurant in Waldport is a fish & chip place with a salad bar on Hwy. 101. **$ to $$. Jeannie's Drift-In Cafe** is located on the bay in the older section of Waldport, at 1260 Port St. This is a good place for breakfast or simple but tasty meals at other times. The cafe has a good view. **$ to $$.**

There's a private RV park in Tidewater (503-528-3251), located next to the floating restaurant. The **Beachside State Park** campground is 4 miles south of Waldport with 20 trailer sites and 60 tenting sites.

NEWPORT

This resort town is located on Yaquina Bay, a deep-water harbor. The sheltered harbor and the adjacent ocean beaches provide a scenic environment for this popular vacation town. There are many places to stay and to eat. The Yaquina Bay oyster is a specialty of the seafood restaurants.

Yaquina Bay State Park, on the spit which shelters the entrance to the harbor, is a wonderful place to stroll with its jetty and ocean views. The **Yaquina Lighthouse** is the oldest building in Newport. It began operation in 1871 and closed three years later when it was discovered that the light couldn't be seen from the north. While the light was never again activated, the building—a Victorian home with a light on top—has been restored and now is a museum furnished with antiques. It's the only wood frame lighthouse on the Oregon Coast.

The lighthouse which replaced it is on display—and still in operation— at **Yaquina Head**, set in a park which has been designated an Outstanding Natural Area. The headland, composed of volcanic lava, is constantly battered by surf. Harbor seals can be seen here along with thousands of sea birds and grey whales in season. Low tide reveals the "Marine Gardens" with a multitude of animal and plant life in the intertidal area. The park was designated in 1980 and is operated by the Bureau of Land Management. There are paved trails throughout the headland.

As a resort town, Newport has a good selection of places to stay, including one of the top B & B places on the whole Pacific Coast: the **Sylvia Beach Hotel** (503-265-5428). It's a small oceanfront hotel especially for book lovers, with each room dedicated to a different famous author. Some of the rooms have fireplaces and the hotel serves a full breakfast to its visitors. Its at 267 NW Cliff Street. **$$**. Another B & B, the **Oar House** (503-265-9571) is a 1900-era house at 520 SW 2nd St., with two rooms and private baths, a whirlpool and sauna. **$$**.

The **Shilo Inn** is a complex of modern hotel and older motel with two restaurants, a lounge, two indoor pools and a handy location on the beach. The inn serves a free continental breakfast. **$$ to $$$**. The **Embarcadero** (503-265-8521 or 1-800-547-4779) is a resort hotel and marina on the bayfront with dining room and lounge, indoor pool, a large whirlpool and sauna. The resort has one and two-bedroom suites with fireplaces and kitchens. **$$ to $$$**. Three miles north of town, on the beach, is a smaller, cozier place: the **Moolack Shores Motel** (503-265-2326). This motel has rooms with beamed ceilings and fireplaces and is close to Beverly Beach State Park.

For campers, there are the state parks and **Pacific Shores RV Resort** (503-265-3750 or 1-800-333-1583), a large RV park 2 miles north of town with hookups, heated pool and sauna. There are all kinds of restaurants and most serve seafood. They include the original **Mo's**, on the waterfront at 622 SW Bay Blvd. **Mo's Annex** is down the street. **The Shanghai Clipper** is in an historic mansion at 333 SE Bay Blvd. All are **$$ to $$$**.

OTTER ROCK, DEPOE BAY & GLENEDEN BEACH

Just north of Beverly Beach State Park, the small community of Otter Rock is located on a the Otter Crest Loop, which takes you to several scenic points including the **Devil's Punch Bowl**, a bowl-shaped rock formation which fills through a deep cavern at high tide. **Devil's Punch Bowl State Park** has a picnic area, a sandy beach and marine gardens are visible at low tide. There's a smaller day-use park at **Otter Crest**—a large high rock above the crashing surf—north of the village of Otter Rock. The shoreline at Otter Crest is host to sea lions, seals and many types of sea birds.

Depoe Bay is another small community overlooking the ocean—with much charm and a rocky bay. This is known as the "world's smallest harbor" and you'll see why. It covers only six acres. It may be small but there's a small fishing fleet here with charter craft available. A privately-owned aquarium is in the village.

Gleneden Beach offers a wonderful wild beach and the more civilized comforts of the famed five-star Salishan resort. There is a loop drive along Gleneden Beach and the local artist community has established several art and crafts shops along the road.

There are places to stay in the three villages. The most notable and in a class by itself is the **Salishan Lodge** on Siletz Bay (503-764-2371 or 1-800-547-6500). This condominium-style resort is on everyone's top-ten list of places to stay in the United States. The resort has a renowned championship golf course, and the dunes and beach are nearby. There are nature trails through the wooded property and along the bay. You can walk for six miles on the central section of the **Oregon Coast Trail**. The dining is truly fine at Salishan and the cuisine has won awards from far and wide, as has the extensive wine cellar. There is also a less formal restaurant (the Sun Room) and a coffee shop, as well as an indoor pool, exercise equipment and indoor and outdoor tennis courts. **$$ to $$$**.

All other places pale beside Salishan but there are good places to stay in the other towns. The **Alpine Chalets** (503-765-2572) at Otter Rock features two-bedroom A-frame cottages with kitchens. **$$**. The **Inn at Otter Crest** (503-765-2111 or 1-800-452-2101) is a very good, secluded resort with ocean-view units, restaurant and lounge. Rooms have kitchens and fireplaces and the inn has a pool, saunas, and tennis courts.

The **Holiday Surf Lodge and RV Park** (503-765-2133 or 1-800-452-2108 OR) has 84 motel-type units and 110 RV spaces at the north end of Depoe Bay. There are two B & B homes in Depoe Bay: **Channel House B & B** (503-765-2140), on the ocean with a whirlpool (**$$**) and **Gracie's Landing** (503-765-2322) on the bay with fireplaces (**$$**).

The **Dining Room at Salishan** is highly recommended. For less formal dining, **Chez Jeanette** on the Gleneden Loop has French cuisine with local produce and herbs, with seafood a specialty. **$$ to $$$** The **Chowder Bowl** in Depoe Bay serves fish & chips and clam chowder. **$ to $$**. There's a **Mo's** here too. **$$**.

LINCOLN CITY

This town came into being when three small towns were amalgamated in 1965. The communities remain as separate entities, joined by seven miles of sparkling ocean beach with Devils Lake providing fresh water recreation. Lincoln City is one of the prime vacation resort towns on the Oregon Coast. It has more ocean-view lodging than any other community on Hwy. 101 and enough natural recreational possibilities to take up several vacations. It's a particularly good family vacation town with several good walking trails, ten state parks within a 15-minute drive and a variety of summer cultural and sports events. Theater West offers several productions each year in the town's tiny theater. The annual sandcastle competition is a major attraction.

Seal watching is a preferred summer activity and the Gray whales pass by Cascade Head and Road's End parks from March through May. Devils Lake and Siletz Bay are good windsurfing locations. There are also two wine tasting rooms in Lincoln City (Honeywood Winery & Oak Knoll Winery). And as we've pointed out before, this is another place for great storm watching during winter months. The Salmon River offers salmon, steelhead and trout fishing. The Siletz River is famous for its chinook salmon. Devil's Lake is stocked with perch and trout and also supports fishing for catfish, crapper and largemouth bass.

There are large and small places to stay here. The larger, resort-style hotels include the **Shilo Inn** (503-994-3655), 187 rooms, on the ocean with a restaurant and lounge, indoor pool and whirlpool. **$$ to $$$**. The **Best Western Lincoln Sands Inn** (503-994-4227 or 1-800-528-1234) is another large resort, an all-suite hotel with full kitchens, a heated pool & whirlpool and free continental breakfast **$$ to $$$**. The **Surftides Beach Resort** (503-994-2191 or 1-800-521-3452, outside Oregon) is also on the ocean with kitchen units, a dining room & lounge, indoor pool, whirlpool and tennis. **$ to $$**. The **Siletz Bay Inn** (503-996-3996 or 1-800-843-4940) on SW 81st St. has ocean views, rooms with kitchens, in-room whirlpools and a good location south of the main town **$$ to $$$**. **Nendel's Cozy Cove** (503-994-2950) is a resort motel at 515 NW Inlet Ave., on the ocean with rooms and suites—some with in-room whirlpools; a heated pool & sauna. **$$ to $$$**.

You have several B & B homes from which to choose, including the **Palmer House Oceanview Inn** (503-994-7932) at 646 NW Inlet in Lincoln City. This B & B inn has private baths and a full breakfast is served. **$$**. The **Brey House B & B Inn** (503-994-7123) is at 3725 NW Keel Ave in town with a good ocean view. **$$**. The **Rustic Inn** (503-994-5111) is a log house with private baths at 2313 NE. Holmes Rd. The **Salmon River Lodge** (503-994-2639) is in a scenic location at 5622 Salmon River Hwy (Hwy 18) with 2 bedroom units and a full breakfast. **$$**.

Camping spots are plentiful, including the large **KOA Kampground** on East Devils Lake Rd. (503-994-2961), the **Tree 'n Sea Trailer Park** (503-996-3801) on 51st Street, and **West Devils Lake State Park** on Hwy. 101.

PACIFIC CITY & OCEANSIDE—THREE CAPES LOOP

The **Three Capes Loop** offers a fascinating drive to several scenes of outstanding natural beauty, as well as several small vacation communities. The loop is an alternative route between Lincoln City and the town of Tillamook and is accessed by taking one of three roads leading west from Hwy. 101, just north of the small town of Neskowin. The northernmost road leads west from Cloverdale. The oceanside route passes by state parks, sand dunes, spectacular seastacks, haystacks and more!

Pacific City is a small vacation village at the south end of the loop road. It's at the mouth of the Little Nestucca River. The beaches, including the sands at **Bob Straub State Park** offer clamming, surf fishing and walking on the spit. Just north of Pacific City is **Cape Kiwanda**. The state park here offers great stretches of wild beach with views of the cape. This is a favorite location for hang gliding. The huge Haystack Rock is here.

Cape Lookout is to the north. Driving from the south, the first feature here is the **Cape Lookout Trail**, a 2.5-mile hiking trail to the tip of the cape. The cape is home to more than 150 varieties of birds. **Cape Lookout State Park** has a scenic stand of Sitka spruce, an ocean beach and a striking half-mile headland. This is the nesting place for a large flock of California murres. The park has a campground with showers and basic campsites, as well as picnic areas.

At the north end of Netarts Bay is the small town of **Netarts**. There is a boat launch here with good bay and surf fishing.

To the north is the resort village of **Oceanside**. The community is close to **Three Arch Rocks National Bird & Sea Lion Refuge** and **Cape Meares State Park**. The inactive lighthouse here offers a wonderful view of the coastline including a sea lion rookery, sea caves and cliffs and the "Octopus Tree". The lighthouse is open from May through September and the park has a picnic area. Drive another ten miles north and you arrive at Tillamook.

Places to stay on the loop include the **House On The Hill** (503-842-6030), a lodge with a commanding view on Maxwell Point and rooms with kitchen facilities. **$$**. The **Anchorage Motel** (503-965-6773) is in Oceanside, close to the sea with kitchen units. **$$**. The **Neskowin Resort** (503-392-3191) is a condo-style resort, located on the ocean in the village of Neskowin with a restaurant and lounge. **$$**.

The **Pacific View Bed & Breakfast** (503-965-6498) is in Pacific City, with good views of the coast and the mountains. **$$**. **Sandlake Country Inn** is another cozy B & B home at 8505 Galloway Rd. **$$**. The **Sea Haven Inn** (503-842-3151) is in Oceanside with nine rooms and ocean views. **$$**.

You may camp at **Cape Lookout State Park** or in several private RV parks, including **Cape Kiwanda RV Park** (503-965-6230), 130 sites, in Oceanside with full hookups and boat launch. The **Pacific City Trailer Park** (503-965-6820) also has full hookups, showers and laundry, close to the beach and stores in the town of Pacific City.

TILLAMOOK

Mention Tillamook and you automatically think of cheese. At least I do. This town—slightly inland on Hwy. 101—is home to the largest and best-known cheese factory in Oregon. Tillamook Cheese makes a famous cheddar and offers a fascinating self-guided tour of the plant, with video monitors increasing your knowledge of the cheese-making process. At the end of the tour there's a store filled with cheese of all ages and other Tillamook products. I highly recommend the five year-old cheddar which is not available in other retail outlets.

Tillamook is a handy base for vacation trips to the Three Capes Loop (see previous page) and to other recreational areas in Tilamook County. The area is a waterfall-lover's delight. Munson Creek Falls is the highest waterfall in the Coast Range, cascading 266 feet over a dramatic cliff. The trailhead is 1.5 miles off Hwy. 101 and the lower trail is a short walk to a picnic area and the base of the falls. The upper trail is longer and requires climbing but it leads to a great view from the falls' mid-point.

There are smaller falls including the Nehalem Falls (eight miles east of Mohler), Clarence Falls (12 miles east of Beaver) and Gunaldo Falls—requiring a good hike—about 11 miles south of Hebo.

For war historians, the old blimp hangars which are leftovers from the Second World War provide an interesting visit. On the edge of town, these huge buildings housed a set of navy blimps used along the coast to track Japanese submarine activity. The buildings are in use today by local firms including a lighter-than-air craft testing facility. You can drive to see them from the outside by going to the entrance of the Port of Tillamook Industrial Park. The county's Pioneer Museum is located at 2106 Second Street and is open Sunday through Friday. On the grounds of the museum is a restored steam logging donkey.

The **Mar-Clair Motel** (503-842-7571) is another of the Best Western group, at 11 Main Ave. in Tillamook. It has a pool, whirlpools and a sauna. **$$.** **McClaskey's Restaurant** is part of the motel operation. The Oregon-based chain Shilo Inns is also represented in Tillamook. This **Shilo Inn** (503-842-7971 or 1-800-222-2244) is on Hwy. 101, north of downtown with standard rooms, several rooms with kitchens, a restaurant, lounge, indoor pool, whirlpool and a fitness center. **$ to $$.** For bed and breakfast accommodation, try the **Blue Haven B & B** (503-842-2265). This country home, at 30235 Gienger Road, has three rooms furnished with antiques and a full breakfast is served. **$. Aldercrest House** (503-842-5246) is another bed and breakfast home, with two rooms at 3280 Aldercrest Road **$ to $$.**

The **Pacific Campground & Overnight Trailer Park** (503-842-5201) is across the road from the Tillamook Cheese factory. The campground has pull-through sites, full hookups, tent sites and showers. The nearest large public campground (including 53 sites with trailer & RV hookups) is in **Cape Lookout State Park**—on the coast (503-842-4981). You get there by taking the Three Capes Loop (see previous page).

GARIBALDI & ROCKAWAY BEACH

Driving north from the town of Tillamook, Highway 101 veers toward the sea again, curving around the north shore of Tillamook bay to the small town of **Garibaldi**. This is a commercial fishing center with shrimp and fish processing plants. The boat basin has a small charter fleet for those who wish to catch some ocean fishing. A marina with public moorage is also available in the harbor.

Barview Park, just north of town, has an excellent jetty shoreline with fishing for rock and ling cod, perch and flounder. The Miami River—a trout fishing stream—is two miles south of Garibaldi.

It's a five-mile drive north from Garibaldi to Rockaway Beach. This is another vacation town with wide sandy beaches and several lakes just inland. Lake Lytle is the largest of the fresh water fishing lakes. **Rockaway Beach State Park** and **Twin Lakes State Park** are day-use parks on Highway 101. Both are just north of the town center and both give access to the beaches and include picnic areas. **Manhattan Beach State Park** is a larger day-use park on the same long stretch of sand, with beach access and a picnic area. This is said to be Oregon's longest stretch of beach (seven miles) although—not having walked and measured the complete coastline—I can't vouch for local bragging.

Garibaldi has two moderately-priced motels, the **Fanta Sea** and the **Tilla Bay** (see below). The **Gracey Manor** (503-322-3369) is a bed and breakfast home at 119 East Driftwood in Garibaldi, with three rooms (for adults) and a view of the bay. **$**. You'll have no problem satisfying your desire to get a room on the beach at Rockaway. The town is stretched along the beach and several motels are located with good ocean views. These include the **Silver Sands Motel** (503-355-2206) at 201 South Pacific with 64 units—some with kitchens, a pool, whirlpool, and sauna. **$ to $$**. The **Surfside Motel** (503-355-2312) has 51 units with oceanview rooms and some with kitchens and fireplaces. There's an indoor pool. **$ to $$$**.

The **Rock Creek Inn** (503-355-8282) has seven oceanfront condo-type units (1 & 2 bedrooms) with kitchens and fireplaces, at 145 North Miller. **$$**. If you prefer the privacy which a cottage offers, try **Broadwater Oceanside Cottages** (503-355-2248) at 105 South 6th. There are four cottages with kitchens. **$$**. A larger home is also available for rent here.

Rockaway and Garibaldi offer several places for campers and RV owners. **Spring Lake RV Park** (503-355-2240) is in Rockaway with 18 spaces, full hookups, showers, hot tubs, laundry and a picnic area. The RV park also rents paddle boats, sailboats and canoes for puttering around the the lake. In Garibaldi, the **Tilla Bay RV Park** (503-322-3405) is attached to a motel at 805 Garibaldi Ave. There are 15 spaces, hookups, showers and laundry. The **Fanta Sea Motel** (503-322-3251) in Garibaldi has RV parking spaces but no hookups, at 302 7th Street. The nearest state campground is in **Nehalem State Park** in the town of **Nehalem**, 11.5 miles north of Rockaway Beach.

WHEELER, NEHALEM & MANZANITA

The three small communities on and near Nehalem Bay are more placid places to stay than the beach resorts of Rockaway Beach to the south and Cannon Beach to the north. **Wheeler** is a tiny village with a public dock and moorage, overlooking Nehalem Bay. Wheeler is centered on Hwy. 101 with several old buildings providing character. The Bayfront Bakery on Hwy. 101 is a good place to stock up for picnics and camp breakfast food.

Nehalem is located where the Nehalem River flows into Nehalem Bay. A large sand spit protects the bay from the ocean surf and this is the southern end of a six-mile stretch of sandy beach. There's a boat ramp to Nehalem Bay and a campground at **Nehalem Bay State Park,** three miles off Hwy. 101. There's a popular arts festival in Nehalem each June and Duck Days are celebrated in mid-February.

Manzanita is to the north of Nehalem, in the center of a seven-mile beach. This is the site of a wrecked Spanish galleon which lies beneath the sea. North of town is **Neahkahnie Mountain**, which offers a trail to the summit, providing good views of the seashore including Cape Falcon, just below the mountain. This is part of the Oregon Coast Trail. **Neah-Kah-Nie Beach**—two miles south of the trailhead—is another popular sunning spot. Highway 101 climbs part-way up the mountain as it leads north along the shoreline and there are several viewpoints with pulloffs on the west side of the road, providing good views of the beaches to the south.

The **View of the West Inn** (503-368-5766) is in Wheeler with excellent ocean views from the motel's balcony. Some of the rooms have kitchen units. **$$**. **Tillman's Terrace Court** (503-368-5464) has cottages including kitchens at 317 Rowe Street in Wheeler. **$$**. The **Coachman Motor Inn** (503-368-5245) at 114 Laneda in Manzanita, has rooms with kitchens along with a bakery and deli. **$ to $$**. The **Sand Dune Motel** (503-368-5163) is not on the beach but close, at 428 Dorcas Lane in Manzanita. **$ to $$**.

The **Wheeler Fishing Lodge** (503-368-5858) is on Hwy. 101 (580 Marine Dr.) with waterfront rooms on the bay. The lodge rooms are furnished with antiques and one room has a whirlpool. **$$**.

The **Inn at Manzanita** (503-368-6754) is a bed & breakfast home with ocean views, in-room whirlpools and fireplaces. Breakfast is served—breakfast in bed if you wish. **$$**. The **Nehalem Bay House Bed & Breakfast** (503-368-7153) overlooks the bay in Wheeler. This home offers two antique-furnished rooms and full breakfast. **$$**.

Nehalem Bay State Park has a campground as well as a horse camp. The **Bunk House Motel** (503-368-6183) has RV parking spaces on Hwy. 101 in Nehalem. There are walk-in campsites in **Oswald West State Park**, north of Manzanita. This park contains most of Neahkahnie Mtn. and the campsites are accessible via a 1/4 mile trail.

CANNON BEACH & TOLVANA PARK

Tolvana Park and **Cannon Beach** are neighboring communities facing the Oregon Islands National Wildlife Reserve. Both towns lie on the Beach Loop sideroad which joins Hwy. 101—north of Neahkahnie Mtn.—and comes out to re-join the highway just north of Cannon Beach.

South of the beach loop are several points of interest on Highway 101. **Cove Beach** and **Falcon Cove** are reached via their own access road which runs west from the highway. **Hug Point State Park** is a 42-acre day-use park four miles south of Cannon Beach, on the highway. There's a good sheltered beach here as well as picnic tables. **Arch Cape** is a small residential community with ocean access, south of the Tolvana loop turnoff.

After you get on the Beach Loop, Tolvana Park appears. You can also get into Tolvana Park by taking Warren Rd. from the highway. There's a day-use park here with beach access and picnic tables. Hane's Bakerie, on the loop road, is a good place to stop for fresh bread and pastries.

Sunset Blvd leads west from Hwy. 101 to the Cannon Beach town center. Cannon Beach is situated on a nine-mile stretch of beach and is one of Oregon's leading summer communities. But beware: the crowds are thick and often boisterous during summer months. The off-season is better!

The Coaster Theater stages plays regularly and the Portland State University runs its summer "Haystack" program. The town was named for several Spanish cannons which were found washed ashore. They came from the sloop *Shark* which was wrecked south of the town in 1846. The Tillamook Head Lighthouse, perched on offshore rocks, was abandoned as a lighthouse in 1957 and is now privately-owned. There's a huge haystack rock sitting offshore, just south of the town center.

The **Gray Whale Inn** (503-436-2848) is a cozy inn with six units at 164 Kenai St. in Tolvana Park, just off the Beach Loop Road. **$ to $$**. The **Hearthstone Inn** (503-436-2266) is another cozy lodge, with four units at Hemlock and Jackson at the north end of Tolvana Park (Loop Road). The rooms have fireplaces, skylights and kitchens. **$$**. The **Surfview** (503-436-1566 or 1-800-345-5676) is a large Hallmark resort, facing the Haystack Rock. The rooms range from standard units to deluxe spa suites. The hotel has a swimming pool and a full-service operation. **$ to $$$**.

The **Best Western Surfsand Resort** (503-436-2274) is a large, modern motel with 74 units at Oceanfront and Gower Street, with a restaurant and lounge, a pool and all the amenities of a major resort. **$$ to $$$**. The **Ecola Creek Lodge** (503-436-2776 or 1-800-873-2749) features large one and two-bedroom suites with kitchens and ocean views. Some of the suites sleep up to ten people. It's located at 208 5th Street in Cannon beach **$ to $$$**.

The **RV Resort At Cannon Beach** (503-436-2231) is at 345 Elk Creek Rd., with full hookups, a pool, store, playground and other facilities. The **Sea Ranch RV Park** (503-436-2815) is a more basic RV park at 415 Hemlock St., with trailer parking, some tent sites and showers

SEASIDE

This it it! The quintessential ocean-side resort town of everyone's faded memory: with an old-fashioned small town atmosphere, the de-rigeur ocean promenade, a main street called Broadway, historic homes fronting the sea, connections with the Lewis & Clark expedition, a river flowing through the middle of town, Victorian bed & breakfast inns facing long stretches of sandy beach, jazz festivals, barbershop quartet contests, a Dahlia Parade, an Octoberfest bash, outdoor historic drama productions, and kite-flying competitions.

In addition to all this, Seaside is a good base for exploration of some excellent scenery. The **Tillamook Head Trail** is a six-mile (one-way) walk to Lookout Rock and a view of the Tillamook Lighthouse. The **Saddle Mountain Trail** is 12 miles southeast of town on Hwy. 26.

North of Seaside—on a loop road—is the famous **Gearhart By The Sea** resort hotel (503-738-8331) where the condo-style units overlook the **Gearhart Golf Links**, a Scottish-style championship course. Seaside also has its own golf course. The **Seaside Aquarium** features Pacific marine life.

Where to stay in Seaside? That's not a real problem. There are moderate and deluxe resort motels with ocean frontage. There are also a number of cozy bed and breakfast inns—many of them historic homes from the turn-of-the-century. Among the resort motels are two Best Western operations: the **Ocean View Resort** (503-738-3344) at 414 North Promenade, on the ocean with a pool and all the amenities of a full-service hotel (**$$ to $$$**); and the **Seashore Resort Motel** (503-738-6368), a slightly more modest motel that also has a swimming pool and whirlpool and is also on the beach at 60 North Promenade. **$$**. The **Shilo Inn Oceanfront** (738-9571) is at 30 N. Promenade with a dining room, indoor pool, sauna, steam room and whirlpool. **$$ to $$$**. The **Shilo Inn Seaside-East** (503-738-0549) is an all-suite hotel with an indoor pool and whirlpool, and all suites have a refrigerator and microwave oven. It's at 900 S. Holladay. **$ to $$**. For those who require kitchen units, the **Hi-Tide Motel** (503-738-8414 or 1-800-621-9876) is on the ocean with large rooms, kitchenettes, fireplaces, an indoor pool and whirlpool. **$ to $$**. The **Ebb Tide Motel** (503-738-8371 or 1-800-468-6232) is at 300 North Promenade with standard rooms and suites, kitchenettes, an indoor pool, whirlpool and fireplaces in all units.

The **Boarding House** (503-738-9055) is a Victorian B & B home with six rooms, all with private bath, and its located on the river at 208 N. Holladay, close to the beach and downtown. **$$**. The **Gilbert Inn** (503-738-9770) is another B & B home: an historic mansion from 1892, with ten rooms—one block from the beach at 341 Beach Ave. **$$**. The **Walker House** (503-738-5520) is well-known for its fine breakfasts and its Alaskan flavor. This 1879 home is at 811 First Ave. and has three rooms.

The **Riverside Lake Resort** (503-738-6779) has 36 camping and trailer spaces with hookups and showers.

ASTORIA

Yankee fur trader John Jacob Astor established what is now the city of Astoria. His ship traveled to the mouth of the Columbia on March 22, 1811 and finally landed in the estuary after battling strong winds and high waves. Within a month, Astor's party had started to build a fort which was then named Fort Astor or Astoria, until 1813 when the encampment was taken over by the British and re-named Fort George. Astoria was restored as a name over the years following the signing of the Oregon Treaty. The first post office on the Pacific Coast was opened here in March, 1847.

So the city is rich in history and the area is replete with historical monuments and museums. These museums and restored forts confirm that Astoria was seen to be an important strategic point on the Pacific Coast. First, during the early exploration days, Russia, Spain and Britain vied for the first sight of new land. The exploration of U.S. Army explorers under Lewis and Clark reached the coast and founded Fort Clatsop in 1805. The conflict between Britain and the U.S. over the Oregon Territory brought a degree of tension to the area and during the Civil War, Fort Stephens was built to keep hostile forces out of the Columbia.

The continuing maritime history of the area is shown in several Astoria memorials. **Flavel House,** now restored as a public museum, was the home of Captain George Flavel, a pioneer river pilot who built this Queen Anne-style home in 1885. Flavel is credited with becoming the area's first millionaire as the result of success in his tugboat and wharfage businesses. The Flavel Home is at 8th and Duane and is open daily. Two other county museums make worthwhile visits. The **Clatsop County Heritage Museum** is at 16th & Exchange St. in what used to be Astoria's City Hall. The museum contains native American artifacts, displays on the immigrant founders of the region and frequent art and photography exhibitions. The **Uppertown Fire Fighters Museum** is the third county museum—at 30th and Marine Drive—originally a brewery building and then re-designed as a firehouse. The museum collection includes vehicles from every era of firefighting, from hand-drawn to motorized.

The **Columbia River Maritime Museum** is located on the river at the foot of 17th Street. Open every day except Christmas and Thanksgiving, the museum celebrates the discovery of the river by Europeans in 1882 and the continuous use of the Columbia since then for exploration, defense, commerce, whaling, fishing and recreation. There are seven major theme exhibits plus an outside exhibit, the Lightship Columbia, which was the last Coast Guard lightship to operate on the Pacific Coast.

The restored **Fort Stevens,** now a state park with a campground and historical displays, was a Civil War relic and then a World War Two defense station. The fort is located in Hammond, on the coast just south of Astoria. **Fort Clatsop National Memorial** commemorates the Lewis & Clark expedition. It's five miles southeast of Astoria, just off Hwy. 101. The original **Fort Astoria** is remembered in a park at 15th and Exchange Streets.

ASTORIA

The most prominent landmark in the city is the **Astoria Column**. The Astor family and the Northern Pacific Railway paid for the construction of the column in 1926. It was designed after Rome's Trajan Column which was constructed in 112 A.D. but this column is built of reinforced concrete with an external sgrafitto frieze. Inside, there is a 164-step circular stairway leading to the top and a platform which offers a panoramic view of the mouth of the Columbia and the surrounding countryside. The monument is situated on Coxcomb Hill, in a residential area close to downtown Astoria.

Charterboat fishing is a popular attraction. The mouth of the Columbia provides some of the finest saltwater fishing in the world: for salmon, sturgeon, rockfish, halibut and ling cod. In midsummer, anglers vie for a chance to fish for shark and tuna. The Astoria Bridge stretches for 4.1 miles over the Columbia, leading to Southwest Washington and several seaside resort towns.

The **Red Lion Inn** (503-325-7373 or 1-800-547-8010) is the Astoria version of this popular chain operation. This one has 124 rooms with balconies and the motel has a dining room and lounge. It's located at 400 Industry Street. **$$**. For a view of the river, there is the **Astoria Dunes** (503-325-7111) at 288 Marine Drive. The motel has coffee in the rooms, an indoor swimming pool, whirlpool and laundry. **$$**. The **Shilo Inn**, another of the Oregon-based chain hotels, is an all-suite motel with microwaves and refrigerators in the rooms, an indoor pool, whirlpool, steam room and fitness center. **$$ to $$$**.

Astoria is one of those locations where bed and breakfast stays offer an historic touch along with the usual comforts and fine eating which characterizes a good B & B. Most of the B & B houses are early Victorian homes, built at or before the turn of the century. **Franklin House B & B Inn** (503-325-5044) is one of these, at 1681 Franklin Ave. It was built in the 1800s and each room is named after a different Pacific Coast lighthouse. A full breakfast is served in the main dining room. **$$**. The **Astoria Inn** (503-325-8153) is an 1890's Victorian farmhouse with a great view of the Columbia River from a wooded property, with queen-size beds and private baths and a harp-making studio on the grounds. A full country breakfast is served to guests. **$$**.

Franklin Street Station (503-325-4314) is a B & B and one of the city's older houses at 1140 Franklin St., three blocks from downtown. The house was built by shipbuilder Ferdinand Fisher and the house is endowed with ornate craftsmanship. All five rooms have private baths. **$ to $$**. The **Rosebriar Inn** (503-325-7427) was built in 1902 by an Astoria banker and was—for a while—a nunnery. There are ten rooms, some with private baths, and a full breakfast is served in the large dining room. The home has been beautifully restored. **$ to $$**. **Grandview B & B** (503-325-0000 or 1-800-488-3250) is another Victorian home, at 1574 Grand Ave., with seven themed rooms and expanded continental breakfast. **$ to $$**.

St. Helens

The city of St. Helens is situated on the south shore of the Columbia River between Astoria and Portland. It's a historic and picturesque town which deserves more than the usual drive-past given it by most tourists. Not only is its location on the Columbia a scenic attraction, but this small city has a charming old-town area. Nearby there are a number of worthwhile recreation areas which deserve a lingering visit.

St. Helen's is the commercial center for Columbia County. This is an area with vast forests sprawling over coastal hills and valleys, providing several opportunities for sideroad and backroad trips. Some of these are covered on page 127. These backroads take you to forest villages like Mist, Veronia and Pittsburg.

St. Helens was first named Plymouth and became a thriving town when Portland was merely a hamlet. However, the Pacific Mail docks in St. Helens burned and the company moved its mail operation to the new town of Portland at the mouth of the Willamette River. This gave Portland an advantage and St. Helens remained a small lumbering town.

Out in the river, **Sand Island** is Oregon's only marine park, with boating, swimming and picnic facilities. A ten-block area of the town was placed on the National Historical Register in 1984. Called Olde Towne, the district features a number of homes and civic buildings which date to the late 1890s and early 1900s. The Old Columbia County Courthouse, located on the riverfront, was built in 1906 of locally quarried basalt rock. A clock tower is perched on top of the building and a periodic steam whistle reminds people of the early river history of St. Helens. The old courthouse is now the County Historical Museum which features displays of marine artifacts, pioneer displays and a regional Indian photographic collection.

History buffs will be fascinated by the **St. Helens Hotel Restaurant and Klondike Bar** which are located in the old 1909 hotel building. The 28-foot bar still remains. The present **City Hall** was first a bank which failed during the Depression in 1932. This building—like the neighboring courthouse—was built with basalt and the two historic structures give a distinctive character to the town.

Columbia City is the nearby village, down-river from St. Helens. There is a scenic walking trail between the two communities, accessed from behind the St. Helens dog pound. **Columbia View Park**, in St. Helens, is a good place to view river traffic. If you're interested in visiting a paper mill, the Boise Cascade plant is open for tours: during summers on Thursdays at 2 pm, and otherwise by appointment (call 397-2900).

There are several places to stay in St. Helens, including two B & B homes. **Cliff-Rose Bed & Breakfast** (503-367-3185) is at 145 South First St. with three rooms and laundry facilities. $. **Hopkins House Bed & Breakfast** (503-397-4676) also has three units, at 105 South First St. $.

The **Village Inn Motel** is located on Highway 30, with standard rooms and a restaurant. $.

PORTLAND

Although it is not on the Pacific Coast, I have included a brief review of Portland because those who travel the coastal routes may wish to spend a night or two in this beautiful city — consistently rated as one of the most livable places in the nation. Situated where the Willamette River meets the Columbia, Portland is a city of riverside walks, parks and a modern downtown district: a good place to base a Pacific Northwest exploration.

This is a livable city for many reasons. First, its not too large with a population of around 400,000 people. Second, the city planners have taken great care to preserve the unique ambience of the city with riverside open spaces, gardens and building-height restrictions for much of the city.

Portland is close to the great outdoors. Within a 30-minute drive, the **Columbia Gorge** offers unparalleled scenery and recreational opportunities including the most popular sailboarding area in the country. The Cascade Mountains are ever-present and close to town with **Mt. St. Helens** to the northeast in the state of Washington and **Mt. Hood** challenging the Portland skyline. Mt. Hood is a prime recreation area for Portland residents and visitors. **Timberline Lodge** is the famous mountain resort hotel and a section of the Oregon Trail provides a historic, high-altitude walk. The **Mt. Hood Railroad**, built in 1906, gives visitors a scenic ride through the Columbia Gorge and the old volcano's foothills.

Portland has a pleasant, moderate climate with the usual wet Pacific Northwest weather during winter months. However, the rain encourages Japanese cherries and camellias to bloom in January and February and spring comes early to this city sheltered by the Cascades. There is an annual flood of blossoms in the spectacular city parks, including azaleas, rhododendrons, roses, dogwoods and other flowering trees of every hue.

Downtown Portland is very civilized, with a free transit zone covering the central core of the city. There are lots of fountains and sculptures on the streets, together with sidewalk cafes, little pocket parks, riverfront activity and a growing number of art galleries. **Powell's Bookstore** is among the largest in the U.S. and a "must" for new and used book buyers. The **Blitz/Weinhard Brewery**—where Portland's famous Henry Weinhard beer is made—is open for tours. You can walk beside the Willamette River or take a river cruise on the Willamette or the Columbia—or both.

Washington Park is the major city park and the location of the Metro Washington Park Zoo. The park also contains the International Rose Test Garden and the Japanese Gardens. There is often live music in the park on summer evenings and kids will be thrilled by a ride on the park's steam train. **Waterfront Park** is another place for summer music as well as the annual "Bite of Portland" international food festival. There are two superb cultural institutions: the **Portland Center for the Performing Arts**, located at SW Broadway and Main includes the city's major concert hall and theatres which host symphony, opera and drama; the **Oregon Historical Center**, at 1230 SW Park Ave., is the city's major museum.

PORTLAND

Portland—like any livable city—is a series of neighborhoods. In Portland, the placement of the rivers create the neighborhoods and in general they're easy to find. **Downtown** includes the Old Town section, at the north edge of the business district. The central core of the city is blessed with a network of parks: more than 5,000 acres of them, including Forest Park—a huge wilderness area— and the Hoyt Arboretum which not only displays an outstanding collection of trees and shrubs but also offers public tours and lectures on the collection. Washington Park with its zoo and Japanese Gardens is also in the downtown area, as is the Western Forestry Center which includes a large amphitheater for theatrical and musical performances. Over 50 miles of trails wind through the Arboretum and Forest Park, all part of the same complex of green spaces.

Southwest Portland gives you your best shot at a panoramic view of the city. The Council Crest Viewpoint is the highest spot in the city, offering great views of the Cascades (Rainier and Hood), as well as the Willamette Valley and the Columbia River.

Northwest Portland is immediately north of the downtown area with chic shops, restaurants, and a colorful collection of Victorian homes. At the extreme northwest edge of the city is **Sauvie Island,** a quiet, protected 20-mile-long island which includes market farms and parks with areas for swimming, picnicking, biking and hiking.

You cross the Willamette River to drive to the **East Side**. The three bridges offer enticing walks with waterfowl viewing and wonderful sunrises over Mount Hood. One of the city's Bohemian communities is on the East Side, centered along Hawthorne Boulevard where you'll encounter crafts shops, antique stores and several fine restaurants. The Rhododendron Test Gardens are located in this section of town, as is Leach Botanical Park which was a private estate and is now owned and operated by the city. Ross Island is a scenic area which is well worth an hour's visit.

Northeast Portland is the largely industrial area of the city which includes the International Airport and most of the city's busy docks, as well as the yacht clubs on the bank of the Columbia River, near the Portland end of the Interstate-5 bridge. The University of Portland is in north Portland along scenic Willamette Blvd. The waterfront promenades—along both the Columbia and Willamette—offer grand scenic walks at any time of day, and particularly in the evenings.

This is a city with pure water (from the slopes of Mt. Hood) and a civilized, cultivated ambience which is hard to match in any other American city. The downtown is fortunate to have several landmark office buildings including the celebrated **Portland Building**, designed in a neoclassical style by architect Michael Graves. Together with the restoration of older buildings in Old Town and well-designed new buildings such as the **McCormick Pier** development and the **Yamhill Market,** Portland is just an outstanding city to live in—or visit.

PORTLAND

The Benson (503-228-2000 or 1-800-228-3000) is downtown Portland's grand old hotel, recently refurbished with excellent dining and full service. **$$ to $$$**. The **Riverside Inn** (503-221-0711 or 1-800-648-6440) is a large hotel with a scenic location at 50 SW Morrison with restaurant, lounge and riverview rooms. **$$**. Also in the downtown area at 1510 SW Harbor Way, the **Riverplace Alexis Hotel** (503-228-3233) is a smaller, deluxe European style hotel with superb service and accommodations, a stylish restaurant, lounge and free continental breakfast There are 74 rooms and 10 condo-suites here and the hotel is beautifully situated on the Willamette River, beside the Waterfront Esplanade. **$$$**. **Nendels**—the northwestern chain—has two motels in the Portland area: The Nendels at 9900 SW Canyon Road (503-297-2551) is in Beaverton, to the west, with a restaurant, coffee shop and outdoor pool **($)**. Their airport inn (503-255-6722) has the same facilities at 7101 NE 82nd Ave. **$ to $$**.

On the southern side of Portland, the **Cypress Inn** (503-655-0062 or 1-800-225-4205) at 9040 SE Adams is a modestly-priced motel with 104 rooms, whirlpool, a restaurant next door and complimentary breakfast. **$**. In a similar price range, the **Best Western Willamette Inn** (503-682-7275) also has kitchens at 30800 SW Parkway Ave. along with a nearby pitch & putt golf course. **$**.

There are a number of fine B & B operations in the city including **General Hooker's** (503-222-4435), a Victorian in an historic neighborhood within a short drive or walk of downtown. There's a roof deck with good views. **$$**. The **Portland Innkeepers**—at the same number—makes reservations at five more of the most attractive B & B inns in the city.

There's camping at **Jantzen Beach RV Park** (503-289-7626 or 1-800-443-7248), at 1503 N. Hayden Dr. The park has full hookups, showers, laundry, etc. For deluxe camping and RV life, the **Mt. Hood RV Village** (1-800-255-3069) is a 214-acre resort with 550 RV sites on the Salmon River including an indoor pool, sauna and whirlpool, store and propane. The 350-acre Wildwood Recreational Park is adjacent. The **Woodburn I-5 RV Park** (503-981-0002) is at the Woodburn Exit-271 with 150 sites, full hookups, heated pool and playground. The best public camping in the Portland area is in **Ainsworth State Park** which is at the base of Mt. Hood, accessed from Interstate Highway 84, part of the Mt. Hood Loop Drive.

There are so many good restaurants in Portland it's hard to know where to start. In the downtown area, the **Mallory Hotel Dining Room** has been a favorite of gastronomes for many years **($$ to $$$)** as has **Louis' Oyster Bar**. **$$ to $$$**. On the East Side: **McMenamin's on Broadway** is a restaurant offering at least 30 microbrewery beers on tap along with gourmet burgers & other dishes in an informal atmosphere **($$)**, and **Salty's** for seafood beside the river. **$$ to $$$**. If a busy scene with entertainment is what you want, you couldn't do better than the **Dakota Cafe** at 239 SW Broadway. **$$**.

SCENIC DRIVES FROM PORTLAND

A **wine tour** close to Portland provides an introduction to some of Oregon's growing number of very good wines as well as a scenic drive for a day or two. Much of Oregon's wine industry is located only an hour's drive south of the city in the Willamette Valley. One wine tour provides an interesting visit to this scenic valley on sideroads in the McMinnville area (see page 127).

For a short tour which includes eight wineries closer to Portland, drive south on I-5 to exit 292. Drive to Tigard and turn west on Hwy. 240 (Scholls Ferry Rd.) to **Ponzi Vineyards** (on Vandermost Rd). This winery is just 15 miles southwest of the city center. From here, continue on Hwy. 210 and turn north on Hwy. 219 to Bunkhalter Rd. and **Oak Knoll Winery** where there is a tasting room and picnic area. Drive north on Hwy. 219 to Hillsboro and turn west on Hwy. 8 to Forest Grove. You now drive south on Hwy. 47 to **Montinore Vineyards** (on Dilley Rd)., and then to **Elk Cove Vineyards** and **Kramer Vineyards**, both on NW Olsen Rd.

Driving northwest from Forest Grove on Hwy. 8, David Hill Rd. is a loop road leading to **Laurel Ridge Winery** which specializes in sparkling wines. Further along Hwy. 8 is **Shafer Vineyard Cellars** where summer jazz sessions are held on Sundays during July and August. The final winery on this drive is **Tualatin Vineyards** which is beyond the village of Gales Creek on Seavy Road. The best way to return to Portland is via Highway 6 and then on the Sunset Highway, (Hwy. 26).

A tour of a completely different type is the **Mt. Hood Loop** drive which parallels some of the original Oregon Trail. This one-day circle drive will lead you around the mountain and along the Columbia River Gorge. The loop starts with Highway 26 from Portland which—after half an hour—takes you into **Mt. Hood National Forest,** south of the mountain. The highway crosses the Salmon River and Sandy River, two excellent recreational streams. **Ramona Falls** is an easy three-mile hike from Lolo Pass Rd. Just off the highway is **Timberline Lodge**, the area's premier ski resort and summer inn. We're now on Hwy. 35 and at the highest point on the tour: Barlow Pass (4,157 ft.). The Pacific Crest Trail crosses the highway at this point. Past the Cooper Lake Ski Area and Cloud Cap Inn, the lava fields near Parkdale provide reminders of the volcano's eruptions.

Then we reach the Hood River Valley with acres of fruit trees, the Mt. Hood Scenic Railroad and the sailboard mecca at Hood River. There are two major resorts in this area: the **Hood River Resort** and the **Columbia Gorge Hotel**. Both offer a unique overnight experience. To the east, The Dalles has been a vacation spot since 1843 when wagon trains came to the end of the main Oregon Trail here.

Returning to Portland, you can take either the unpaved Lolo Pass Road which provides a great backroad experience, or I-84 which speeds you to the scenic waterfall route, a 22-mile loop drive to **Ainsworth State Park** and seven waterfalls.

Southwest Washington

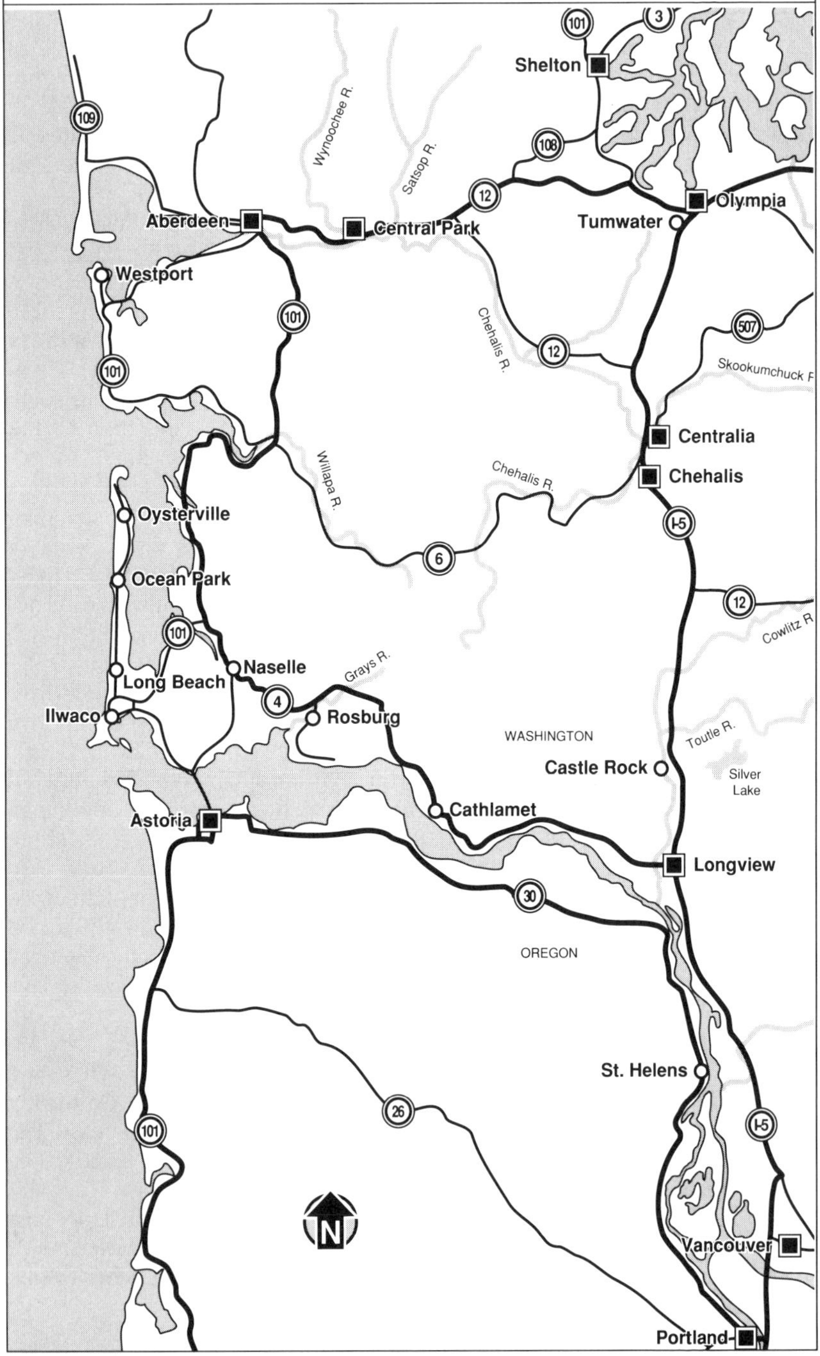

WASHINGTON'S SOUTH COAST

For most vacationers, Southwest Washington means the Long Beach Peninsula. From Cape Disappointment—across the mouth of the Columbia River from Astoria Oregon—to Leadbetter Point on Willapa Bay, this 28-mile stretch of wide sand spit offers vacation towns, state parks, historic sites, wildlife preserves and the "world's longest beach drive".

The drive to and from Long Beach can be just as fascinating as being on the peninsula. From the east, the route from **Vancouver Washington** (across the river from Portland) leads past a steady succession of picturesque old logging and farming towns, state and county parks with campsites, and superb fishing spots along the **Columbia River** and its tributaries. These include the **Elochoman** and **Grays** rivers and both are famous for salmon and steelhead.

Southwest Washington also means taking the ferry to **Puget Island** and its sandy beaches and quiet parks. It's the last ferry operating on the Columbia River. Puget Island is near the town of **Cathlamet** where a small but fascinating local museum displays artifacts of the early logging and agricultural history of the region. This is also where rare Columbian whitetailed deer are preserved in a special wildlife refuge. The town of **Skamokawa** has preserved its historic homes and other buildings in its National Historic District and a remarkable collection of old homes, barns and churches near **Grays River Bridge** and **Nasselle** wait to be photographed.

But the main attraction is that long stretch of beach on the peninsula, while several other attractions make a vacation here worthwhile. The sheltered waters of Willapa Bay provide an excellent place for sailing and boating. The Willapa National Wildlife Refuge includes an island preserve in the bay. The resort towns of **Long Beach**, **Ocean Park**, **Ilwaco** and **Oysterville** feature a range of lodges, inns, motels and B & B homes.

The **Fort Canby restoration**, at the southern tip of the peninsula, is an interpretive center which re-traces the journeys of Lewis and Clark. The early history of the area is available to be explored, as well, in the **Columbia Historical Museum** and the **Ilwaco Heritage Museum**. The historic district in Oysterville adds to the pioneer aura of the peninsula.

The **Cape Disappointment Lighthouse**—at Fort Canby—faces the mouth of the Columbia River. The **North Head Lighthouse** is at the end of a trail, two miles from Ilwaco. There are three state parks in the area: **Leadbetter Point State Park** at the extreme northern tip—three miles north of Oysterville—is a day-use park with hiking trails, wildlife observation and beach activity. **Fort Columbia State Park** is two miles west of the Washington side of the Megler-Astoria Bridge. This park has picnic areas, hiking trails and a youth hostel which is the only place to stay in the park. **Fort Canby State Park** has 250 campsites, a boat launch, walking trails, picnicking, jetty fishing and the Lewis & Clark Interpretive Center. It is—by far—the most popular visitor spot on the peninsula.

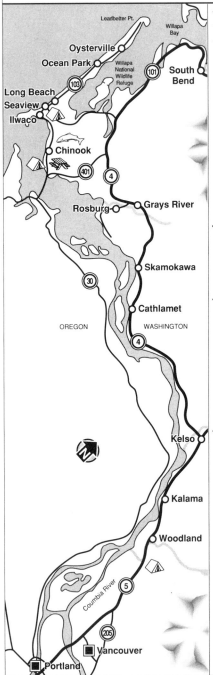

Vancouver This day's drive begins in the city of Vancouver Washington, across the Columbia River and north of Portland, Oregon. The first leg of the trip is on Interstate 5 which parallels the Columbia River in a northwesterly direction. The city has motels, hotels, gas stations, restaurants and stores. Old Fort Vancouver—now restored—was a stockade fur-trading post for the Hudson's Bay Company and, in its day, the area's most important settlement.

Junction-Hwy. 502 to village of Battle Ground and Lewis & Clark Scenic Railway tour. The train station is in the downtown area of Battle Ground.

Junction-Highway 103 to Merwin Lake, Yale Lake, the villages of Ariel & Cougar; the lava tubes at Ape Caves, the Swift Creek Reservoir and the Mt. St. Helens National Monument.

Woodland Gas, food, motels.

Kalama Town with gas, food, stores.

Junction-Longview Turnoff To town of Longview, on Columbia River. Motels, gas, restaurants, stores. Alternate route to Hwy. 4 and Long Beach Peninsula.

Kelso-To Highway 4 Gas, stores, cafes, stores, motels. Take Highway 4 west to Cathalmet and the Long Beach Peninsula.

Longview (downtown off Highway 4) The highway passes Longview, leading west toward the coast. The **Columbia River Bridge** crosses to Rainier, Oregon and Hwy. 30 which joins Portland to Astoria & the Oregon Coast.

Highway Log

Cathlamet Gas, cafe, store, hotel, motel, RV park. Small, scenic village with pioneer museum.

Whitetailed Deer Refuge This is one of two wildlife reserves in the U.S. for the rare Columbian white-tailed deer.

Skamokawa Gas, store, RV park. Town with preserved historic district. Tours are available through Vista RV Park. Tavern has historical photographs on display.

Grays River The covered bridge is the last one remaining in Washington.

Rosburg Gas, store, cafe. 20 miles from Cathlamet. Take Hwy. 403 south to **Altoona** & Columbia River. Continue on Hwy. 4 toward Long Beach peninsula.

Naselle Gas, cafes, store, motels, RV park. Small town in agricultural area. Look for picturesque old homes and barns. Radar Ridge, off Hwy. 4, offers good views from an old deserted radar installation.

Junction-Highway 401 Southern route to Long Beach Peninsula and Astoria Bridge (12 miles).

Megler Gas, cafes, stores in village at north end of **Megler-Astoria Bridge**. Take the bridge to Astoria and the Oregon Coast.

Chinook Village with gas, cafe, store, RV parks, campgrounds.

Fort Columbia State Park Day-use park on Columbia River with picnicking, trails, youth hostel.

Ilwaco Town at southern end of Long Beach Peninsula with gas, motels, B & B homes, stores, RV parks, state campground, heritage museum, murals on buildings.

Fort Canby Restored fort at mouth of Columbia River—now a state park with interpretive center, jetty, trails & campground.

Seaview Gas, lodge, trailer park, B & B homes, store, restaurant, pub.

Long Beach The largest of the peninsula towns, with gas, restaurants, resorts, motels, stores, B & B homes, RV parks, camp-grounds. The new Long Beach Boardwalk offers a 1/2-mile walk over the sand with fine ocean views. The town has a series of murals on buildings depicting local historical events and wildlife scenes. Other attractions include beach driving, amusement arcade, city park with tennis court, Lewis & Clark Monument and Willapa National Wildlife Refuge.

Cranberry Bogs From Hwy. 103, take Pioneer Road or Cranberry Rd. east toward Sandridge Rd. (the east peninsula shoreline road).

Rhododendron Nurseries North of the Cranberry Bogs on Sandridge Road.

Loomis Lake State Park. Day-use park for fishing, canoeing, picnicking.

Klipsan Beach Wide beach with parking.

Ocean Park Gas, restaurants, stores, B & B homes, camping.

Surfside Last public beach access on Hwy. 103.

Nahcotta & Oysterville Towns reached via Sandridge Rd. on east side of peninsula.

Leadbetter State Park is at the peninsula's north tip via Sandridge Road.

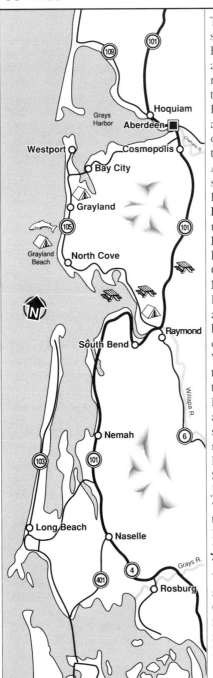

This route provides an extremely scenic drive along the Willapa River to Willapa Bay and then along the Pacific Coast to the resort community of Westport at the southern edge of Grays Harbor. Highway 105 continues in a northeast direction to the mouth of the Chehalis River and across the bridge to the town of Aberdeen and access to the southwest corner of the Olympic Peninsula.

Rosburg Gas, store, cafe. 20 miles from Cathlamet. **Junction-Highway 4 & 403** Hwy. 403 leads south to **Altoona** & the Columbia River.

Naselle Gas, cafes, store, motels, RV park. Small town in agricultural area with historic old homes and barns. Radar Ridge, off Hwy. 4, offers views from a deserted Cold War radar installation. There are two primitive campgrounds along this road, at Western Lake & Snag Lake. Trails lead around the lakes and a gravel road continues to the summit with superb views of the nearby hills as well as Mt. St. Helens, Mt. Rainier and Oregon's Saddle Mountain.

Just south of Naselle is a sideroad which runs for five miles beside the south bank of the Naselle River.

Junction-Highways 4 & 101 Take Hwy. **101 west** to the Willapa National Wildlife Refuge and the Long Beach peninsula. (See Page 158 for the map and log for this route). Take **Hwy. 101 north** for the rest of this drive to Raymond & Aberdeen.

Highway Log

Nemah Small village at the edge of the Willapa Hills. Gas, cafe, store.

Loop Road to Bay Center This sideroad leads to a peninsula and the village of Bay Center. Gas, cafe, store, private campground. There are good views of the north part of Willapa Bay, the northern tip of the Long Beach Peninsula and islands in the bay.

South Bend Small town near the mouth of the Willapa River. Motels, restaurant, private RV parks.

Raymond On the south bank of the Willapa River. This town has motels and a private RV Park as well as gas, cafes and stores.

Loop Road to Willapa and Hwy. 6 Across the Willapa River bridge, Highway 101 continues north, the inland route to Cosmopolis and Aberdeen. Just north of the bridge is a sideroad leading southeast to the village of Willapa and then joining Hwy. 6 just south of the village of Menlo.

Junction-Highways 101 & 105 Take **Highway 105** to continue the coastal drive to Tokeland, Westport and Aberdeen.

Junction-Tokeland Road This sideroad runs south from Hwy. 105 to the village of Tokeland and views of Willapa Bay from the north shore.

North Cove Gas, cafe, store. Village near **Cape Shoalwater** at northwest corner of Willapa Bay.

Grayland Beach State Park Camping & picnic facilities.

Grayland Village on the Pacific Coast. Gas, cafe, store.

Twin Harbors State Park Camping, picnic tables.

Junction-Westport Rd. To Westport Take this road north to the village of Westport—located at the southern side of the mouth of Grays Harbor—and the passenger ferry to Ocean Shores (see below).

Westhaven Lighthouse Historic Site, picnic facilities.

Westhaven State Park Day-use park with ocean views, picnic tables.

Westport Gas, cafe, store. Small village with a scenic location near the tip of a peninsula at the mouth of Grays Harbor.

Ferry to Ocean Shores This is a passenger-only ferry which crosses the mouth of Grays Harbor to the town of Ocean Shores, the northern beaches and the Olympic Peninsula.

Bay City Gas, store. Small village on south shore of Grays Harbor.

Markham Small village.

Junction-Hwys 105 & 101 Highway 101 is the inland route leading south to Raymond, the Long Beach Peninsula and Highway 6 which runs east to Chehalis and Interstate-5. Cross the Chehalis River Bridge north to the city of Aberdeen.

Aberdeen Town at the mouth of the Chehalis River with gas, motels, cafes, RV parks, stores, fishing charters and other tourist services. For strip maps, highway logs and details on the Olympic Peninsula, see pages 166-183.

Junction-Highway 12 Take Hwy. 12 east to Montesanto & Olympia (via Hwy. 8).

LONG BEACH PENINSULA

The Washington Coast is made up of two vastly different landscapes. To the north, the Olympic Peninsula is a scene of dense forests and craggy seashore. On the other hand, the coast in Pacific County—at the extreme southwestern corner of the state—is just about one long beach: from the Columbia River to Point Grenville in the large Quinalt Indian Reservation. Much of the latter coastal shoreline is on long sand spits or peninsulas which shelter river mouths and deep harbors. It's a vastly unexplored section of the state, since most travelers stay around Puget Sound or on the Olympic Peninsula.

However, the Long Beach Peninsula—a 24-mile sand spit—has long been a popular vacation spot and the site of many summer homes. The modern history of the peninsula began with the arrival of the Lewis & Clark expedition in 1804. From the late 1800s, people have been coming here to enjoy the expanse of beach and the quiet lifestyle of the peninsula.

In those days, there were no roads leading to the peninsula from the east and steamers brought visitors down the Columbia River. Now, the peninsula is a 3.5-hour drive from Seattle and about 2.5 hours from Portland.

The chief product of the peninsula (or more correctly Willapa Bay) is oysters—millions of them. Oyster farmers grow and harvest huge quantities of oysters each year (it's a $20 million industry) and some of them have probably found their way to your table already. Should you visit the peninsula, you can be sure that they'll be available in the restaurants and cafes here.

As on the Oregon Coast, the Long Beach Peninsula has become a winter haven for storm watchers. The waters off Cape Disappointment are particularly rough and the winter winds and waves are stupendous.

Aside from the 28 miles of uninterrupted beach, the outstanding natural attraction of the area is the **Willapa National Wildlife Refuge**. Part of the refuge is on the mainland, close to Highway 101 as it approaches the peninsula. The other part is Long Island in Willapa Bay. This is the longest estuarine island in the United States and it is a marvelous piece of Northwest nature. There are cool, damp coastal forests including an old-growth grove of huge coastal red cedars. This grove covering some 270 acres is one of the few remaining reproducing climax forests in all of the Pacific Northwest. The cedars range from five to seven feet in diameter and grow to a height of 160 feet. But the cedar grove is only a small part of this diverse island. There are five campgrounds with 25 sites in all. Canoeing and kayaking are popular pursuits and canoeing is one way to get to the island from the mainland portion of the Refuge or from the Nahcotta boat basin. There are sandy beaches, salt water marshes and tidal flats to explore.

The Wildlife Service operates an information center at the mainland portion of the refuge and has information including campground locations and interpretation materials.

LONG BEACH PENINSULA

Beach Driving:

In the "old days", around the turn of the century, the regular stagecoach service ran up the beaches of the peninsula to Oysterville, where a ferry took passengers to South Bend. The beach is recognized as a state highway and the practice of driving on the beach has lasted until today. It may seem odd, to some, to be able to drive on this long stretch of beach but thousands of local residents and visitors do it for recreation.

Portions of the beach are closed to vehicles and on those portions which are open, the speed limit is 35 miles an hour and 25 mph on the approaches. All-terrain-vehicles are not permitted on the beach because they are not licensed (now you see why the beach is classed as a highway). The northern four miles of beach—at Leadbetter Point—are closed except during razor clam season and the southernmost 2.5 miles of beach is closed year-round. You're encouraged to drive only on the hard, wet eastern sand and not on the softer western portion which is razor clam habitat. Driving in the dunes is prohibited.

Fishing:

The peninsula is a lure for anglers who come here for sea, bay and river fishing. Personal-use licenses are necessary for all anglers and in this area, only Pacific Ocean fishing has limited openings, with the summer season starting in June or early July. There are no closures for **salmon** fishing in the Columbia River and you may fish the length of the lower river from the Megler-Astoria Bridge to the Interstate-5 Bridge at Portland. Anglers have a daily limit—through December 31—of six salmon, 12 inches or longer including two adult salmon. Below the Astoria Bridge—including at the Fort Canby Park jetty—the season runs until March 31st. Updated season information is usually available in April from the Washington State Dept. of Fisheries and charter boat offices.

Bottomfish include a wide variety of local fish including Pacific cod, tom-cod, Pacific hake, pollock, sole, flounder (but not Pacific halibut), lingcod and other species including sculpin and ratfish. The bottomfish season is year-long. Lingcod has a 3-fish limit and all species of rockfish have a 15-fish limit. Charter boats based in Ilwaco take visitors out on bottomfishing trips. **Sturgeon** fishing requires a personal-catch record and license for catching sturgeon in the Columbia River and Willapa Bay. Freshwater angling hours are from one hour before sunrise to one hour after sunset. The minimum size is 40 inches with a maximum size of 72 inches. Tagged fish are required to be reported.

Sport Crabbing is permitted along the peninsula, including the Columbia River and Willapa Bay (and also Grays Harbor to the north). The season extends from December 1 through September 15. The catch limit is six Dungeness crabs measuring at least 6 1/4 inches across the back.

Loomis Lake is stocked with **rainbow trout** for the annual season opening in April.

LONG BEACH PENINSULA

State Highway 103 runs north along the western shore of the peninsula from Ilwaco to Ocean Park. Most of the inns and motels are along the highway with the majority in Long Beach.

Ilwaco:

The **Inn at Ilwaco** (206-642-8686), at 120 Williams St. NE, is a bed and breakfast inn which was built as a church in 1928. This New England-style inn has nine rooms (seven with private bath) and a full breakfast is served to guests. As with most bed and breakfast homes, the inn has a no-smoking policy. **$ to $$. Heidi's Inn** (206-642-2387) is at 126 Spruce Street. This older motel has been remodeled and has in-room refrigerators and free coffee. There's also a shared kitchen for use by guests, an indoor whirlpool and laundry. **$ to $$.**

Fort Canby State Park has a large campground, suitable for tenters, trailers and RVs. There are two RV parks in Ilwaco: **Beacon Charters and RV Park** (206-642-2138) and **The Cove RV & Trailer Park** (206-642-3689).

Seafood is on the menu of almost every place to eat on the peninsula. In Ilwaco, the **Reel-Em-In Cafe** is a longstanding local hangout with a good view of the harbor. **Smalley's Gallery** is another waterfront restaurant with clam chowder and fish and chips the mainstays. Both are in the **$ to $$** range.

Seaview:

This is mainly a residential community but Seaview offers a quieter atmosphere than the busier, more commercial motel district of Long Beach which is just to the north; B & B homes predominate. **Pouslbo Bed & Breakfast** (206-642-4393) offers a European touch. **$$.** The **Shelburne Inn** (206-642-2442) is one of the peninsula's most historic buildings, built in 1896, and is the last original hotel still welcoming guests. The inn is furnished with antiques and the traditional breakfasts are an attraction. **$$. Gumm's Bed and Breakfast** (2206-642-8887) is located near the Ocean beach and unlike some B & B homes, Gumm's welcomes children. The inn includes suites and has a hot tub. **$$.**

The **Souwester Lodge and Trailer Park** (206-642-2542) has a campground with hookups off the beach access road in Seaview. The historic lodge building which dates from 1892 is the site of the "Fireside Evenings", a series of concerts and lectures in the style of the old Chautauqua camp meetings which were popular here as well as in other locations across the country at the turn of the century.

Long Beach:

This is where most of the action is for visitors, from beach driving to shopping, as well as the majority of the peninsula's motels and restaurants. The **Land's Inn Bed and Breakfast** is located in the dunes: a secluded spot, with a path to the beach, ocean views and private baths. **$$.** The **Scandanavian Gardens Inn** (206-642-8877) has four rooms and a suite, all with private bath, sauna and whirlpool, and a Scandanavian buffet for breakfast. **$$.**

Long Beach (continued):

The **Chautauqua Lodge** (206-642-4401) is the largest motel on the peninsula with 180 units on the ocean with fireplaces, kitchenettes and the **Potlatch Restaurant** and lounge. The motel has an indoor pool, whirlpool, a sauna and recreation room. It's located at 304-14th Street NW, 14 blocks north of the Long Beach town center. **$$**. **Nendels** operate a regional chain of motels in Washington and Oregon. The Long Beach motel (206-642-2311 or 1-800-547-0106) has 72 units, on the ocean, with a heated outdoor whirlpool, in-room coffee and the **Lightship Restaurant & Bar. $$. Our Place At The Beach** (206-642-3793) is a smaller motel in a dunes setting, with 25 units with an ocean view and some have kitchens and fireplaces. There are two whirlpools and an exercise room. **$ to $$. The Breakers** (206-642-4414 or 1-800-288-8890) is a condo-style resort with one & two-bedroom units with kitchens & ocean views, near the golf course.

The **Super 8 Motel** (206-642-8988) is one of the budget chain of motels at 500 Ocean Beach Blvd. with some ocean-view rooms, free continental breakfast and laundry. This motel is located in the downtown area close to shopping and restaurants. **$**.

Anthony's Home Court (206-642-2802) has a motel and trailer park at 1310 Pacific Hwy. with weekly and monthly rates.

Seafood is plentiful at any Long Beach restaurant and we recommend the **Lightship Restaurant** at Nendels (see above). Other good places to eat include **The Tides** which specializes in huge breakfasts as well as seafood and steaks at other hours. The **Dog's Salmon Cafe** is an unpretentious place at 2nd and Pacific.

Ocean Park:

North of Long Beach, Ocean Park has less of the carnival atmosphere and offers B & B accommodation and campgrounds. **The Coast Watch Bed & Breakfast** (206-665-5976) has large rooms, queen-size beds, private baths and a private path to the beach. There are two secluded suites on the dunes. **$$**. With a forest setting, **Weather Beach Haven** (206-665-5976) is located on three shaded acres. The **Surfside Inn** (206-665-5211) is a time-share condo-style motel which welcomes overnight guests. It's on the ocean with kitchens, a heated pool and hot tub. **$ to $$**.

The **Westgate Motor & RV Park (206-665-4211)** has a scenic setting on the ocean. The RV park has some cabins as well as RV and trailer spaces with hookups. It's two miles south of Ocean Park. There are two other trailer parks: **Ocean Air** (206-665-4027) and **Evergreen Court** (206-665-6351).

Nahcotta:

The quieter side of this sand spit is the east side, accessed via Sandridge Rd. which runs the length of the peninsula. In Nahcotta, a picturesque fishing and oyster village, the **Moby Dick Hotel** (206-665-4543) is a B & B inn with ten rooms on Willapa Bay. **$ to $$**.

THE OLYMPIC PENINSULA

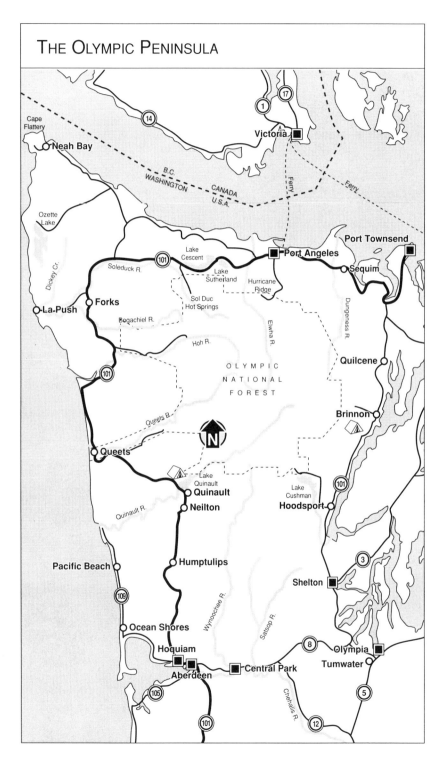

DRIVING THE OLYMPIC PENINSULA

For the purposes of this book, the Olympic Peninsula is the area bordered by the Chehalis River at the south, the Strait of Juan de Fuca at the north, and the Hood Canal on the east. The peninsula has the most diverse geography in Washington State with its dramatic mountain range, the sand of the Olympic beaches and the verdant rain forest in Olympic National Park.

The big question for Olympic visitors is whether to drive clockwise or counter-clockwise. This—of course—largely depends on where you come from, but I have found that if you're entering the peninsula from Interstate 5 in the vicinity of Olympia, a clockwise trip makes a great deal of sense—to catch the southern beaches first and then move on to the National Park and forest areas and then return to Olympia skirting the Olympic National Forest and the Hood Canal. And this is how our circle route is laid out in the highway logs which follow.

We will also explore the **Kitsap Peninsula** as an alternative way of proceeding south on the last leg of the tour.

Our tour begins in Washington's capital city, **Olympia**, at the southern end of Puget Sound. The first 31 miles is on Highway 8, a freeway joining Interstate-5 and the town of **Montesano**. Highway 12 then continues for another eleven miles to **Aberdeen**, at the mouth of the Chehalis River. Highway 109 leads through the town of **Hoquiam**, on Grays Harbor (a large bay), to the **Olympic beaches** and the resort towns of Ocean Shores, Ocean City, Copalis Beach, Pacific Beach, Moclips and the native village of Taholah, in the Quinault Indian Reservation. This drive, by itself, provides quite a satisfactory vacation experience. But the main attractions of the Olympic Peninsula lie to the north.

From Hoquiam, we take the coast route 101 on our circle route around the peninsula. Passing through the village of Humptulips, it's a drive of 38 miles to the **Lake Quinault** area and the edge of the Olympic National Forest. A loop road runs around the lake, taking you to sandy beaches, thick rain forest and glacier-fed steelhead streams.

Then it's west to the coast and the village of **Queets** in the northwest corner of the Quinault reservation. The highway hugs the sea for about 15 miles of Olympic National Park shoreline and then moves inland again to **Forks**, the logging town which is the headquarters of **Olympic National Park**. A scenic sideroad runs west to the sea and the village of **La Push**, home of the Quileute Indians. Another sideroad, north of Forks, leads to Hwy. 112 which runs along the shore of the Strait of Juan de Fuca—west to the native village of **Neah Bay** and to **Cape Flattery**.

Highway 101 continues west to **Port Angeles** and through the town of **Sequim**—close to several important wildlife refuges—until it turns south along the Hood Canal where there are access roads into the **Olympic National Forest**. We pass through several scenic communities including **Quilcene**, **Brinnin** and **Hoodsport** as we return to Olympia.

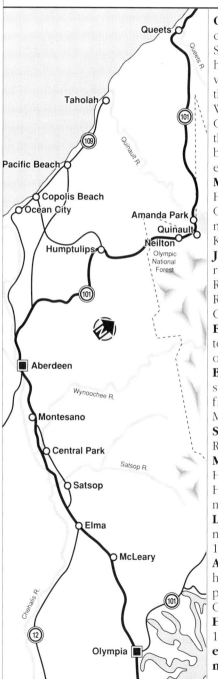

Olympia Washington's capital city, at the southern end of Puget Sound. The city has a range of hotels, motels, stores and other visitor services including tours of the legislative building on Capital Way. The Nisqually Delta, near Olympia, features walking trails through the forest and viewing of birds including great blue herons, eagles and hawks.

McCleary Gas, cafe, store. On Highway 8, 15 miles from Olympia. State Hwy. 108 runs northeast to join Interstate-5 at Kamilche.

Junction-Highway 12 This road runs southeast along the Chehalis River to Malone, Porter, Oakville & Rochester. to meet I-5 north of Centralia.

Elma Gas, cafe, store. Small town, seven miles from McCleary on sideroad.

Brady Gas, store. Village on sideroad. A backroad leads north from Brady to the villages of Matlock and Dayton and to **Schafer State Park** on the Saltsop River.

Montesano Town to junction of Hwys. 8, 107 and 12. Take Highway 12 to Aberdeen (11 miles).

Lake Sylvia State Park One mile north of Montesano on Highway 12. Camping, picnic tables.

Aberdeen Gas, motels, B & B homes, restaurants, stores, RV park. City at the mouth of the Chehalis River. Attractions include **Hoquiam's Castle**, a restored 1897 mansion, **Poulson's Museum** on Hwy. 101. & the **Bowerman Basin** for bird watching.

Highway Log

Hoquiam Gas, restaurants, motels, stores, campground. Town on Grays Harbor, four miles west of Aberdeen.

Sidetrip to ocean beaches:
Take Highway 109 west to Hoquiam and the ocean beaches.
Junction-Backroad leading north from Hwy. 109 to Copalis Crossing and along the Humptulips River to the village of Humptulips.
Junction-Highway 109. Take Hwy. 109 south to town of Ocean Shores and north to Ocean City, Copalis Beach, Pacific Beach and Moclips.
Ocean Shores gas, motels, B & B homes, stores, restaurants. Seaside community at the south end of the Olympic Beaches. A passenger-only ferry runs to the Long Beach Peninsula at Westport.
Ocean City State Park On the beach with camping and picnicking, north of Ocean Shores.
Ocean City Gas, cafe, store, motel, RV park, campground. Small resort village on the ocean.
Copalis Beach Gas, cafes, store, motels, RV parks, campground. Resort community just north of Ocean City. A backroad leads east to Copalis Crossing and Humptulips.
Griffiths-Priday State Park a day-use park with picnic tables on the beach, north of Copalis Beach.
Pacific Beach State Park On the ocean at Pacific Beach, north of Copalis Beach. Camping, picnicking, beach access.
Pacific Beach Gas, motels, cafes, stores, camping. A backroad leads

southeast to the villages of Aloha, Carlisle and Copalis Crossing, then joins the backroad which runs beside the Humptulips River.
Moclips Gas, store, motels, restaurants. Small resort village.
Taholah (at north end of Hwy. 109) Native village, in the Quinault Indian Reservation.

Return to the Olympic Loop Drive:
Take Hwy. 101 north at Hoquiam for the clockwise drive around the Olympic Peninsula.
Humptulips Village with campground & RV park, 22 miles north of Hoquiam on the Humptulips River.
Neilton Village just south of Lake Quinault.
Quinault On sideroad to the east of Highway 101. The main community in the Lake Quinault recreation region. Gas, cafes, store, lodge, motels, RV parks. At entrance to Olympic National Forest with trails and primitive forest campsites. and southwest corner of Olympic National Park. The **Hoh Valley**, with the finest rain forest in the state is just north of Quinault. The **Quinault Valley** has another superb rain forest. Lake Quinault has good fishing. There is a Forest Service ranger station in Quinault with information on park facilities and trails.
Amanda Park Village just north of Quinault. Hotel.
Junction-Sideroad to Clearwater
Queets Native Village, 27 miles west of Quinault turnoff on Hwy. 101.

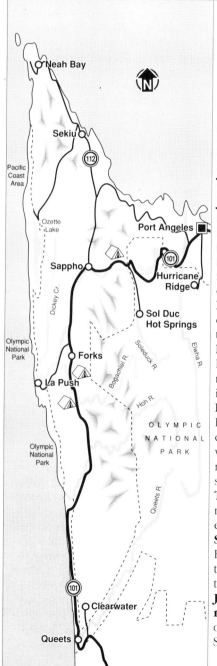

Queets Indian village, part of the Quinault Indian Reservation. The highway now leads north along the Pacific Coast, through the shoreline section of Olympic National Park. The shoreline is protected to the Makah Indian Reservation, at the northwest tip of the peninsula.

Kalaloch Small village with National Park ranger station.

Junction-Sideroad To Hoh Indian Reservation.

Junction-Hoh River Road This road leads east to the Hoh Rain Forest in Olympic National Park and the rain forest trail. There is a ranger station at the end of this road—at the trailhead—and campsites beside the road.

Bogachiel State Park Just south of Forks with camping, picnic tables, on Bogachiel River.

Forks Gas, motels, restaurants, RV parks, national park information center. This logging town is situated inland.

La Push Gas, cafe, store, motels, RV park. Small Quileute native community on the coast accessed via a sideroad leading west, just north of Forks. There is a ranger station in La Push.

Tyee Small community, eight miles north of Forks at the south end of Lake Pleasant.

Sappho Village at junction of Hwy. 101 and sideroad running through Olympic National Forest to join Hwy. 112.

Junction-Sideroad leading north to Hwy. 112 and the Strait of Juan de Fuca, Clallam Bay, Sekiu and Neah Bay.

Highway Log

Sidetrips—to Strait of Juan de Fuca, Cape Alava and Neah Bay

The sideroad leading north from Sappho joins Highway 112 after a drive of about seven miles. Highway 112 leads west to the northwest sip of the Olympic Peninsula and the village of **Neah Bay** and leads east along the Strait to Joyce and Port Angeles. There is also a fascinating sideroad which leads southwest from Hwy. 112 to **Cape Alava** and the Ozette Trails in the northern portion of the national park shoreline section.

Should you wish to spend time in this area, and drive to Port Angeles via Hwy. 112, you may pick up the tour route at Port Angeles with the strip map on the next page.

Junction-Hwy. 112 Turn west for Neah Bay and Cape Alava.

Clallam Bay Gas, motel, RV park, camping, store. Small town on the Strait of Juan de Fuca. This is a prime sports fishing center.

Sekiu Small community on the strait, just west of Clallam Bay.

Junction-Road to Cape Alava This sideroad leads southwest to Cape Alava, Lake Ozette and the Ozette Trails. Lake Ozette is the third largest lake in the state. There is a national park ranger station here and the Ozette Indian Reservation is at the end of this road. Trails lead through forests and meadows to the cape.

Neah Bay Gas, store, motels, camping. This community is in the Makah Indian Reservation. The road leads to **Cape Flattery**

and views of high cliffs, caves and high seas. **Neah Bay** is 62 miles west of Port Angeles.

Return to Olympic Peninsula Loop Tour:

We now pick up the loop tour at Sappho, 13 miles north of Forks. Hwy. 101 leads through the Olympic National Forest for 17 miles, to Fairholm and the northern edge of Olympic National Park.

Fairholm Gas, cafe, store. Village at the western end of Lake Crescent. There is a national park ranger station near Marymere Falls. A sideroad leads southeast, from just west of Fairholm to **Sol Duc Hot Springs** where there are visitor accommodations including a hot springs resort with cabins and an RV park. Lake Crescent, within the national park, requires no fishing license.

Junction-Sideroad to Piedmont & Joyce. This road leads north, along the east shore of Lake Crescent to meet with Hwy. 112 at Joyce.

Elwha Small community on Elwha River, a fishing stream. The **Elwha Dam** is near the junction of Hwy. 101 and Hwy. 112.

Junction-Hwy. 112 This hwy. leads west to Joyce, Clallam Bay and Neah Bay.

Junction-Elwha River Road This sideroad leads south through Olympic National Park to fishing spots and hiking trails, along the Elwha River and the Glines Canyon Dam.

Port Angeles Gas, motels, stores, RV parks & ferry to Victoria, B.C.

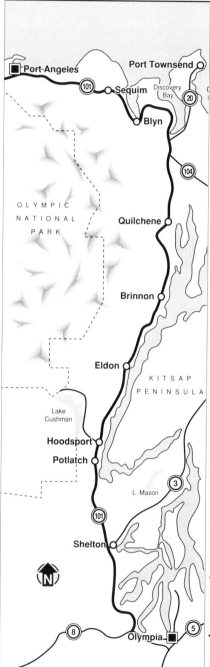

Port Angeles Gas, motels, B & B inns, stores, restaurants, RV parks. Town on the Strait of Juan de Fuca. Ferry to Vancouver Island (Victoria).

Highway 101 heads west through the town of Sequim and then turns south to follow the shore of the Hood Canal—a long fiord— through Quilchene and Hoodsport and then cross-country to Olympia and Interstate-5. An alternate route leads down the Kitsap Peninsula with access to Port Townsend, Edmonds and Bremerton with additional alternate routes to **Olympia** and to **Tacoma** and I-5.

Junction-Loop Route to Dungeness About 12 miles from Port Angeles, this road leads north to the village of Dungeness with access to the Dungeness National Wildlife Refuge. The loop returns to Hwy. 101 at Sequim.

Sequim Gas, motels, RV parks, stores, restaurants, museum. There are several saltwater resorts near Sequim, as well as attractions in the Dungeness Valley.

Sequim Bay State Park just east of Sequim, with camping and picnic areas.

Blye Gas, cafe, store. Small village on Sequim Bay.

Gardiner Small village near mouth of Discovery Bay.

Discovery Bay Gas, cafe, stores. Junction of Hwy. 101 and Route 20-to Port Townsend, Hadlock, Irondale & the Port Townsend Bay resort area.

Junction-Hwy. 104 To Hood Canal Bridge (15 miles).

Highway Log

Alternate Route through Kitsap Peninsula:
Highway 104 leads southeast to the Hood Canal Bridge, to the towns of the Kitsap peninsula including Edmonds, Poulsbo, Winslow, Bremerton and Port Orchard. This is a scenic alternate route to either Olympia or Tacoma.

Hood Canal Bridge The bridge crosses the mouth of the Hood Canal. At the east end of the bridge, a road leads east to the city of **Edmonds** which is nine miles from the bridge.

The road leads south, down the Kitsap Peninsula for seven miles to a turnoff to the towns of **Poulsbo** and **Winslow**. Both have visitor services (see Kitsap pages which follow).

16 miles south of the Poulsbo turnoff is the turnoff to the city of **Bremerton** with its large naval base and picturesque downtown.

Junction-Hwy. 300 To Belfair, and Hwy. 3-to Shelton and Hwy. 101.

Junction-Hwy. 106 To Union and Hwy. 101 (20 miles). One mile east of this junction is the highway to Gig Harbor and Tacoma (25 miles).

Turnoff to Port Orchard & Southworth (11 miles).

Return to Olympic Peninsula Circle Tour:
Junction-Hwy. 104 Highway 101 leads south toward Dabob Bay and the village of **Quilchene**. There is a National Park Forest ranger station here as well as gas,

cafes, store & RV parks. From Quilchene, Hwy. 101 leads in a southwest direction along the Hood Canal. The **Mt. Walker Viewpoint** is off the hwy. just south of Quilchene.

Brinnon Gas, motels, cafes, store, camping. A road leads into the Olympic Wilderness National Forest from Brinnon.

Dosewallips State Park South of Brinnon (camping & picnicking)

Eldon Gas, cafe, store.

Hoodsport Gas, motels, stores, cafes. This small town on the Hood Canal is a handy base for **Olympic National Park** activity. A road leads to the Hoodsport Trail (walks and picnicking, Lake Cushman State Park (camping, picnicking), Mt. Washington, and the Mt. Skokomish Wilderness. There's a ranger station at the end of the road where there are trails into Olympic National Park.

Potlatch Village just south of Hoodsport.

Potlatch State Park Just south of Potlatch (camping, picnics).

Junction-Highway 106 To Union, Belfair and Kitsap Peninsula towns.

Junction-Forest Road Leads northwest into Olympic National Forest and Skokomish River from a point just south of the Skokomish Indian Reservation.

Junction-Highway 3 To Allyn, Port Orchard and other Kitsap Peninsula towns.

Shelton Town at Hwy. 101 & Hwy. 3 junction with gas, motel, store, cafes.

Olympia State Capitol, I-5.

SOUTH OLYMPIC BEACHES

The beach communities of the southwest corner of the Olympic Peninsula offer a quieter, less developed alternative to the busier resort towns of the Long Beach Peninsula or the Oregon Coast.

Ocean Shores began a large-scale development as a tourist resort in the 1960s but their great plans didn't materialize. Thus, we have a quiet dunes community with summer homes, a good 18-hole golf course and plenty of places to beachcomb and to go clamming and fishing. At the tip of the peninsula is the Marine Interpretive Center at **Ocean City State Park**. The state park facilities include a campground with trailer hookups and tent sites, plus placid water for canoeing and kayaking.

Ocean Shores—at the southern end of the peninsula—boasts six miles of sand beaches, a three-mile long lake, a good collection of motels with beach access & ocean views, and the golf course. Highway 109 continues north along the peninsula through **Ocean City**, **Copalis Beach**, **Pacific Beach**, **Moclips** and at the end of the road is the Quinault Indian Reservation and the village of **Taholah**.

Most of the resort motels are in Ocean Shores, including the **Sands Resort** (206-289-2444 or 1-800-841-4001) with 79 ocean-front units with kitchens. There's an indoor pool, sauna and whirlpool and some rooms have their own hot tubs. **$$**. The **Grey Gull Motel** (206-289-3381 or 1-800-562-9712) is a condominium-style resort; all units face the ocean and have kitchens. The motel includes a heated outdoor pool and a sauna. **$$**. The **Gitchee Gumee Motel** (206-289-3323 or 1-800-562-6373) is another place with kitchen units and free coffee, an indoor-outdoor pool and fireplaces. **$ to $$**. The **Polynesian Resort** (206-289-3361 or 1-800-562-4836 WA) has 72 condo-style units with kitchens. Some rooms have fireplaces and there is an indoor pool, sauna, whirlpool, restaurant and lounge. **$$**.

The **Ocean Front Lodge** (206-289-3036) is a bed and breakfast inn in Ocean Shores. **$ to $$**.

1.5 miles south of **Pacific Beach**, the **Sandpiper Beach Resort** (206-276-4580) is a motel with kitchen units and ocean views from every room. The hotel has no telephones or television sets in the rooms, offering a more peaceful way to spend a beach vacation.

Ocean City (north of Ocean Shores) also offers accommodation including the **Pacific Sands Resort** (206-289-3588), a smaller motel with only nine units, some with fireplaces. The resort has a heated pool and is near the golf course. **$ to $$**.

There are several motels at **Moclips** just north of Ocean City and several offer floodlit surf scenes. The **Hi Tide Ocean Beach Resort** (206-276-4142) is on Razor Clam Beach with deluxe condominium-style units including kitchens and fireplaces. **$$ to $$$**. The **Ocean Crest Resort** (206-276-4465) offers ocean views, fireplaces in the rooms, an indoor pool, sauna, hot tub, exercise room, spa services and a dining room.

The northern state park—with camping—is **Pacific Beach State Park**.

OLYMPIC NATIONAL PARK

The Park & The Forest:
The small mountains on the Olympic Peninsula were a fortress not to be breached by the earliest settlers of the Oregon Territory; until 1889, when an exploration party sponsored by the Seattle *Press* newspaper crossed the mountains. Even the native Indians of the peninsula rarely penetrated the loftiest of the meadowlands around Mt. Olympus, for the peak held spiritual properties.

However from 1890 on, the logging industry was quick to notice the great opportunity to harvest the abundant rain forests on the west side of the peninsula and logging began in earnest—much to the consternation of naturalists who lobbied successfully to create the Olympic Forest Preserve in 1897. The Preserve became the Olympic National Monument and then, in 1936: Olympic National Park.

So the center of the peninsula, with Mt. Olympus as its crown, has been fully reserved from forestry. The **Olympic National Forest,** where the logging is still done, almost surrounds the parkland. Only recently has the northern spotted owl controversy brought calls for further cutbacks in Olympic Peninsula logging and the government's withholding of additional major tracts of forest from harvesting has angered the logging community while pleasing environmentalists. Over the years, the size of the park has decreased and increased as the whims of government saw fit, from its original 615,000 acres, to the present area of 922,000 acres—1,400 square miles.

Ecology:
No other region in the western hemisphere has the variety of ecological systems to be found in Olympic National Park. There are three distinctly different ecosystems. The Olympic beaches on the Pacific Ocean are the most northerly strip of wilderness beach in the lower 48 states. This strip of seaside land—separated from the mountain sections of the park—has rocky headlands, wide grassy meadows and beaches which are often piled with stacks of driftwood logs, brought in by the tides and the sometimes-fierce ocean surf.

At the lower levels of the park are the forest valleys. On the west side of the peninsula, there is the rain forest—the most highly treasured temperate rain forest in North America. The valleys have been carved by rivers flowing from mountain glaciers and then gathering rain water which is plentiful at almost any time of year, particularly in the winter. The Queets, Quinault, Bogachiel, Soleduck, Elwa valleys and—more than the rest—the Hoh River valley receive between 150 and 200 inches of rain each year. The rain nourishes the heavy stands of fir, spruce and hemlock with an amazingly varied population of plants on the forest floor, including club moss, fern, oxalis, huckleberry, bunchberry, skunk cabbage and bedstraw.

Summers in the forest are quite sunny and the vision of golden shafts streaming through the canopy, highlighting the incredibly green mosses, provides amazement at nature's wonder and gives life-long memories.

OLYMPIC NATIONAL PARK

Geography and Wildlife:

Think of the park as a medieval crown. At the top, in the center—the diadem—is Mt. Olympus, the highest in the range at 7,976 feet (2,430 meters). This is a peak for only the most experienced mountain climbers but hikers can easily penetrate the mountain meadows beneath the peaks and the glaciers, by taking trails from the Hoh or Soleduck valleys.

To the west of Olympus is a chain of north/south peaks which stand above Hood Canal like sentinels. These are the mountains which are seen from Seattle and throughout the Puget Sound area.

Along the west half of the peninsula are the long river valleys and the rain forests. The mountaintop precipitation of around 200 inches a year has created more than 50 active glaciers in the mountains. Below the glaciers is a network of mountain meadows, and the park's trail system passes through many of these meadows—within reach of several of the glaciers.

The meadows are wonderful places for wildlife viewing. Visitors usually see blacktailed deer grazing within a few yards of the trails. Marmots are everywhere, sunning on rocky ledges and hurrying to eat as much as they can before the long winter begins. Mountain goats and black bears are often seen in the distance, and sometimes close-up!

The lower-level meadows are resplendent with flowers—blankets of them. Here too are the deer who seem to regard humans as part of the area's natural environment. At the westernmost edge of the peninsula is the beach portion of the park and Highway 101 explores eleven miles of the strip with parking places along the way.

Trails & Visitor Facilities:

Year-round visitor centers are located at 3002 Mt. Angeles Rd. in Port Angeles and in the Hoh Rain Forest There are slao information centers at Storm King on Lake Crescent and at Kalaloch, on the coast.

The strip of park beaches runs north from Queets to the Makah Indian Reservation at the northwest tip. Although there is no prepared trail along the strip of beaches, hikers do walk the beaches and the headlands and it's possible to walk from the south end of the strip (at Kalaloch Lodge), all the way north along the shoreline through La Push to the tip of the peninsula and Cape Flattery. You can camp along the way and a week's vacation should do it. **Kalaloch Lodge** (206-962-2271) is a year-round operation just north of Queets, a perfect spot for clamming, beach activity and winter storm watching.

The **Quinault Valley** has two roads leading into the wilderness and to trailheads at the end of the roads which run along the north and south banks of the Quinault River. There are summer ranger stations on both routes with park campgrounds on each side of Quinault and within short hikes beyond the two trailheads. There are commercial resorts and RV parking at Quinault and Amanda Park (see page 170). Chief among these is Lake Quinault Resort, a famous old wilderness inn.

OLYMPIC NATIONAL PARK

The **Hoh Valley**—south of Forks—has the most heavily hiked trails in the national park. This is the rain forest at its best, although people who like privacy get more benefit from the Bogachiel, Elwa and Soleduck valleys. A road leads from Highway 101 east, up the Lower Hoh Valley, passing a string of park campsites situated on both sides of the road. At the end of the road which climbs into the upper valley, to the real rain forest, there is a ranger station and the trail which leads to Mount Olympus. This trail connects with the trail from Soleduck Hot Springs, so it is possible to penetrate deep into the mountains by foot although roads do not traverse the park. The trails meet at **High Divide,** near the **Seven Lakes Basin**, an enormous valley—carved by glaciers—which is dotted with crystal clear ponds.

Just north of Forks, an unpaved road leads west along the **South Sikum River**, past the Klahartie campsite and ending at **Rugged Ridge.** Highway 101 cuts through the wandering Soleduck Valley, turning westward, skirting the south shore of **Crescent Lake**, a large body of water which hosts a collection of resorts and park campgrounds. Just west of the lake is a sideroad leading south to **Soleduck Hot Springs.** This is a popular summer resort with several hot pools, an RV park and the trailhead for the High Divide trail which takes hikers on a seven-mile (one-way) tour to the heights of the park. As mentioned earlier it is possible to join the Hoh Trail for the descent into the rain forest.

The most accessible and popular park attraction is **Hurricane Ridge.** At an elevation of 5,200 feet (1,585 meters), it is reached by driving up a winding 17-mile road which ends at a parking lot and the Visitor Center. Here there are picnic areas, flower-covered meadows and truly spectacular views into the Olympic Mountains. Deer watching is a fascinating activity for children and adults alike.

The **Elwa Valley** has the longest drainage system in the park. This area is accessed by a road leading south from from Highway 101, half way between Crescent Lake and Port Angeles. The trails here, less-traveled than the busier Hoh and Soleduck trails, are nonetheless exciting. The advantage here is the low elevation. The **Olympic Hot Springs** are beside Boulder Creek, a tributary of the Elwah River. The east side of the park has its own attractions, particularly the **Dosewalips** trails, south of Quilcene. A gravel road leads up the steep hills, through a strip of National Forest land along the north fork of the Skokomish River. Two main trails fan out from above the ranger station and campground. The northern trail leads between Mt. Mystery and Wellesley peak to Claywood Lake; the southern branch trail follows the Dosewalips River to Enchanted Valley (where there is a ranger station), beside Chimney Peak. At the south, at Hoodsport, there is another road which enters the park to reach **Lake Cushman**, the **Staircase** campground and ranger station at the Skokomish River trailhead.

For more detail contact the park office, listed at the back of this book.

LAKE QUINAULT

This is the place to stay while exploring the rain forests of Olympic National Park. **Quinault** is located on its namesake lake, offering great fishing plus stream fishing for steelhead along Highway 101 between Quinault and the Hoh River which is a few miles north. A road from Quinault leads into the park and several trail systems. Basically, visitors to the national park have the choice of staying in Quinault or in the town of Forks. Quinault is the rustic alternative, closer to nature and the record-size trees of the region. This area also includes the small village of **Amanda Park** which is on Hwy. 101. Quinault is located a mile down the forest road which continues on into the park. There is a ranger station for the National Park on South Shore Road. There's another ranger station off North Shore Road with trails leading into the park and Olympic National Forest. Outdoor lovers will want to hike the park trails to remote primitive campsites and the locations of these campsites are found in leaflets available at the two ranger stations in the area.

In Amanda Park, the **Amanda Park Motel** (206-288-2237) is located right on Hwy. 101 (look behind Amanda Park Mercantile) **$**. **Lochaerie Resort** has a beautiful site on Lake Quinault. The resort has rustic cabins with kitchens and a rocky beach. It's off the highway, four miles along North Shore Road.   The **Lake Quinault Resort Motel** (206-288-2362) is also on North Shore Road, on the beach, with kitchen units, picnic area and boat rentals. **$ to $$**.

Amanda Park Mercantile is the general store on the highway with a good stock of food (some take-out), hardware, gas, and fishing licenses.

In Quinault, The **Lake Quinault Lodge** (206-288-2571 or 1-800-562-6672 WA) is the major resort hotel. This is an old fashioned hotel, built in 1926. A new addition has 92 rooms. The resort has a very good dining room, lounge, indoor pool, sauna, whirlpool, a game room, in and canoe & paddle boat rentals. Some of the rooms have gas fireplaces and balconies with views of the lake. **$$ to $$$**.

The **Rain Forest Resort Village** (206-288-2535) is 3.5 miles from Highway 101 along South Shore Road. The resort has cabins with kitchens as well as the "Village Inn" with rooms and suites, all with private bath and most have lake views. There is a restaurant and lounge with good views of the lake and the resort offers boating and canoeing. There is also an **RV Park** at the Resort Village with full hookups, a store, gas, laundry and tenting sites. There's a dock and even a seaplane landing.

The village of **Humptulips** is located on Highway 101, sixteen miles south of Amanda Park. The **Riverview Campground and RV Park** (206-987-2216) has RV and trailer spaces with hookups and tenting sites.

A back road—a few miles north of Humptulips—runs in a northeast direction, crosses the north fork of the Humptulips River and pokes through the southern edge of the Olympic National Forest. Another interesting backroad drive goes south from Humptulips to the coastal beaches.

FORKS, LA PUSH & NEAH BAY

The town of **Forks** has been caught up in the Spotted Owl controversy more than most of the traditional logging communities of the Pacific Northwest. Because much of the town's logs come from National Forest land on the peninsula, the environmental campaign has affected this community to a great degree. The **Forks Timber Museum**—on Hwy. 101 just south of town—provides historical background.

As a lumber town and the commercial center for this part of the peninsula, Forks has a good supply of stores, cafes and other services for visitors. And Forks is in the center of an amazing recreation area which offers something for everyone. The town is in the midst of six top fishing rivers where anglers fish for salmon, steelhead, rainbow trout and sea-run cutthroat. The remarkable Hoh River Rain Forest is just southeast of town. At **La Push,** the home of the Quileute Indians, the coast offers secluded sandy beaches, swimming and more sport fishing. Northwest of Forks, accessed by a side road via Hwy. 112, is **Ozette Lake** and the Ozette trails in the Olympic National Park forest and the strip of shoreline park.

Neah Bay is located at the extreme northwest tip of the peninsula, in the Makah Indian Reservation. The road continues to the ocean and Cape Flattery, a wind-swept rocky shore with crashing waves.

With all this only a short driving distance away, its a shame not to schedule a couple of days for recreation based in Forks. There are several cozy bed and breakfast homes in Forks including **Manitou Lodge** (206-374-6295). This is a modern cedar home situated in ten acres of rain forest. **$ to $$.** The **Miller Tree Inn** (206--374-6806) is another B & B, a country house dating from 1917, located on three acres near the Hoh rain forest, There are six rooms here, three with private bath; children over four are welcome and full breakfast is served. **$ to $$.** The **Misty Valley B & B** (206-374-9389) has a great view above the Sol Duc River valley and full breakfast is served in the main dining room of the house, on the deck with a view, or even in your room. **$ to $$.** The **River Inn On the Bogachiel** (206-374-6526) is a chalet-style building on the river, 2.5 miles from downtown Forks, with whirlpool and full breakfast served. **$.** The **Forks Motel** (206-374-6243) is a standard motel with 61 units, heated pool and free coffee—on Highway 101 in Forks. **$ to $$.** The **Far West Motel** (206-374-5506) is on Highway 101 north of Forks. **$ to $$.** The **Rain Forest Hostel** is located on Highway 101, south of town (call 206-374-2270).

There are motel and RV facilities in **La Push. La Push Ocean Park** (206-374-5267) is a motel with rooms and cottages including kitchens, fireplaces and ocean views. There is also camping here. The **Shoreline Resort** (206-374-6488) has full hookups beside the beach and a laundry.

In **Neah Bay,** the **Snow Creek Fishing Resort** (206-645-2284) has RV and tent sites. The **Thunderbird Motel** (206-645-2450) has rooms with kitchens and an RV park. The **Tyee Motel** (206-645-2223) and RV Park has much the same facilities.

PORT ANGELES

Port Angeles is the seat of Clallam County and home to the people who run the Olympic National Park and Forest. There's a National Park interpretation and information center on Race Street. The **Hurricane Ridge** area of the park lies high above the town, at the 5,200 foot level, offering a panoramic view of the strait and the surrounding park wilderness. This is an organized and developed family recreation area with skiing in the winter and hiking & picnicking from May through September. **Hurricane Lodge** (206-928-3211) is open during the summer months and for day-use during the winter season.

An excellent place to catch views of the strait and the mountains is **Ediz Hook**, the long sand spit which shelters the Port Angeles harbor. Drive to the Hook on Marine Drive. You can walk to the end of the spit.

The **Coho Ferry** takes cars and passengers across the strait to Victoria on Vancouver Island. There are four daily round trips from mid-May to mid-September. For the rest of the year, there are two trips per day—each way (call 206-457-4491 for information). Boat moorage is available at Port Angeles Boat Heaven (call 206-457-4505).

The **Marine Laboratory** on the City Pier features displays of local marine life including a touch tank. The lab is operated by Peninsula College. The **City Pier** has an observation tower at its end, providing a great view of the area. The pier also features a picnic area, a promenade deck, public beach and short-term boat moorage. For some local history, go to the **Clallam County Historical Museum**, on the second floor of the old County Courthouse at 4th and Lincoln. The **Peninsula Golf Club**, on Lindberg Road, has an 18-hole course which is open to the public.

Near town: **Marymere Falls** with a 90 foot drop is 20 miles west via Hwy. 101 and accessed by taking a 3/4 mile trail from the Storm King station. **Sol Duc Hot Springs Resort**—on the Soleduck Road—has three hot pools, a freshwater pool with 32 cabins, an RV park, restaurant and the trailhead to the Seven Lakes Basin area in the park (for information, call 206-327-3583). Where else to stay? The **Red Lion Inn** (206-452-9215) is a chain motel at 221 North Lincoln with 187 units and a heated pool on the waterfront, close to the ferry landing. **$$**. The **Super 8 Motel** (206-452-8401) is a budget chain operation at 2104 East First, with 62 units, laundry and free 24-hour coffee. **$**. There are a dozen bed & breakfast homes in Port Angeles including the **Tudor Inn** (206-452-3138), a 1910 Tudor-style house at 1108 South Oak, with antique furnishings, an English garden and full breakfast. **$ to $$**. **Harbour House** (206-457-3424) is at 139 West 14th. It's a Cape Cod-style home—one block north of Hwy. 101—which welcomes children. **Anniken's B & B**, at 214 East Whidby has a European ambience with good views and full breakfast. **$**.

For camping, the **KOA Kampground** (206-457-5916) is 6 miles east of town with 90 sites, cabins & heated pool. The **Log Cabin Resort** (206-928-3436) is on Lake Crescent in the park with hookups, showers and cafe.

SEQUIM & PORT TOWNSEND

Sequim (pronounced squim) is a small agricultural town, slightly inland from **Dungeness Spit**, the longest natural sand jetty in the United States. The Dungeness Loop Road meets Highway 101 just east of Sequim and along the shore of Dungeness Bay, for which the crab is named. There is a marine park at the spit which has been designated the Dungeness National Wildlife Refuge. The **Dungeness Recreation Area** is a county park on the headlands of the spit. The park has a campground with 65 sites, showers and picnic areas. **Sequim Bay State Park**, with a campground and picnic facilities, is just east of Sequim on Hwy. 101. There are a half-dozen RV parks in or near Sequim including **Rainbow's End RV Park** (206-683-3863), on Hwy. 101 west of town, with full hookups and a trout pond & stream. The **Silver Sands Resort** (206-683-4050) is at 662 West Sequim Bay Rd. The **South Sequim Bay RV Park** (206-683-7194) is on Old Blyn Highway, south of town.

For motel accommodation in Sequim, the **Best Western Sequim Bay Lodge** (206-683-0691 or 1-800-528-1234) has 30 rooms and several suites in a quiet setting. The lodge has a heated pool and restaurant. **$$**. The **Juan de Fuca Cottages** (206-683-4433) are on Dungeness Bay with full kitchens plus beaches and golfing nearby. **$$**.

Port Townsend is a charming Victorian seaport at the northeastern tip of the Olympic Peninsula. The town has more Victorian architecture than any town north of San Francisco and is an excellent place to visit or stay for awhile, especially during the renowned annual jazz festival or during the fall Festival of Wooden Boats. It is a handy and picturesque place to stay while exploring the eastern trails of the Olympic National Park and Forest including the Mt. Townsend trails, the Dosewallips Trail and a series of trails which begin with the Dungeness Trail. For information on the eastern trails, see the rangers in the Quilcene park station on Hwy. 101.

The **Starrett House Inn** (206-385-3205) is an historic Victorian B & B home at 744 Clay Street. **$ to $$**. Another Victorian B & B (dating from 1889) is the **Old Consulate Inn** (206-385-6753) at 313 Walker (at Washington). This home has splendid views of the water. **$ to $$. Holly Hill House** is another historic home in the uptown district, at 611 Polk Street. **$ to $$**.

There are several fascinating old hotels in Port Townsend, including the **Palace Hotel** (206-385-0773 or 1-800-962-0741 WA), opened in 1889 and situated in the historic Victorian district. The hotel has suites with Victorian furniture, private baths and free continental breakfast. **$$ to $$$**. The **Manresa Castle** (206-385-5750) is another old hotel with a Victorian restaurant & lounge at 7th and Sheridan. The rooms have private baths and good views. **$$**. At **Port Hadlock**, just south of Port Townsend, the **Port Hadlock Inn** (206-385-5801 or 1-800-395-1595) is an excellent resort inn which began life in 1910 as a wood alcohol plant. The resort includes a marina, restaurant and tennis courts. **$$ to $$$**.

ALONG THE HOOD CANAL

The Hood Canal is a narrow fiord which separates the Olympic and Kitsap peninsulas. This is a major waterway for pleasure and working boats including submarines which are based at the Bangor naval base. Highway 101 skirts the west shore of the canal. hugging the Olympic Peninsula. and providing access to several prime recreation areas in Olympic National Park and Forest. There is a ranger station on the highway at the village of **Quilcene**.

From the highway one can see at close hand the peaks of the Olympic Range including (from north to south) Mt. Clark, Mt. Deception, Buckhorn Mtn, Mt. Constance, Mt. Anderson, Mt. Jupiter, the Brothers and Mt. Duckabush. There are three state parks with campgrounds within a short drive from the highway. **Dosewalips State Park** is on the highway at Brinnon. **Lake Cushman State Park** is on the forest road north of Hoodsport and **Potlatch State Park** is off the highway at the southern end of the canal.

If you want a roof over your head, there are places to stay along the Hood Canal and in **Quilcene** which is situated on Dabob Bay, a finger running north from the canal. The **Quilcene Hotel** (206-765-3447) has standard rooms in this little community on the highway. **$ to $$**.

Brinnon is a village 12 miles south of Quilcene and **Pleasant Harbor Marine Park** is a scenic recreation site for boaters. The **Bayshore Motel** (206-796-4220) is on the highway. **$**. Aside from the state park here, **The Cove RV Park** is also right on the highway with hookups and showers.

Mike's Beach Resort (206-877-5324) is on the highway beside the Hood Canal at Lilliwaup, another small village about 20 miles south of Brinnon. **$ to $$**.

Hoodsport is the largest of the Hood Canal towns, but that's only in comparison to the other villages, which are tiny. Wine seekers may stop here to sample the wares of the **Hoodsport Winery** which has its tasting room on Highway 101, a mile south of town. It's open daily from 10 am to 6 pm. The **Sunrise Motel and Resort** (206-877-5301) has motel units and a campground. The **Lake Cushman Resort Campground** (206-877-9630) is north of Hoodsport on the same road which leads to the state park. Not surprisingly, the private resort has more sophisticated facilities than the public campground,. The **Rest-A-While RV Park** (206-877-9474) is right on Highway 101 at Hoodsport.

Potlatch is the location of a state park with campground along with a few other places to stay. The **Canal Side Motel** (206-877-9422) has standard units on the highway. **$**. **Minerva Beach Mobile Village** (206-877-5145) has some RV and trailer sites with hookups.

At the extreme southern end of the Hood Canal is **Union**, located on Hwy. 106 seven miles southeast of Potlatch. This is one of the roads which lead to Belfair and Port Orchard on the Kitsap Peninsula. The **Alderbrook Inn Resort** (206-898-2200) has motel-type units on the canal. **$ to $$**.

KITSAP PENINSULA

Lying between the Hood Canal to the west and Puget Sound to the east, the Kitsap has several scenic and unusual communities including **Poulsbo**, founded by Norwegian settlers and still bearing many cultural reminders of those pioneers. Then there are **Bremerton**—with its large naval shipyard, **Port Orchard**, near the south end of the peninsula, and **Edmonds**—near the northern tip. The route down the peninsula provides an alternative drive to and from the Olympic Peninsula.

Bainbridge Island (with the town of **Winslow**) is connected to the Kitsap by bridge—near Poulsbo—and is also serviced by a ferry. You can take the car ferry from the tiny seaport of **Kingston** to Edmonds, just north of Seattle. **Port Gamble,** across the Hood Canal Bridge from Hwy. 101, is the only company town still left in the state. Its raison d'etre is the oldest continuously operating lumber mill in North America. Among buildings to visit here is St. Paul's Episcopal Church which was built in 1870. There's a historical museum beneath the old fashioned General Store.

Poulsbo is eight miles from the Hood Canal Bridge, a town which remembers its pioneer Norwegians in its restaurants, street decor and its special occasions. Viking Fest is held in mid-May, the Scandia Midsommarfest in mid-June and the Traditional Lutefisk Dinner in October. The summer festival "Arts by the Bay" is staged in mid-July and again in mid-August. Places to stay in Poulsbo include the **Cypress Inn** (206-697-2119 or 1-800-752-9981 WA), on Hwy. 305 with standard rooms and units with kitchenettes and whirlpools, a laundry room and free continental breakfast. **$ to $$**. The famous **Mitzel's Restaurant** is next door. **Poulsbo's Evergreen Motel** (206-779-3921) is also on Hwy. 305 with swimming pool, whirlpool and free coffee. Some rooms have kitchenettes. **$ to $$**. The **Manor Farm Inn** (206-779-4628) offers rural relaxation in a quiet setting at 26069 Big Valley Rd. NE. **$$**. The **Glen Cedar RV Park** (206-779-4305) has hookups and showers.

Bremerton may be an industrial town—with its naval shipyard—but it is an extremely pleasant community which was recently rated as the best place to live in all of the U.S. The downtown area has been refurbished and Bremerton has a range of accommodation including an exclusive, secluded inn: **Wilcox House** (206-830-4492). This is an estate dating from the 1930s, located on Hood Canal with spectacular views of the Olympic Mountains. The grounds are park-like, there's a pier, the breakfasts are renowned. **Nendels Suites** (206-377-4402) at 4303 Kitsap Way has 102 one and two-bedroom units with kitchens, and some include a whirlpool. There's also a heated pool. **$$**. The **Super 8** (206-377-8881) is another link in the budget chain with basic rooms, laundry and free morning coffee. **$**.

Campers head to the three state parks on the peninsula. **Ilahee State Park** is three miles north of Bremerton off Hwy. 306. **Scenic Beach State Park** is 12 miles northwest of town, on the Hood Canal. **Belfair State Park** is south of Belfair, via Hwy. 300. All have campgrounds and picnic areas.

PUGET SOUND

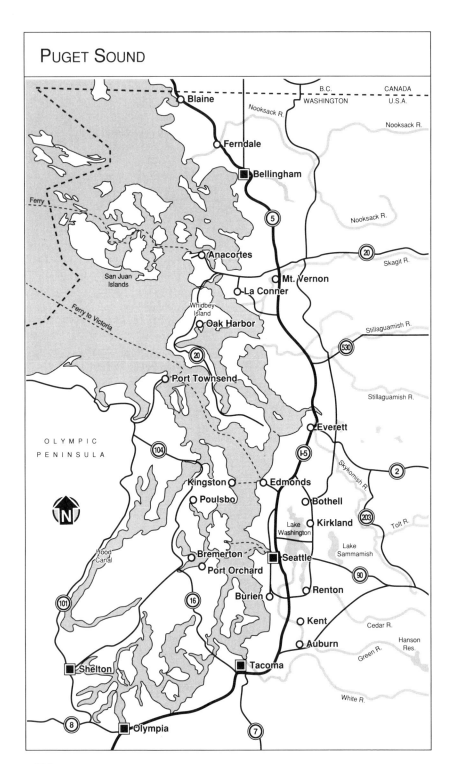

PUGET SOUND

Peter Puget was an officer in the crew of Capt. George Vancouver when the intrepid British explorer found the body of water which now bears his name. Since that day in 1792, the Puget Sound area has been a haven for pirates; then a location for lumber mills, shipworks, airplane manufacturers, and a host of other major industries; then a starting place for thousands of Klondike Gold Rush adventurers in 1898. It is now home to those who live in the State of Washington's three major cities, Seattle, Tacoma and Olympia. Puget Sound contains islands of every description, large and small. Whidby Island, at the north end of the Sound, is the longest island in the contiguous U.S.

The coastline of Puget Sound is filled with hundreds of bays. The Hood Canal, a long fiord, makes a dramatic departure from Puget Sound at its south end, creating the Kitsap Peninsula. Washington State Ferries criss-cross the Sound, taking passengers and cars to the islands and to other points on the mainland including the Olympic Peninsula.

The main highway artery for the Puget Sound area is Interstate-5 which runs north and south near the Puget Sound shoreline. It connects the three cities and many other communities which lie along the Sound, all the way north to the Canadian border.

The communities of the Sound all have their own charm. At the extreme southern end is **Olympia,** the capital city of Washington, dominated by the capitol's neo-classical dome. **Gig Harbor** is a small nautical town with New England-style architecture and an enticing summer music and art program. Nearby **Tacoma** displays its early history as a Hudson's Bay trading post at Fort Nisqually, and its art and artifacts in the Tacoma Art Museum and the Washington State Historical Museum.

A short drive north is **Seattle,** Washington's urban gem—the Evergreen City. Seattle has it all: a waterfront on Elliot Bay, part of Puget Sound; lakes within the urban area; hills to vary the city scene; a prosperous industrial community and bedroom communities which are fascinating towns and cities in themselves; the nearby Cascade Mountains provide year-round activity from skiing to swimming in mountain lakes, fishing in trout streams, relaxing in getaway resorts and hiking the park trails.

North of Seattle, the city of **Everett** boasts the largest one-story building in the world: the Boeing Aircraft plant. The town of **Anacortes** is the gateway to the San Juan Islands and **Bellingham** with Mt. Baker dominating the skyline is the northern coastal city. Puget Sound is a boaters' paradise with its sheltered waters, islands, marinas, and secluded coves for overnight anchorage. **Whidby Island** provides a scenic alternate route north from Seattle for those driving to visit the San Juan Islands or going on to Canada, along with resorts you may wish to visit for a while.

It's no wonder that each year, several of the cities and towns on Puget Sound are named in national surveys as the best places to live in all of the United States. They make great places to visit too!

OLYMPIA

The capital city for Washington, Olympia is best known to outsiders for its government buildings, especially the 267-foot Capitol Building with its masonry dome in a neo-classical style, and the beer which bears the city's name. The **Capitol Campus** is a tree-shaded park with graceful buildings surrounded by gardens.

As with the other Puget Sound cities, Olympia is dominated by the awesome sight of Mount Rainier, a few miles away to the southeast. **Mt. Rainier National Park** is a summer playground for the population of the entire area. For spectacular views, take Highway 7 and then Sideroad 706 and Windy Ridge Road, for the scenic drive up Mt. Rainier. Sunrise is at the highest point on the mountain accessible by car and offers the best views of the mountain's glaciers along with forests and sub-alpine meadows. Along the way, off Hwy. 7, **Northwest Trek Wildlife Park** is a 600-acre attraction which offers close-up views of wildlife native to the Pacific Northwest region.

Less well-known but as important for ecological purposes is the **Nisqually National Wildlife Refuge**, close to Olympia along Interstate-5 (take exit 114). The marshes here provide a resting and wintering area for migratory birds using the Pacific Flyway. The wildlife refuge is open daily during daylight hours. In Olympia, the Farmers' Market on North Capitol Way is a great place to shop for fresh foods or to eat in one of several distinctive cafes.

As a government town, Olympia is well-served with hotels and motels and also has a surprising number of B & B inns and RV parks.

The **Westwater Inn** (206-943-4000 or 1-800-562-5635) is a large hotel with 192 rooms and several hot-tub suites, two restaurants, a nightclub and a heated outdoor pool. It's in the downtown area of the city at 2300 Evergreen Park Drive. **$$ to $$$**. The **Golden Gavel Motor Hotel** (206-352-8533) is more of a standard motel at 909 Capitol Way. **$ to $$**. There's another **Super 8 Motel** (206-459-8888 or 1-800-848-8888) at 4615 Martin Way, in nearby Lacey off I-5 with free coffee and low prices. **$**.

The **Harbinger Inn** (206-754-0389) is a restored 1900-era B & B home with views of the water at 1136 East Bay Drive. **$$**. The **Puget View Guesthouse** (206-459-1676) is a waterfront cottage on Puget Sound, in a quiet, private setting. **$$**. **Sylvester House** (206-786-8582) is another good bed and breakfast inn at 1803 Capitol Way. **$$**.

Campers and RV owners have a wide range from which to choose in the Olympia area. The **American Heritage Campground** (206-943-8778) at 9610 Kimmie Ave. SW is open during summer months and has RV, trailer and tent sites. **Olympia Campground** (206-352-2551) is at 1441 83rd Avenue and is open year-round with full hookups for RVs and trailers and tent sites. Both of the above campgrounds take toll-free reservations at 1-800-323-8899. **Millersylvania State Park** (206-753-1519), with campground, is located at 12245 Tilley Rd. S—off I-5—south of Olympia.

TACOMA & GIG HARBOR

Tacoma is Seattle's "little sister". It was—in its early days as a Hudson's Bay post—a much larger and more important community than Seattle. But even if it is now not as large as Seattle, Tacoma has definite attractions for visitors which shouldn't be underrated.

Gig Harbor is a small, picturesque fishing village just a few miles west of Tacoma via the Tacoma Narrows Bridge.

First the home of the Puyallup and Nisqually Indian tribes, the Tacoma area was settled by Europeans when the Hudson's Bay Company opened a trading post, three miles up the Nisqually River, in what was then the Oregon Territory. In 1852, Nicholas Delin built a sawmill and cabin in what is now downtown Tacoma. He was the first settler. Tacoma grew with the completion of the railroad in 1873 and Union Station, with its dome of copper, stands as a reminder of that early railroad history. The local economy is fueled by Fort Lewis (army) and McChord Air Force Base.

There are several museums and restorations in the area which explain all of this history. The **Washington State Historical Society Museum** has the state's largest collection of Indian and Alaskan artifacts. The **Fort Lewis Museum** and **McChord Air Force Base Museum** both have significant military artifacts and displays. The Fort Lewis Museum chronicles the history of military matters in the area from the first Lewis & Clark expedition in 1806. The McChord Museum includes a collection of vintage aircraft. The **Ohop Pioneer Farm Museum** takes visitors back to the 1800s with hands-on activity including milking, butter churning and grain grinding (call 206-832-6300). Antique Row is a collection of old shops along Broadway, St. Helens and Commerce, in Tacoma's historic district.

Point Defiance Park, located on a five-mile drive around the waterfront, is one of the Pacific Northwest's best urban parks. It includes several gardens, old-growth forest and the **Point Defiance Zoo and Aquarium**, with displays organized around a Pacific Coast theme. There is also a striking Southeast Asian complex with sharks, eels and tropical fish.

Fort Nisqually, transplanted to its present site in Point Defiance Park, contains the original buildings from the Hudson's Bay post of 1833. There are daily demonstrations and the fort celebrates a variety of festivals throughout the tourist season, including Queen Victoria's birthday (May 24). Overlooking the action in Tacoma's harbor, **Fireman's Park** is built atop Schuster Parkway. Its focal point is a high totem pole carved by Alaskan Indians. The Port of Tacoma has an observation tower, at One Sircum Plaza, offering good views of the busy harbor and the Sitcom Waterway. It's on the top floor of the building and is open 24 hours a day.

Crossing the Tacoma Narrows Bridge is not the challenge which travelers faced in 1940. Three months after its completion, high winds shook and collapsed the bridge, which has since been called "Galloping Gertie". Gig Harbor is five miles from the west end of the bridge. The scenic village features boutiques, craft shops and, at last count, 17 restaurants.

TACOMA & GIG HARBOR

The **Gig Harbor Jazz Festival** is held the second weekend of August (call 206-627-1504).

Kopachuck State Park and **Penrose State Park** are in the Gig Harbor area. Penrose Park is on the nearby Key peninsula, down Hwy. 302 and then along the sideroad to Longbranch. It has a campground, picnic area and boating facilities. Kitchen shelters are available here. Kopachuck Park features camping, beach hiking, clamming, scuba diving and fishing.

Dash Point State Park, about five miles northeast of Tacoma off Hwy. 109, has a large campground with trailer hookups, swimming, picnicking and beach activity. It is open year-round. The **Maze on the Meadow**, on Peacock Hill in Gig Harbor, is a walking maze planted with 500 Douglas fir trees.

Where to stay? The **Tacoma Sheraton Hotel** (206-572-3200) is the city's new, large downtown hotel, at 13209 Broadway Plaza, with 319 rooms, restaurants and lounges. **$$ to $$$**. The **Quality Hotel** (206-572-7272) is one of that chain's larger hotels, close to the Tacoma Dome and I-5 (exit 133). It has 162 rooms and suites, a restaurant and lounge. **$$**. **Nendels Inn** (206-535-3100) is another in this regional chain of motels, at 8702 South Hosmer, with 144 rooms, heated pool, laundry, and free coffee. There a restaurant next door and it's close to Tacoma Mall, the largest shipping center in the state. The **Best Western Tacoma Inn** (206-535-3880) is at 8726 S. Hosmer with indoor pool. **$$**. A **Days Inn** (206-475-5900) is located at 6802 S. Sprague, off I-5 at exit 129 with 118 rooms and six suites with restaurant, lounge and heated pool. It's one mile south of the Tacoma Mall and three miles south of the Tacoma Dome.

There are several B & B establishments in Tacoma including **Keenan House Country B & B** (206-752-0702) at 2610 Warner St. N. which offers breakfast to its guests and has dining at night for the public. **Traudel's Haus B & B** (206-535-4422) is located at 17th Ave. Court E in Tacoma.

In Gig Harbor, the **Gig Harbor Motor Inn** (206-858-8161) is at 4709 Fosdick Dr. NW with a swimming pool. **$ to $$**. Gig Harbor also has several good B & B places with views of the scenic waterfront including the **Ketch Krestine B & B** (206-858-9395 or 858-9421). You can't get much closer to the water than this: it's a 100-foot tall ship which was built in 1903 to be a Baltic trader. **$ to $$**. **No Cabbages B & B** (206-858-7797) is at 7712 Goodman Drive NW. **$$**. **The Parsonage** (206-851-8654) is another quaint B & B home at 4107 Burnham Dr. **$$**.

For camping, we've mentioned the state parks nearby (see above). There are several private RV parks in the area including the **Gig Harbor KOA** (206-858-8138). As with other KOA RV parks, this has full hookups and other facilities including trailer and tenting sites, store, etc. at 9515 Burnham Drive. In Tacoma, **Camp Benbow's Lake Tanwax Retreat** (206-879-5426) is at 32919 Benbow Drive East. **River Road Motor Home Court** is at 7824 River Road E. in neighboring Puyallup (south of Tacoma).

SEATTLE

The Emerald City:
Located in the center of western Washington and on the eastern shore of Puget Sound in a spectacular setting between the Sound and the Cascade Mountains.

Less than 150 years old, a young city straining at its boundaries but with no major urban sprawl because of the felicitous geography with hills, lakes, and those green, green forests.

A city with historical markers, including the early settlement by Scandinavian loggers and fur traders, the great fire of 1889 which nearly destroyed the complete downtown district, the frenzied gold rush stampede of 1897 and 1898 which saw thousands of adventurers leave from Seattle for the Yukon and Alaska, the steady immigration to Seattle by people from around the world, giving the city an international flavor; the 1962 World's Fair which brought Seattle into being as a major metropolitan center and kick-started the cultural and economic life of the whole urban area which is now King County—including major adjoining cities such as Bellevue and Everett.

Well-known for its abundant rainfall, yet the amount of rain which falls yearly in the area is less than that in the major eastern U.S. cities.

It's the mist which makes it seem like so much more. And it's the rain and mist which provide the verdant setting for this sparkling city, nestled between Puget Sound and Lake Washington.

Downtown Seattle, like the rest of the huge urban area, is a series of neighborhoods and experiences. The business district is centered around Fifth Avenue, Pine & Olive, with major department stores including the original Nordstrom, Frederick & Nelson and The Bon Marché. There's a new trade and convention center—built over Interstate-5—which includes the area's visitor information bureau. The newly-completed **Westlake Mall**, between Pine and Olive, is a shopping and office complex at the end of the downtown monorail line which leads to the Seattle Center.

The **Seattle Center** is the city's lasting benefit from the World's Fair. This complex of public space—parkland, the Pacific Science Center, the Coliseum arena, a 40,000 square foot exhibition hall, and the Space Needle tower—was the site of the fair and is the present-day location of festivals, athletic events, international art exhibits, restaurants and shops. It's the site of the **Folklife** (folk music) festival—held in May—and the unique **Bumbershoot Festival** which features hundreds of performers of all musical genres along with art and crafts shows each Labor Day weekend.

The **Pike Place Market** has to be the city's soul. This historic complex of buildings perched over the Elliot Bay escarpment has probably America's finest farmers' market as well as seafood stores, cafes, shops and housing, on what seems to be a myriad of levels. This is the oldest continuously-operating farmers' market in the United States. A series of staircases lead down to the downtown Seattle waterfront.

SEATTLE

The **Waterfront** is spread along Alaskan Way, serviced by the city's only remaining street-car line which begins at Pioneer Square in the original 1800s historic district. The piers which once saw ships loaded with Klondike gold rush stampeders sailing for Alaska and the Yukon now house distinctive seafood restaurants and cafes, many with outdoor patios; city attractions including the Seattle Aquarium, summer concerts, souvenir shops and the busy Washington State Ferry terminal at the Coleman Pier. There's a hotel on one of the piers with amazing waterside rooms. The unique **Waterfront Park** has no grass but a waterfall fountain, viewpoints, benches and picnic areas. **Myrtle Edwards Park** at the north end of the waterfront is linked to the Elliot Bay Bikeway—a promenade to a fishing pier.

Pioneer Square is the historic district between the waterfront and the Kingdome with wonderfully-restored buildings constructed after the great fire of 1889 and containing art galleries, book stores, restaurants, clubs, taverns and the **Underground**. After the fire, the downtown district was raised a whole storey to correct the terrible drainage, and the old streets and some buildings are still there. A tour will take you underground to a warren of old shops lit by filtered sun from skylights. Pioneer Place Park has a distinctive Pergola built of wrought iron and a 60-foot Tlingit totem pole honors the memory of Chief Seattle. His bust is also on display in the park. The **Elliot Bay Book Company**, on First Avenue, is the city's largest bookstore with its own basement cafe—a landmark in itself. Seattle citizens are considered to be the country's most serious readers and buyers of books.

The **International District**—hard-by the Kingdome—is a small but distinctive quarter combining Chinese, Japanese and Southeast Asian shops and restaurants.

From almost everywhere in Seattle, you can see the hills which rise above the city in the West Seattle area. Queen Anne Hill and Capitol Hill are the most notable, each with its own network of parks and scenic viewpoints. Magnolia Boulevard, on **Queen Anne Hill**, leads to Discovery Park, the city's largest and most varied piece of parkland. A former army base, this park features groves of trees, dunes, picnic areas, a museum and a native cultural center. Queen Anne Hill has the Seattle Center at its base.

Capitol Hill is mainly residential with Broadway as its main street. Here there are cafes and bars, the Cornish College of the Arts and St. Mark's Cathedral on 10th Avenue East. Volunteer Park is a 40-acre green space on the northern heights of the hill. It has a circle drive and the Seattle Art Museum with its large Asian art collection. Some of Seattle's older residences—renovated and preserved—are in this area.

To the north of downtown Seattle and the hills is the **Duwamish Waterway** which connects large Lake Washington to little Lake Union and beside the the community of Ballard through the Chittenden Locks (popularly called the Ballard locks), to Elliot Bay and Puget Sound.

SEATTLE

The **University of Washington** campus anchors Seattle's northern neighborhoods and Lake Washington provides a beautiful setting for these residential communities. The **Woodland Park Zoo** is at the north end of Fremont Ave. Originally a private estate, the zoo features plenty of room for animals to roam and an outstanding rain forest setting for the resident gorillas. There's also an African Savannah section with lions, elephants, hippos, zebras and giraffes. **Woodland Park** also includes a children's theater and an arboretum; the east side of the park contains tennis courts, pitch and putt golf and a walking trail to Greenlake. The university was founded in 1861 and is blessed with beautiful gardens, an arboretum and several museums. The **Thomas Burke Memorial Museum**, at the north entrance of the campus, has a good collection of native Indian art and artifacts. The **Henry Art Gallery** has an excellent collection of 18th & 19th-century art and features traveling exhibitions.

To the east of Lake Washington is the city of Bellevue and the major Seattle suburb. The "Eastside" also includes the towns of Kirkland, Issaquah and, to the north, Lynwood and Woodinville (home of St. Michelle Winery, Washington largest winemaker on a lovely estate with frequent summer concerts).

Where to stay? Downtown Seattle holds the city's major hotels. The **Alexis Hotel** (206-624-4844) is the nonpareil, a small intimate European-style hotel on First Ave. in the downtown area with renowned service and gourmet cuisine in the famed dining room. **$$ to $$$**. The **Seattle Sheraton Hotel & Tower** (206-621-9000) is located near the Seattle Center and the downtown district on 6th Ave. It's a modern high-rise hotel with room and suites, restaurants and lounges. **$$ to $$$**. The **Meany Tower Hotel** (206-648-6440) is located on Brooklyn Ave in Northeast Seattle, just down the street from the University of Washington, close to Lake Washington and Interstate-5. The hotel has large rooms with great views and the Meany Grill restaurant **$$**. The **Super 8 Motel** is in the south end, near the airport at 3100 S.192nd with laundry & free coffee. **$**.

Bellevue has a string of hotels, adjacent to Interstate 405, including the **Bellevue Hilton** (206-455-3330) at 100-112th Ave. NE with a pool, restaurant & bar, adjacent seafood and Mexican cafes. **$$**. **Days Inn** (206-643-6644) is a budget motel on 156th Ave. SE (off the I-90 freeway) with balconies, whirlpool and adjacent restaurant. **$**.

There are many B & B homes in the Seattle area. For reservations at a number of these, call the Pacific B & B agency at 206-784-0539. The **Chambered Nautilus** (206-522-2536) is a B & B inn, an old Georgian house in the university district with private & shared baths. **$$**. **B & B at Mildred's** (206-325-6072) is an 1890 Victorian house with three rooms and a 3-bedroom apt. on 15th Ave. E near Volunteer Park. **$$**.

The nearest RV park to Seattle is **Trailer Haven** (206-362--4211), at 11724 Aurora Ave. N. with full hookups, showers & laundry.

SEATTLE—RESTAURANTS & SIDE TRIPS

One could spend a whole week or two just eating in the Seattle area: in seafood cafes along the waterfront and in the suburbs, in some of the country's finest gourmet restaurants and hotel dining rooms, and even on a scenic train ride in the Mount Rainier foothills. Perhaps the following listing will help you decide!

There are two hotel dining rooms which deserve some reverent attention. I've already mentioned the Alexis Hotel dining room. This is a small intimate restaurant with flawless service and fine cuisine. $$$. It is fully matched by Fullers, the dining room in the downtown Sheraton Hotel. Over the past five years, **Fullers** has won a nationwide reputation for its fresh Pacific Northwest cuisine featuring local seafood, an extensive wine list and service at the same consistent level. $$$. **Ivar's Acres of Clams** and several additional cafes around town are the legacy of the colorful Ivar Haglund. Ivars is joined on the waterfront by several other seafood cafes which include outdoor patio dining on Elliot Bay. **$ to $$**. The cafes in the **Pike Place Market** are inexpensive places to eat, with views of Elliot Bay. The **Union Square Grill** near the convention center downtown, features a long bar with an astonsihing variety of beers (draft and bottled) and a fancy restaurant next door.

To the east of Seattle lie the Cascade Mountains, dominated by **Mt. Rainier,** southeast of the city. With a day's return drive, you can experience the majesty of Rainier and the National Park which bears its name. To get there, take I-5 south, past Tacoma and exit to Highway 512 which runs east to the junction of Hwy. 161. Turn south on Hwy. 161 and drive through Eatonville (26 miles) and turn left on Hwy. 7. After 10 miles (at Elbe) take Hwy. 706 to Ashford and on along a winding mountain road to the **Mt. Rainier National Park Visitor Center** and the Paradise Lodge.

This summer-only road continues along the mountain base to join Hwy. 123 which leads north to the sideroad to **Sunrise** and the panoramic views from a visitor centre and viewpoint at the top of the road. This is the highest spot on Mt. Rainier accessible by car. You can return to Seattle by continuing north on Hwy. 123 and then Highway 410 which leads to the Valley Freeway (to Kent) and to I-5 just north of Tacoma. You may, of course choose to do this trip via the reverse route, to arrive at Sunrise just before sunrise. It's an unforgettable view. The **Mt. Rainier Scenic Railroad** takes a 40-mile excursion from the village of Elbe and on weekend evenings, it becomes a dinner train (call 206-569-2588).

Other easy side-trips include a day-trip to "Twin Peaks" country. **Snoqualmie Falls** is the small mountain town where the cult TV series was filmed. With its dramatic waterfall, the town has always been a tourist attraction but now the action is intense. The town is 25 miles due east of Seattle, via Interstate-90. The Snoqualmie River cascades 268 feet through the now familiar rock gorge. The **Salish Lodge** overlooks the falls as it did in the TV series (206-888-2556 or 1-800-826-6124).

PUGET SOUND FERRIES

The Washington State Ferry system is a vital part of the Puget Sound area transportation system, serving tourists and residents who live on islands or on the Kitsap and Olympic peninsulas and who commute to work in Seattle.

The ferries generally cross Puget Sound from east to west and vice-versa. Service is expanded on some routes during the busier summer months. In the Seattle-Tacoma area there are five ferry terminals and we'll list them from south to north.

There is a short ferry crossing from **Fort Defiance** (Tacoma) to the south end of **Vashon Island** (Tahlequa). The schedule is approximately hourly both ways from 6 am to 1 am.

Ferries depart from **Fauntleroy** (south of Seattle) to **Vashon Island** and to the Kitsap Peninsula (Southworth). These commuter runs are more frequent in the early morning and late afternoon with runs during the day at least hourly.

From the Coleman Dock in downtown **Seattle**, ferries run to **Bainbridge Island** (Winslow) and to the **Kitsap Peninsula** (Bremerton). These are also commuter routes with frequent runs in the morning and afternoon periods. Crossing time to Winslow: 35 minutes; to Bremerton: 60 minutes.

From **Edmonds**, north of Seattle, a ferry cruises to the **Kitsap Peninsula**, to the small port of Kingston. Crossing time is 30 minutes.

Mukilteo is the southern suburb of Everett, north of Edmonds. A ferry leaves **Mukilteo** for the south end of **Whidby Island**, at Clinton. This run takes 20 minutes and the schedule is frequent.

While on Whidby Island, you can take a short ferry ride from **Keystone**, half way up the island, to **Port Townsend**, the picturesque community at the top of the Kitsap Peninsula. Crossing time is 30 minutes.

At the north end of Puget Sound (the Gulf of Georgia—to be more accurate) there is ferry service from **Anacortes** which stops at four of the **San Juan Islands** (**Lopez, Shaw, Orcas** and **San Juan**). All ferries do not stop at all of the islands. Once a day (more during summer months), the ferry continues on to Sidney on Vancouver Island permitting travelers to drive to Victoria and points north on Vancouver Island. The first ferry leaves Anacortes at 6 am with at least nine sailings to one or more islands during the day (more during weekends and summer weekdays). The ferry stops more frequently on Orcas and San Juan.

For information on all Puget Sound ferries, call the followng telephone numbers:

Schedule information: (you get people at these numbers) 206-464-6400 or 1-800-542-7052 or 0810 (WA)

Recorded Schedule Information: 206-624-4500, then press 2840 or 1-800-252-4550, then press 2840

International sailings (Victoria): 604-381-1551 or 656-1531.

WHIDBY ISLAND

This long, thin island snakes up Puget Sound from just north of Seattle to the top of the Sound, near the town of Anacortes. It forms a land bridge for travelers who can use the island route to make their way north toward Canada or to the San Juan Islands. From the south, you get there via a ferry from Mukilteo, to the south of the city of Everett. From the north, there's a bridge at Deception Pass State Park.

Whidby is a fascinating island, with some strange customs. The island's transit system (busses) doesn't charge fares. You ride for free! It's funded by a 3% sales tax and vehicle taxes. It's the loganberry capital of the U.S. **Whidby's Greenbank Farm** grows more loganberries than any other farm in the world and the berries go into making the island's famous liqueur and jams. The island has an underwater park—next to the ferry landing at Keystone—where divers can see a panorama of undersea life including fast-moving scallops, giant barnacles and gherkins.

Deception Pass State Park, is on the island—and off the island—with the bridge joining the two sections which are separated by a narrow passage of water flowing through high cliffs. There is camping here as well as scenic beachcombing and walking trails on both sides of the pass. The pass was named after Spanish captains failed to see the cut between Whidby and Fidalgo Islands and the British—who came later—found it and named it Deception Pass.

The island is a mixture of green farmers' fields, marshy wetlands and picturesque villages along the coast. You'll want to visit **Greenbank Farm**, and sample the loganberry products. It's located about half-way up the island just north of Greenbank. The wetlands are at the south end of the island, around Useless Bay, with tidal and fresh water marshes and many small islands. More than 100 types of birds inhabit Useless Bay. There are beaches at four state parks in South Whidby: Possession Beach, Freeland, Maxwelton Beach and South Whidby. All have picnic areas. The villages of **Clinton** and **Langley** (at the south) and **Coupeville** (toward the north) are all on the east side of the island overlooking sheltered water. All are quaint little towns with resort accommodations. **Oak Harbor** is the major community on the island, near the north end with a naval air base nearby.

The **Inn at Langley** (206-221-3033) is a popular resort in the southern island community. It has a respected dining room and a great view of Saratoga Passage. **$$ to $$$**. Most of the resort inns are in and near Coupeville including **The Coupeville Inn** (206-678-6668) **$$**, and the **Captain Whidby Inn** (206-678-4097) which is constructed of madrona logs, and has a restaurant, lounge & units with kitchenettes. **$$**. The **Inn at Penn Cove** (206-678-8000) at Coupeville, is a B & B which has two adjacent Victorian houses. The rooms have private baths. **$$**. The **Colonel Crockett Farm B & B** (206-678-3711) is an 1855 Victorian farm house overlooking Admiralty Bay on the island's west side. There are four rooms and a buffet breakfast is served. **$$**.

ANACORTES

This town on Fidalgo Island is separated from the mainland by Swinomish Channel over which a bridge takes visitors rushing to catch the ferry to the San Juan Islands. Some arrive in Anacortes too late to make the ferry and so some advice on where to stay is necessary. And even if you don't arrive late, you may wish to stay in or around Anacortes.

Fidalgo Island was named for Lt. Salvador Fidalgo, an officer on the explorer ship *San Carlos.* Ship Harbor—now Anacortes—was settled in 1860 and was a Pacific whaling station. There are now two oil refineries on the island as well as fish processing plants. Fidalgo provides the highway link to Whidby Island (to the south) and to the ferry terminal beyond Anacortes which takes cars and passengers to four of the San Juan Islands and to Victoria B.C.

Boating is very big in Anacortes. It is the site of several large marinas and shipbuilding companies. Anacortes sounds Spanish and it is. But the town was named for Anna Curtis, the wife of a Canadian who bought land around Ship Harbor and named the area for his wife—but with a Spanish accent.

You may wish to visit **Washington Park**, the town's largest and a fine place for cycling, picnicking or walking. There's a campground here. **Causland Memorial Park** includes a World War One memorial with walking paths, floral displays and mosaic walls. The **Anacortes Museum** displays artifacts from close to home and across the Pacific Northwest region.

The **Ship Harbor Inn** (206-293-5177) or 1-800-852-8568 WA or 1-800-235-8568 Canada) is convenient for those who are waiting for the ferry to make its first run in the morning. It overlooks the ferry terminal and is a place to leave your car if you opt to walk or bicycle your way around an island or two. The inn has fireplaces in some of the rooms and kitchen units. **$ to $$**. The **Anacortes Inn** (206-293-3153 or 1-800-327-7976 WA) is downtown but less than 15-minutes' drive from the ferry at 3006 Commercial St. It has a heated pool. **$ to $$**.

The Majestic (206-293-3355) is a small, older hotel in the European style with 23 rooms, all decorated differently with decks and views, hot tubs and wet bars. The hotel boasts a Victorian pub with dining and a good collection of beers and "spirits". **$ to $$**.

There are several B & B homes in Anacortes which will provide you with cozy, intimate lodging, including the **Admiral's Hideaway** (206-293-1016) at 1318 30th Street with swimming pool. **$$**. Continuing on a nautical note, the **Albatross** (206-293-0677) is at 5708 Kingsway. **$ to $$**. The **Hasty Pudding House** (206-293-5773) is at 1312 8th Street in Anacortes. **$ to $$**. Another B & B, the **Cap Santé** (206-293-0602) is located at 906 9th Street.

The Sunset **B & B** is at 100 Sunset Beach—a picturesque spot—with a restaurant and room service. **$$**.

La Conner & Chuckanut Drive

The whole town of La Conner is a Registered Historic Site. The only word I can think of to describe La Conner is *"quaint"*. It's a New England—styled seaport but it's not on the sea. It's located on Swinomish Channel, near Puget Sound, on the mainland just south of Fidalgo Island. It's connected to the island and the Swinomish Indian Reservation by the Rainbow Bridge, an award-winning piece of construction which opened in 1958. The town was settled in 1868 when Thomas Hayes opened a trading post where Totem Pole Park is now located. In 1870, John Conner purchased the post and established a post office, re-naming the town from Swinomish to La Conner—to honor his wife Louisa A. Conner. Who said northwest people weren't creative?

La Conner is a community of fishermen, writers, artists, crafts people and farmers. Some service the growing tourist trade. The village is a getaway location for Seattleites who come here to walk along the channel, eat seafood in the restaurants, drink in the tavern and stay in the cozy hotels and B & B places. There's a sizeable charter boat business here with anglers sailing into Puget Sound to catch salmon and other fish. The town experiences a huge smelt run in the winter months as millions of the little fish swarm up the channel.

Built as a bank, the **Town Hall** is a triangular-shaped building which is one of the original buildings here; next door is the **Magnus Andersen Cabin**, an early pioneer home, built in 1869. The **Gaches Mansion** at 2nd and Benton was built in 1891. Its 22 rooms have been restored and the house is open for weekend viewing. Its 2nd floor is home to the **Valley Museum of Northwest Art**. The **Skagit County Museum** on 4th Ave. houses a collection of local farming and pioneer artifacts with pictorial displays on Skagit Valley agriculture and Mount Baker. The museum is open Wednesday through Sunday.

The **La Conner Country Inn** (206-466-3101) is a modern, yet cozy, motor hotel with fireplaces in every room and free continental breakfast. It also includes the excellent restaurant **Barkley's of La Conner**. **$$ to $$$**. The **Heron** (206-466-4626) is a Victorian inn with private baths, hot tub and continental breakfast. **$$**. The **Heather House** (206-466-4675) is a B & B home at 505 Maple Ave. **$$**. The **Rainbow Inn B & B** (206-466-4578) has eight rooms in a country home with hot tub and full breakfast served. **$$**.

Camping is permitted in **Pioneer Park**, next to the Rainbow Bridge. The **Potlatch RV Resort** (206-466-4468) has full hookups and other camping facilities at 410 Pearle Jensen Way.

Running north from Highway 20 is Highway 11: **Chuckanut Drive**. This is one of the most scenic short drives on the Pacific Coast, hugging the shoreline cliffs as it winds along Puget Sound. It is definitely our preferred route to Bellingham and points north. Along the way are two seafood restaurants, the **Oyster Bar** and the **Oyster Creek Inn**. Both are recommended. **Larabee State Park**, with a campground, is on the Drive.

BELLINGHAM AND POINTS NORTH

Interstate-5 connects the city of **Bellingham** with the more southern cities of Washington state. This is a growing urban center with a busy port including the recently-established **Alaska State Ferry Terminal.** Once a week the large car ferries dock here to pick up travelers to the Alaskan Panhandle. Bellingham and the smaller communities to the north are in Whatcom County, the gateway to Canada and to the northern Cascade Mountains. **The Whatcom County Museum of History & Art** is in the old, ornate, former City Hall.

Mt. Baker—a high volcano—dominates the skyline throughout this area. The mountain is in the center of the **Mt. Baker Wilderness Area**, a protected tract of forest which encompasses several separate activity regions, including the popular **Mt. Baker Ski Area** on the north side of the mountain reached by taking Highway 542 from just north Bellingham. This highway is also part of the **North Cascades International Loop Drive** which runs south of the international border, breaching the Cascades and then circling through southern British Columbia before returning to the U.S. at **Blaine,** the northernmost town on the Puget Sound coast.

Between Bellingham and Blaine there are two small communities on the I-5 corridor: **Ferndale** and **Birch Bay**. The charming village of **Lyndon**—settled by Dutch immigrants—is inland, 25 miles from Bellingham and close to the Canadian border in the fertile Nooksack River Valley.

This part of Washington is fast becoming a resort region which is typified by the deluxe **Inn at Semi-Ah-Moo** near Birch Bay (206-371-2000 or 1-800-854-2608 US or 1-800-854-6742 Canada). What used to be a fish cannery has been expanded into a seaside golf resort and conference center. The resort has a scenic seafood restaurant, cruises to the San Juan Islands and all the other amenities of a first-class resort. **$$ to $$$**.

Another fine resort is **The Resort at Sudden Valley** (206-734-6430) at 2145 Lake Whatcom Blvd., eight miles from downtown Bellingham. The resort has a championship golf course and Lake Whatcom is nearby. **$$ to $$$**.

For an overnight stay in Bellingham, the **Park Motel** (206-733-8280 or 1-800-732-1225) is at 101 N. Samish Way, just off I-5 at exit 252. The motel has a sauna and whirlpool and serves continental breakfast. **$ to $$**. The **Coachman Inn** (206-671-9000 or 1-800-732-1225 US) is at 120 N Samish Way with 60 rooms, swimming pool, a sauna and whirlpool. **$ to $$**.

Springcrest Farms (206-966-7272) is a country B & B home at 6058 Everson St. (via Goshen Rd.) in Bellingham. **$ to $$**. The **Willows Inn**, another B & B, is at 2579 West Shore Drive on Lummi Island, just north of the city. **$ to $$**. The nearest public campground is at **Larrabee State Park**, on Chuckanut Drive, south of town. There are RV parks to spare in Birch Bay including **Ball Bay View RV Park** on Jackson Rd. (206-371-0334); **Beachside RV Park** (206-371-5962) on Birch Bay Dr.; and **Birch Bay RV Resort** (206--371--7922) on Harbor View Rd. There are public camping in **Birch Bay State Park**, at 5105 Helwig Road.

SAN JUAN ISLANDS

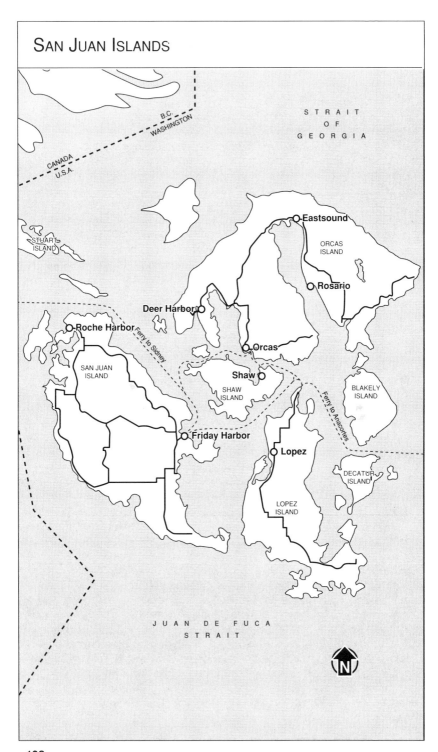

STRAIT OF GEORGIA

B.C. WASHINGTON

CANADA U.S.A.

STUART ISLAND

Eastsound

ORCAS ISLAND

Rosario

Deer Harbor

Roche Harbor

Ferry to Sidney

Orcas

SAN JUAN ISLAND

Shaw

SHAW ISLAND

BLAKELY ISLAND

Ferry to Anacortes

Friday Harbor

Lopez

DECATUR ISLAND

LOPEZ ISLAND

JUAN DE FUCA STRAIT

N

SAN JUAN ISLANDS

The 273 islands of the San Juan archipelago can only be described as magical. I have returned time and time again to these tranquil islands which make up the northwest corner of the southern 48 states and find each time a remarkable sense of repose and rejuvenation.

The Lummi Indians, who first inhabited the islands, believed that human life began in the wilderness of San Juan Island and that the islands were sacred places. Explorations by Spanish, Russian, British and (later) Americans made life difficult for the natives but today's island residents believe that the islands are indeed special — and they are!

Washington State car ferries bring visitors to the four largest islands from Anacortes. In order of ferry landings they are: Lopez, Shaw, Orcas and San Juan. Some of the ferry runs end in Sidney on Canada's Vancouver Island.

The islands — particularly San Juan Island — are steeped in history. Spanish explorers Perez Heceta and Lopez de Haro arrived to chart the waters in the 1770s and 1780s. The English arrived in 1792 when Capt. George Vancouver charted the interior channels and bays and convinced the Russians to withdraw. But the Hudson's Bay settlements piqued American interest in the area and in 1841, an expedition under Capt. John Wilkes brought the beginning of a period of international conflict over these gems in the sparkling blue waters of north Puget Sound.

The infamous "Pig War" began when an American farmer shot a Hudson's Bay Company pig which was rooting through his potato patch. The incident brought British troops to San Juan Island and precipitated a lengthy but peaceful "war" over which country owned the archipelago. The matter was settled by arbitration, by — of all people — Kaiser Wilhelm I, in 1872. He ruled in favor of the United States and the British withdrew. The two garrison sites — "British Camp" and "American Camp" — are now parts of a national park which commemorates the period of conflict.

The side roads of the islands provide drivers and cyclists with peaceful recreation. There are state and county parks throughout the island chain. Some of Washington state's prime resorts are located here, along with many bed and breakfast homes which provide restful stays in sea-side locations and in the verdant countryside.

San Juan Island is the most populated with the county seat in Friday Harbor. **Orcas Island** is known as the "Resort Island", for the vacation resorts which are located on this upsidedown U-shaped island. Chief among these is the famed Rosario Resort. **Lopez Island** has less accommodation but makes a wonderful day-long visit with overnight stays possible in several rustic resorts. Lopez with its waterfront parks, high bluffs and two public camping parks is ideal for nature lovers who wish to stroll on sand spits and to view nature at its best. **Shaw Island** has no overnight lodging and few campsites but provides a peaceful, rural ambience for day visitors.

SAN JUAN ISLAND

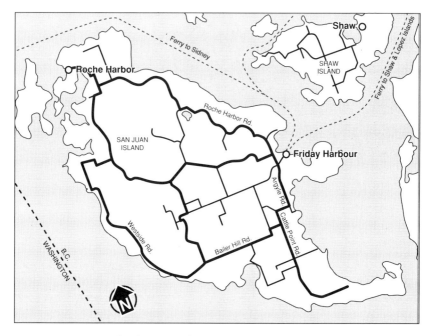

San Juan is the busiest of the islands and the most populated but this is only relative to the other islands. Compared to the mainland, life here is relaxed with rural countryside everywhere but in the center of the small town of **Friday Harbor**.

Friday Harbor is the seat of San Juan County. It's the final island stop on the ferry route from Anacortes and the scene of a celebrated Dixieland Jazz festival held each July. The island has the most varied terrain of the San Juans — with small mountains, agricultural valleys and a stunning coastline which is accessible by car or bicycle.

Overnight facilities are available in Friday Harbor and around the island and range from an historic resort at Roche Harbor to B & B homes scattered across the island, to two modern motels in Friday Harbor. There are two private RV parks and one public campground in the county park at Smallpox Bay.

The earliest settlement was San Juan Town, located at the southwest edge of the island where the American Camp portion of the national park now commemorates the early history of the island. Few traces of the settlement remain and the focus of life on the island is Friday Harbor.

The University of Washington operates two scientific facilities which are open to the public. North of Friday Harbor is the marine laboratory where tours are available. A 200-acre biological preserve on False Bay offers a fine opportunity to observe intertidal life at low tide.

SAN JUAN ISLAND - FRIDAY HARBOR

This small town is home to 1,000 people with a short main street and several fine public amenities including the new San Juan Community Theater & Performing Arts Center which offers a variety of live entertainment. The public marina is a favorite of boats from the U.S. and Canada and includes a B & B sailing ship.

The **San Juan Historical Museum**, at 405 Price Street, is a homestead from the 1890s with displays of local pioneer artifacts. It's open Wed-Sat. from 1 pm to 4:30 pm from early June through Labor Day. The **Whale Museum**, located in the second-oldest building in Friday Harbor at 62 First St. North, is devoted solely to whale life and features a 2/3rds scale skeleton of an Orca and a lifesize model of a baby Humpback whale. Exhibits include data on the Orca pods which feed in the waters off the San Juans. It's open from 10 am to 4 pm in summer months (admission fee).

Art galleries, book stores, cafes and grocery stores are found on Spring Street and connecting streets. The National Park Service operates a visitor information center on Spring Street. Here you may obtain a map for an historic walking tour of the town. Cycling is a favorite way of getting around the island and bicycles may be rented from Island Bicycles at 380 Argyll (call 206-378-4941) Many visitors leave their cars on the mainland and use bicycles to tour the island. Mopeds provide another way to get around, and are available from Suzie's Moped at Churchill Square, just above the ferry departure lanes (call 206-378-5244).

There are two motels which offer standard rooms. The largest is the **Inn at Friday Harbor** on Spring Street (206-378-4351 or 1-800-752-5752). The motel has large rooms, an indoor swimming pool and whirlpool. **$$**. The **Island Lodge** (206-378-2000 or 1-800-822-5753) is located on Guard Street, 1/2 mile from the ferry landing, with standard and housekeeping rooms and suites, a sauna, whirlpool, barbecue area and several llamas to entertain guests. **$ to $$**.

Bed and Breakfast homes are plentiful and located in town and around the island roads. The **San Juan Inn** (206-378-2070) is right in the middle of the downtown area, close to the ferry landing on Spring Street. It's a charming Victorian building furnished with brass and wicker. **$$**. **Hillside House** (206-378-4730), 365 Carter Avenue (off Guard St.) has six rooms just above the town — a quiet setting, private and shared baths and full country breakfast. **$$**. **Duffy House** (206-378-5604), 760 Pear Point Rd., has six rooms with shared baths plus a waterfront cabin and private beach. **$$**. **Blair House** (206-378-5907) is at 345 Blair Ave. surrounded by Douglas firs, with six rooms and a cottage, heated pool and hot tub. **$$**. **Wharfside Bed & Breakfast** (206-378-5661) is the Jacquelyn, a 60-foot ship docked at Friday Harbor. This unusual and well-equipped B & B has two cabins, one with a private head. The forward cabin has a double bed & two bunks. The aft cabin has a queen-size bed. Betty & Clyde Rice serve breakfast in the main salon or on the poop deck, if weather permits. **$**.

San Juan Island — Roche Harbor

Fifteen minutes' drive from Friday Harbor, the resort at Roche Harbor is one of the most unusual and intriguing vacation places on the whole Pacific Coast. Situated just north of the British Camp portion of San Juan Islands National Park, Roche Harbor is another historic site which is imbued with British and American spirit.

First a Hudson's Bay trading post servicing the nearby British encampment, limestone was discovered in the surrounding hills and thirteen quarries were developed then a lime and cement shipping operation was started in the mid 1800s. The property and business changed hands several times until the early 1880s when Roche Harbor was purchased by John S. McMillin who turned the operation into a multi-million dollar industry. By 1886, he had built a complete village with a hotel (Hotel de Haro), houses for his workers and a church. The limeworks quickly became the largest lime operation west of the Mississippi and ships carried McMillin's lime to ports throughout the length of the Pacific Coast. Lime production was the main activity of Roche Harbor until 1956 and the McMillins prospered although the lime baron was in constant trouble with government departments including the tax collector. Part of the McMillin legacy is a dramatic and eerie mausoleum — in the woods near the village — he built for the burial of his immediate family.

In 1956, the Tarte family purchased the whole village and have turned it into a resort which includes a large marina, an excellent restaurant, the Victorian Hotel de Haro — looking exactly as it did in the early days of the century— and condominium units which provide more modern accommodation for visitors. In front of the hotel is a formal garden, in the English style. Several island state parks lie just offshore.

For period atmosphere, Roche Harbor can't be equalled in the Pacific Northwest. The hotel, which in its limestone days housed such dignitaries as Theodore Roosevelt, is a gem which may lack untramodern conveniences but makes up for it in charm. The restaurant overlooks the harbor and serves superb local seafood. The chapel—very popular for weddings—is the only privately-owned consecrated Roman Catholic church in the U.S. A short walk to the north takes you to the McMillin Mausoleum. A walk to the south takes you to British Camp and the Mt. Young trail. The resort has its own paved airstrip. You can buy fish and shellfish directly from fish boats in the marina.

The resort celebrates its past with special observances including a daily lowering of the colors — at sunset. Flags are lowered while the national anthems of Britain and Canada are played. The American flag is lowered to the strains of Sousa's Stars and Stripes Forever. Resort staff march in formation on the dock and the cannon fires a final salute. This marks the end of the day and the start of party-time — on the many visiting boats and in the resort's bar. It's a festive place! For information and reservations, write Roche Harbor, WA 98250 or phone 206-378-2155.

AROUND SAN JUAN ISLAND

American Camp is located near the southeast end of the island, accessed by driving down Cattle Point Road. The national park site has a great walking beach, a one-mile historic trail to the American redoubt and past the site of the Hudson's Bay farm, the home of the fateful wandering pig which nearly brought the British and American sides to combat. Cattle Point, at the tip of the island, has its own picnic park and small cove beach.

Driving north along the island's west shore you'll find several points of interest including three parks. **False Bay** is indeed false, half of the time. At low tide the water disappears to leave a mud flat with tide pools. This is a University of Washington Biological research site and its open to the public. Moving north along West Side Road, **Lime Kiln State Park** offers picnicking and a view of the Lime Kiln Lighthouse. This is the nation's only whale-watching park where one can often see pods of killer whales feeding on the abundant salmon close to the shore. **San Juan County Park**, to the north, is on Smallpox Bay. There are 18 campsites here and space for a few more tents. Scuba diving, beachcombing and picnicking are popular activities in this park. On the northeast side of the island is the **Reuben Tarte Picnic Area**, on a tombolo — a small rocky peninsula which connects two coves. This is a good area for scuba diving and snorkeling. **Jackson Beach Park** is south of Friday Harbor, a good place for sunning on the long sandy beach. Finally, in Friday Harbor, **Sunken Park** is close to the downtown area: a good place for picnics near the ferry landing.

Several fine **Bed & Breakfast homes** are situated outside of Friday Harbor by the sea or in the rural valleys. **Trumpeter Inn** (206-378-3884) is just north of San Juan Valley Road on Trumpeter Way. There are six rooms with private bath — a find for true romantics. **$ to $$**. Probably the most outstanding B & B inn is Olympic Lights, on the sea near British Camp with magnificent view of the Olympic Mountains. Four rooms share two baths while the fifth room has a private bath. Full breakfast is served. This Victorian farmhouse on Cattle Point Road is a perfect base for beach walking and exploring the parks on the west shore of the island. **$$**. The **States Inn** (206-378-6240) is a nine-room B & B located in a verdant valley on West Valley Road. There's a 2-bedroom suite with sitting room and all rooms have private baths All of the rooms bear the names of different states and are designed with regional decor. **$$ to $$$**. The **Moon & Sixpence** (206-378-4138) is on Beaverton Valley Road, an inn with a weaving studio in the rural countryside. This is a remodeled dairy farm which offers rooms in the farmhouse and in outbuildings. There are three rooms, a suite and a one-room cabin. **$$**. **Westwinds** (206-378-5283) has a suite situated on ten acres at the foot of Mt. Dallas, near Lime Kiln Park. **$$$**.

Snug Harbor Resort (206-378-4762 or 1-800-542-SNUG) is on Mitchell Bay, near Roche Harbor, with a marina, several campsites and 9 cabins **$**. **Lakedale Campground** (206-378-2350) on Roche Harbor Rd., has RV and tenting sites and several small lakes nearby for boating and canoeing.

ORCAS ISLAND

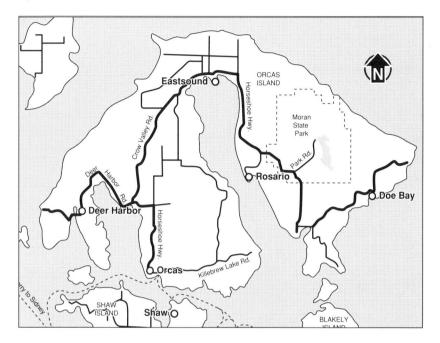

Orcas Island takes its name — not from its whale shape — but from the Viceroy of Mexico in 1792. East Sound, the channel which almost cuts the island in two, creates magnificent views from almost every angle.

The prominent landmark on the island is Mt. Constitution, the highest point in the San Juans. Much of the mountain including the summit is part of **Moran State Park,** given to Washington by Robert Moran, a shipping and ship building magnate who built the estate which became the well-known Rosario Resort. Rosario and several other resorts make Orcas a preferred year-round destination for vacationers. From the summit of Mt. Constitution one can see the entire archipelago and onward to Vancouver Island and the Olympic Peninsula, and — on a clear day — as far as Mt. Rainier to the southeast and Mt. Baker to the west. It's a breathtaking vista.

Eastsound, the island's largest community, is situated on the thin sandy piece of land which joins the two halves of the island. The village has retained its period charm over the years and it has a tranquil laid-back ambience. The ferry landing is in **Orcas** at the southeast corner. The main road leads through the middle of the island to Eastsound and on to Moran State Park and then to the tail of the whale at Obstruction Pass where there is a small park with a public beach. Nearby, **Doe Bay** features a hot spring resort. **Deer Harbor** is on the eastern peninsula with several resorts and a marina. On all parts of the island are charming inns and resorts with accommodation for every taste, from rustic cabin-type fishing resorts and Victorian inns to the deluxe spa atmosphere of Rosario.

ORCAS ISLAND

Orcas has a stunning coastline with many bays and inlets, providing space for marinas, resorts, beaches, whale-watching spots and relaxing in the unspoiled wilderness of this varied terrain.

The chief outdoor attraction is the 4600-acre **Moran State Park**, 13 miles from the Orcas ferry landing and only two miles from the village of Eastsound. As you enter the park you're five miles from the summit of Mt. Constitution but it is possible to drive all the way on a paved road. Bicycling up to the top is a challenge! Hiking trails start mid-way up the mountain, leading to the summit and a unique viewing tower built during the Depression from a design brought to the island by Robert Moran, who admired the stone lookout towers in the Caucasus mountains.

From the summit, there is a 360 view of Puget Sound, southwestern British Columbia, the Olympic Mountains and, in the distance, the thrilling peaks of Mt. Rainier and Mt. Baker.

Mt. Constitution is only one of the many things to experience in this large park. **Cascade Falls** is an impressive waterfall. **Mountain Lake**, near the summit, is a fine fishing lake with a 3.6 mile walking trail circling the lake. **Twin Lakes** are small and secluded lakes which are reached by walking past Mountain Lake on the trail up Mt. Constitution.

At the bottom of the mountain is **Cascade Lake**, which you pass just after entering the park. This lake is on the highway between Eastsound and the village of Olga and the developed campsites are in this area. Cascade Lake is a popular boating, canoeing and fishing lake with swimming and hiking opportunities.

The most accessible public beach on the seashore is at **Obstruction Pass**, on the southeast side of the island. There's a half-mile walk from the road. This is a scenic, secluded beach with a small camping area and a picnic site.

There is also a short stretch (60 feet) of beach just north of Eastsound at the end of North Beach Road. Several other beaches around the island are accessible by boat.

There are many places to stay on Orcas, from rustic to deluxe.

The premier resort is **Rosario** (206-376-2222 or 1-800-562-8820). It is centered around the famous Moran Mansion which is steeped in Washington history. Robert Moran made his considerable fortune building ships for the Klondike Gold Rush and later built the first U.S. battleship, the USS Nebraska. Moran moved to Orcas Island in 1905 after doctors told him that he had only a year to live. He began building a large mansion for his family and brought his shipwrights to the island to build the house. It was constructed like a ship — with teak and mahogany interior finishings. The wood was brought into Cascade Bay and milled on-site. He even built his own electric power station. The home's roof was covered with six tons of copper. Moran lived there until his death in 1942, 34 years after his doctors forecast his immediate demise.

ORCAS ISLAND

Rosario is now a holiday resort which deserves its superb reputation. The mansion includes a stepped dining room with good views and excellent cuisine. The magnificent music room on the second floor contains a pipe organ which is played daily for the enjoyment of guests. Moran was no musician and bought a player organ which he pretended to play for his guests, but the resort's resident organist really does play it. There's a spa with pool and sauna on the lower level and the resort features spa-week packages. Rosario is popular during holiday weekends with special stay & eat packages. One of my most memorable Christmas vacations was spent here. There are 179 rooms and suites ranging from quiet cottages to modern motel-type rooms and condominium suites. A large outdoor pool is perfect for family swimming and there is a marina with store and cafe on the property. The resort is a short drive from Moran State Park and only a short walk to Cascade Lake. **$$ to $$$**.

The **Orcas Hotel** (206-376-4300) is just above the island's ferry landing. This beautifully restored Victorian has rooms decorated in period style. The hotel's English pub is a perfect stop to pass the time while waiting for the ferry. There is a dining room in the hotel. **$$**. The **Outlook Inn** (106-376-2200) is in Eastsound, another historic building with 49 restored rooms and a Victorian dining room specializing in West Coast seafood. **$$**. Also in Eastsound is the **Landmark Inn** (206-376-2423), a condominium-style resort with motel units as well and good views of the sound. The hotel has one and two-bedroom units, some with kitchens, fireplaces and private decks. **$$**. **Smuggler's Villa Resort** (206-376-2297) is on the north shore with 20 two-bedroom condo-type units with kitchens, hot tub, sauna and pool, tennis court and boat moorage. **$$**. **Beach Haven Resort**, at Eastsound, has 12 50-year-old housekeeping cottages (1-4 bedrooms) with showers and wood stoves, on a 10-acre property. **$$**.

The island has a number of excellent bed and breakfast operations including the **Turtleback Farm Inn** (206-376-4914), a wonderful farmhouse with antique furniture in a quiet rural setting, full breakfasts and gardens. **$$**. **Kangaroo House** (206-376-2175) is in Eastsound, a restored 1907 home with period furniture, a garden for strolling and renowned breakfasts. **$$**. **Liberty Call Bed & Breakfast** (206-376-5246) is just east of the ferry landing at Orcas. This is a small operation with two rooms. **$**.

Olga is a small village south of Eastsound near the whale's head, close to Moran State Park and Doe Bay. Here the **Lieber Haven Resort** (206-376-2472) is a B & B with 12 apartment-style units in a quiet rural setting. **$$**.

Campers and RV owners will head to Moran State Park where there are campsites at Cascade Lake or to the small primitive campground at Obstruction Pass. There is, however, a private RV park and campground on the island, **West Beach Resort** (206-376-2240) which has 36 sites with hookups plus 36 tenting sites and 13 cabins **($ to $$)** located on a good beach with a stunning sunset view over the water.

Lopez Island

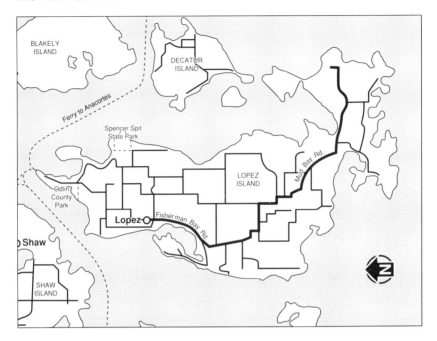

Lopez is normally a day-adventure for most travelers. It's a handy stop as the first ferry landing on the San Juan islands ferry trip, permitting tourists to drive off the ferry and spend a few hours on the island and then go on to stay on Orcas or San Juan islands. There are fewer places to stay on Lopez which also adds to the number of day trippers.

Lopez does have its charms, however, and I would recommend visiting Lopez for several reasons:

First, there are two parks on the island which are quite different from the natural areas on the larger islands. The gentle landscape of **Odlin County Park,** on the west side of the island near the ferry landing, features 82 acres of woods and beach with picnicking and boating opportunities. There is a small campground in the park with 30 sites. **Spencer Spit State Park** offers a different view of the water from the northeast side of the island. Three miles from the ferry landing with a mile-long sandy beach, Spencer Spit provides walking trails, a covered picnic area and 42 campsites. The spit connects Lopez with Frost Island at low tide and popular pastimes here include clamming, fishing and crabbing.

Lopez Village is in the north-central section of the island and there are cafes and stores here for obtaining camp supplies and picnic food.

With flat terrain, Lopez is a favorite of cyclists who can "do" the island in a day. The public campsites are perfect as bicycle camps.

The slow and out-of-time ambience of the island is characterized by the down-home restaurants and the soda fountain at the Lopez Island Pharmacy.

LOPEZ ISLAND & ISLAND RESTAURANTS

The one resort on this island is **The Islander Lopez** (206-468-2233) on Fisherman Bay, just a short drive from Lopez Village. The resort includes a marina with space for 50 boats, sail and motorboat charters, bike rentals and a swimming pool and hot tub. The resort has 32 rooms, 10 with kitchens, as well as four cabins, a restaurant and cocktail lounge. **$$**. The **Inn at Swifts Bay** (206-468-3636) is a recently opened bed and breakfast home. The tudor-style building sits on three wooded acres with a private beach a short walk away. The inn has four rooms, two with private bath. There is a whirlpool, a spa at the edge of the woods and full breakfast is served. **$$**. **McKay Harbor Inn** (206-468-2253) has a beach-side location — a 1920 home with gardens and full breakfast in an unspoiled setting. The beach is a prime attraction here. **$$**

For those who like to stay in rustic cabin-type accommodations, try **Marean's Blue Fjord Cabins** (206-468-2749) on Jasper Cove. There are three cedar log cabins with kitchens, decks and fireplaces. There are nature trails from the property, one of which leads to the beach. **$$**.

Restaurants on the Islands:

Restaurants on Lopez include **The Galley**, located on Fisherman Bay. This dining place which specializes in seafood dishes has overnight moorage for visiting boats along with rooftop dining overlooking the bay. **Gail's Restaurant** has a homey setting in Lopez Village with the kind of food your grandmother used to cook. It's not fancy but it is certainly cozy.

Orcas Island has the best restaurants in the San Juans, in keeping with its reputation as the "Resort Island". **Bilbo's Festivo** in Eastsound serves Mexican cuisine in the appropriate environment. It's open for lunch and dinner and makes a good contrast if you're eating mainly in the resort dining rooms. **Christina's Restaurant**, also in Eastsound, serves fresh seafood dishes at very low prices. The **Ship Bay Oyster House** in Eastsound has a varied menu which includes seafood, steaks and chops. **Sonnie's Deli** is for lighter eating: soups, sandwiches and deli foods. Good hotel dining rooms open to the public include the **Outlook Inn** in eastsound, The **Orcas Hotel** (the dining room or the pub) at the ferry landing and the deluxe **Rosario Resort** dining room.

Friday Harbor and the rest of San Juan Island have fewer restaurants but the quality is high. A polular breakfast and lunch spot is the **Bistro**, on the waterfront at the ferry landing in Friday Harbor. Their beer-batter cinnamon bread is a breakfast treat and they serve the best coffee in town. On Spring Street, the **Springtree Eating Establishment & Farm** serves northwest cuisine (seafood, lamb, etc.) at breakfast, lunch and dinner. There's an intriguing treed entrance and an outdoor patio here, and the food is flavored with herbs from their own farm on the island. The **Roche Harbor Resort Restaurant** offers great seafood in an 1880s setting. It's unique. **King's Market** on Spring Street is the best place to pick up picnic supplies and camp food. The store has a vast selection of northwest wines.

Shaw Island

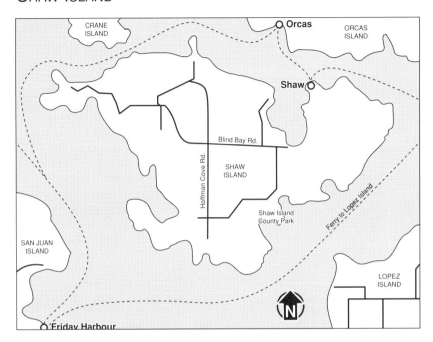

Shaw is the smallest of the islands served by the ferry system and the least visited. It has no overnight accommodation except for a few campsites so most visitors have to plan in advance to visit Shaw and then catch a later ferry to another island or back to the mainland.

Shaw lies in the center of the group of islands and thus has sheltered water all-around. The island is approximately eight square miles in size and 100 people live there year-round. Unlike some of the smaller out islands in the archipelago, Shaw Island homes have electricity, a store and roads. The only commercial enterprise open to the public is the **Little Portion Store**, beside the ferry landing. It, the post office and the ferry landing are operated by Franciscan nuns. The **Shaw Island Historical Museum** is a log cabin across from the historic one-room schoolhouse, at the corner of Blind Bay Rd. & Hoffman Cove Rd. It'ss open on Saturdays and Mondays.

The one park on the island is **Shaw County Park**. It's located at the south end of the island. The property was once a military reservation, until the Shaw Island residents purchased it for public use. It has one of the best beaches in the San Juans and this is one of the few places in the island chain where the water gets warm enough for swimming. There are 12 campsites and a boat launch in the park, along with toilets and drinking water. Nature trails lead along the shoreline and through the woods. The park is 6 miles from the ferry landing. There is no restaurant on the island so visitors should stock up at the store and head for the County Park to enjoy picnic fare.

Southwestern British Columbia

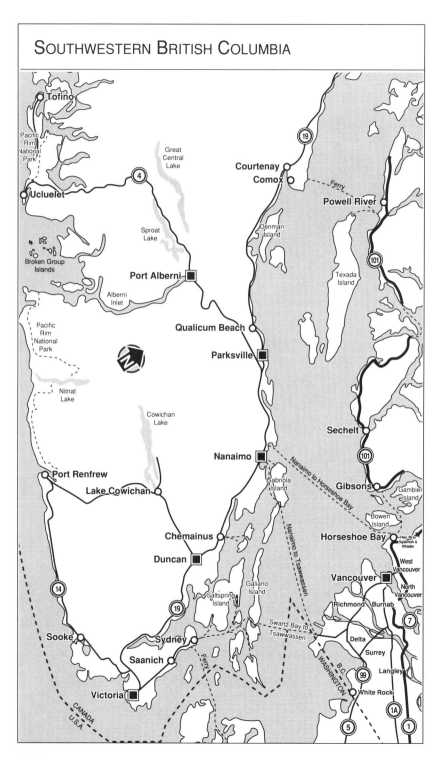

Tofino
Pacific Rim National Park
Ucluelet
Great Central Lake
4
Courtenay
Comox
19
Ferry
Powell River
Denman Island
Broken Group Islands
Sproat Lake
Texada Island
101
Port Alberni
Alberni Inlet
Qualicum Beach
Pacific Rim National Park
Parksville
Nitnat Lake
Cowichan Lake
Sechelt
101
Nanaimo
Gabriola Island
Nanaimo to Horseshoe Bay
Gibsons
Gambier Island
Port Renfrew
Lake Cowichan
Bowen Island
Chemainus
Nanaimo to Tsawwassen
Horseshoe Bay
Hwy. 99 to Squamish & Whistler
Duncan
West Vancouver
Vancouver
North Vancouver
14
Galiano Island
Saltspring Island
Richmond
Burnaby
7
19
Swartz Bay to Tsawwassen
Sooke
Sydney
Delta
Surrey
Saanich
99
Langley
Ferry
Victoria
CANADA U.S.A.
B.C. WASHINGTON
White Rock
1A
1
5

British Columbia's South Coast

Much of the coastline of British Columbia is accessible only by boat. The famous and beautiful Inside Passage is an example of the thousands of miles of forested mountain coast which cannot be reached by road. From the northern border of Washington State, to the rain forests of the Alaskan Panhandle, the B.C. Coast is a largely unspoiled wilderness of staggering proportions and awesome beauty.

The adventure locations in this book touch only the road-accessible southwestern coast: the true Pacific Coast — on Vancouver Island — and the inland coast of the Strait of Georgia sheltered by the mountain chain which runs the length of Vancouver Island. Here, the short strip of coastline called **The Sunshine Coast** provides rustic sea-side delight in a string of small villages.

We also cover the east, west and south coasts of **Vancouver Island.** The West Coast is rugged, wild and largely uninhabited. Highways run through the forests and across the mountains to Pacific Rim National Park and the small fishing villages of Tofino and Ucluelet. The south coast route from Victoria to Port Renfrew provides a scenic day-trip or a longer vacation exploration. The road ends at the starting point of the West Coast Trail, part of Pacific Rim National Park and an extremely rugged week-long journey for experienced hikers. The east coast of this large island is more placid country. Here, the smooth waters of the Strait of Georgia lap against long beaches where small resort towns offer accommodation ranging from rustic cabins to deluxe resorts including several of Canada's prime fishing resorts.

On the east side of Georgia Strait, south of the Sunshine Coast and adjoining the U.S. border, is the spreading urban area of **Vancouver** and its surrounding suburbs. The Southwestern B.C. area, called the Lower Mainland by residents, includes the the sophisticated City of Vancouver which boasts an international flavor after more than 100 years of immigration from around the world, the "North Shore' communities of North and West Vancouver and the sprawling bedroom communities of Burnaby, Richmond, Surrey, Delta, Coquitlam and the agricultural Fraser Valley. Vancouver has one of the most felicitous natural environments of any world city with sea, mountains and the great Fraser River blending to provide amazing vistas from every angle. The north shore mountains provide handy ski hills and provincial parks while downtown Vancouver is ringed with sandy beaches.

North of Vancouver the Sea to Sky Highway (Hwy. 99) cuts along the impressive shore of Howe Sound to the paper town of Squamish and up into the Coast Mountains to **Whistler,** B.C.'s renowned international ski resort — where skiing is a year-round activity.

Southwestern B.C. is now North America's third most popular vacation destination, after California and Florida. Nowhere else is there the same combination of urban sophistication and outdoor adventure possibilities. Just north of the U.S. border, this corner of B.C. is accessible and welcoming.

GETTING THERE — B.C. FERRIES

British Columbia Ferry Corp. (a government operation) operates car ferries throughout the province including 27 routes along the B.C. coast. For ferry schedules, write: B.C. Ferry Corporation, 1112 Fort Street, Victoria, B.C. V8V 4V2. For up-to-date information from a real person — not a computer— phone **(604) 669-1211** (Vancouver). Here are the major ferry routes:

Mainland to Vancouver Island:
- Vancouver (Tsawwassen) to Victoria (Swartz Bay). 17 sailings per day (summer). 8 sailings per day (winter), 1 hour, 35 minutes.
- Vancouver (Horseshoe Bay) to Nanaimo. 16 sailings per day (summer). 8 sailings per day (winter), 1 hour, 35 minutes.
- Mid Island Express: Tsawwassen to Nanaimo. 4 sailings per day, 1 hour, 45 minutes. For information on these routes, phone 669-1211

Vancouver Island to Southern Gulf Islands:
- Swartz Bay to Salt Spring Island (Fulford Harbour), 10 sailings per day, year-round, 30 minutes. Information, Victoria: 656-0757.
- Swartz Bay to Pender Island (Otter Bay), Mayne Island (Village Bay), Galiano Island (Sturdies Bay), & Saturna Island. Schedule depends on day of week and time of year. Information, Victoria: 656-0757.
- Crofton to Salt Spring Island (Vesuvius Bay), 11 sailings per day year-round, 20 minutes. Information, Victoria: 656-0757.
- Chemainus to Thetis Island & Kuper Island, 10 sailings per day, year-round, 25 minutes. Information, Victoria: 656-0757.
- Nanaimo to Gabriola Island, 17 sailings per day year-round. Duration: 20 minutes. Information Line, Nanaimo: 753-6626.

Vancouver Island to Northern Gulf Islands:
Ferries run from Bulkley Bay to Denman Island and from Denman Island to Hornby Island. The ferry to Quadra Island runs from down-town Campbell River. At the northeast tip of the island, a ferry runs from Port McNeill to Cormorant Island (Alert Bay) & Malcolm Island (Sointula). For information on these ferries, call (604) 753-1261.

Inside Passage & Queen Charlotte Islands:
The Queen of the North sails from Port Hardy to Prince Rupert through the Inside Passage. There are five sailings per week during summer months and reservations are required. For information and reservations, call Vancouver, (604) 669-1211; Victoria, (604) 386-3431, 7 am-10 pm daily; Seattle Washington (206) 441-6865, 8:30 am - 4:30 pm, Mon.-Fri. For travel to the Queen Charlotte Islands, ferries run between Prince Rupert & Skidegate. June through September: four to five sailings weekly. For vehicle reservations, phone the Inside Passage numbers. For more-detailed information on travel to northern Vancouver Island or throughout B.C., I suggest that you use our companion book "British Columbia Adventures".

THE SUNSHINE COAST

Lying along the east coast of Georgia Strait — a few kilometers northwest of Vancouver — is the Sunshine Coast. It is aptly named because of its location in the rain shadow of Vancouver Island which brings this stretch of coastline unusually-dry weather. Because of the 45-minute ferry ride from Horseshoe Bay, the communities of the Sunshine Coast are a world apart from the hustle of the Lower Mainland. The communities along this stretch of Highway 101 are all small, scenic places with a relaxed lifestyle and a growing number of tourist facilities including many resort lodges, bed & breakfast inns, campgrounds and an extensive system of district and provincial parks. Some of the country's best scuba diving is here, in the hundreds of bays and inlets of this inner coast. There is excellent saltwater fishing at any point along the drive.

To get to the Sunshine Coast, drive to Horseshoe Bay in West Vancouver and board the ferry to Langdale. This pleasant cruise takes you past the islands of Howe Sound to the ferry landing which is just south of **Gibsons**. Highway 101 — the final, northern leg of the continental coastal route — runs the length of the Sunshine Coast for 88 miles (142 kilometers) to the village of Lund. Hwy. 101 takes you past and through some of the most scenic communities in the province. The town of **Sechelt** is located on the southern edge of the Sechelt Peninsula. To the north, **Halfmoon Bay** is home to the two major fishing and vacation resorts of the area. **Pender Harbour** is a beautiful sheltered bay and is the area name for three separate communities lying around the bay: **Madeira Park**, **Garden Bay**, and **Irvine's Landing**.

Continuing north, the highway passes Ruby Lake and ends, temporarily, at **Earl's Cove**. This is the site of a ferry terminal where a free ferry takes you across Jervis Inlet to **Saltery Bay** and the northern stretch of the Sunshine Coast. Farther north, **Powell River** is a paper mill town where a ferry crosses Georgia Strait to Nanaimo on Vancouver Island. Another ferry links Powell River with Texada Island.

Another 17 miles (28 KM) north is the end of the highway at **Lund** — a scenic fishing and tourist village — founded by Scandinavian settlers in the early 1800s.

With its extensive park systems, the Sunshine Coast has become a favorite destination for campers and RV owners, as well as anglers who come here each year to fish for salmon. Trails throughout the area offer scenic hiking experiences and opportunities for bird and whale watching.

The busy season here begins in mid-June and continues until the end of September. During these periods it is advisable to reserve your accommodations in advance. If you're planning to stay in public park campgrounds you should plan your driving schedules and ferry crossings so that you arrive early enough in the day to have a place to stay. This said, the Sunshine Coast offers a relaxed vacation experience in timeless beauty and a chance to get away from the busier aspects of life in B.C.

Sunshine Coast (Hwy. 101)   Vancouver to Powell River
179 KM (144 miles)   2 hours

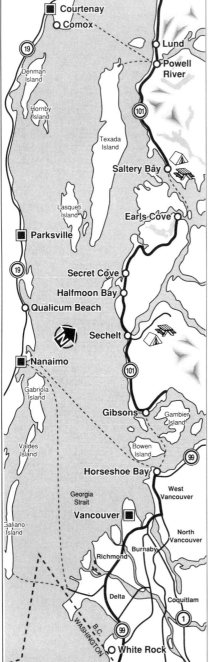

Ferry to the Sunshine Coast:
The ferry ride from the Horseshoe Bay terminal to Langdale on the Sunshine Coast is a pleasant 45 minute cruise across Howe Sound. From Vancouver, the terminal is reached by driving across one of the two bridges to the north shore of Burrard Inlet (Lion's Gate & Second Narrows) and taking the Upper Levels Highway (Hwy. 1) west to the village of Horseshoe Bay. Here you will find several good restaurants, a beer-brewing oyster bar, a pub and deli.

Langdale Ferry Terminal
Turn left after leaving the ferry for Gibsons and the Sunshine Coast. Turning right leads to the Port Mellon paper mill where tours are available. **Beach Access Park** is off Pt. Mellon Rd., with swimming & picnic tables.

Gibsons, with an infocentre, gas, stores, motels, restaurants and marina**. Soames Hill Park** on a hill offers a lookout, hiking trail and picnicking.

Secret Beach Park (take Ocean Beach Drive in Gibsons), has picnic tables & swimming.

Roberts Creek Provincial Park half-way between Gibsons and Sechelt has a picnic site and a public campground in the forest.

Davis Bay south of Sechelt has a beach and a district park with swimming and a boat launch. Gas, store, motels, restaurants.

Selma Park at the south edge of Sechelt has a boat launch.

Sechelt, town with gas, stores, motels, camping and RV parks, located at the southern shore of Sechelt Inlet.

Porpoise Bay Provincial Park, off Porpoise Bay Rd., just north of Sechelt. Camping, beach, picnic area, canoeing.

Halfmoon Bay, village with store, gas & lodges. **Welcome Beach Park**, a wilderness park has a nature & hiking trail, take Francis Rd. **Cooper's Green Park** in Halfmoon Bay has picnic tables, boat launch, playground & fishing. **Smuggler's Cove Park** (take Brooks Rd.) has a hiking trail to a scenic cove.

Pender Harbour: gas, stores, pubs, B & B homes & motels. The communities of **Madeira Park**, **Garden Bay** & **Irvine's Landing** are situated around this scenic bay. **John Daly Park** (on Garden Bay Rd.) has a picnic area & walking trail. **Katherine Lake Park**, with camping & swimming is off the road to Irvine's Landing, north of Garden Bay.

The Infocentre for the Pender Harbour area is in Madeira Park, call (604) 883-2561.

Sakinaw Lake north of Pender Harbour, boat launch.

Ruby Lake, just south of the Earl's Cove ferry landing has two boat launches & a restaurant.

Road to Egmont, 1 KM south of ferry landing leads to a small village and the trail to **Skookumchuck Narrows Provincial Park** and view of tidal rapids.

Earl's Cove, ferry landing & cafe, 51.5 miles (83 KM) from Langdale ferry. 45-minute ferry trip across Jervis Inlet.

Saltery Bay ferry terminal.
Saltery Bay Provincial Park, camping, day-use area with picnic tables, swimming, boat launch, scuba diving.

Kent's Beach, private campground.
Palm Bay, private campground.
Myrtle Point, Private RV park & **Myrtle Rocks Marine Park.**

Powell River, town 19 miles (31 KM) from Saltry Bay ferry. Gas, motels, B & B homes, restaurants. Ferries to Nanaimo (Vancouver Island) & Texada Island. **Willingdon Beach Park**, municipal campground with beach on Marine Avenue with showers, playground, nature trail. **Haywire Regional Park**, camping on Powell Lake with showers, boat launch, beach, trails to lakes. Start of **Powell Forest Canoe Route** connecting 12 lakes over a route of 35.5 miles (57 KM). Map available at park or Infocentre, 6807 Wharf St., beside ferry landing-downtown call (604) 485-4701.

Sliammon Village, Indian community, fish hatchery, north of Powell River.

Dinner Rock Park, a rustic forest campsite, south of Lund.

Lund, small village at north end of Hwy. 101. Motel, gas, marina, restaurant, pub. Launching point for Desolation Sound boating.

Copeland Islands Marine Park, near Lund, across Thulin Passage.

Finn Bay Wreck Site, just north of Lund with undersea wreck of 65 foot boat "Adventurer".

Okeover Arm Provincial Park, take road leading east from Lund. Park has primitive campsites and a boat launch.

SUNSHINE COAST

After the ferry ride to **Langdale**, Hwy. 101 runs north to **Gibsons**, a picturesque fishing village where the long-running TV series "Beachcombers" was filmed for 19 years. The series is now off the air but the scenery of Gibsons is familiar to millions of people around the world.

Back near the Langdale ferry landing the Soames Point Hiking Trail, 2 KM beyond the ferry terminal, provides a good view of the surrounding area including the Strait of Georgia and Vancouver Island—across the strait. The Gibsons Infocentre is on Lower Marine Dr., call 604-886-2325. The Elphinstone Pioneer Museum in Gibsons is open daily during summer months. The shell collection is one of the largest in Canada and the museum also features displays and artifacts on Coast Salish life (phone 604-886-8232). Take the scenic seawall walk from Government Wharf—a ten-minute stroll to Lower Gibsons. There is good cross-country skiing in this area from January through March.

Roberts Creek Provincial Park, 10 KM north of Gibsons on Hwy. 101 has campsites and picnic tables, a waterfall and good beachcombing. This is a popular spot for hunting for mussels and oysters at low tide.

Sechelt, 25 KM (15 miles) from the Langdale ferry landing is the major town on the Sechelt Peninsula. The local Infocentre is in the downtown area (phone 604-885-3100). There is a fine display of rhododendrons in **Rockwood Lodge Gardens** next to the Infocentre on Cowrie St. The garden is free and open year-round. The local Arts Centre hosts the annual festival of the Written Arts, a writers festival.

Porpoise Bay Provincial Park, on Sechelt Inlet is 4 KM from town on a side-road. There is a sandy beach here, fishing for coho and cod and a camping area. There is access from the park to **Sechelt Inlets Marine Recreation Area,** accessible by boat or canoe. There are eight sheltered campsites east of the peninsula.

Smuggler Cove Provincial Marine Park, 20 KM (12.5 miles) north of Sechelt off Hwy. 101 has reefs for diving, five walk-in campsites and a trail to a beach. This is one of a growing number of marine parks established by the B.C. government, located on the coastline of Vancouver Island and in the Sunshine Coast/Howe Sound area on the mainland. If you own or rent a boat while on the Sunshine Coast, you may wish to travel north to Desolation Sound — north of Powell River—the site of Canada's largest marine park with more than 60 kilometers of shoreline, several off-shore islands and impressive views of the glacier-clad Coast Mountains. The waters there are warm enough for scuba diving.

Pender Harbour is situated in a beautiful cove. The area includes three scenic villages: **Madeira Park,** to the south, **Irvine's Landing** on the north side at the mouth of the harbor and **Garden Bay**. There are several resorts, a campground and marinas in the Pender Harbour area with diving facilities and 9-hole golf course. The summer Infocentre for Pender Harbour is in Madeira Park, call 604-883-2561.

SUNSHINE COAST

Egmont, off the highway via Egmont Rd. (just south of Earl's Cove), is a small village which offers supplies, moorage and access to **Skookumchuck Narrows Provincial Park**. This park on the northeast tip of the peninsula overlooks the narrows. A 90-minute walk leads to Narrows & Roland points where there are picnic areas and views of tidal rapids

The **Earl's Cove ferry terminal**, 17 KM beyond Madeira Park, provides a free ferry to **Saltery Bay** on the north side of Jervis Inlet. This is a 50 minute ferry ride and Hwy. 101 continues its northward run to the pulp mill town of Powell River. **Saltery Bay Provincial Park** is on the north side of the ferry crossing with campsites, swimming, boat launch and picnic facilities. There are several campsites between the landing and Powell River.

Powell River is the site of ferries to Comox on Vancouver Island and to Texada Island. Tourist facilities include a hotel, several motels and campgrounds. The local Infocentre is at 6807 Wharf St. (485-4701). The **Powell Forest Canoe Route** features a chain of 12 lakes providing a 50 KM route with 5 miles of portages.

Sunshine Coast Accommodation:

Gibsons: The **Cedars Inn**, on Hwy. 101 (886-3008) has a summer pool, hot tub, saunas and some rooms with kitchenettes. **$$**. **Cassidy's B. & B.** (886-7222) has an ocean view and hot tub **$**. **Sunshine Lodge** on North Road (886-3321) has a heated pool, kitchenettes & fireplaces. **$$**.

Sechelt: The **Driftwood Inn** is in downtown Sechelt (885-5811), on the waterfront with some housekeeping rooms, restaurant, and a beach. **$$**. **Willows Inn B & B** (885-2452) has a separate cottage at Roberts Creek. **$$**.

Halfmoon Bay: The Jolly Roger Inn (885-7184 or 1-800-6630180) is a deluxe condo-style resort on Secret Cove with dining room, lounge and marina plus fishing charters. **$$ to $$$**. **Lord Jim's Resort Hotel** (885-7083**)** off the highway overlooking Malaspina Strait has lodge rooms & cabins, a restaurant, heated pool and fishing charters **$$ to $$$**. **B & B By The Sea,** has one room plus a private cottage. **$$**.

Pender Harbour: Lowe's Motel & Campground (883-2456) has housekeeping cottages and campsites with hookups and showers, rental boats, moorage, laundry and a beach with picnic tables & barbecues **$$**. **Madeira Marina** has a motel and campground overlooking Pender Harbour. There are 2-bedroom housekeeping units and campsites with hookups as well as boat rentals, moorage and a water taxi service **$**

Garden Bay: The **Duncan Cove Resort**, on Sinclair Bay Road (883-2424) has a motel, housekeeping cottages and campsites with hookups, showers, boat rentals, and laundry. **$ to $.**

Powell River: The Inn at Westview, 7050 Alberni St. (485-6281) is a hotel with dining room **$**. **Haywire Regional Park**, 7 miles north of town at 5776 Marine Dr. has campsites, showers, beach & boat launch. **Oceanside RV Park**, 4 miles south of town on Hwy. 101 has hookups, tent sites, showers, beach and a golf course across the highway.

VANCOUVER ISLAND

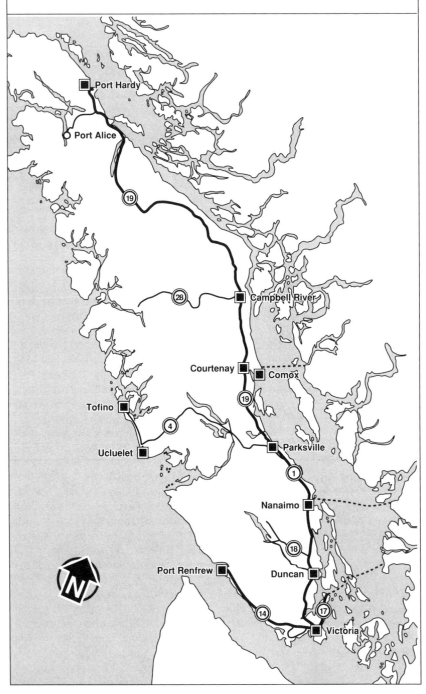

Port Hardy

Port Alice

19

28

Campbell River

Courtenay
Comox

19

Tofino

4

Ucluelet

Parksville

1

Nanaimo

18

Port Renfrew

Duncan

14

17

Victoria

VANCOUVER ISLAND

Stretching north and south for 480 kilometers (300 miles), Vancouver Island is the largest island off the west coast of North America. Its spine is the mountain range which separates the island into two zones: the sheltered and mild east coast with its beaches and resort communities, and the wild, rugged west coast which is largely uninhabited.

Near the southern tip of the Island is **Victoria**, a decidedly un-Canadian city with a quaint Victorian-English charm exhibited by the many tea rooms, woolen shops, double decker busses and other accouterments of English life which set Victoria apart from other B.C. cities. While there are such pseudo-English tourist establishments as a replica of Anne Hathaway's Cottage and the Royal London Wax Museum, this part of Vancouver Island is filled with unique things to see such as Fort Rodd Hill, a British fort built to keep Americans south of the perceived British border during the short and silly 'Pig' War, and the renowned Butchart Gardens in Sidney north of Victoria. With its light rainfall (27 inches average) and temperate climate, Victoria is a prime tourist destination for Americans and Canadians. The Trans-Canada and Island Highways branch out from downtown Victoria, steering you to a variety of urban and sea-side tourist centers.

Sooke, an hour's drive from downtown Victoria, is a scenic fishing and logging town on Juan de Fuca Strait. Another hour, driving west, is **Port Renfrew**, a picturesque village now attracting international interest as the trail head for the West Coast Hiking Trail.

Duncan, north of Victoria, is close to the Cowichan Lake area. The lake, noted for its fish and resort lodges, is a magnet for summer vacationers. The **Cowichan Valley** is home to the Cowichan Indian Band, well-known for its native crafts including Cowichan sweaters.

Ten years ago, **Chemainus** was a logging village in decline. Local people took matters into their own hands and gave the town a new focus by organizing the painting of murals depicting local history and culture on many of the town's buildings. Today, there are 26 large murals on the sides of downtown buildings, reflecting the local logging heritage. Thetis and Kuper islands are a short ferry ride away.

Nanaimo, the "Harbour City", is the home of the renowned Nanaimo Bar (not a pub, it's a famous dessert square). The harbor is of interest to visitors with its constant action, scenery and seawall walk. There are several good pubs too—be sure to try the Village Inn in nearby Lantzville. North of Nanaimo, the Island Highway (Hwy. 19) runs through an almost steady stream of water-side vacation towns. **Parksville** is the turn-off point for Highway 8, Port Alberni and Pacific Rim National Park.

Our tour of the Vancouver Island coast covers the lower third of the island. We deal with the whole island in more detail in the two companion books: "Alaska-Yukon Adventures" features the Island Highway as a north-bound route toward Prince Rupert and the Alaskan Panhandle; "British Columbia Adventures" covers the entire province.

VICTORIA & AREA

Anchoring the southeast corner of Vancouver Island, the city of Victoria has become one of the continent's favorite tourist destinations. Conde Nast Traveler magazine listed Victoria as one of the five most pleasant cities in the world to visit — not an easy achievement for what was only 100 years ago a rowdy trading post inhabited by con men and other undesirables who flocked to the town to fleece Klondike Gold Rush stampeders. Established by the Hudson's Bay Company when the Oregon Treaty was signed, Victoria has lost its rough & ready atmosphere and is an oasis of English gentility, where the Union Jack waves in the summer breezes and high tea has become a standing tradition. Because Victoria has developed this more-English-than-England theme, it has become an extremely popular tourist city. The people are friendly, the pace is leisurely and a variety of attractions and recreation bring people back to Victoria again and again. It is also a popular retirement place.

The **Inner Harbour** provides a focal point for visitors, with the local infocentre located under an art deco tower. Here are the terminals for ferries to Seattle and Port Angeles WA, and seaplane flights to Vancouver. Across the harbor are the B.C. Parliament Buildings which sparkle at night with hundreds of lights. An excellent introduction to the province is a visit to the **Royal B.C. Museum**, located next to the Parliament Buildings. This major museum concentrates on B.C.'s natural history and native heritage. More history can be soaked up at **Fort Rodd Hill**, a former British bastion from 1896, now operated as a national historic site. **Bastion Square** in the downtown area is the site of old Fort Victoria (1843). **Craigdarroch Castle**, a Victorian mansion built by coal magnate Robert Dunsmuir, is open for tours.

The Victoria area is blessed with many gardens and parks. The most famous and extensive of these is **Butchart Gardens**, located in Sidney near the Swartz Bay ferry docks. At any time of the year Butchart Gardens provides a panorama of flowers, trees and shrubs in what was once a huge gravel pit. The gardens of **Government House**, the residence of B.C.'s Lieutenant Governor, are open to the public daily. The city has a wide range of hotels, motels and bed & breakfast places, some of them surprisingly inexpensive during the off-season. Travel by car to the outskirts of Victoria is recommended: to **Saanich Inlet**, **Sidney** and **Cowichan Bay** where boat rentals, guides and tackle are available. **Sooke,** west of Victoria, is part of a scenic natural area, perfect for picnics or for sophisticated dining (more on this later).

Golf courses within the city including Uplands, Cedar Hill and Gorge Vale. Glen Meadows Golf Club is at West Saanich & McTavish.

At the top of the food list is the **Empress Hotel Dining Room** on the Inner Harbour and the dining room of the **Oak Beach Hotel** on Beach Dr. Both hotels have a good ambience and fine cuisine. **Pagliacci's** at 1011 Broad St. is a less formal place—pasta is the specialty—with jazz at night. **Buchart Gardens** has a restaurant amidst the flowers.

VICTORIA & AREA

There are many many good places to stay in the Victoria area. The **Captain's Palace** at 309 Belleville St., downtown on the Inner Harbour (388-9191), has rooms with atmosphere in three former mansions, breakfast included. **$$ to $$$.** **Stay 'N Save Motor Inn**, 3233 Maple St., off Hwy. 17 north (383-5111): This chain motel is 1 km from downtown, restaurant. **$$.** The **Brentwood Inn**, at 7176 Brentwood Dr., Brentwood Bay (652-2912) is five minutes from Butchart Gardens with some housekeeping units, restaurant, pub & a dinner cruise is available. **$$.**

The **Empress Hotel**, 721 Government St. (downtown on Inner Harbour, 384-8111, 1-800-828-7447) It's called the "Grand Old Lady" of Victoria with good reason. It's an institution, newly restored to its early grandeur. Tea is served in the lobby each afternoon. Hotel amenities include a pool, restaurants and lounges and it is next to the Victoria Conference Centre. **$$ to $$$.** **Hotel Grand Pacific** is in downtown Victoria at the Inner Harbour. This is Victoria's newest large hotel with pool, sauna, whirlpool, fitness center, dining room and lounge. **$$ to $$$.** **$$.** The **Oak Bay Beach Hotel**, 1175 Beach Drive (598-4556), is a Tudor inn on the water with a distinctive atmosphere and excellent service. The staff serves high tea each day in the lobby. The hotel has a restaurant, pub, and yacht cruises—with dining—are available. **$$ to $$$**

There are many fine bed and breakfast operations in the Victoria area. Here are some of the best: **Portage Inlet House**, 993 Portage Rd. (479-4594), is on a secluded site overlooking Portage Inlet. This solar heated house has 3 rooms plus a "Honeymoon Cottage". Full breakfast is served. **$$.** The **Lilac House, at 252 Memorial Crescent** in Victoria (389-0252), is an 1892 Victorian house in the old community of Fairfield, near Juan de Fuca Strait. There are three antique-furnished rooms here, with full breakfast. **$.** **Charlotte's Guest House**, 338 Foul Bay Rd., Victoria (595-3528) is an oak-shaded home with fine views of Georgia and Juan de Fuca straits in the Gonzales neighborhood (take Fairfield Rd. east to Foul Bay Rd.) There are two rooms with full breakfast including home baking. **$.** The **Oak Bay Guest House**, 1052 Newport Ave. (598-3812) is a 1912 B. & B. inn with private baths. As well, two reservation services book B & B homes: Garden City B & B Service (604-479-9999) and All Season B & B Agency (604-655-7173 or 595-2337).

Fort Victoria RV Park & Campground, 340 Island Highway (Hwy. 1A) is on The Gorge waterway in the town of View Royal, 6 KM from downtown Victoria, with hookups, sani-station, tenting sites, showers & laundry. The **Goldstream Park Campground** is on the Trans-Canada Highway (Hwy 1) 17 KM from downtown Victoria. This is a basic public campground with showers, set amidst towering Douglas fir trees. **KOA Victoria East**, Mount Newton Cross Road, 18 KM north of Victoria in Saanichton (652-3232) is a large RV park overlooking the water with hookups, pull-through sites, showers, store, propane & laundry.

Vancouver Island Drives

This brief summary introduces the main roads in the southern third of Vancouver Island and some of the attractions along the way. For more detailed information on the towns and cities of the Island, see the highway logs and pages on the towns of the area which follow.

Highway 14 & West Coast Road—Victoria to Port Renfrew:
This short and pleasant drive covers the 111 KM (70 mile) road which runs along the coastline of the Strait of Juan de Fuca, on the south end of the Island. This route can be done as a day trip out of Victoria or, better still, as a vacation jaunt which could take a weekend or several days. The West Coast Road, also known locally as the Sooke Road, is suitable for overnight stays for visitors who are pulling tent trailers, camping in tents, driving RVs or who want to enjoy the luxury of several deluxe inns. There are several communities along the way which can serve as a vacation base. Of these, Sooke is the preferred place—about a third of the way to the Pacific coast. With its impressive bay sheltered by a large spit of land, as well as a supply of good accommodations and food, Sooke is an ideal vacation destination.

Between Victoria and Sooke, the road is Highway 14. West of Sooke, it's called the West Coast Road. At the end is Port Renfrew, long a logging community which only recently has been gearing up for an increased number of tourists who are making the trip to hike the West Coast Trail. Visitors also go there to see the unusual Botanical Beach Provincial Park, three KM from the village. Between Sooke and Port Renfrew are several strikingly scenic beaches with good sand and some with picnic facilities. The Juan de Fuca beaches are attracting a growing interest from surfers and windsurfers.

The West Coast Road is also a way to begin a circle route which could end back in Victoria by joining the Trans-Canada Highway at Duncan, north of Victoria. From Port Renfrew, the mainline logging road mentioned earlier takes you to Lake Cowichan. From there, Highway 18 runs east to join the Trans-Canada just north of Duncan. For details on facilities and services along the West Coast Road, see page 230.

The Island Highway:
What B.C.ers call the Island Highway is actually two highways — as the government sees it. The route between Victoria and Nanaimo is part of the Trans-Canada Highway system and is called Hwy. #1. The rest of the north/south route along the eastern shore of the Island—all the way to the northern tip and Port Hardy — is called the Island Highway (Hwy. # 19). This is a favorite route for vacation travelers. Along the way, north from Victoria, are an almost continuous string of seaside communities until you reach the towns of Courtenay and Comox (at mid-island). All of these small resort towns cater to tourists from afar as well as vacationing B.C.ers.

Vancouver Island Drives

The sheltered waters of the Strait of Georgia provide a perfect setting for resort motels and hotels, RV parks and a few private campgrounds. Some of the most popular provincial camping parks are along this route.

The major cities and towns along the Island Highway include **Nanaimo**, site of one of the mainland ferry terminals; **Courtenay** and **Comox** in the center of mid-Island country; and **Campbell River** which is well-known as a superb salmon fishing center. The highway then moves north, passing through a vast wilderness, leading to **Port Hardy** and the terminus of the car ferry to Prince Rupert. Tourists use the Island Highway to provide an alternate and time-saving route to Southeastern Alaska, sailing on the ferry "Queen of the North" to Prince Rupert and transferring there to one of the local Southeastern Alaska Ferries. This is also a fascinating way to move northward, driving from Prince Rupert along the Stewart-Cassiar Highway to the Yukon and theAlaskan interior.

The Island Highway offers swimming and fishing lakes along the way—by the hundreds—in addition to walking and hiking trails every few kilometers. There is a wide profusion of motels, hotels and resorts with cabins, as well as a range of campgrounds (private and public) and RV parks with hookups and drive-through sites.

North of Campbell River, however, there is little in the way of this kind of human comfort—until you get to the North Island communities—but much beautiful wilderness scenery.

Our suggested drive is from Victoria, in the south, to Nanaimo and a short distance north to **Parksville** where Highway 5 leads west to the Pacific Coast.

Highway 4—The Road to Pacific Rim Park:

Port Alberni is the major town on this road which runs for 181 KM (113 miles) between Parksville and the West Coast. However, the major attractions for tourists are two smaller fishing villages and a wonderful national park between the villages. The communities are Tofino and Ucluelet. Tofino has always been a fishing community and has become home to an eclectic collection of outdoors lovers, artists and craftsmen. Ucluelet has its economy based on logging but, in recent years, has become a tourist center—particularly for whale-watching expeditions.

Pacific Rim National Park is the jewel of Vancouver Island parks. It offers miles of sandy, surf-swept beaches where driftwood logs pile up like matchsticks. The park has campsites (drive-in and walk-in), walking & hiking trails, and those miles of sandy beaches to walk along—perfect for beachcombing. There is also a variety of accommodation near the park including motels, beach-side cabins and private campgrounds and RV parks. It's hard to miss with a vacation in or near the park. The road is paved all the way to Tofino.

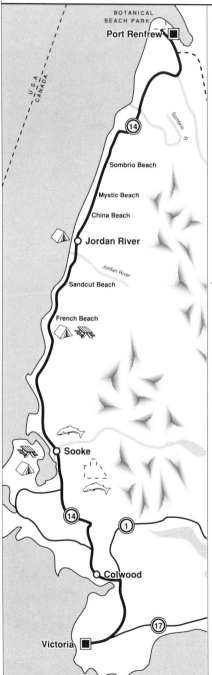

This trip is easily done in one day, or can provide several days or even a week of outdoor adventure on this rugged coastline beside the Strait of Juan de Fuca. The road has a string of scenic sand beaches—highly recommended.

Downtown Victoria Take Highway 1 to the Colwood overpass. Follow the Sooke cutoff signs onto Hwy. 14.

Colwood This small city is 18 KM (11.2 miles) from downtown Victoria. Fort Rodd Hill Historic Site is a restored British fort at the entrance to Esquimalt Harbour.

Junction—Metchosin Road This road is an alternate route to Sooke via Metchosin and several interesting regional parks including **Albert Head Lagoon, Witty's Lagoon, Devonian and East Sooke** parks. Brochures are in the Colwood Infocentre, 697 Goldstream Ave. (478-3242).

Matheson Lake Provincial Park (take Happy Valley Rd. at the end of Metchosin Rd.) Canoeing, swimming, fishing. A trail circles the small lake.

Sooke KM 44 (mile 27.3) Gas, motels, hotel, restaurants, stores. A scenic fishing and logging town, Sooke is an ideal base for exploring the parks and trails along the Juan de Fuca coastline. The **Sooke Museum** (on Hwy. 14) is a pioneer museum with Coast Salish native artifacts, logging equipment, a salmon barbecue and afternoon teas.

Highway Log

The Sooke Harbour House is a small hotel with a renowned restaurant specializing in west coast foods. There are several fine B & B houses in the area as well. See page 230 for details. From Sooke, the West Coast Road travels past several great beaches. Last gas here before Port Renfrew.

French Beach Provincial Park KM 64.5 (mile 40) Campsites & two picnic areas, forest trails and views of the Olympic range.

Sandcut Beach KM 71 (mile 44.4) A forest recreation area. A trail takes you to a fine beach & along Sandcut Creek.

Jordan River KM 76 (mile 47.2) Store, cafes. A forestry village. There are two free RV parking areas on the beach.

China Beach Provincial Park KM 81 (mile 50.3) This is an excellent day-use park with a beautiful beach, trails through mixed forest (cedar, fir, hemlock) & rockhounding. The wind is sometimes quite strong here. Tie down your hat!

Mystic Beach KM 83 (mile 51.6) A trail leads to the shore where a waterfall cascades to a secluded beach. This is one of several forest recreation sites along the rd.

Sombrio Beach KM 91 (mile 56.7) A scenic forest beach with several caves at one end. For a short walk to the beach, take the western access road. The clear cut here brought protests when the area was logged.

Road to the Red Creek Fir KM 110 (mile 68.3) A 17 KM gravel road leads to Canada's largest Douglas fir tree, more than 900 years old. Follow the Red Creek signs to a parking lot & trail.

Port Renfrew KM 111.5 (mile 69.3) Gas, cafes, cabins, hotel, store, camping. This village is at the mouth of the San Juan River, and is near the southeast end of the West Coast Trail—part of Pacific Rim National Park. An information center is located on the road to the trailhead.

Logging Rd. to Cowichan Lake: A 54 KM (33.5 mile) road leads to the Cowichan Lake district from Port Renfrew. Cowichan Lake is one of the most popular recreation areas on Vancouver Island. This mainline logging road is partially paved and there are two forest campsites along the way. Fairy Lake forest park is 3 KM from the San Juan River bridge, another convenient place to camp.

Botanical Beach Provincial Park: 3.5 KM from the end of Hwy. 14. Check the papers for low-tide hours and visit then. This park has hundreds of tidal pools cut into the shoreline rock. Many are filled with a wonderful variety of marine life. Gray whales migrate past the park. A word of warning! The access road to Botanical Beach is very rough and it is sometimes difficult to drive farther than about the half-way point during the wet months.

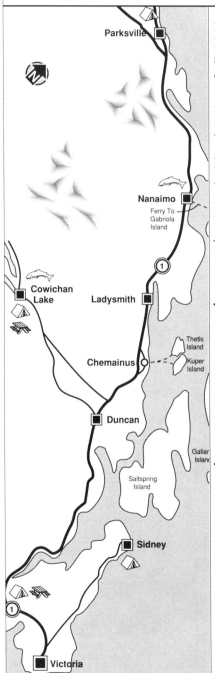

Hwy. 1, the Trans-Canada route, leaves Victoria and follows the shoreline of Saanich Inlet after cutting through Goldstream Provincial Park. The mountain ridges forming the spine of the island can be seen to the west.

Victoria KM 0 (mile 0) The starting point is downtown Victoria, near the Inner Harbour. The Victoria Infocentre is here (phone 368-2127). See pages 221 to 225 for Victoria details.

Junction—Cloverdale Road KM 2 (mile 1.2) To Hwy. 17 for the airport and B.C. ferries at Swartz Bay.

Junction—McKenzie Ave. KM 5 (mile 3.1) To Hwy. 17 and the University of Victoria.

Rest Stop (Portage Inlet-on east side of rd.) Picnic tables & boat launch.

Thetis Lake Park KM 11.5 (mile 7.1) Swimming, picnic tables, canoeing & fishing for bass & trout.

Junction—Millstream Road KM 13 (mile 8) Turn north for 31 KM (19 miles) to Lone Tree Hill Park (Douglas firs, eagles). Turn south for 1 KM to Mill Hill Park (hiking trails).

Goldstream Provincial Park KM 18 (mile 11) Camping, nature trails, visitor center. This park has stands of very high Douglas firs amid a mixed forest. There is an annual chum salmon run on the Goldstream River which peaks every four years.

Highway Log

Junction—**Shawnigan Lake Cutoff** KM 28 (mile 17.4) to a resort and recreation area which includes **Memory Island Provincial Park** (beaches) & **Shawnigan Lake Provincial Park** (swimming, boating, picnicking).

Malahat Drive The scenic drive over Malahat Mountain begins here. The summit provides views of the mountains and inlet.

Bamberton Provincial Park KM 35.5 (mile 22) Camping, swimming, picnic tables.

Mill Bay KM 45 (mile 28) Visitor Infocentre on Hwy. 1. The ferry travels to Brentwood Bay near Butchart Gardens. Gas, stores.

Junction—Cobble Hill Road KM 48 (mile 29.8) West to Cobble Hill & Shawnigan Lake. East to Cowichan Bay.

Cowichan River: At the south entrance to the city of Duncan. This popular fishing river has a 19 KM trail offering anglers great rainbow, steelhead & salmon.

Duncan KM 62 (mile 38.5) Gas, stores, motels. Infocentre on Hwy. 1, downtown (746-4421). A city of 20,000, Duncan is home to the Cowichan Indian Band, best known for crafts including the famous Cowichan sweaters.

B.C. Forest Museum KM 64 (mile 39.8) A popular attraction with outdoor attractions including a steam train and sawmill as well as other features including displays on the history of the B.C. forest industry.

Junction—Hwy. 18 KM 65 (mile 40.3) To the town of Lake Cowichan (28 KM-17.3 miles), Bamfield, Carmanah Park, the West Coast Trail & Port Renfrew.

Crofton KM 74 (mile 46) A pulp mill town with ferry to Salt Spring Island. Infocentre at the museum, next to ferry terminal.

Junction—Hwy. 1A KM 89 (mile 55) to **Chemainus.** Gas, stores, Infocentre in a rail caboose on Chemainus Rd. The town is famous for the murals on the downtown buildings, depicting local history. A ferry runs to Thetis & Kuper islands. See page 139.

Ladysmith KM 91 (mile 51.5) Infocentre on Hwy. 1. Stores, cafes, gas, arboretum & museum.

Junction—Yellow Point Rd. KM 96 (mile 59.6) to Roberts Memorial and Hemer day-use parks (picnicking, water sports).

Nanaimo KM 112 (mile 70) The "Harbour City". Gas, hotels, motels, restaurants, stores. Travel Infocentre at Hwy. 19 & Bryden St. At Nanaimo, the Island Highway to Port Hardy changes to # 19. The ferry terminal is at Departure Bay, at the end of Hwy 1. Please see page 231 for Nanaimo details.

Lantzville Rd. KM 134 (mile 83) A small seaside community. Gas, a great pub, stores, camping.

Parksville KM 154 (mile 95.6) Gas, stores, motels, pub, camping. A resort community with golfing & a fine beach.

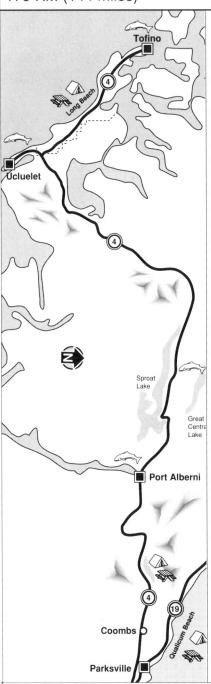

A vacation or side-trip to the Vancouver Island west coast and Pacific Rim National Park is highly recommended.

Highway 4 begins in Parksville and runs west through the lumbering & fishing city of **Port Alberni** to the two colorful west coast villages of **Tofino** and **Ucluelet.** Between the two towns is the Long Beach section of **Pacific Rim National Park**, a long stretch of rugged coastline including the 30-kilometer Long Beach, much of which is glistening white sand.

The rustic country village of **Coombs** is at the 9 KM (5 mile) point. Look for goats grazing on the general store's roof. Coombs hosts a country and bluegrass festival in July.

Port Alberni is 42.5 KM (26.4 miles) from Parksville. The highway provides access to several provincial parks. After leaving Port Alberni, the highway crosses the Mackenzie mountain range, descending beside Kennedy Lake to the coast. The highway comes to an end at the Tofino/Ucluelet Road. Turn left for Ucluelet, 8 KM (5 miles) down the road. Turn right for Tofino which is 34 KM (21 miles). See pages 234 & 235).

The Long Beach section of the park lies between the villages. Look on the right (east) side of the road for the park information center.

Highway Log

Our highway log begins at the junction of the Trans-Canada Hwy. (#1) & Highway 4, where Highway 4 leads west from Parksville.

Turnoff for Englishman River Falls Provincial Park KM 5 (mile 3) The park is 9 KM (5.6 miles) off the highway. Waterfalls, swimming and fishing.

Coombs KM 9 (mile 5.6) A small, rustic village with a country store. Look for goats on the roof.

Little Qualicum Falls Prov-incial Park KM 17.7 (mile 11) On the south shore of Cameron Lake. One of the few spots to fish for brown trout.

Cameron Lake Picnic Park KM 21.5 (mile 13.4) On the highway.

Beaufort Picnic Park KM 24.5 (mile 15.2)

Macmillan Provincial Park KM 25.6 (mile 16) Includes Cathedral Grove, a preserved stand of Douglas fir trees—some of the tallest in the province.

South Port Alberni Road KM 41 (mile 25.5) Turnoff for the drive to **Bamfield** along a 101 KM (63 mile) logging road. Bamfield is near the Broken Group Islands and is the northeast trailhead for the West Coast Trail.

Turnoff to Port Alberni KM 42.5 (mile 26.5) Turn southwest for the city. The city's Infocentre is located at 2533 Redford Street. For Port Alberni details, see page 232.

Sproat Lake Provincial Park KM 57 (mile 35.5) Beaches & camping.

Junction—Tofino/Ucluelet Road: KM 140 (mile 87) Turn south to the picturesque village of Ucluelet for gas, restaurants, B & Bs and motels. Turn north for Pacific Rim National Park and the village of Tofino. This comm-unity, a fishing village, also has gas, motels, cafes and recreational activities including tours of Clayquot Sound and neighboring islands. See page 235 for details.

Pacific Rim National Park:

Thundering surf, long beaches, rugged rocks and forest make up the superb Long Beach portion of B.C.'s newest national park. Long Beach is the most accessible part of the park, with sand beaches running for 16 KM. The tides have brought in huge driftwood logs which are piled along the beaches: sun bleached and glistening. The place to start your visit is the main park center at Lost Shoe Creek where you can obtain trail maps and camping information. The Wikaninnish Centre contains displays on the park ecology. Huge murals show ocean life including whales, fish and seabirds. There are film showings & a dining room in the building. Long Beach is a haven for surfers and a wonderland for those who enjoy nature at its best — including walks on the trails, swimming in the ocean or exploring the driftwood-covered shoreline. See pages 233 & 234 for park information.

SOOKE & PORT RENFREW (WEST COAST ROAD)

Many travelers who visit towns along the West Coast Road keep their accommodations in Victoria. That's too bad, because staying in an inn or bed & breakfast home along the highway gives you a chance to see more and to savor the atmosphere of this unique corner of the island.

The famed **Sooke Harbour House** is at 1528 Whiffin Spit Road in Sooke (642-3421). This small hotel is unique and operates on a bed and breakfast + lunch plan. It features a superb restaurant and modern rooms—most of which overlook Juan de Fuca Strait. It is expensive (room rates vary from $125 to $240) and worth every penny for the food alone. The hotel building is surrounded by a herb garden, providing fragrance and fresh herbs for the hotel's kitchen. Whiffin Spit is a minute's walk from the hotel with the town a 2 minute drive away. **$$$**.

Malahat Farm Bed & Breakfast on Anderson Rd. is just west of the town (642-6868). One of the best bed and breakfast experiences in the province, the breakfast fixings come from the farm. Rooms are filled with antiques and comfortable high old-fashioned brass beds. **$$ to $$$**. **Ocean Wilderness** is a bed & breakfast home off Hwy 14, just a ten minute drive west of Sooke (646-2116). The house is located on the Strait of Juan de Fuca in a forest setting with bald eagles in the trees and whales passing by. The rooms are large with canopied beds. **$$$**. The **Tideview Bed & Breakfast** (642-9650) and **Altman's Bed & Breakfast** (642-3030) are both on the waterfront via Dufour Rd. Both are **$$**.

Point No Point, a resort 24 KM (15 miles) west of Sooke has a scenic location and log cabins with kitchens and fireplaces. The resort has a good restaurant which is open for lunches and afternoon tea. **$$**.

Sooke Community Park on Phillips Road (642-6244) has camping by the river and a sani-station. **Sunny Shores Resort & Marina**, 5621 Sooke Rd. (642-5731) has hookups, pool, sani-station, showers, laundry and a small motel with marina nearby. **Sooke Harbour Marina & Campground**, 6971 West Coast Rd. (642-3236) has hookups, showers, laundry, sani-station, boat rentals & boat launch.

Port Renfrew Accommodation:

Port Renfrew Hotel, at the end of the road in town (647-5541). This is an old original building right on the waterfront beside the public dock. It has a restaurant and a colorful pub—filled in the summer by people from around the world, most of them wearing hiking boots. **$**. **Bay View House Bed & Breakfast,** 65 Wickaninnish (647-5536), operated by Charlie & Marlo Baxter with the full house available for 5-6 people or individual rooms with continental breakfast. Daily & weekly rates. **$**. **Beach-view Bed & Breakfast,** 11 Queesto Drive (647-5459) has two rooms and a self-contained cabin (weekly bookings only) with full breakfasts available. **$**. **Pacheenaht Band Campsite**, at the mouth of the San Juan River in Port Renfrew, has tent and trailer sites, boat launches and a sand beach. The **Port Renfrew Marina,** on Gordon River Rd. (647-5430), has RV parking spaces and a sani-station.

NANAIMO

Nanaimo was a coal town when it was founded by the Hudson's Bay Company in 1852. With a population of 50,000, Nanaimo is the Island's second largest city and a year-round fishing, logging and transportation center. An important confection was invented here in 1950 when a local woman won a contest for dessert squares and the 'Nanaimo Bar' was born.

Newcastle Island, a provincial park with good hiking and tent camping, is a short ferry ride from downtown. Nanaimo offers a walking tour with several historic buildings in the downtown area.

Bungee jumping came to Nanaimo in 1990. The 140 foot jump is 13 KM south of town 200 meters off the Island Hwy. at the Nanaimo Lakes turnoff. The "Bungee Zone" is open daily during spring, summer and fall months.

The Nanaimo city visitor infocentre is at 266 Bryden Street (on the Trans-Canada Highway) downtown, phone 754-8474.

The ferry terminal — for mainland ferries — is at Departure Bay, just north of downtown Nanaimo at the end of the Trans-Canada Highway. Phone 753-6626 (recorded message); general information: 753-1261.

Accommodation in Nanaimo and area is plentiful. Downtown hotels and motels are standard business-style operations. The more interesting fishing lodges and small inns are outside of town. The **Colonial Hotel** is at 950 Terminal Ave. (754-4415). Some of the rooms have kitchen units and there is a swimming pool, sauna and coffee shop. **$** The **Best Western North Gate** is a large modern motel at 6450 Metral Dr. (390-2222) This is on Hwy. 19, next to a shopping centre. The motel has a restaurant and a pub. **$$**.

The **Coast Bastion Inn**, at 11 Bastion St. downtown (753-6601) (1-800-663-1144), is a full-service hotel with dining room, coffee shop, pub, sauna, whirlpool. The Coast chain of hotels has properties in several B.C. cities and all are well-operated hotels. **$$ to $$$**.

The **Inn of the Sea Resort** on Yellow Point Road, south of Nanaimo, is 13 km (8.7 miles) north of Ladysmith off Hwy. 1 (245-2211). This is a popular fishing and vacation inn. The rooms & suites have sea views. There is a pool, whirlpool, tennis and dining room. **$$ to $$$**.

Triple E Tent & Trailer Park, 8 KM (5 miles) south of Nanaimo on Hwy. 19 (754-3611) Full & partial hookups, showers, laundry. **Beban Park Campground**, 2300 Bower Rd. (758-1177), Civic campground, close to downtown, 1 1/2 KM west of Hwy 19. **Jingle Pot Campsites**, 4012 Jingle Pot Rd. (758-1614). 6 KM (4 miles) north of Nanaimo. Partial & full hookups, shaded campsites, showers, laundry, store.

For food, I suggest the following: The **Harbour Lights Restaurant**, 1518 Stewart Ave. (753-6614) serves steak and seafood. Closed Sundays. **$$**. The **Lighthouse Bistro & Pub,** 50 Anchor Way (754-3212), a pier-top restaurant in the waterfront area. Seafood is the specialty. **$$**. **Chez Michel**, 10 Front Street (754-1218) has a fine location with French cuisine. **$$$**.

PARKSVILLE & PORT ALBERNI

Parksville is a placid vacation base for many visitors to Vancouver Island. It is within easy driving distance of Nanaimo and Victoria and at the junction of the Island Highway (Hwy. 19) and Hwy. 4—the road to Port Alberni and Pacific Rim National Park, Tofino and Ucluelet on the West Coast. This is a resort and retirement community with good golfing, beach activity and is close to a number of fine outdoor attractions and activity areas. **Englishman River Falls Provincial Park** is 5 KM (3 miles) west of Parksville on Hwy. 4. There is a good public campground here and hiking trails through the forest. The park has a day-use area with picnic spots, swimming, and good trout fishing. **Rathtrevor Provincial Park** south of Parksville offers some of the warmest salt-water swimming in B.C. You have the chance to spot some of the 150 bird varieties seen here.

Tyh-Na-Mara Resort, 2 KM south of town off Hwy. 19 (248-2072 or 1-800-663-7373). This is the area's fancy resort hotel with all the facilities: condo-type hotel accommodations, log cottages, indoor pool, a sea-side location and walks through the arbutus & fir forest. **$$$**

Graycrest Resort, on Rathtrevor Beach, south of town (248-6513), is a new resort complex with condo-type units, full kitchens, pool, sauna, laundry, restaurant nearby. **$$ to $$$**

Madrona Beach Resort, 1045 East Island Hwy. (248-5503) on the water at Rathtrevor Beach has townhouse-style units including kitchen, fireplace, 2-bedroom suites, etc. Also 1 bedroom and studio units. **$$ to $$$**

Sea Edge Motel, on the highway close to downtown (248-8377). 1 or 2-bedroom sleeping & housekeeping units. Laundry, playground. **$$**

French Creek Cottages & Campground, West Island Highway (248-3998). 1 to 3 bedroom housekeeping cottages with an ocean view, restaurant and pub. **$$** The adjacent campground has showers, laundry and shaded sites but no hookups. **Craig's On-The-Sea Campground & RV Park**, 3 KM (2 miles) south of town on Northwest Bay Rd. (248-5928). Waterfront sites, hookups, showers, laundry, sani-station, beach, store, playground, boat launch. **Big Tent & RV Park**, Island Highway, on the Englishman River (248-6249) has hookups, store and a sani-station.

In **Port Alberni**, the **Hospitality Motor Inn** is at 3835 Redford St., near the main entrance to town from the highway (723-8111 or 1-800-663-6677). This motor hotel has standard rooms, a restaurant and pub. **$$**.

The **Greenwood Motor Inn**, 4850 Beaver Creek Rd. (723-1244 or 1-800-663-6678) is also a motor hotel with dining room, pub and lounge. **$$**.

The **Timberlodge & RV Campground**, Port Alberni Highway (723-9419) has a lodge with standard and housekeeping units, a heated pool, sauna, dining room and lounge. **$$** The campground has shaded and open sites, hookups, showers and laundry. **Dry Creek Public Campground**, on Napier Street off 3rd Ave. (723-6011), is a municipal campground beside a creek with shaded sites and partial hookups, showers, sani-station, boat rentals, propane and store.

PACIFIC RIM NATIONAL PARK

Pacific Rim National Park is the main reason visitors come to the West Coast communities of Tofino and Ucluelet. This is Canada's newest national park, established in the 1970s. It is comprised of three separate units: Long Beach, the Broken Group Islands and the West Coast Trail. The park was created to interpret the great forces and influences of the Pacific Ocean on these three unusual landscapes. The park's main Visitor Centre is located in the Long Beach section, just off the Ucluelet/Tofino road north of the Highway 4 junction. The information desk here has full details on the three units in the park, including maps of walking and hiking trails within the park, campsite availabilities and interpretive brochures.

Long Beach is the most accessible and most popular unit of the park. Stretching for 11 KM (7 miles) between Ucluelet and Tofino, this is a long string of wide sandy beaches swept by surf which, during storms, is awe-inspiring. The several stretches of beach are separated by rocky headlands which jut out into the ocean. There are drive-in and walk-in campsites. Green Point is the major campsite, a typical national park campground. The primitive walk-in sites are at the north end of Long Beach via a 1 KM trail. Visitors hike the beaches, headlands and the forest trails. There are several good viewpoints along the road including Radar Hill, the site of an old World War II installation which provides an excellent view of the beaches, ocean and nearby mountains.

The beach at Wickaninnish is the most impressive of the Long Beach unit, with huge piles of driftwood logs haphazardly stacked as if a giant had thrown a handful of toothpicks. This is also the location of the Wickaninnish Centre, an interpretive building with films and displays on the whales and other marine life. This building has a good restaurant with a magnificent view of the thundering surf below.

Surfing is a popular activity on Long Beach but the favorite pastime is strolling along the beaches looking for razor clams and oysters and watching the colorful sea birds which follow the tides for their food. There are tidal pools along the headlands which contain a wide variety of sea life including mussels, sea stars, limpets, hermit crabs, varieties of seaweed and barnacles. The park is on the Pacific Flyway which makes bird watching during spring and fall seasons a real delight. Some birds winter in the park as well. There are several interesting nature trails in the Long Beach unit; one of the most fascinating is a short bog trail with stands of stunted shorepine, peat moss and the Labrador tea plant.

The Broken Group Islands are accessed by boat from Bamfield or Ucluelet. The Lady Rose sails daily from Port Alberni, landing on Gibraltar Island as well as at Bamfield. Toquart Bay, accessible via a logging road, is also a gateway to the islands for private boats. The waters of Barkley Sound are studded with reefs and morning fog often shrouds the islands. The islands are rugged with few beaches or tidal flats but there are sheltered inlets at Hand, Gibraltar and Jacques islands.

PACIFIC RIM NATIONAL PARK

If you are planning a trip to the Broken Group islands, you should have Marine Chart 3670 which combines park information and navigation information.   It's available for $8 from the Canadian Hydrographic Service, Chart Sales and Distribution Office, Institute of Ocean Sciences, 9860 West Saanich Road, Box 6000, Sidney B.C. V8L 4B2.

The West Coast Trail spans a distance of 77 kilometers (48 miles). The original trail was established during the 1800s as a lifesaving trail. Because of the great winds and surf which pound this rugged part of Vancouver Island and the isolation of the area, a trail was necessary for shipwrecked mariners whose ships foundered off the coast.   The trail was re-constructed during the 1970s and completed for hiking in 1980.   It provides a rugged experience which tests self-sufficiency. Most people take five or six days, or longer, to hike the full length of the trail. It is not a recommended experience for neophyte hikers but, for the experienced, it is a thrilling challenge which offers wonderful scenery including crashing surf, majestic inlets and a seemingly unending panorama of wildlife, old growth and new forests, craggy landscape and pristine beaches.

The northern trail head is located at Pachena Bay which is 5 KM from the village of Bamfield on Barkley Sound. The southern trail head is across the San Juan River from Port Renfrew. Hikers arrive at Bamfield by car, on a 60 KM (37 mile) logging road from Port Alberni or by taking the passenger ship "Lady Rose" from Port Alberni. For information on the ship's schedule, phone 1-800-663-7192. Port Renfrew is accessible by car from Victoria via Highway 14 (the West Coast Road, see pages 225 & 230). You can also get to Bamfield and Port Renfrew on logging roads which start from Lake Cowichan. There are several private operators who run hikers from Port Renfrew across the San Juan River to the southern trail head. There's also a park information kiosk in Port Renfrew. A useful contour map of the West Coast Trail is available by writing the Ministry of the Environment, 553 Superior Street, Victoria B.C., V8V 1X4.

Tofino is a laid-back fishing village which offers several special attractions to visitors. A short flight or an hour's boat ride take you to Hot Springs Cove and a natural island hot spring with several pools descending from the source to the sea. Tour boats take visitors through Tofino Inlet to Meares Island. Whale Watching is a prime spring attraction in both Tofino and Ucluelet. The Tofino Infocentre is at 351 Campbell Street (604-725-3414).

Ucluelet, at the south end of the Tofino/Ucluelet Rd., has a small fishing fleet and is home to loggers and others who work in the nearby coastal forests. Sports fishing is popular with plentiful salmon, cod, halibut and red snapper. The town Infocentre is at 1620 Peninsula Road. You can also go to the Municipal Office at 200 Main Street for information. There is a map posted outside this building which offers a bird's eye view of Ucluelet and its attractions.

Suggested places to stay in **Tofino** include the **Pacific Sands Beach Resort**, 1421 Pacific Rim Highway (Ucluelet/Tofino Rd.) (725-3322). Housekeeping cottages and motel units near Pacific Rim Park with 9-hole golf course nearby. **$$**. **Orca Lodge**, on Hwy. 4 KM south of town near the park (725-3344) has rooms with private bath, restaurant and lounge, fishing packages. **$$**. The **Crystal Cove Beach Resort**, 3 KM south of town (725-4213), has self-contained log cottages **($$)** and a campground with hookups, showers, shaded and open sites on and away from the beach. **Mackenzie Beach Resort**, 2 KM from town on Mackenzie Beach features 1 & 2 bedroom log housekeeping cottages, indoor pool **($$)** and 16 campsites. **Duffin Cove Resort Motel**, in town on the water (725-3448) has standard motel units and cabins with laundry, near stores and restaurants. **$$**. **Maquinna Lodge**, 120 First St. in the town center (725-3261), is an older hotel which has a dining room and lounge, cold beer & wine store, fishing charters arranged. **$**. The **Bella Pacifica Campground** on Mackenzie Beach near the Hwy. (725-3439) has a large campground with hookups, showers and laundry.

There are several interesting places to east in Tofino, including **The Loft**, 346 Campbell Street (725-4241). This is the place for full meals, well cooked and presented food served with a west coast flair. Seafood is a specialty (of course). Open from 7 am to 9 pm. **$$ to $$$** The **Alleyway Cafe** (725-3105) is almost hidden. Look for the Bank of Commerce on Campbell St. and then walk behind the bank. It's open from 9 to 9, serving soup, sandwiches, salads, pizza. **$ to $$**. **Weigh West Pub**, on the waterfront near the fishing harbor, serves typical pub food including fish and chips, sandwiches, etc. plus draft and bottled beer. **$**.

In **Ucluelet,** the **West Coast Motel**, on the main street overlooking the harbor (726-7732) has sleeping and housekeeping rooms and suites with 1 or 2 bedrooms, some rooms with whirlpool, indoor pool, sauna, squash court, restaurant. **$$**. The **Canadian Princess Resort** (726-7771 or 1-800-663-7090) is a ship in the harbor with staterooms plus on-shore units, dining room and lounge. Fishing charters can be arranged in advance. **$ to $$**. **Burley's Bed & Breakfast**, 1078 Helen Road, on the inlet (726-4444) is a comfortable lodge having private rooms with shared baths, a lounge with fireplace, decks and lawn near the beach. **$** The **Pacific Rim Motel** is just off the main street overlooking the harbor (726-7728) with standard and housekeeping units — some with views of the water. **$**. **Island West Resort RV Park & Marina** at the foot of Bay Street (726-7515) has five motel units and a campground with partial hookups, showers, sani-station, boat rentals, boat launch, moorage, touring charters. **Ucluelet Campground**, a large campground overlooks the bay (726-4355) with showers, flush toilets, hookups, boat rentals.

For dining in Ucluelet, try the **Canadian Princess Resort ($$ to $$$)** or the **Whale's Tale** restaurant **($$ to $$$)**. Both specialize in seafood.

GULF ISLANDS

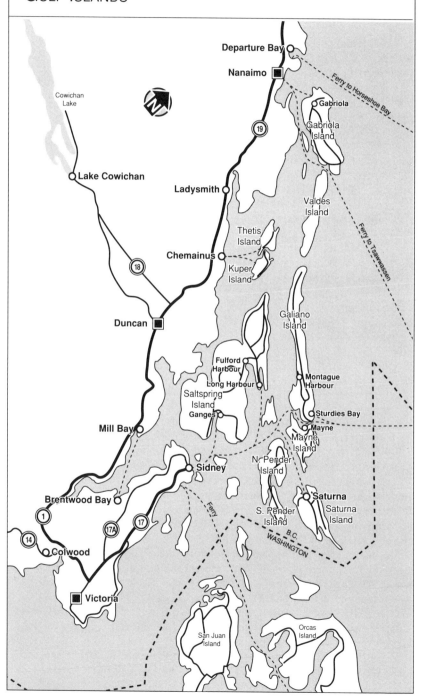

Cowichan Lake

Departure Bay

Nanaimo

Ferry to Horseshoe Bay

Gabriola

Gabriola Island

Ferry to Tsawwassen

Lake Cowichan

Ladysmith

Valdes Island

Thetis Island

Chemainus

Kuper Island

Galiano Island

Duncan

Fulford Harbour

Long Harbour

Montague Harbour

Saltspring Island

Ganges

Sturdies Bay

Mayne

Mill Bay

Mayne Island

Sidney

N. Pender Island

Brentwood Bay

Saturna

S. Pender Island

Saturna Island

Colwood

B.C.

WASHINGTON

Ferry

Victoria

San Juan Island

Orcas Island

SOUTHERN GULF ISLANDS

Nesting in the Strait of Georgia—off the calm side of Vancouver Island—the southern Gulf Islands offer relaxed holiday getaways in a quiet, bucolic environment. Separated from the San Juan Islands by just a little bit of water and the unseen U.S. border line, the Canadian Gulf Islands hark back to an earlier age when people were close to the land and were more aware of their natural surroundings.

The Gulf Islands lack much of the sophistication and glitz of neighboring Vancouver and they do not have the English manor-house ambience of Victoria. But that's not what we're looking for on these Islands in the Strait. You should expect sparkling water, quiet winding roads through lush farmland and forests, with accommodations to suit the ambience: fine bed and breakfast homes; some outstanding intimate restaurants serving fresh West Coast cuisine; fascinating provincial parks with cobble beaches; bird life including bald eagles; animal life including island deer and killer whales; hiking along the coastlines and through the forests or golfing on some of the islands. The islands offer a chance to get away to a more peaceful kind of recreation, similar to that available on the neighboring San Juan Islands — but with a Canadian difference.

The most southerly of the islands are the more populated and more accessible: **Salt Spring, Pender, Mayne, Saturna and Galiano**. These are reached by ferry from Swartz Bay near Victoria or from Tsawwassen near Vancouver on the mainland. They all have accommodations and attractions for travelers, although Salt Spring and Galiano are more geared to tourist traffic. Pender is actually two islands, joined by a bridge where a peninsula was blasted away to create a narrow ship passage.

Thetis & Kuper islands are reached from Chemainus — off the Trans-Canada Highway, north of Victoria. **Gabriola** Island is reached from the harbor in Nanaimo. These three smaller islands are more suitable for day visits while visiting the southern portion of Vancouver Island

There are more Gulf Islands to the north of Nanaimo but they are not part of this book. The northern islands (Denman, Hornby, Quadra, Cortes, Malcolm & Cormorant) are covered in detail in the companion book "British Columbia Adventures".

The southern islands are becoming increasingly popular as residents of the Vancouver area look for interesting weekend getaways in quiet surroundings. Several new bed and breakfast inns have opened in recent years and the islands have continued their tradition of serving fine food in distinctive restaurants.

The southern islands have become a haven for sea kayakers who flock to the archipelago to paddle throughout the quiet waters between the islands and to camp along the shore, in one of several provincial and local parks. The islands also appeal to cyclists who can easily do a tour of an island in a single day, using the rural sideroads which are free from heavy traffic.

GULF ISLANDS

Like the San Juans to the south, the Gulf Islands are composed for the most part of sandstone and shale. Only the southern part of Saltspring Island is volcanic in nature.

Much of the shoreline of the southern islands is rocky and rugged, often with cliffs which the sea erodes. Vegetation on the islands is primarily Douglas fir, with groves of madrone (arbutus) and some Garry oak. There is also some western red cedar. Salal is the dominent plant in the underbrush, along with salmonberry and huckleberry. Parks on the islands present ample opportunity to walk through the forests. One of the great benefits of visiting these islands is the wealth of wildflower life on the spring meadows. Stonecrop, blue camas and satin flower are predominant.

The pods of killer whales (Orca) which inhabit the north Puget Sound area also come to visit these islands. It's a thrillling experience to watch these families as they stop to feed on the abundant local salmon, with fins piercing the calm waters betwen the islands and their frequent gliding through the surface into the air. Whales are not the only wildlife to be seen here. Thousands of Steller's and California sea lions inhabit the B.C. waters. Up to 1,000 sea lions (of both types) winter in the Gulf Islands and more can be seen along the east coast of Vancouver Island.

Harbor seals breed in Georgia Strait and can be seen along the island coastlines, more likely from a boat than from the shore.

The Gulf Islands provide superb opportunities for birding, with sea birds nesting throughout the southern islands. Species include cormorants, gulls, tufted puffins, guillemots and the great blue heron. Should you stay overnight on one of the islands, you'll no doubt be serenaded in the night by one or more of the many loons who live in the area. Loons are most populous in April and May when they are flying north on the Pacific Flyway to their northern nesting grounds.

The king of Gulf Island birds is the bald eagle. Eagles are common on the islands and you'll see their huge stick nests atop many trees along the shorelines.

The people of the Gulf Islands are an independent lot. They are fiercely proud of their beautiful surroundings and will do almost anything to preserve their environment and their lifestyle. A recent movement on Galiano has succeeded in having the residents purchase the island's mountain from MacMillan Bloedel, the forest company — to be preserved for public use. The government of British Columbia has recognized the unique nature of these islands and has assigned their care and planning to the "Islands Trust" whose members are elected from each of the 13 major islands.

There is a moderate pace on the islands which makes them perfect for cycling. I suggest that if you have bikes, bring them along. You'll appreciate leaving your car or RV at your campsite or inn and exploring the country roads of the island at your leisure by bicycle.

GALIANO ISLAND

Galiano is my personal favorite of the southern Gulf Islands, partly because of its natural ambience and also because of the very fine restaurants and bed & breakfast places on the island. The ferry arrives at Sturdies Bay and the Infocentre is just up the hill (phone 539-2233). There are miles of old logging roads and trails for walking. It is possible to hike the entire east coast, a trek of some 20 KM.

Here are some of the natural highlights of the island:

Montague Harbour Provincial Park has 87 acres of shell and gravel beaches, a lagoon and a sheltered harbor as well as two campgrounds (one for motorists, the other for cyclists and boaters). There are signs of the existence of Indian settlements here, including a midden on the Gray Peninsula.

Bellhouse Park is on a rocky peninsula at Burill Point, near the Sturdies Bay ferry landing. This is a natural area with a few picnic tables overlooking Active Pass. Across the pass is Mayne Island and on a good day — which is almost any day — you can see the peak of Mount Baker in Washington state.

Another park overlooking Active Pass is **Galiano Bluffs Park**. Drive along Bluff Drive and stop at this lovely local park to watch the ferry and other marine traffic sailing through the pass. A good place to dip your canoe into the water is **Retreat Cove**. This is a small bay which is reached by driving down Porlier Pass Drive.

A particularly good trail runs beside Porlier Pass to Coon Bay. This walk takes about 50 minutes. Drive to the Indian reserve at the end of Porlier Pass Rd. Please ask permission to cross the private property where the trail begins.

The new **Woodstone Country Inn** (539-2022) is a superb B & B inn with a fine restaurant in a rural setting **$$ La Berangerie** (539-5392) has an outstanding restaurant with rooms above, in a great wooded setting. **$ to $$. Sutil Lodge** (539-2930) is a heritage house at Montague Harbour with 1930s rooms, shared baths, free canoes and dining. **$ Madrona Lodge** has cedar cottages by the sea with moorage, rowboats and bicycles. **$ Bodega Resort** (539-2677) has log chalets with kitchens on a hill in a farm setting. **$ to $$**

Some eating places deserve special mention. The **Pink Geranium** (539-2477) is a unique, reservations-only restaurant serving superb food in a home setting. Book here several weeks in advance, they're not open every day. **La Berangerie** (539-5392) is open daily with fresh west-coast food and Huguette Benger's French flair. It's a must if you're visiting Galiano.

For a pub meal, there's the **Hummingbird Inn** at Sturdies Bay. It has take-out service and a picnic area. The **Trincomali Bakery**, across from McLure Rd. has fresh bread, pastries & cappucino—a good place to pick up picnic supplies.

PENDER ISLANDS

There are two Pender islands: South and North. Separated by a narrow canal, they are joined by a bridge. From the canal you can see both Browning Harbour and Bedwell Harbour which have visitor facilities including moorings, motels, stores and restaurants. The two islands stretch for 16 KM (10 miles). There are miles of good beaches here, three lakes, a 9-hole golf course and a frisbee golf course in the woods. Scuba divers are attracted by the octopus off South Pender. This is a tranquil, rural island with a distinctive charm.

The islands can be toured by car, on a 45-kilometer (28 mile) drive. Don't be confused by the ever-changing names on the main road which takes you from south to north. On the north island it's called Bedwell Harbour Rd. which becomes Armdale Road. In the center of the north island it changes to Canal Rd. and keeps that name on the south island.

The 40 miles of shoreline include many small bays and beaches, mostly cobble.

The ferries land at **Otter Bay**. Port Washington Road leads from this small, quiet community and heads to join Bedwell Harbour. Rd and your drive to the southern end of the island and on to the south island. Tourist services are available at Driftwood Centre, where there is a small shopping mall with a cafe, grocery, liquor store and post office. While you're here, be sure to visit Razor Point by taking Razor Point Rd., across from the shopping center. The road runs along the shore of Browning Harbour. There's a government wharf at the end of the road along with a small beach — a good spot for picnics.

After you cross the canal on to the south island, turn on to Spalding Road which leads to **Bedwell Harbour**. There is a resort and marina here, including a restaurant and pub. One of the most scenic spots on the islands is at Gowlland Point which has excellent views of the San Juan Islands. Campsites are at **Beaumont Provincial Marine Park** and at **Prior Centennial Park**. For information, call the island Infocentre: (604) 629-6550.

The largest hotel is the **Bedwell Harbour Resort** (629-3212) with rooms, cottages, a marina, restaurant, pub and store. **$$** The **Eastridge Chalet Inn** (629-3353) is a modern motel which has a few RV parking spaces in mid-island. It is closed during December and January. **$$**.

Bed & Breakfast places offer a preferred way to stay. One of the best is **Cliffside Inn On-The-Sea** (629-3221), on Armadale Rd. (for adults) in a wonderful setting with its own beach plus a dining room and breakfast included. **$$ to $$$**. **Pender Lodge** (629-3221) has rooms & cottages, a restaurant, lounge, pool, & tennis. **$$ to $$$**. **Cutlass Court B & B** (629-6141) is 6 miles (10 KM) from the ferry terminal with private & shared baths and hot tub. **$$**. **Corbett House Bed & Breakfast** (629-6305) is 2 miles (3 KM) from the ferry landing on Corbett Road. This is a restored old farmhouse with period rooms, country furnishings and an orchard setting. **$$**.

MAYNE ISLAND

Mayne is an even smaller and less settled island than Pender and is perfect for quiet weekends or vacations where walking, enjoying nature and just relaxing are prescribed. The ferry lands at **Village Bay**, where there is a community of modern homes. **Miners Bay**, about 1.3 miles away, is the older community on the island with quite a different atmosphere.

700 people live on the island. Some farm, others commute to work in Victoria or Vancouver. Mayne has long been an apple-growing center and is famous for its King apples. There are orchards and sheep and poultry farming bolster the island economy. Miner's Bay was a turn-of-the-century tourist resort town with several Victorian hotels and more pubs than was safe for the tiny community. There are still good examples of Victorian architecture in Miners Bay. The old island goal is now a museum. and a number of fine old mansions look over the bay.

Campbell Bay has a fine swimming beach. **Mount Parke,** the highest spot on the island, has scenic hiking trails. Sight-seeing cruises are available at Miner's Bay to observe sea lions and other wildlife. There are docking facilities at Horton Bay & Miners Bay. A community of artists and crafts people on the island exhibit their work in several outlets. **Dinner Bay Park** is a day-use park with picnic tables and a beach. Phone the Infocentre at 539-5311. Mayne is a magnet for scuba divers who explore Enterprise Reef and Conconi Reef as well as the wreck of the Zephyr, which went down in 1872.

Mount Parke offers some of the best hiking on the island. A 77-acre park is being developed here. There are great views of Active Pass and other islands from the peak. **Navy Channel**, which runs between Mayne and Pender islands provides an interesting walk. To get there, take Marine Drive to Navy Channel Road. From the intersection, walk for about 15 minutes down Navy Channel Road, along the shore of the channel. There is a view of Pender Island across the water.

Like the other islands, cycling is a preferred mode of transportation — and exercise—on Mayne. The public roads don't have a great deal of traffic and make excellent cycling paths with fresh scenery around every corner. **Mariner's Way**, around Crane Point, is one. **Edith Point Rd**. is another.

There is no public campground on Mayne Island and people who visit the island stay in one of several inns and bed and breakfast homes.

For history buffs: **Springwater Lodge** (539-5521) is an 1890s hotel, said to be the oldest continual operation in B.C. There are rooms and four cottages plus a dining room overlooking Active Pass. **$ to $$**.

Blue Vista Resort, on Bennett Bay, has cabins with fireplaces, kitchens & decks. **$ Fernhill Lodge** (539-2544) is a B & B inn on Fernhill Rd. with historic theme rooms. **$$ Gingerbread House** (539-3133) is a restored Victorian home on Campbell Bay Rd. **$$**. **The Root Seller Inn** (539-2621) is a B & B lodge on Village Bay Rd. **$$**.

Salt Spring Island

With 8,000 residents, Salt Spring is the largest and most populated of the Gulf Islands: 32 KM (20 miles) long and 12 KM (8 miles) wide. It was explored by the Spanish and British in the 1700s and settled in the 1850s. Most residents live in or near the town of **Ganges** — in the middle section of the island.

Other communities include **Vesuvius** (on the northwest coast) and **Fulford Harbour** at the southern end of the island. Salt Spring has become a haven for artists and the island has become a center for arts and crafts, particularly around the Ganges waterfront.

Visitors will see sheep farms across the island and Salt Spring lamb is known by gastronomes around the world. The island has miles of hiking trails, forests and scattered beaches along the coastline. Because of its position in the shadow of Vancouver Island, it has a large amount of sunshine each year. The infocentres are in Ganges and Fulford Harbour.

The island's name comes from a series of briny springs at the island's north end. It is the only island in the Gulf of Georgia with salt springs.

You can get a good orientation to the town of Ganges by driving up **Chatsworth Road** where there is a good viewpoint showing the Ganges waterfront. You can see the Chain Islands which lie in the harbor and the surrounding countryside. **Mouat Park** near Ganges is a quiet reflective place near the town center. **Ruckle Park** at Beaver Point is an unusual island park which was originally a pioneer homestead and farm. This park has camping facilities and picnic sites with the homestead on display; the farm remains in operation.

Mt. Maxwell Park has an excellent viewpoint on the summit. The peak is 595 metres (1,952 feet) and from here you can see the smaller Gulf Islands beyond Fulford Harbour and over to Vancouver Island. On the lower part of Mt. Maxwell are several limestone caves with stalagmites and stalactites. Unfortunately, the caves are hard to find because of the steepness of the mountain at that level.

Along Musgrave Road is **Drummond Park**, the location of an ancient Indian petroglyph which has a storied past. The carving of a seal was found in the water at Fulford Harbour and moved for safe-keeping to the local airstrip. The province moved it again and finally it has found its rest in the park. There are several beaches in this area, in front of the park and down the road.

A tiny park is found at the end of Beddis Road, at **Beddis Beach**. The beach is made up of broken shells and gravel. The views are wonderful — including those of North Pender, Prevost Island and Swanson Channel.

Ferries to the island run to Ganges — from the mainland terminal at Tsawwassen — and to Fulford Harbour from the terminal at Swartz Bay on Vancouver Island. There is also an inter-island ferry which connects the southern island ferry terminals.

SALT SPRING ISLAND

The village of **Ganges** has a full range of shops and other services for travelers. There are supermarkets, a post office, gas stations and places to eat. Because of the large group of artists and crafts people who live on Salt Spring, Ganges has several art and crafts shops where there is excellent local art, pottery, weaving and other crafts on sale.

You have a wide range of places to stay on Salt Spring, from deluxe to woodsy. Bed and breakfast operations are plentiful across the island and these seem to be in sync with the laid-back pace of island life.

Hastings House (537-2362), a member of the exclusive Chateaux & Relais, is a luxury hideaway inn with a fine dining room. **$$$**. This is, without question, the finest place to stay on the island if you like to be pampered in a unique inn with a genteel country ambience.

Cusheon Lake Resort, 171 Natalie Lane (537-9629), is a secluded waterfront resort with log chalets, swimming, canoeing, fishing and hot tub. **$$ to $$$**. The **Arbutus Court Motel**, 770 Vesuvius Bay Rd. (537-5415) has standard rooms & housekeeping suites. **$**. The **Harbour House Hotel** is on the Ganges waterfront at the Harbour's End Marina (537-5571) with standard rooms, a restaurant, pub and shopping nearby. **$$**.

Bed and breakfast places include a cottage or rooms at **Applecroft Farm** near Ganges (537-5605); the **Southdown Farm**, 121 Beaver Pt. Rd. (653-4322) with large rooms, a whirlpool and children welcome. The **Inn at Precious Meadows**, 177 Vesuvius Bay Rd., (537-5995) has a cottage and rooms with gardens on 11 acres. For couples who want seclusion there is **Ambrosia Orchard**, a cottage at 197 Walker Hook Rd. (537-4156). At least 20 B & B homes are on the island. For information on Salt Spring B & B inns, call the Ganges Infocentre at 537-5252. All B & B homes have prices in the (**$$**) range.

Campers have a choice on Salt Spring. **Ruckle Provincial Park** is located 6 miles (10 kilometers) from the Fulford Ferry terminal, at the end of Beaver Point Rd. The park has 40 walk-in waterfront campsites and space for a few RVs in the parking area. **Mouat Provincial Park** in Ganges has 15 drive-in sites and this is the place for RV drivers to stay.

There are several good restaurants on Salt Spring including the charming **Vesuvius Inn** which overlooks Stuart Channel; the **Fulford Inn Pub** which offers pub lunches indoors or on a patio overlooking Fulford Harbour; and the **Waterside Bistro** in Ganges with an international menu and water views. Try the **New Deli Cafe** in Ganges, and the **Seaside Kitchen**—serving seafood on the Vesuvius waterfront.

The most sophisticated and renowned restaurant on the island is the dining room at **Hastings House**. The dining room is open to the public and reservations are necessary. The food is always fresh, using local and regional meats, seafood, vegetables and herbs, and the cooking is so good that the hotel serves as a cooking school several times each year. It's pricey but for well-trained palates, it's worth it. For reservations, phone 537-2362.

SATURNA, THETIS & KUPER ISLANDS

Saturna:

This is a smaller island with its own charm. Saturna is reached from the other southern Gulf Islands via the inter-island ferry or from the Tsawwassen and Swartz Bay ferry terminals. 350 people live here making this the least populated of the islands which are served by ferry. The ferries land at Lyall Harbour where there is a gas station, liquor store & pub.

Saturna is primarily a day-tripping island. Ferry service to the island is not as frequent as to the other more heavily populated islands and visitors should plan carefully to avoid being disappointed.

People often come to Saturna on a to visit **Winter Cove Marine Park** and to cycle along East Point Road. The park has a loop trail and day-use facilities including picnic tables, a boat ramp and fire pits.

East Point is particularly scenic and the drive along East Point Rd is rewarding. The lighthouse at East Point was built in 1888. This area is best explored at low tide. The water holds kelp beds and this is a good place to view sea birds including cormorants, guillemots, murres and grebes. There are bald eagles in the area as well.

The highest point on Saturna is **Mount Warburton Pike**. This 490 meter (1608 foot) hill has a gravel road which is most suitable for 4x4s and which makes a good hiking trail. To get there, take Narvaez Bay Road from East Point Road and turn on Harris Road across the road from the general store. The summit is 4.5 kilometers (2.8 miles), offering good views of the Pender islands, Vancouver Island and the San Juans. The mountain is inhabited by feral goats, descendants of farm animals which went wild near the turn of the century. The road passes through an ecological reserve which preserves a grove of Douglas firs.

There are no campsites on Saturna but for those who wish to sample this remote and rugged island, there are several B & B homes.

Boot Cove Lodge (539-2254) is a restored turn of the century inn with 3 rooms & shared bath, breakfast included and evening meals by reservation. **$**. **East Point Resort** (539-2975) is on a sandy beach with housekeeping cottages and a boat ramp. **$$**. **Breezy Bay Bed & Breakfast** (539-2937) is an old farmhouse with 4 units & shared bathroom with a full breakfast and dinner by reservation. **$**. Eating places other than the above are situated at Saturna Point near the ferry landing, including a pub which serves food. There's an annual lamb barbecue on the July 1st. weekend.

Thetis & Kuper:

These islands are usually done as a day-trip from the ferry terminal in Chemainus which is located off Highway 1, north of Victoria.

Thetis Island has accommodation at **Overbury Farm Resort** (246-9769) There are self-contained units with kitchens as well as summer cabins, a dining room, beach and boating. Weekly rates during summer season, daily at other times. **$$**.

VANCOUVER & THE LOWER MAINLAND

Residents of the sprawling area surrounding Vancouver call this part of the province the "Lower Mainland" More than half of the population of B.C. lives in this southwestern corner of the province—a total of slightly more than 1.5 million. Southwestern B.C. includes more than twenty cities and towns and the fertile Fraser Valley: the agricultural heartland of the province. The Lower Mainland's major geographical feature is the Fraser River which winds through the area and ends in a large delta. The Fraser estuary is a major resting place for millions of migrating birds in spring and fall seasons. It is an unparalleled environment which is now feeling the encroachment of the fast-developing urban areas.

Vancouver and the surrounding communities are located in one of the most spectacularly beautiful urban regions on the continent. Vancouver itself is almost surrounded by water, with the Coast Mountains to the north. English Bay provides a string of sand beaches stretching from Stanley Park to the Fraser River. There are beaches in the central core of the city.

The city of **Vancouver** is the hub of the Lower Mainland. It houses the business and financial center for B.C. and the Port of Vancouver. The core area of the city is on a peninsula called the **West End**. At the tip of the peninsula is **Stanley Park**, one of the world's great urban green spaces. On any day of the year, one can visit Stanley Park and tour the Vancouver Aquarium with its whales and other sea life, view a good totem pole collection, see a cricket game; walk around the "Seawall" which encircles the park, running under the Lions Gate Bridge, and past several good restaurants; ride on the miniature train through a zoo; play tennis, pitch and putt golf or lawn bowls; sun on the grass or on one of three beaches; have a picnic; and walk on several kilometers of nature trails through the second-growth forest.

Vancouver's **Chinatown** is, after San Francisco's, the largest outside of China. It is a wonderful collage of neon signs, fruit and vegetable stores spilling out onto the sidewalks, restaurants serving every type of Chinese and southeast Asian cuisine, and other retail outlets catering to the needs of the area's large Chinese community. There are herbal medicine stores, shops with kitchenwares and import outlets.

Vancouver is a city of neighborhoods which have their own flavors. The downtown peninsula (the West End) is separated from the West Side by English Bay. Here, ocean freighters anchor as they wait to enter the harbor. Around English Bay are a number of beaches starting at Stanley Park and ending at the University of British Columbia at Point Grey. English Bay is the site of the annual international fireworks competition which brings hundreds of thousands of people to the beaches in late July and August.

Other popular attractions include the **Capilano Suspension Bridge**, on Capilano Road in **North Vancouver** (across the Lions Gate Bridge from Stanley Park). There's a narrow swing bridge over the canyon of the Capilano River, offering superb views and garden walks.

Vancouver & Area

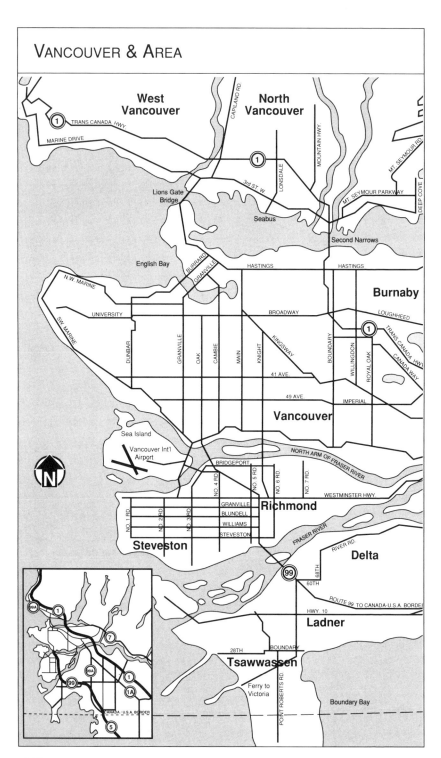

West Vancouver

North Vancouver

TRANS CANADA HWY.

MARINE DRIVE

CAPILANO RD.

MOUNTAIN HWY.

MT. SEYMOUR RD.

3rd ST. W.

LONSDALE

MT. SEYMOUR PARKWAY

DEEP COVE

Lions Gate Bridge

Seabus

Second Narrows

English Bay

BURRARD

GRANVILLE

HASTINGS

HASTINGS

N.W. MARINE

Burnaby

UNIVERSITY

BROADWAY

LOUGHHEED

TRANS CANADA HWY.

SW MARINE

DUNBAR

GRANVILLE

OAK

CAMBIE

MAIN

KNIGHT

KINGSWAY

BOUNDARY

WILLINGDON

ROYAL OAK

CANADA WAY

41 AVE.

49 AVE.

IMPERIAL

Vancouver

Sea Island

Vancouver Int'l Airport

NORTH ARM OF FRASER RIVER

BRIDGEPORT

NO. 4 RD.

NO. 5 RD.

NO. 6 RD.

NO. 7 RD.

WESTMINSTER HWY.

GRANVILLE

BLUNDELL

WILLIAMS

STEVESTON

Richmond

NO. 1 RD.

NO. 2 RD.

NO. 3 RD.

FRASER RIVER

RIVER RD.

Steveston

Delta

68TH

99

60TH

ROUTE 99 TO CANADA-U.S.A. BORDER

HWY. 10

Ladner

28TH

BOUNDARY

Tsawwassen

Ferry to Victoria

POINT ROBERTS RD.

Boundary Bay

N

99A

1

7

99

99A

1

1A

CANADA-U.S.A. BORDER

5

Vancouver

The Lower Mainland is endowed with many gardens which are in a beautiful state year-round, thanks to the mild climate and timely rains. Perhaps the finest of the gardens is **Queen Elizabeth Park** at 33rd Ave. & Cambie St. The gardens, created in two former stone quarries, are at the city's highest point. They have a wide variety of flowers and ground covers and native & tropical plants abound inside the dome of the Bloedel Floral Conservatory. The Civic Arboretum was Canada's first civic tree and shrub collection. **VanDusen Botanical Gardens**, another civic park at 37th Ave. & Oak St. contains several garden areas including an oriental garden, a children's garden, a hedge maze, a hanging garden and rare shrubs and flowers. There is a fee here, phone 266-7194.

Dr. Sun Yat Sen Classical Garden, at the edge of Vancouver's Chinatown (578 Carrall St., 687-7133) is the only authentic classical Chinese garden outside of mainland China. Built by artisans from Suzhou, the garden is a harmonic wonder: quiet, reflective and thought inspiring. It is open daily with an admission fee.

The **UBC Botanical Garden** is on the campus of the University of British Columbia. Open daily, this is one of Canada's foremost botanical displays: a living gallery of plants from around the world used for education and recreation. There are more than 10,000 species in eight separate sections. The Asian Garden contains more than 400 species of rhododendrons and giant snow lilies. There are also herb, physick, alpine, B.C. native, and contemporary gardens as well as a garden shop. Phone 228-4208 for information. **Nitobe Memorial Garden**, on the UBC campus, is an authentic Japanese garden with tea house, open daily during summer months and weekdays from mid-October through mid-March. Created by Dr. Kannosuke Mori in 1960, this garden provides quiet strolls in a tranquil wooded setting which changes with the seasons.

Stanley Park, at the tip of the downtown peninsula, a forest, zoo, aquarium, children's play areas and several gardens. The rose garden near the entrance to the park is notable. **Park & Tilford Gardens**, is next to a busy shopping mall in North Vancouver (Cotton Rd. & Brooksbank Ave.) Built by the distillery which has since disappeared, the garden continues to be an urban delight. It is particularly beautiful at night with hundreds of small twinkling lights along the paths.

In Richmond, the suburb to the south of Vancouver, the **Richmond Nature Park** at 11851 Westminster Highway (at #5 Rd.) features a preserved bog with a pond and four trails ranging to a mile in length. The Nature House has displays of birds and other bog life. The park is open daily, call 604-273-7015. Two provincial parks in the immediate Vancouver area may be of interest. **Mt. Seymour Provincial Park** in North Vancouver has good views of the harbor, Indian Arm and the surrounding area. **Cypress Provincial Park** in West Vancouver offers views from above English Bay. Both parks have picnic areas and ski hills.

VANCOUVER

Downtown Vancouver is hotel-central for the Lower Mainland area and the large and higher-priced hotels are close to shopping and the business district. Several have positions on or near the waterfront with wonderful views. The **Hotel Vancouver**, 900 West Georgia Street, (1-800-268-9411, Canada or 1-800-828-7447, USA.) is Vancouver's venerable landmark hotel, well preserved and restored in the center of downtown with pool, sauna, shops, restaurants including roof-top dining. **$$**. The **Pan Pacific Hotel** at 999 Canada Place (662-8111 or 1-800-663-1515) is located on a harbor pier overlooking Burrard Inlet. This deluxe hotel is part of a Japanese chain of resort hotels. Restaurants serve French, North American and Japanese cuisine. There is a pool, sauna, health club, lounge, and great views from the Canada Place promenade. **$$$**.

The **Four Seasons Hotel**, at 791 West Georgia St. (689-9333 or 1-800-268-6282) is a superb hotel close to everything in the shopping and business district and connected to the Pacific Centre shopping mall. The restaurants are excellent and the hotel has pools, sauna, whirlpool, lounges and an exercise room. **$$$**. For more of a European touch, try the **Wedgewood Hotel**, 845 Hornby Street (689-1234 or 1-800- 663-0666). This is a smaller, cozy hotel in the central part of downtown across from Robson Square with restaurant, lounge, coffee shop, and a comfortable ambience. **$$$**. The **Westbrook Hotel** at 1234 Hornby St. (689-7777 or 1-800-663-0666) is also close to the shopping and business district. This modern hotel has suites with kitchen facilities, a pool, sauna and restaurant. **$$$**.

Nearby in the West End is the **Sylvia Hotel**, 1154 Gilford Street (at Beach Ave. (681-9321). This ivy-covered hotel is an older, cozy place facing the beach and English Bay and has a new, modern wing. It has rooms (some with kitchens) and suites with a restaurant and lounge overlooking the bay where sunsets are often spectacular. **$ to $$$**.

Outside of the downtown area there are several moderately-priced hotels, all chain operations: The **Sheraton Inn Plaza 500,** 500 West 12th Ave. (873-1811 or 1-800-325-3535) is across the corner from City Hall, with convenient shopping, restaurant and lounge. **$$ to $$$**.

The **Relax Plaza Hotel** is at 3071 St. Edwards Dr. in the suburb of Richmond (278-5155 or 1-800-661-9563). Ten minutes from the Vancouver International Airport and 20 minutes from downtown Vancouver, this hotel is close to Hwy. 99 with a restaurant, lounge, pool, whirlpool and free airport shuttle. **$$**. Just down the same highway (# 99) is the **Stay 'N Save Motor Inn**, 10551 St. Edwards Dr., Richmond (273-3311 or 1-800-663-0298). This motel provides basic but good accommodation at reasonable prices (there's another one in Victoria). This motel has an adjoining restaurant and a laundry. Some rooms have kitchen units. **$$**.

The **Inn at Westminster Quay**, 900 Quayside Dr., New Westminster (520-1776 or 1-800-663-2001) is beside the Fraser River with a public market and SkyTrain transit station nearby, and a 30-minute drive to Vancouver. **$$**.

VANCOUVER

For campers and people with RVs, **ParkCanada RV Inn** is at 4799 Hwy. 17, via 52nd Street (Tsawwassen), close to the ferry terminal (943-5811). This RV park has full hookups, store, showers, with golf and a waterpark nearby. **KOA Vancouver** is in Surrey, the large eastern suburb, at 14601-40th Ave. at the junction of King George Hwy. and Hwy. 99 (594-6156). The **Dogwood Campground** is near Hwy. 1 at 15151-112th Ave. in Surrey (583-5585), an RV park with full hookups, tent sites, pool & laundry.

Vancouver and area are blessed with a wide range of fine dining rooms, ethnic restaurants and bistros with food from every conceivable corner of the world, so it's not possible to list all of the delightful places to eat throughout the Lower Mainland. I have a long list in the book "B.C. Adventures", and here we cover the highlights including some local favorites which have service-with-a-flair along with good food.

Settebello at 1133 Robson St., in the Robson Fashion Court (681-7377), is one of Umberto Menghi's many success stories. This place serves Italian cuisine with a light touch, including many fresh varieties of pizza. There's a good wine list, an outdoor patio and friendly service. **$$**.

Raintree, at 1630 Alberni is near Stanley Park (688-5570). This restaurant opened a few years ago and instantly began to influence the way other Vancouver restaurants thought about cooking. The food is Pacific Coast cuisine—always fresh and always current with a wonderful wine list. Their high apple pie is an architectural wonder. **$$ to $$$**. Downstairs is **Leon's Bar & Grill**: less expensive and less formal, but with the same fine kitchen. Near the Raintree, English Bay offers good views along with your meal. The prime location for beach-side dining is the **English Bay Cafe**, across from the beach at Denman St. and Beach Ave. (669-2225). Seafood is the specialty here but a variety of food is available in the downstairs Bistro or the upstairs dining room. The Bistro has a deck overlooking the bay. **$$ to $$$**. The length of Denman Street is packed with restaurants.

Long a haven for seafood lovers is **The Cannery**, on the Burrard Inlet harborfront at 2205 Commissioner St. (254-9606). The Cannery has an extensive fresh sheet each day and a enormous wine list which concentrates on California wines. **$$$**.

The downtown hotels offer fine dining including seafood at **Fish & Co.** in the Hyatt Regency Hotel, 655 Burrard at Georgia St. (682-3663). The restaurant has fresh entrees each day which are listed on blackboards; **Seasons**, in the Four Seasons Hotel (791 West Georgia St., 689-9333) is a typical Four Seasons' experience: superb **$$$**. The **Timber Club** and **The Roof** restaurant in the Hotel Vancouver offer dining with a touch of occasion—the Roof in particular has that old 30's style ambience with dancing after dinner most evenings. Prices in both are **$$$.** One of the finest operations for many years in downtown Vancouver is **The William Tell**, now located in the Coast Georgian Court hotel at 765 Beatty St., near the B.C. Place dome. Its cuisine is Swiss, as you might imagine. **$$$**.

MORE INFORMATION SOURCES

California:

Anderson Valley C of C
P.O. Box 275, Booneville CA
95415

Arcata Chamber of Commerce
1062 G Street, Arcata CA 95521
(707) 822-3619

**Armstrong Redwoods State
Reserve** 17000 Armstrong Woods
Rd., Guerneville CA 95446
(707) 869-2015

Audubon Canyon Ranch
4900 Hwy. 1, Stinson Beach CA
(415) 868-9244

Avenue of the Giants Assoc.
P.O. Box 1000, Miranda CA 95553
(707) 943-3108

Bodega Bay C of C
P.O. Box 146, Bodega Bay CA
94923 (707) 875-3422

Crescent City-Del Norte C of C
P.O. Box 246, Crescent City CA
95531 (707) 464-3174

**Eureka/Humboldt County
Convention & Visitors Bureau,**
1034 Second St., Eureka CA 95501
(707) 443-5097

Ferndale C of C
P.O. Box 325, Ferndale CA 95536
(707) 786-4477

**Fort Bragg/Mendocino Coast C
of C** P. O. Box 1141, Fort Bragg
CA 95437 (707) 964-3153

**Fort Humboldt State Historic
Park** 3431 Fort Ave., Eureka CA
95501 (707) 445-6567

Fort Ross Historic State Park
(707) 847-3286

Garberville/Redway C of C
P.O. Box 445, Garberville CA
95440 (707) 923-2613

Healdsburg C of Commerce
217 Headsburg Ave., Healdsburg
CA 95448 (707) 433-6935

Humboldt Redwoods State Park
P.O. Box 100, Weott CA 95571
(707) 946-2311

Leggett Valley C of C
P. O. Box 218, Leggett CA 95455
(707) 925-6214

McKinleyville C of C
P.O. Box 2144, McKinleyville CA
(707) 839-2449

**Mendocino Coast State Parks &
Beaches** (707) 937-5804

**Mendocino County Conv &
Visitors Bureau,** P.O. Box 244,
Ukiah CA 95482 (707) 462-3091

**Muir Woods National
Monument** Mill Valley CA
(415) 388-2595

Petaluma C of C
215 Howard St. Petaluma CA
94952 (707) 762-2785

Point Reyes National Seashore
Point Reyes CA 94956
(415) 663-1092

Redwood Empire Association
1001-One Market Plaza, Spear
Tower, San Francisco CA 94105
(415) 543-8334

Redwood National Park
1111 Second St., Crescent City CA
95531 (707) 464-6101; Del Norte
Coast Redwoods State Park (707)
445-6547 or (707) 458-3310;
Jedediah Smith Redwoods State
Park (707) 458-3310 or (707) 464-
9533; Prairie Creek Redwoods
State Park   (707) 488-2171

Rio Dell/Scotia C of C
715 Wildwood Dr., Rio Dell CA
95562 (707) 764-3436

Russian River Region Inc.
14034 Armstrong Woods Rd.,
Guerneville CA 95446
(707) 869-9009

Sonoma Coast State Beach
(707) 875-3483

**Sonoma County Conv. &
Visitors Bureau**
100-10 4th St., Santa Rosa, CA
95404 (707) 575-1191

Sonoma Valley Visitors Bureau
453 First Street East, Sonoma CA
95476 (707) 996-1091

**Trinidad Chamber of
Commerce** P.O. Box 356,
Trinidad CA 95570
(707) 677-0591

Ukiah Chamber of Commerce
495 E., Perkins St., Ukiah CA
95482 (707) 462-4705

West Marin C of C
P.O. Box 1045, Pt. Reyes Station
CA 94956 (415) 663-9232

Willits Chamber of Commerce
15 S, Main St., Willits CA 95490
(707) 459-4113

Oregon: (503)

Bandon C of C
P.O. Box 1515, Bandon OR 97411
347-9616

Brookings-Harbor C of C
P.O. Box 940, Brookings OR
97415 (469-3181)

Cannon Beach C of C
P.O. Box 64, Cannon Beach OR
97110 (436-2623)

Charleston Information Center
P.O. Box 5735, Charleston OR
97420 (888-2311)

Depoe Bay C of C
P.O. Box 21, Depoe Bay OR
97341 (765-2889)

Florence Area C of C
P.O. Box 26000, Forence OR
97439 (997-3182)

Gold Beach C of C
510 S. Ellenburg St., Gold Beach
OR 97444 (247-7526)

Lincoln City Visitors Center
P.O. Box 787, Lincoln City OR
97367 (994-8378)

Lower Umpqua C of C
P.O. Box 11, Reedsport OR 97467
(247-3495 or 247-2155 OR)

McMinnville C of C
417 N. Adams, McMinnville OR
97128 (472-6196)

Mount Hood Recreation Assoc.
P.O. Box 342, Welches OR 97067
(622-3101)

Newport C of C
555 S.W. Coast Hwy., Newport
OR 97365 (1-800-262-7844)

North Bend C of C
P.O. Box B, North Bend OR 97459
(756-4613)

Northwest Oregon Visitor Ctr.
25 SW Salmon, Portland OR 97240
(222-2223)

Oregon Coast Association
P.O. Box 670, Newport OR 97365
(336-5107)

Oregon State Parks
525 Trade St. S.E., Salem OR
97310 (378-6305)

Oregon Tourism Division
775 Summer Street NE, Salem OR
97310 (543-8838)or 1-800-547-
7842 (outside Oregon)

Portland/Oregon Visitors Ctr.
26 S.W. Salmon, Portland OR
97204 (222-2223)

Port Orford C of C
P.O. Box 637, Port Orford OR
97465 (332-8055)

Rogue River C of C
P.O. Box 457, Rogue River OR
97537 (582-0242)

Siskiyou National Forest
200 NE Greenfield Rd., P.O. Box
440, Grants Pass OR 97526

MORE INFORMATION SOURCES

(479-5301); Gold Beach Ranger District (247-6651); Chetco Ranger District (469-2196)

Siuslaw National Forest
4077 Research Way, Corvallis OR 97339 (750-7000)

St. Helens C of C
174 S. River Hwy., St. Helens OR 97051 (397-0685)

Seaside C of C/Visitors Bureau
P.O. Box 7, Seaside OR 97138 (738-6391)

Southwestern Oregon Visitors Assoc., 88 Stewart Ave., Medford OR (779-4691 or 1-800-448-4856)

The Dalles Area C of C
404 W. 2nd Street, The Dalles OR 97058 (296-2231)

Tillamook C of C
3705 Hwy. 101 N., Tillamook OR 97141 (842-7525)

Waldport C of C Visitors Center
P.O. Box 669, Waldport OR 97394 (563-2133)

Yachats Area C of C
P.O. Box 174, Yachats OR 97498 (547-3530)

Washington: (206)

Anacortes C of C
1 Swinomish Channel, Anacortes WA 98221 (293-4687)

Bellingham/Whatcom County Visitor & Conv. Bureau, 904 Potter St., Bellingham WA 98226 (671-3990)

Birch Bay C of C
4897 Birch Bay-Lynden Rd., Birch Bay WA 98239 (371-7675)

Blaine Visitor Center
900 Peace Portal Rd., Blaine WA 98230 (332-4544)

Bremerton Area C of C
P.O. Box 229, Bremerton WA 98310 (479-3579)

Everett Area C of C
1710 West Marine View Dr., Everett WA 98201 (252-5181)

Forks Chamber of Commerce
P.O. Box 1249, Forks WA 98331 (374-3333)

Gig Harbor C of C
P.O. Box 1245, Gig Harbor WA 98335 (851-6865)

Grays Harbor C of C
P.O. Box 450, Aberdeen WA 98520 (532-1924)

Island County Visitors Council

(Whidby Island) P.O. Box 152, Coupeville WA 98239 (321-5005)

Kingston C of C
P.O. Box 78, Kingston WA 98346 (297-3813)

La Conner C of C
P.O. Box 644, La Conner WA 98257 (466-4778)

Long Beach Peninsula Visitor's Bureau, P.O. Box 562, Long Beach WA 98631 (642-2400)

Lopez Island C of C
P.O. Box 102, Lopez Island WA 98261 (486-3800)

Mount Rainier National Park
Tahoma Woods, Star Route, Ashford WA 98304 (569-2211)

National Forests/National Parks Service
1018 First Ave., Seattle WA 98104 (442-0170)

Northwest Washington Tourism Assoc. Box 922, Langley WA 98260 (221-TOUR)

Ocean Shores Convention Ctr.
P.O. Box 382, Ocean Shores WA 98569 (1-800-874-6737)

Olympia Visitor & Conv. Bur.
P.O. Box 7249, Olympia WA 98507 (357-3370)

Olympic National Park
Visitor Center, 600 E. Park Ave. Port Angeles WA 98362 (452-4501)

Olympic Peninsula Tourism Council, 120 Washington, Bremerton WA 98310 (1-800-443-7828, ext 30)

Orcas Island C of C
P.O. Box 252, Eastsound WA 98245 (376-2273)

Port Angeles Visitor Center
121 E. Railroad, Port Angeles WA 98362 (452-2363)

Port Townsend Visitor Ctr.
2437 Sims Way, Pt. Townsend WA 98368 (385-2722

South Bend C of C
P.O. Box 335, South Bend WA 98586 (875-5533)

Poulsbo C of C
19044 Jensen Way NE, Poulsbo WA 98370 (779-4848)

San Juan County C of C
(San Juan Islands)
P.O. Box 65, Lopez WA 98261 (468-3663)

San Juan Island C of C

P.O. Box 98, San Juan Island WA 98250 (378-5240)

Seattle/King County Visitor Information, 666 Stewart, Seattle WA 98101 (461-5840)

Sequim/Dungeness Valley C of C
P.O. Box 907, Sequim WA 98382 (683-6197)

Southwest Washington Regional Information Program
P.O. Box 876, Longview WA 98632 (425-1211)

Tacoma/Pierce County
Convention. & Visitors Bureau, P.O. Box 1933, Tacoma WA 98401 (627-2836)

TRIS (Trails Information System) phone 442-0170

Washington Coast C of C
P.O. Box 430, Ocean Shores WA 98569 (289-4552)

Washington State Ferries
801 Alaskan Way, Seattle WA 98104 (464-6400)

Washington State Parks, 7150 Cleanwater Lane, Olympia WA 98504 (753-2027)

Westport/Grayland C of C
P.O. Box 306, Westport WA 98595 (345-6223)

British Columbia:

Canada (604)

B.C. Ferries
1112 Fort Street, Victoria B.C. V8V 4V2 (386-3431, Victoria or 669-1211, Vancouver)

Pacific Rim National Park
P.O. Box 280, Ucluelet, B.C. V0R 3A0 (726-4212 (summer) (726-7721-off-season)

Tourism Assoc of Southwestern B.C., 304-828 West 8th Ave., Vancouver B.C. V5Z 1E2 (876-3088 or 1-800-667-3306 US)

Tourism Assoc. of Vancouver Island, 302-45 Bastion Square, Victoria B.C. V8W 1J1 (382-3551)

Tourism British Columbia
Parliament Buildings, Victoria B.C. Canada V8V 1X4

Tourism Vancouver
Pavilion Plaza, 1055 Dunsmuir St. Vancouver B.C. V7X 1L3 (683-2000)

Tourism Victoria
6th floor, 612 View Street, Victoria B.C. V8W 1J5 (382-2160)

INDEX

Index

INDEX

INDEX

British Columbia Adventures

Explores all of this vast province from the U.S. border to the Yukon border; from the Rocky Mountains to the Pacific Ocean. This guide includes national and provincial parks, places to stay & eat, and things to see & do in Vancouver and Victoria, and across the mountain wilderness. **256 pages. $12.95**

Pacific Coast Adventures

Explores the Pacific Coast drive from the Golden Gate Bridge to British Columbia's Sunshine Coast. Regions covered include the Oregon Coast, California's coast wine country, Washington's Olympic Peninsula and Puget Sound, the San Juan Islands and Southwestern British Columbia including the Gulf Islands and Vancouver Island destinations. **256 pages. $12.95**

Rocky Mountain Adventures
(April, 1992)

Covers the entire length of the Rocky Mountain ranges from the northern Canadian Rockies to the Sangre de Cristo range in Colorado and New Mexico. Included are highway routes, mountain resorts; mountain trails, national, state & provincial parks; and places to stay and eat — in British Columbia, Alberta, Idaho, Montana, Colorado and New Mexico. **320 pages. $12.95**

Alaska-Yukon Adventures
(April 1992)

The complete guide to highway travel, attractions, parks and places to stay and eat in Alaska, the Yukon Territory, and Canada's Western Arctic including the Alaska Highway, the Dempster Highway to Inuvik N.W.T. and the Mackenzie/Liard Highway route to Fort Simpson & Yellowknife N.W.T. The book includes access routes from B.C., Alberta, Idaho and Montana. **256 pages. $12.95**

TO ORDER DIRECT (from the U.S. only): For each book send an additional $2 postage & handling to Western Traveller Press, 822—717 Simundson Drive, Point Roberts, WA 98281.